AF607982

SHAKESPEARE IN QUÉBEC

Nation, Gender, and Adaptation

Shakespeare in Québec

Nation, Gender, and Adaptation

JENNIFER DROUIN

UNIVERSITY OF TORONTO PRESS
Toronto Buffalo London

Toronto Buffalo London
www.utppublishing.com

ISBN 978-1-4426-4797-8

Publication cataloguing information is available from Library and Archives Canada

This book has been published with the help of a grant from the Canadian Federation for the Humanities and Social Sciences, through the Awards to Scholarly Publications Program, using funds provided by the Social Sciences and Humanities Research Council of Canada.

University of Toronto Press acknowledges the financial assistance to its publishing program of the Canada Council for the Arts and the Ontario Arts Council.

University of Toronto Press acknowledges the financial support of the Government of Canada through the Canada Book Fund for its publishing activities.

Contents

Acknowledgments

The initial intention of this book was to bridge Canada's "two solitudes" by bringing together Québécois texts in French and scholarly criticism and theory in English. Along the way, I crossed many bridges myself, and it is with much gratitude that I acknowledge those who helped me here. First, I thank Leanore Lieblein who provided not only careful readings of the entire manuscript but also crucial archival material and unpublished manuscripts, and, most importantly, graciously shared her deep knowledge of Shakespeare in Québec. I also obtained unpublished manuscripts from Nathalie Claude, Mark Fortier, Caroline Garand, Madd Harold, Laurie Maguire, Yves Sioui Durand, and Nancy Thomas, as well as Daniel Gauthier at the *Centre des auteurs dramatiques*, and photos from Robert Gurik. During my time at McGill University, I was fortunate to work with a mighty triumvirate, which in addition to Leanore included Paul Yachnin and Michael Bristol. I am grateful to Paul for his sharp mind, his warm mentorship, and his leadership steering the *Making Publics* team. Mike's voice has been in my head throughout much of the composition of this book as I continue to endeavour to be like Mike, a scholar equally rigorous, articulate, and generous. Erin Hurley also read part of this manuscript and shared her own work on Québec with me.

McGill University provided funding towards the completion of this project, as did the Université du Québec à Trois-Rivières where it first began and Allegheny College. The University of Alabama's Research Grants Committee, College of Arts and Sciences, and Department of English all provided generous research and travel funding. I also received financial support from the Québec Fonds pour la Formation des chercheurs et d'aide à la recherche (FCAR, now FQRSC) and the

Social Sciences and Humanities Research Council of Canada (SSHRC). Work in progress was presented at a number of conferences, including those organized by the Association of Canadian College and University Teachers of English, the British Shakespeare Association, the Canadian Association for Commonwealth Literature and Language Studies, the Canadian Association for Theatre Research, the International Shakespeare Association, the International Shakespeare Conference, the North East Conference on British Studies, and the Shakespeare Association of America, and I thank my fellow participants for their careful responses to my work. I presented an overview of this book to members of the Groupe de recherche identités et cultures at Université du Havre and the Institut de recherche sur la Renaissance, l'âge Classique et les Lumières at Université Montpellier III. I am grateful to Sarah Hatchuel, Nathalie Vienne-Guerrin, and Claire Bowen for their hospitality and the opportunity to experience the linguistic and cultural differences between Québec and *la mère patrie* during my month in France.

Portions of this book have previously appeared in print as "Daughters of the Carnivalized Nation in Jean-Pierre Ronfard's Shakespearean Adaptations *Lear* and *Vie et mort du Roi Boiteux*" in *Theatre Research in Canada/Recherches théâtrales au Canada* 27.1 (spring 2006); as "Nationalizing Shakespeare in Québec: Theorizing Post-/Neo-/Colonial Adaptation" in *Borrowers and Lenders: The Journal of Shakespeare and Appropriation* 3.1 (fall/winter 2007), which was reprinted as "Nationalizing the Bard: Québécois Adaptations of Shakespeare since the Quiet Revolution" in *Native Shakespeares: Indigenous Appropriations on a Global Stage*; and as entries on *Hamlet-le-Malécite* and Michel Garneau's *Macbeth* in the online anthology of the *Canadian Adaptations of Shakespeare Project*, edited by Daniel Fischlin. The publishers have graciously given their permission to reprint this work.

For support both scholarly and moral, I thank my book buddies, Joyce Boro, Fiona Ritchie, and Alanna Thain, with whom I have untaken this journey. Joyce and Fiona took time away from their own manuscripts to read and provide feedback on chapter 2. Anne Quéma commented on and helped me refine the first two chapters. Feedback from the two readers for the University of Toronto Press further improved the final manuscript, and I am grateful to my editors Suzanne Rancourt and Leah Connor at UTP for steering this project from beginning to end. Jim Bulman, Soledad Caballero, and Jennifer Hellwarth at Allegheny College deserve thanks for their warmth and kindness, as do colleagues and friends in Montréal and across Canada, including

Wes Folkerth, Chris Fox, Deb Hoffmann, Ric Knowles, Susan Knutson, Vin Nardizzi, Julie Norman, Joan and Peter Oliver, Nicole Prévost, and Jessica Slights, as well as my two families back home in Nova Scotia for whom I am sure this process has seemed as long and daunting at times as it did to me.

At the University of Alabama, my friends and colleagues in the Hudson Strode Program in Renaissance Studies, in the English department, and across campus have been supportive, including David Ainsworth, Alex Cook, David Deutsch, Ed Geisweidt, Steffen Guenzel, Nic Helms, Tricia McElroy, Jennifer Purvis, Wendy Rawlings, and Kirk Walter. Sharon O'Dair has not only been a fabulous director of the Strode Program; she has also offered a keen critical eye and a willing ear at many stages throughout the life of this project, providing incisive and invaluable critique that has made the entire book stronger than it would have been otherwise. I am particularly grateful to her for being more than a colleague and for her support and friendship over many years, in the past and undoubtedly in the future.

Finally, this book would not exist were if not for the late Guy Drouin who made me fall in love with Québécois literature and culture. Joanne Biron and Michel Gignac continue to nourish me with poetic words in Québécois. During the composition of a significant portion of this manuscript, I was actively involved in the Parti Québécois at many levels, and I am grateful to the three leaders with whom I worked – Claude Villeneuve, president of the Comité national des jeunes, Daniel Turp, MNA for the riding of Mercier, and Bernard Landry, former premier and leader of the official opposition at the time – and from whom I learned much about Québec that I could not have learned from scholarly books alone. I remain inspired by the selflessness of Monsieur Landry's mantra, "la patrie avant le parti, et le parti avant les ambitions personnelles," a poignant expression of the idea that "the needs of the many outweigh the needs of the few or the one." This philosophical perspective is what makes politics and responsible citizenship matter so much to me. *Ce livre est dédié à toutes celles et à tous ceux qui ont milité et qui militent toujours pour que le Québec devienne un pays souverain, indépendant, et libre.*

SHAKESPEARE IN QUÉBEC

Nation, Gender, and Adaptation

Introduction

It is common practice in Québec to contrast "la langue de Molière" and "la langue de Shakespeare."[1] Yet, in a Québec that prides itself on still speaking Molière's tongue, it is puzzling to find a remarkably rich history of adaptations of Shakespeare since the Quiet Revolution, a period of massive social reform inaugurated in 1960. More than thirty such French-language adaptations of Shakespeare have been written in Québec – and an impressive number of translations and innovative stage productions have been performed as well – making Shakespeare a far more creative force in Québec than Molière. The surprising existence of Québécois Shakespeare raises an important question: why has Shakespeare become one of Québec's major authors?

By uniting the Québécois language and Shakespeare's texts, Québécois adapters embrace cultural hybridity, appropriate Shakespeare's canonical authority, and legitimize their local struggle for national liberation. Canonical difference provides Québécois authors with the freedom to manipulate Shakespeare's texts freely for their political purposes, just as others have manipulated his plays in service of various political agendas transhistorically and transculturally. The lack of investment in, and indoctrination by, the British literary canon, coupled with what Michael Bristol has identified as Shakespeare's big-time status as a pop celebrity, make his texts both worthy of adaptation and sufficiently culturally distant to become objects of play. The irreverent, and hence liberating, attitude of Québécois towards Shakespeare is captured in the nickname they have given him: "le grand Will." In Québec, Shakespeare is *grand*, a big-time author worthy of a certain reverence, yet Québécois playwrights are not afraid to bring him down to size, to make him their own, and to develop an affectionate relationship with him on a first-name basis (Lieblein, "Re-making" 178–9).

Québec's unique social history makes it an ideal case study of how Shakespeare's big-time status works in a nation that has complex colonial, postcolonial, and neocolonial relationships with France, Britain, and English Canada. As a former settler colony of France (with a lingering colonial inferiority complex), which was then conquered by the British in 1759 only to be subsumed shortly thereafter into the Canadian confederation, which many Québécois consider a form of neocolonial tutelage, Québec has been both a colonizer of the First Nations and has been colonized itself. Québec's rare status as a nation without full political sovereignty results, however, in its adapters choosing to appropriate Shakespeare in order to advance the nationalist social project more often and more radically than issues related to gender and sexuality, making the treatment of gender in Québécois Shakespeares an anomaly in the larger Western context.

Through close textual readings of the adaptations with an eye to discerning the points of divergence between the Shakespearean "source" texts and Québécois authors' rewritings of them, focusing in particular on representations of nation and gender, this book seeks to explain why contemporary Québécois playwrights appear so obsessed with rewriting Shakespeare, what changes they make to the Shakespearean text, and how the differences between Shakespeare and the adaptations engage the nationalist, feminist, and queer concerns of contemporary Québec society. The readings do not enumerate translation differences but investigate the radical changes to content that allowed Québécois playwrights to advocate subversive political discourses and to contribute to the hot debates of the Quiet Revolution in the 1960s, the 1970 October Crisis, the 1980 and 1995 referenda, the rise of feminism, and the emergence of AIDS. By tracing the changing political discourses over the course of four and a half decades, these chapters show not only how Shakespeare has been adapted in Québec but also how Québécois adaptations have evolved in response to changes in the political climate.

Chapter 1, "Postcolonial Shakespeares and Gendering the Québec Nation," begins by examining the postcoloniality of Canada followed by the postcoloniality of Québec. Although postcolonial approaches to Québécois literature remain rare, the applicability of postcolonial studies to Québec has begun to take place in the last decade, notably through a special issue of *Québec Studies* devoted to the topic. Parallels between the Québec sovereignist movement and African decolonization were established during the Quiet Revolution, however, and thus justify approaching the adaptations in this light. Comparing Québec with other

Commonwealth countries and nations with similar national liberation movements reveals that Québécois Shakespeares are less like Canadian Shakespeares than like those from Australia, New Zealand, Scotland, and Catalonia. Shakespeare was not used, however, as a colonizing tool by the educational system in Québec in the way his works participated in the anglicization of India. Following an identification of notable characteristics of these other national Shakespeares, the chapter moves into a discussion of the history of Québec from the Conquest through the Quiet Revolution, focusing on the evolution of different nationalist discourses and the changing rights and roles of women and queers in Québec society during this period. Nation and gender intersect during the Conquest through the metaphor of rape, and the ramifications of Québec's rape complex continue to the present day through homophobic tropes, which Robert Schwartzwald calls the "fear of federasty" – a verbal re-enactment of the symbolic pederasty imposed on the Québec nation by traitors considered complicit with the federal colonizer. The complicated relationship between nation and gender also manifests itself in the political sphere through the popular feminist slogan "Pas de Québec libre sans libération des femmes! Pas de femmes libres sans libération du Québec!"[2] One would expect a certain degree of sympathy among Québécois nationalists for the emancipation of women, especially since the nation itself is frequently figured as a mother. Under the rule of the nationalist Parti Québécois, Québec has often enacted progressive legislation granting rights to women and queers before other parts of Canada did, yet the nationalist movement itself has had very little engagement either theoretically or practically with the feminist and queer movements – a reality reflected in the preponderance of the national question over representations of gender and sexuality within this corpus of plays. Nationalism is not, however, a static entity in Québec and nationalist discourses have evolved over time, existing in plural, and often contradictory, forms today.

Chapter 2, "A Theory of Shakespearean Adaptation," flows from this theorization of nation and gender through the notion of the transformation of a group's own sense of otherness into a more fully realized collective selfhood, a principle underlying nationalism but also part of postcolonial adaptation, which involves making a Shakespeare that is foreign, alien, and other fit into a local culture's self-identity so the adapted text is a product of both, its composite parts discernible but inseparable. The primary concern of this chapter, however, is to define "adaptation" itself because the current trend of applying the term to myriad cultural products without distinction dilutes its critical usefulness. I argue the need for a more rigorous application of qualifying adjectives to the cross-generic and cross-media adaptations that compose Shakespeare studies' various branches: textual adaptation, stage production, novelistic, and cinematic adaptation. Once distinctions between genres and media are established, it then becomes possible to identify different types of adaptations based upon how characters and plots are transformed into new narratives, which may also be classified by an open-source system of adjectives that enlarges our analytical toolbox without placing restrictions on future creations. Following this theorization of "adaptation," the chapter ends with a consideration of this book's other two key terms, "Québécois" and "of Shakespeare," to conclude that a Québécois adaptation of Shakespeare is a play, written by an author born or living in Québec, that rewrites significantly Shakespeare's text yet retains sufficient ties to Shakespeare to constitute more than a passing allusion to his titles or characters.

Chapters 3 through 6 treat the plays chronologically in order to demonstrate the parallel evolution of discourses of nation and gender within the plays and Québec society at large, particularly the progression in nationalist discourse from the rejection of defeatism in the 1960s to the issue of language in the 1970s, the post-referendum disillusionment in the 1980s, and the tension since the 1990s between plurality and pluralism in a nation that requires a united identity in order to achieve full political sovereignty.

Chapter 3, "The Quiet Revolution: *Passer à l'action*," looks at the first ever adaptation of Shakespeare in Québec, Robert Gurik's *Hamlet, prince du Québec* (1968). Gurik situates Québec's quest for sovereignty in terms of Hamlet's problem of ceaseless thought versus the urgency to take action, and he transforms Hamlet's most famous soliloquy into a reflection on freedom: "Être ou ne pas être libre!" (51).[3] The play espouses the nationalist imperative to throw off the *né pour un petit pain* defeatism inculcated by the church and to *passer à l'action* so that one day there will be "un... Qué... bec... libre,"[4] the dying command Hamlet-Québec gives to Horatio-Lévesque. The play's nationalism manifests itself through anti-ecclesiasticism, neo-Marxism, and parallels with African decolonization, and it is articulated in terms of Québec's socio-political, linguistic, and economic inequality within the framework of Canadian federalism. However, since there were no female political leaders at this time, the adaptation does not contain any female roles. Instead, the Queen represents the male-dominated Catholic Church, and Ophelia is aligned with former Premier Jean Lesage, resulting in a masculinist vision of how a Québec *libre* should develop.

Chapter 4, "Tyrants and Usurpers: Tradapting the Conquest," turns to Michel Garneau's two "tradaptations" of Shakespeare's *Macbeth* and *The Tempest*. Garneau's *Macbeth de William Shakespeare: Traduit en québécois* (1978) takes up the challenge to protect and promote the Québécois language issued by Michèle Lalonde in "La deffence et illustration de la langue quebecquoyse" (1973), which is modelled on Joachim du Bellay's *Deffence et illustration de la langue françoyse* (1549).[5] Writing during the debate about *Loi 101*,[6] Garneau invents an eighteenth-century dialect spoken prior to the Conquest of New France by Britain. He conflates the play's action in medieval Scotland with that of the Conquest as well as the 1970s neocolonialism believed to have resulted from it, linking all three layers of his palimpsest through a single nationalist discourse centred on the country's usurpation by a tyrant and its desperate need for liberation. Usurpation also figures prominently in *La tempête* (1989), but, contrary to Shakespeare's Prospero, Garneau's Prospero/Québec commits no wrongs against his brother Antonio/English Canada and nothing justifies the usurper's treachery of stealing Prospero's *seigneurie* from him. As in Gurik's play, however, Garneau's tradaptations provide little space for women characters. In his later play Miranda fares better than in Shakespeare because her inheritance of the usurped nation is predicated on her intelligence and self-sufficiency rather than her womb; however, in his earlier play Lady Macbeth is more circumscribed by eighteenth-century New France gender norms than those of medieval Scotland, losing her ambition and becoming a domestic companion. Norms governing masculinity are challenged, but Conquest/rape imagery and the fear of federasty continue to manifest themselves because, in keeping with allusions to the Conquest as one of the tradaptations' palimpsestuous layers, the masculine is as potentially penetrable and conquerable as the usurped nation.

Chapter 5, "The First Referendum: Daughters of the Carnivalized Nation," concentrates on Jean-Pierre Ronfard's *Lear* (1977) and *Vie et mort du Roi Boiteux* (1981),[7] adaptations of Shakespeare's *King Lear* and *Richard III* respectively. Ronfard's adaptations use carnival and magic realism to parody the bastardized state of the nation whose corruption and decay can be eliminated only by the rise to power of strong-willed women. Straddling the 1980 referendum, Ronfard's plays carnivalize the nation, rendering it grotesque through a focus on bastardy, a pertinent theme for a Québec nation still considered illegitimate as a full political entity, at best Canada's limping, bastard cousin. Whereas in the pre-referendum *Lear* the declining state of the nation and the urgency to rescue it figure prominently, in the post-referendum *Vie et mort du Roi Boiteux* the obvious degeneration of the nation is relegated to the background in favour of a focus on gender relations and sexuality until the nation finally acquires a female ruler at the play's end. The later play's inquiry into women's social, political, and marital roles corresponds to the historical rise of the feminist movement in Québec and the increased social presence of women's issues following the temporary decline of the national question after the referendum loss. Ronfard's adaptations figure daughters as the survivors, inheritors, and sources of regeneration for fictional, bastard nations that pass through the disorder of carnival and then hover on the precipice of a new social order which will be more inclusive of women, and to some extent immigrants, that is, of the "others" to whom carnival gives leave to rule.

The sixth chapter, "The Second Referendum: Plurality without Pluralism," examines the explosion of adaptations since the 1990s. At least twenty-seven adaptations have been written since then by playwrights from various sociocultural backgrounds, including the first Québécois adaptations written by women, queers, and aboriginals. These plays testify to Québec's ongoing ideological struggle between the need for a homogeneous definition of the nation if it is to unite and achieve sovereignty and the need for expressions of diversity by the various social groups within the nation. A plurality of new voices emerges during this period, but this diversity does not necessarily signal a turn away from nationalism in favour of the Canadian brand of pluralism, multiculturalism, which is absent from this corpus since Québec policy privileges intercultural integration instead. The explosion of new voices is embodied in the *38* event (1996), a series of thirty-eight monologues about each of Shakespeare's plays written by thirty-eight different playwrights under thirty-eight years of age. Marked by individualism, each monologue is a personal interpretation of a single play and lacks intertextual, thematic exchange with the others. Other adaptations showcasing new voices during this period include Pierre-Yves Lemieux's *À propos de Roméo et Juliette* (1989) in which a gay Mercutio asserts his homoerotic desire for Roméo during the emergence of AIDS, Normand Chaurette's *Les Reines* (1991) which features the queens from Shakespeare's first tetralogy, Antonine Maillet's *William S* (1991) in which many of Shakespeare's women characters confront the Bard, and Yves Sioui Durand and Jean-Frédéric Messier's *Hamlet-le-Malécite*

(2004) in which an aboriginal man seeks to play Hamlet while living the plot in his own life. This plurality could be seen as a temporary turn away from the use of the Bard as a medium for nationalist discourses since he is appropriated by groups arising from new social movements concerned with gender, sexuality, and ethnicity; however, nationalism remains a salient feature of Québécois adaptations, as we see in Madd Harold and Anthony Kokx's bilingual *Henry. Octobre. 1970.* (2002). Set during the October Crisis, this play presents the English-French bitterness of the battle of Agincourt as ongoing in the modern era, but unlike Shakespeare's *Henry V* it portrays the French more favourably than the English, who are rapists both culturally and literally. By sympathizing with the plight of exploited francophone workers, turning Michèle Lalonde's poem "Speak White" into a rallying cry, and de-demonizing and even heroizing the FLQ, the adaptation unquestionably endorses the sovereignist movement.

The concluding chapter, "Québec v. Canada: Interculturalism and the Politics of Recognition," draws on the sum of these readings to argue that Québécois adaptations cannot be subsumed under the heading of "Canadian" plays. The national question permeates the collective consciousness, so forms of alterity, such as gender, sexuality, and ethnicity, are not prominent in this corpus of texts. Despite more attention to gender in plays since the 1990s, the rape of women's bodies (symbolizing the rape/Conquest of the nation) and federasty continue to surface. While less concerned with gender, Québécois adapters challenge the fundamental principle underlying modern Canadian nationhood: the belief in one multicultural nation *a mari usque ad mare*, united "from sea to sea" as Canada's national motto proclaims. Québécois adaptations operate within the ideology of "two founding nations" because Québec has never bought into the idea of Canadian multiculturalism, which both Québécois and English Canadian scholars recognize was conceived in order to undermine Québec's identity as a nation. Rather than multiculturalism, Québec has adopted the policy of "interculturalism," which was brought to the political forefront in the "reasonable accommodation" debate that led in 2007 to the Bouchard-Taylor Commission. After a brief discussion of interculturalism, the chapter presents some possible explanations, both practical and theoretical, as to why nationalism tends to trump issues of gender and sexuality in contrast to the larger Western experience where new social movements gave rise to identity politics focused on issues such as feminism or queer rights. On a practical level, authorship, education, linguistic difference, and social progress all play a role in making Québec a unique case study in the larger Western context. On a theoretical level, this oddity can be explained by Nancy Fraser's discussion of the redistribution-recognition dilemma whereby some social groups seek redistribution of resources and others seek cultural recognition. In Fraser's view, the problem is that redistribution requires group dedifferentiation while recognition requires group differentiation. Québec is what Fraser calls a "bivalent collectivity" that seeks both political and economic redistribution as well as cultural recognition. Québec is also bivalent in that it is concerned with both differentiation from Canada and dedifferentiation of its own immigrants whom it tries to integrate into the collective national identity. This chapter ends by bringing together the practical and the theoretical explanations to this problem with the example of Pauline Marois, the leader of the Parti Québécois. During a 2011 political crisis, Québécois nationalism's gender trouble played out on Marois's public image.

Finally, the book's appendix charts chronologically the thirty-seven adaptations of Shakespeare in Québec whose publication details can be confirmed. This chronology lists the year, title, author, the Shakespearean source text(s) from which a play is adapted, publication details, production details of the earliest performance, and any translations.

Chapter One

Postcolonial Shakespeares and Gendering the Québec Nation

Ric Knowles opens *Shakespeare and Canada* with an autobiographical narrative. He identifies himself as a "white, male, settler/invader [who] stands *as* postcolonial subject" and who participated in the "1970s Canadian nationalist movement" during which Canadian drama was "coming of age" and supposedly "breaking *free* of what it consider[ed] to be the pernicious influence of the mother country, her Bard, and his theatrical outpost in Southwestern Ontario" (14, 13). Knowles recounts feeling like Miranda when she expresses amazement at this "brave new world/That has such people in't" (5.1.183–4). He claims that she is an "(almost) second-generation settler/invader [speaking], not about the new world, but the old one – or, more accurately, speaking about debased representatives of old world culture on a temporary sojourn in the colonies" (17). Like Miranda, as a teenager he too was awestruck by the old world colonial project, by the costumes, language, and accents of the actors in a production of Shakespeare in Stratford, Ontario. He goes on to describe his "first pilgrimage to England" "while working on [his] PhD" "in search of authenticity, authority, cultural identity" on his "purchased-in-Canada Brit-Rail pass through train stations named after characters in Shakespeare's history plays" (19). After searching for authority and authenticity in Canadian Shakespeare, and struggling at the same time with his own postcolonial identity, Knowles came to the conclusion that Miranda, as both settler and invader, as "inheritor, and perhaps reluctant agent of colonization, who is both implicated in and subjected to the inequities and injustices of the imperial project" (16), embodies a third position that usefully breaks down the Prospero/Caliban binary of colonizer/colonized that still haunts postcolonial theory today. The third space symbolized by Miranda might represent a more nuanced approach to Shakespeare that is less focused on shoring up or repudiating his authenticity, but might, in fact, allow for both simultaneously – a claim which, I argue, is exactly the dual role that Shakespeare performs in Québec.

Many assumptions are at work here, and one in particular merits closer attention: the postcoloniality of Canada. The postcoloniality of settler colonies has long been contested, and in the collection *Is Canada Postcolonial?*, edited by Laura Moss, several prominent critics, including George Elliott Clarke, Neil Besner, Diana Brydon, Terry Goldie, and Stephen Slemon, theorize all sides of the question without arriving at a consensus, or, as Moss sums it up, they arrive at a "typical Canadian response": "an unequivocal 'yes… and no… and maybe'" or "'it depends'" (7). According to Moss, one's stance on Canada's postcoloniality depends on whether or not one chooses to:

- focus on Canada as a member of the British Commonwealth;
- focus on the vastly different histories of the countries in that Commonwealth;
- view Canada as both an invader and settler colony;
- view Canada as holding two solitudes and/or other solitudes;
- see Canada as a nation of immigrants;
- see Canada continuing the colonization of First Nations people;
- isolate Canada as a member of the G8 and a powerful player in globalization;
- isolate Canada as a country with pockets of poverty;
- define Canadian primarily as "not American";
- think of a Molson "I am Canadian!" identity;
- consider multiculturalism in Canada to be more than a series of folklore festivals; and/or
- consider Canada to be a nation of writers from widely diverse ethnic and cultural backgrounds. (7–8)

I am inclined to come down on the Yes side of the question of Canada's postcoloniality, not merely because of my views of Canada vis-à-vis these political, historical, and identitary questions, but also because, like Knowles, I have a similar response to Shakespeare and have made the same PhD research trip in search of authenticity on a purchased-in-Canada BritRail pass, beginning in Stratford-upon-Avon and covering most of England, Scotland, and Wales, passing not only through train stations named after characters in Shakespeare's history plays but also through cities and regions mentioned in nearly every piece of literature I had read since childhood, from *David Copperfield* to *Mutiny on the Bounty*. In seeking to escape the dreariness of rural Nova Scotia, the obvious place to turn (at least in the days before cable TV or the Internet) was the "classics" of "English" literature, of which Shakespeare is the epitome. Given the hoopla, when I was in grade 1, over the visit of the recently married Prince and Princess of Wales to my town (Shelburne, settled by United Empire Loyalists and named after the English earl who became prime minister during the American Revolution), not to mention the visit of the queen herself just a year earlier for the signing of our constitution and granting of our new sovereignty, is it any wonder that England, and its cultural heritage, would figure prominently in my six-year-old mind as the source of "civilization" and "refinement"?[1] Thus, thirty years after Knowles's pilgrimage of postcolonial self-discovery, I and others in my generation of scholars (the tail end of Gen-X) continue to experience Shakespeare as a central figure in the formation of our (post-?)colonial Canadian identity. In this, I am not alone, for in the afterword to her volume *Shakespeare in Canada* Diana Brydon claims that the "work in this collection provides ample proof, were proof required, of Denis Salter's assertion that Canadian anglophilia has 'sought to authorize Shakespeare himself as a natural – that is, stable, lasting, pervasive – symbol of imperial colonial relations. English Canadian actors' attitudes towards Shakespeare [...] have therefore tended to be predicated on the assumption that it is they who must adapt themselves to Shakespeare, not Shakespeare who must adapt himself to them'" (408). While Canadian Shakespeares now appropriate the Bard for their own purposes, as a nation our initial engagement with Shakespeare has been mediated through colonial anglophilia.

But what, then, is the colonial status of Québec? Surely Shakespeare cannot be a determining factor in identitary affiliation for Québécois, 80 per cent of whom are francophone and are not so directly exposed to British culture.[2] Yet, Québec has an even more complex relationship vis-à-vis its European ancestors, the First Nations, and Canada's English-speaking majority. The Québécois people are or have been in colonial, anti-colonial, neocolonial, or postcolonial situations at different times in their history vis-à-vis different groups, sometimes in multiple types of relationships simultaneously.[3] Following exploration by Jacques Cartier in 1534 and the foundation of Québec city by Samuel de Champlain in 1608, Europeans, including the French, colonized the

First Nations of North America, first via the fur trade and various wars and later via more direct assimilation tactics designed to deprive aboriginals of their rights. The settlers of New France, however, and in particular the *filles du roi* recruited to bolster the population, came to be regarded in France as inferior colonials, as illustrated most notably in Voltaire's famous declaration in *Candide* that New France was nothing more than "quelques arpents de neige" not worth the cost of war.[4] Evidence of a lingering colonial inferiority complex vis-à-vis France, particularly in regard to language and culture, can still be seen in Québec today.[5] *La Conquête*, a singular and imposing conquest, and subsequent abandonment by the mother country then forced the colonists of New France into a new colonial relationship with England. Following the Conquest by the British on the Plains of Abraham in 1759, France gave up its claim to New France in the Treaty of Paris in 1763, turning the French colonists into British subjects. The Royal Proclamation issued by George III in the same year created the Province of Québec (later divided into Upper and Lower Canada by the Constitutional Act of 1791), and it sought, among other goals, to assimilate the French colonists and increase the power of the ruling anglophone minority, notably by excluding Catholics, and hence French Canadians, from administrative positions. The assimilation strategy was articulated most famously in Lord Durham's *Report on the Affairs of British North America*, whose purpose was to illuminate the causes of the failed Patriots' Rebellion of 1837–8 which had been mostly led by French Canadians with support from several Englishmen and Irishmen. In his report, Durham claims that the French are "a people with no history, and no literature" (149), and since their culture was unworthy of preservation he recommended assimilating the French into the English minority via the Union of Upper and Lower Canada, which took place the following year. Since the explicit objectives of Union, as proposed by Durham, were to assimilate the French and exploit the greater economic assets of Lower Canada in order to sustain the less developed Upper Canada, it is not surprising that French Canadians since then, and Québécois today, have perceived the relationship between Upper Canada/Ontario/English Canada and Lower Canada/Québec as neocolonial. The term "neocolonial" appears frequently in the writings of some of Québec's more radical nationalists during the 1960s and 1970s, such as Pierre Vallières's *Nègres blancs d'Amérique*,[6] and has continued to appear more recently in the writings of Pierre Falardeau, among others.[7] The emotional outpouring of appreciation for Falardeau's devotion to the nationalist cause following his death on 25 September 2009 testified that despite being branded as too polemical, in particular for his accusations of neocolonialism against corporations and government agencies, he was respected by many Québécois for saying out loud what more astute politicians dared not.[8]

Despite the frequent use of the terms "colonial" and "neocolonial" by nationalists to describe Québec, the use of postcolonial theory to analyse Québécois literature has been slow to materialize. In Québec, and in French literary studies in general, the debate has lagged behind for reasons explored seriously for the first time in the journal *Québec Studies* in 2003. In a special issue devoted to the question "en quoi la littérature québécoise est-elle postcoloniale?,"[9] critics such as Amaryll Chanady, Vincent Desroches, Obed Nkunzimana, and Robert Schwartzwald argue convincingly that Québec is postcolonial and that Québécois literary studies would be greatly enhanced by the application of postcolonial theory to Québécois texts. Chanady suggests that perhaps "it is this complex status of Quebec as colonial/postcolonial/colonized that explains a possible reticence to Anglo-American postcolonial and colonial discourse analysis. Whereas a society with well-entrenched cultural institutions and global cultural hegemony can afford to reflect critically on itself, a society that feels threatened by its marginality in a global context may feel a greater need for legitimation by celebrating its literary accomplishments and establishing an autonomous tradition in literary criticism" (34). She further qualifies how Québec's complex colonial heritage might make scholars adverse to this type of literary analysis: "postcolonial criticism always has an ambiguous status in settler societies, such as those of the Americas, where the hegemonic institutions are Western. Whereas it is easy to criticize Eurocentrism, racism, and neocolonialism in African francophone societies that have acquired their independence from the European colonizer, the (auto)criticism of Western hegemony in settler societies seems paradoxical" (34). Both Chanady and Schwartzwald suggest, though, that postcolonial studies and Québec studies can mutually inform, and transform, each other. For Schwartzwald, what is at stake in bringing postcolonial studies and Québec studies into dialogue is a demonstration of "the pertinence of Quebec's enactment of a postcolonial *protocol* to a general discussion of the negotiation between multiple identitarian positions and national communities that drives postcolonial theory" ("Rush" 129, italics in original). It is precisely this negotiation of multiple identitary positions within Québec's national community that we see emerge through its adaptations of Shakespeare, and which I will address more directly in this book's concluding chapter.

National Shakespeares

If we accept the premise that Québécois literature shares several characteristics with other settler societies and postcolonial literatures, a comparative study of Shakespeares in Canada and other postcolonial Commonwealth countries provides a fruitful context in which to situate an analysis of Québécois Shakespeares. Since Québec's Quiet Revolution, there has been an impressive proliferation of adaptations in English Canada mirroring the number written in Québec, but the content of Canadian adaptations presents significant differences. Québécois adaptations, as we shall see in later chapters, tend to focus primarily on issues surrounding the national question, while Canadian adaptations – influenced no doubt by official discourses on multiculturalism and less concerned with defending the language and culture of the stronger of the two founding nations – demonstrate as a whole a greater interest in diversity, both in terms of cultural diversity, such as the contributions of First Nations peoples, and gender diversity, such as the role of women and queers within the Canadian mosaic.

Canadian adaptations of Shakespeare make their appearance earlier than Québécois adaptations. English Canadians' desire to adapt Shakespeare can reasonably be attributed both to their anglophilia and to their greater familiarity with his texts. The first known adaptation of Shakespeare with Canadian content, according to the *Canadian Adaptations of Shakespeare Project (CASP)*, is the anonymous romance novel *Ottawah, the Last Chief of the Red Indians of Newfoundland* (1848) which uses the structure of *The Tempest* to recount the genocide of Beothuks (although, in keeping with colonialist thought, their extinction is blamed on the Micmacs rather than European settlers). This first appropriation of Shakespeare's texts to tell a decidedly Canadian story is emblematic of several other adaptations that use Shakespeare to bring attention to the stories of First Nations peoples, including Warren Graves's *Chief Shaking Spear Rides Again, or, The Taming of the Sioux* (1975), Tomson Highway's *Dry Lips Oughta Move to Kapuskasing* (1989),[10] Yvette Nolan and Philip Adams's *Shakedown Shakespeare* (1997), Daniel David Moses's *Brébeuf's Ghost* (2000),[11] and Yvette Nolan and Kennedy Cathy MacKinnon's *The Death of a Chief* (2005).[12] In Québec, however, the first adaptation of Shakespeare to adopt a First Nations perspective does not arrive on stage until 2004 with *Hamlet-le-Malécite*, which was co-written by Yves Sioui Durand and Jean-Frédéric Messier and produced by Ondinnok, the only aboriginal theatre troupe in Québec.

Gender has been a prominent feature in English Canadian adaptations of Shakespeare, more so than in Québec. As early as the turn of the twentieth century, Hubert Osborne's adaptations *The Shakespeare Play: A Drama in Rhythmic Prose* (1911) and *"The Good Men Do": An Indecorous Epilogue* (1917) speculated about Shakespeare's views of women and his relationships with his wife, his daughters, and the Dark Lady.[13] More recently, Ann-Marie MacDonald's *Good Night Desdemona (Good Morning Juliet)* (1990) and Djanet Sears's *Harlem Duet* (1996), feminist plays that also speak to issues of queerness and race, have captured the popular attention of the Canadian public. Both won the Governor General's Literary Award in the category of Drama and have had multiple performance runs.[14] Other adaptations, such as Timothy Findley's *Elizabeth Rex* (2000), which also won a Governor General's award, Margaret Clarke's *Gertrude and Ophelia* (1993), and Margaret Atwood's monologue "Gertrude Talks Back" (1992) queer Shakespeare by rewriting gender roles, both the author's and those in his plays.

In terms of mass appeal, perhaps no version of Shakespeare reached more Canadians than the television adaptations performed by the widely popular sketch comedy duo Johnny Wayne and Frank Shuster. Various forms of the *Wayne & Shuster* show were staples on CBC television's Saturday evening programming from the 1950s through to the late 1980s, and they have been occasionally rebroadcast as specials since the 1990s on both CBC and The Comedy Network. Skits such as "The Shakespearean Baseball Game" (1958), "Rinse the Blood Off My Toga" (1955), and "The Macbeth Murder Case (Or Hassle at the Castle)" (1988) were this particular Shakespearean's first introduction to the Bard. Other Shakespearean sketches include "Hamlet, The Kid from Elsinore" (1964), also titled "Hamlet, The Fastest Soliloquy in the West," and "Murder at the Stratford Festival." As television adaptations, these sketches testify to new media's ability to whet the general population's appetite for Shakespeare in a way that traditional stage productions – which were and still are inaccessible or prohibitively expensive in rural parts of Canada – cannot. First performed in black and white in 1958, and redone in colour in 1971 with a slightly altered script, "The Shakespearean Baseball Game," also titled "A Comedy of Errors, Hits, and Runs," is spoken approximately in blank verse. The script deftly mixes low-brow and high-brow culture, relying for laughs on both farcical slapstick (Johnny gets beaned in the head with a baseball) and the audience's knowledge of a mash-up of thirty-three Shakespearean-derived puns and quotations, primarily from *Richard III*, *Julius Caesar*, *Macbeth*, and *Hamlet* (e.g., "A hit, a hit, my kingdom for a hit!"; "Pitchers, catchers, shortstops, lend me your ears"; "So fair a foul I have not seen! [...] Get thee to an optometrist!"; "Now cracks a noble head. Good night, sweet catcher. Flights of shortstops sing thee to thy rest").[15] While similar television adaptations of Shakespeare do not exist in Québec – ostensibly due to the audience's unfamiliarity with the Bard – Wayne and Shuster's witty parodies do share a common trait with Québécois adaptations, and with Australian Shakespeares too: affectionate derision.

Australia is, of course, the settler society and Commonwealth country that most closely resembles Canada historically and socio-politically. According to John Golder and Richard Madelaine, editors of *O Brave New World: Two Centuries of Shakespeare on the Australian Stage*, "Catering for specifically Australian tastes and attitudes scarcely became possible until Australian society claimed post-colonial status: one index of this is the way in which the composition of locally-based Shakespeare touring companies (a phenomenon in themselves) became more Australian" in contrast to the British styles propagated by the Old Vic and the RSC (10). They conclude that Australian Shakespeares – by which they mostly mean productions, but which can include adaptations – do have a distinct style that has emerged from the continent's colonial history: "What we now think of as our post-colonial approach appears to be more 'laid-back,' a term that is always likely to feature in any assessment of where we are now, and may amount to a casually-subversive attitude" (12). This laid-back attitude that masks subversiveness is in keeping with larrikinism, which has characterized Australian Shakespeares since the 1970s and which is akin to the derision found in many Québécois adaptations. Larrikinism, perceived by many Australians as "one of their most cherished national traits," can be defined as "a blend of rebelliousness and cheeky irreverence" that embodies "a spirit of anti-authoritarianism harking back to Australia's origins as a penal colony and the antipathy between convicts and their overseers" (Squires). Applied to Shakespeare, larrikinism amounts to deriding the Bard's authority to dictate Australian cultural practices.

Larrikinism is, according to Adrian Kiernander, most clearly seen in the productions and adaptations of John Bell, an actor and director who co-founded the Nimrod Theatre, which operated in Sydney from 1970 to 1987, and then founded the Bell Shakespeare Company in 1990. In 1971, members of Nimrod created a burlesque Christmas show called *Hamlet on Ice*, whose "rough irreverence seems not only to capture the larrikin spirit of much of the early Nimrod's attitude to the classics, but also to hark back to Australia's early nineteenth-century passion for burlesques of Shakespeare" (241).[16] Other productions that embody Bell's larrikin approach to Shakespeare include a 1972 production of *Measure for Measure* that Kiernander praises for its "carnivalesque quality" (242), Nimrod's production of *Richard III* that "presented the English nobles as 'robber barons and larrikins'" (245), a 1978 production of *The Comedy of Errors* that "successfully maintained the technique of carnivalising Shakespeare for Australian audiences" (245), and the "company's most successful production to date [...] in respect to the complexity and sophistication of its Australian post-colonial qualities [...] *Henry 4*, Bell's 1998 conflation of Part One and Part Two of *Henry IV*" (248). Kiernander claims that this production had a "focus on a criminal underworld" and the "overriding image of the production was the one now increasingly familiar of the British as a wrangling collection of football hooligans" (248, 250–1). Bell's staging of the play as "a production intending to question the lingering influence of British culture in Australia [...] exposed a vision of the metropolitan centre as characterised by a hooligan mentality, where the hegemonic appearance of elegant civilisation was only a facade. By focusing on the less attractive aspects of English culture it worked as an attempt from within a part of the former empire to provincialise the centre" (252). However, insofar as "white Australian society is still conscious of, and celebrates, its origins in a convict settlement, this play might evoke a special sympathy here for the misrule and anti-establishment behaviour in the world of Falstaff" (248). Bell's work taints the British with hooliganism, thereby de-civilizing colonial authority, while at the same time it leaves space for the celebration of larrikin hooliganism in local culture, essentially attributing a positive force in contemporary Australian society to the brutalities of England's colonial past.

Richard Huber's 1998 play *Hamlet: He Was a Grave Digger* is another "vigorously 'larrikin' piece" which Lisa Warrington describes as "a postmodern deconstruction which plays with archetypes and overtly dislocates Shakespeare's text, placing it in a parodic version of Australia" (137). Compared to some of the "irreverent Shakespearean travesties" mentioned above, this play makes Australia's ties to its colonial past even more explicit by featuring "convoluted pseudo-Shakespearean lines in exaggeratedly refined English accents," "a pianist playing 'God Save the King,'" and a ghost "draped in a union jack" (138). Huber's play, Warrington esteems, is "an iconoclastic rewriting, which seeks to deconstruct and dislocate Shakespeare as a cultural authority, repositioning *Hamlet* as an Antipodean farce" (139). Thus, although as an anglophone settler colony Australia resembles Canada in several sociocultural and political respects, its larrikin Shakespeares more closely resemble Québécois adaptations which, as we shall see, also employ Shakespeare's text in a spirit of anti-authoritarianism, in contrast to English Canada's greater reverence for the Bard.

New Zealand's adaptations of Shakespeare share Australia's Antipodean irreverence and larrikin-like dislocation of the Bard's authority, but New Zealand, too, continues to mix defiance with deference by maintaining "at least a residual adherence to a colonial literary past, exemplified by the relatively recent demise of regional Shakespeare Societies" (Warrington 125). As in Australia, and for that matter Canada, "homegrown professional theatre did not take firm root in New Zealand prior to the 1960s" (126n4), notes Warrington, thus producing "a paradox which sees the continued pre-eminence of Shakespeare as a cultural icon" at the same time that adaptations begin to emerge to challenge his status (125). Among the bicultural adaptations that challenge New Zealand's colonial legacy are *Manawa Taua/Savage Hearts* (1994), co-written by Maori playwright Willie Davis and David Geary, a *Pākehā* (a term describing non-Maori New Zealanders usually of British descent), and *Romeo and Tusi* (1997), by Oscar Kightley and Erolia Ifopo. The first play is set "on the eve of New Zealand's nineteenth-century Land Wars" and features "a Maori chieftain who travels to Europe to extract a promise from Queen Victoria that his ancestral lands will not be taken from him" in exchange for him playing the role of "Othello on his return to the colony, as a means of spreading the civilising influence of art" (128–9). Warrington describes the last play as "a loose Shakespearean parody masking a serious theme of racial tension between New Zealand's indigenous Maori and immigrant Pacific Islanders" that features "parody, outrageous political incorrectness, one-liners, slapstick, quick comic reversals and the undermining of authority," all of which are "associated with the tradition of clowning in Samoa called *fale aitu*" (130, 131–2). Significantly, New Zealand boasts two feminist adaptations by Jean Betts, *Revenge of the Amazons* (1983) and *Ophelia Thinks Harder* (1993). Warrington compares the latter to

Ann-Marie MacDonald's *Goodnight Desdemona (Good Morning Juliet)* and Paula Vogel's *Desdemona: A Play about a Handkerchief* (1977). Resolutely feminist, *Ophelia Thinks Harder* chastises the intersecting institutional structures that have held back women's social progress, taking a no-holds-barred approach not seen in Québécois adaptations, as we shall see in chapter 6. In addition to challenging their colonial legacy, anglo-Commonwealth playwrights appear more committed to challenging patriarchy as well.

Scotland also shares a complex colonial history close to that of Québec, but given its proximity to England this nation has a different relationship to the Bard. Like Québec, Scotland currently has an independence movement arising from a past political union contracted without the full consent of its people, that is, without a referendum and despite widespread popular opposition. The relationship between England and Scotland has often been predicated upon the clash of national identities. Notable events in the history of the two nations include the annexation by England in 1296, the Wars of Scottish Independence (1296–1328; 1332–57), the union of the Scottish and English crowns with the ascension of James VI in 1603, the Act of Union in 1707 that united England and Scotland into the United Kingdom of Great Britain and dissolved the Parliament of Scotland, the reconvening of the devolved Scottish Parliament in 1999, and the formation of a minority government in 2007 and a majority government in 2011 by the Scottish National Party with a promise to hold a referendum on independence.

Scholars have not uncovered many Scottish adaptations of Shakespeare, but rumour has it that an "eager, absurd cry of 'Weel lads; what think you of Wully Shakespeare now?' is said to have greeted the 1756 Edinburgh premiere of John Home's Scottish tragedy *Douglas* (produced successfully the following year by Garrick in London […])," which, according to Robert Crawford, "is evidence of Scots seeking a rival to England's great dramatist" (128). The relationship between Shakespeare and Scotland has not escaped competitive rivalry, and Crawford demonstrates how Shakespeare came to be known as "the Bard" only "as a result of later Scottish cultural dynamics in the mid-eighteenth century" and that his acquisition of the title was "hastened by the career of another, very different poet" also known as "the bard," that is, Robert Burns (124). Crawford claims that the "widespread, and now global development of Shakespeare as national 'bard' is a direct reaction to the momentum of Scottish culture, and is bound up with the long-running currents of English-Scottish rivalry," but he also cautions that it "would be quite wrong, though, to suppose that Shakespeare was not venerated in Scotland" (129).

The competition between Scottish culture and Shakespeare as the cultural epitome of its English neighbours can be seen in the drive to translate Shakespeare into Gaelic and Scots. Indeed, the goal of translating Shakespeare directly into another language is to demonstrate the value of that language, and the culture with which it is associated, based on the assumption that any language semiotically rich enough to translate Shakespeare holds intrinsic cultural value.[17] J. Derrick McClure analyses several Scottish translations of Shakespeare, lingering in particular on three translations of the same passage from "the Scottish play": David Purves's *The Tragedie o Macbeth* (1992), Robin Lorimer's *Shakespeare's "Macbeth" Translated into Scots* (1992), and Edwin Morgan's "The Hell's-handsel o Leddy Macbeth" in his *Rites of Passage* (1976). McClure praises Lorimer's work because it follows the Shakespearean source text most closely and appears to be deliberately concerned with fidelity and demonstrating the potential of the Scots language to render Shakespeare accurately. In contrast, McClure assesses Morgan's vocabulary as the richest of the three and appreciates the creativity of his poetic talent, asserting that "his translation is a new work, offered not as an imitation or re-statement but an independent poetic artefact" (233). Yet, he takes issue with omissions and moments of infidelity in Purves's work, claiming that he has "failed to accept the full implications of a translator's role," such as when Purves translates "pall thee in the dunnest smoke of Hell" (1.5.50) as "Hap ye i the darkest plaid o Hell" (231). In choosing the term "plaid," a traditional piece of tartan cloth, when the Scottish word "reek" is an option for translating "smoke," it would seem that, like Morgan, Purves is not intent on producing a direct translation of Shakespeare at all but rather an adaptation or, perhaps more accurately, what Michel Garneau calls a "tradaptation." While McClure is right to point out that wrapping oneself in plaid conveys comforting warmth rather than "the nightmarish terror of Shakespeare's image" (231), this seems to be precisely the point since plaid has become an easily identifiable symbol of Scottish identity to people around the world. The texts of Purves and Morgan can both therefore be seen as "tradaptations" that straddle the border between loyal translation and creative adaptation, as we will see in the work of Garneau.

Catalonia, a non-Commonwealth nation with a burgeoning nationalist movement similar to Québec's, also has a long history of Shakespeare translations that reflect Catalan concerns but adopt a somewhat surprising stance on the colonial relationship between the source text and the target language. In her book *Shakespeare in Catalan*, Helena Buffery claims that when translated into Catalan Shakespeare is "more often than not, an 'establishment' Shakespeare, born of a desire for cultural normality and universality" (1). As is the case for translations of Shakespeare in Gaelic and Scots, translating Shakespeare into Catalan is, she argues, a "process, by which a national culture persuades of its distinctness and distinction through positioning itself in relation to other cultures" (4). During and after the *Noucentista* period, Catalan translations and accompanying paratexts were perceived as "contributing to the 'reciprocal' process of universalizing Catalan through texts of recognized cultural value and appropriating the imperialist values of other cultures so approved in the dominant nationalist political discourse of the early decades of the twentieth century" (11). This desire to elevate Catalan national culture by virtue of the language's ability to produce beautiful renditions of Shakespeare does not mean, however, that the history of Catalan Shakespeares is not also marked by derisive adaptations characteristic of Australia and Québec. Buffery also notes that "it is within the comic tradition of *sainets* that we can perceive perhaps the earliest manifestations of Catalan Shakespeares" (25). These *sainets*, which were comic sketches often played at the Teatre de Barcelona, depicted lower-class life from a satirical point of view, and in this sense they can be likened to Australian larrikinism. She points out that touring productions by foreign theatre companies and Shakespeare-inspired operas "led to a spate of parodies or what are often known as 'travesties' of certain plays" (26), that is, derisive adaptations akin to those in Australia, New Zealand, and Québec. Shakespeare's dual nature, as elevator of a national culture and as a source of ridicule, points to a pattern in nations whose colonial history is not unlike Québec's, demonstrated perhaps most poignantly in the "representation of Shakespeare as a kind of saviour for Catalan culture" whose "sweet and prudent oracles" can, according to Cebrià Montoliu in the introduction to his translation of *Macbeth*, "make you forget the deep lack of your tragic past" (Buffery 128). Tragedy, far from unknown by nations seeking recognition of their political sovereignty, can often be offset with comedy, and it comes perhaps as no surprise that larrikinism and *sainets* would play an important role in the Shakespearean history of such nations, just as many of the Québécois adaptations in this book often turn Shakespeare's tragedies into comedies for their local audience.[18]

Most work on postcolonial Shakespeares has focused on India because of the long and complex colonial relationship between India and England, but India's relationship to Shakespeare differs significantly from Québec's because of cultural attitudes towards adaptation and the role of the educational system. "In the Indian literary tradition," Poonam Trivedi writes, "translation, adaptation, rewriting and transformation are sanctioned practices of literary creation" and recognized as "legitimate modes of alterity"; as such, "the initial indigenous response to Shakespeare in India was to adapt and Indianize" ("It is" 47). While the earliest Shakespeares were "freewheeling adaptations [...] and often added song and dance to facilitate local reception," some were "critical appropriations which challenged colonial hegemony" (47). Adaptation into "an indigenous theatrical idiom remained the mainstream mode" in popular culture, including after independence in 1947 which has seen the adaptive tradition evolve into "a deconstructive 'play' with the text and themes of Shakespeare" (47). However, Shakespeare's popularity in India arose not only through adaptation in popular culture but also through the educational system. While his works were "introduced to India in 1755 as part of the entertainment apparatus of the trading enterprise" (47), it was "with the opening of institutions like the Hindu College of Calcutta in 1817," Trivedi explains, "that the systematic study of English literature began and Shakespeare was enshrined in the classroom" ("Introduction" 14). In fact, Francis Barker points out that the "first time it was possible to take exams in Shakespeare" was not in England but rather "as entrance qualifications for natives wishing to join the Indian Civil Service under the Raj" (262n13). Trivedi argues that after "the Education Act of 1835 and the official promulgation of English as the language of administration and government-funded education, there was a decisive shift. Shakespeare was moved from the fashionable and cultural to the imperial and ideological axis," which produced "a schism (which lasts till today) between the English-educated elite and the vernacular-speaking masses" (15). As a result, "there developed two mutually exclusive streams – of an 'academic' literary Shakespeare led by Anglicized Indians and a popular Shakespeare on stage, transformed and transmuted in translation" (15). In India, then, Shakespeare was both a tool of colonization in the educational system and a tool of resistance to that colonization in popular culture.

This was not the case in Québec where Shakespeare was not taught in the schools in order to promulgate England's greatness. Rather, from the foundation of New France through the Conquest until the Quiet Revolution, education was largely controlled by the church. The BNA Act of 1867 confirmed education as a provincial jurisdiction and in Québec confessional-based schools were either Catholic for francophones or Protestant for anglophones. The educational authority conferred on Catholic priests and nuns allowed them to protect the French language and culture from the influence of the wealthier and more powerful anglophone minority, that is, from those who spoke Shakespeare's tongue. In response to the five-volume *Parent Commission Report* published in 1963–4, the Liberal Party led by Jean Lesage subjected Québec's inadequate educational system to a wave of modernizations, including the creation of a Ministry of Education (MEQ) and improved training for secular teachers, although the Catholic and Protestant school commissions remained in place until the PQ replaced them in 1998 with linguistic school boards. Still today, Shakespeare is not part of the MEQ's official curriculum for francophone students. Individual teachers have discretion to assign whatever literature they choose and tend to gravitate towards Molière for drama. Francophone Québécois are thus more likely to have encountered Molière's plays than Shakespeare's during their formative years, and when they go to see either a theatrical production or an adaptation of Shakespeare they are likely much less familiar with his plays than an anglophone educated in nearby Ontario or across the globe in India.

Nation and Gender from the Conquest to the Quiet Revolution

While the adaptations that are the subject of this book only begin to appear after the Quiet Revolution, contemporary discourses about nation and gender in Québec are marked by the *Conquête* of the French by the British in 1759, the most notable imprint on the collective consciousness of Québec. The French were jolted from a dominant to a dominated collective subject position, and the conquered nation could arguably be likened to a woman. In the case of both francophone Québécois and women, the demographic majority is disempowered and minoritized in terms that are gendered and sexualized; the conquered nation is raped and plundered.[19] As a collective consciousness, the Québec nation acts, ostensibly, like a raped woman who has never fully healed from its wounds; instead, it must learn to live with or, to employ a Québécois colloquialism that highlights its linguistic colonization, "dealer avec" the scars of its past trauma.

The Conquest/rape parallel explains why the spectre of what Robert Schwartzwald calls "federasty" has haunted Québécois literature since the Quiet Revolution. "Fédéraste" is a pun that associates federalists with pederasts. Through this displacement of the abject, an oppressed nation gets one over on Québécois who have sold out to federalist oppressors. The "fear of federasty" betrays a reactionary response to political oppression that attempts to turn the tables on these national traitors by figuring them as effeminate and penetrable, hence weak ("Fear" 179–81). When Québécois authors resort to depicting federalist politicians as "fédérastes," they manifest the national rape suffered during the Conquest that continues to pervade their collective unconsciousness. They transform the passivity implicit in the common sentiment of "on s'est fait fourrer" into verbal sodomitical agency.[20] By inflicting the linguistic equivalent of ritualized sexual violence, they escape the feminized victim position and in turn they effeminize federalist *compradors*. Relying on such homophobic insults to gain the symbolic upper hand in a political struggle is, of course, problematic since queers become casualties of this linguistic war alongside the federalist mimic men who are the primary target.

The Conquest/rape metaphor appears in several Québécois adaptations of Shakespeare where the rape of women's bodies symbolizes the rape of the nation. Corneille's story in Ronfard's *Lear* illustrates how rape is a tool of conquest by soldiers in war, and Judith's dream in Ronfard's *Vie et mort du Roi Boiteux* figures rape as part of a civilizing mission as she imagines the rape of her body as a fit revenge for her husband's colonial rape of aboriginal culture. In *Henry. Octobre. 1970.* Katherine's rape stands in not only for the military conquest of a Québec that has been taken hostage by soldiers, but it also symbolizes Canada's cultural imperialism and neocolonial domination. *Henry. Octobre. 1970.* also contains several homophobic scenes and epithets, and it is an example of how the fear of federasty privileges nationalism over queerness and fails to acknowledge the contributions of queers to the nation's identity – such as those of the famous gay author Michel Tremblay, whose literary use of *joual*,[21] or working-class slang, advanced Québec's claim of a distinct language and culture to the point that Québécois is called "la langue de Tremblay." The repetition within Québécois adaptations of Shakespeare of the motif of a feminized, raped nation can thus be read as an awareness of the victimized *complexe de colonisé* that it has borne since the Conquest, a collective psychological wound that it has been trying to heal since the Quiet Revolution.

Between the Conquest and the Quiet Revolution, the history of Québec is marked both by resistance to England and English Canada and by domination by the Catholic Church. Nationalist discourses encouraging the approximately 95 per cent French Catholic majority to resist colonial rule and assimilation by the English minority were always present, as seen in the popularity of the Parti canadien which became the Parti patriote in 1826 and whose leader Louis-Joseph Papineau played a key role in the Patriots' Rebellion of 1837–8. The Rebellion arose partly in response to the British Parliament's refusal of the 92 Resolutions adopted in 1834 by the Lower Canada Legislative Assembly, which primarily demanded reforms such as the creation of responsible government. Papineau and then Robert Nelson, among others, were forced to flee to the United States where Nelson, an anglophone and the provisional president of the proclaimed but never actualized Republic of Lower Canada, wrote the *Déclaration d'indépendance du Bas-Canada*. This declaration of independence contained several progressive ideas for the period, including equal rights for all aboriginals (referred to as *sauvages*), the abolition of the death penalty (except for murder), the abolition of feudal land management, the abolition of debtor's prison, and the instauration of vote by secret ballot, in addition to rights recently proclaimed in other parts of the world, such as freedom of religion, freedom of the press, and trial by jury.

After the failed Patriots' Rebellion and then Confederation, French Canadian nationalism continued to flourish, but it transformed from the Patriots' overtly political nationalism into clerical nationalism. Coming to the defence of *Canadien* (as Québécois were called until Union) and later French Canadian language and culture, much of this affirmation was articulated by *ultramontaniste* priests. From Latin, meaning "beyond the mountains," that is, beyond the Alps, ultramontanism began in 1840 and peaked between 1867 and 1896; in this ideology Roman Catholic priests supported the pope as supreme head of the church, as opposed to Gallicanism and other tendencies opposed to papal jurisdiction. Ultramontane nationalism linked nation and religion; in the words of Monseigneur Laflèche, bishop of Trois-Rivières from 1870 to 1898, "la foi sera le ciment de la nation" (qtd. in Monière,

Développement 179).[22] Laflèche was against state education, thought the government must legislate to make people respect God's law as interpreted by the Catholic Church, and preached obedience to the British crown. Idealizing French Canada's colonial past, ultramontanism valorized rural agriculture (such as "défricher la terre") over urban industrialization (which was seen as Anglo-Saxon) (181).[23] As Louis Balthazar summarizes it, "Être Canadien français, cela voudra dire d'abord être fidèle à la foi de ses ancêtres, maintenir les cadres familial et paroissial intacts, demeurer enraciné dans la terre ancestrale, résister à l'industrialisation" (72).[24] The primary duty of French Canadians was to defend the Catholic religion and the French language in their New World "foyer" [home]. The family became a microcosm of the minority nation in which traditional values were preserved. These values formed a linked triad underlying the ideology of "la survivance" [survival]: family, language, religion. As homemakers responsible for teaching their children language and a sound moral upbringing, women carried the burden of transmitting these traditional values and ensuring the survival of the nation (Lamoureux, "Nationalisme" 51–2). In advocating a passive nationalism concentrated in family life rather than overt political action, this ideology produced the attitude that French Canadians were "nés pour un petit pain," which ties into the domesticity of the "revanche des berceaux" survival strategy.[25] Clerical nationalism continued under the leadership of Premier Honoré Mercier, as well as *Le Devoir* newspaper founder Henri Bourassa (especially after the First World War conscription crisis) and the priest and historian Lionel Groulx, lasting until after the Second World War.

The power of the Catholic Church facilitated the rise to power of Maurice Duplessis whose Union nationale party ruled Québec from 1936 to 1939 and from 1944 to 1960. The fifteen-year period of Duplessis's second reign until his death in 1959 is often called *la Grande noirceur*, or the Great Darkness, in the historical consciousness of many Québécois, although some historians have critiqued this blanket description. The darkness of this period refers to multiple social conditions at the time: widespread patronage and corruption in government, anti-unionism, censorship, a large economic gap between francophone workers and anglophone "bosses," and few social programs for the masses, except the education and health care provided by the Catholic Church. The Catholic Church was also corrupt as an institution; priests and nuns economically exploited and physically and sexually abused thousands of children who later came to be known as *les orphelins du Duplessis*, or Duplessis's orphans. Duplessis's extremely close ties with the church solidified his power. The Union nationale used the campaign slogan "Le ciel est bleu, l'enfer est rouge" in order to cloak their own blue-logo party in the appearance of virtue and to vilify the opposing red-logo Liberal party.[26] These difficult economic and social conditions were, however, met with resistance. For instance, the 1948 *Refus global* manifesto, written by Paul-Émile Borduas and signed by a group of artists known as *les Automatistes*, helped pave the way for the explosive changes of the Quiet Revolution after Duplessis's death.

The emergence from this great darkness was first termed the "Quiet Revolution" by a writer for the Toronto-based newspaper *The Globe and Mail* in order to explain to English Canada the massive social reforms that were quickly taking place in Québec under the Liberal government of Jean Lesage (1960–6), which had campaigned under the slogans "C'est le temps que ça change" in 1960 and "Maîtres chez nous" in 1962.[27] Important reforms continued to take place under Daniel Johnson's and Jean-Jacques Bertrand's rebuilt Union nationale government from 1966 to 1970, thus characterizing the entire decade as the Quiet Revolution period. Much of this social change can be summarized under the concept of *l'État-providence*, or the welfare state, which stands in marked contrast to Duplessisme: highlights include the creation of free universal health care; public television; the Caisse de dépôt et placement and the Régie des rentes du Québec (societies responsible for managing state funds and pension funds); a Ministry of Cultural Affairs, Ministry of Revenue, Ministry of Natural Resources, Ministry of Justice, and Ministry of Education; the system of CÉGEP colleges and the Université du Québec network; the Office de la langue française; and Montréal's Metro subway system. Under the leadership of René Lévesque, the minister of natural resources at the time, the Liberal government nationalized hydroelectric power and consolidated eleven private electricity companies in the state-owned Hydro-Québec. Other major changes included the creation of the Confédération des syndicats nationaux (CSN), increased unionization, and a new labour code. Québec hosted Expo 67 in the spring and later that year welcomed General Charles de Gaulle, who famously shouted "Vive le Québec libre!" from the balcony of Montréal's city hall.[28] The majority of people abandoned, practically overnight it seemed, the Catholic Church which had heretofore ruled every aspect of socio-political life. The Quiet Revolution, and the feelings of pride, accomplishment, and self-sufficiency that it engendered, inaugurated a wave of nationalist – and sovereignist – sentiment that has grown relatively steadily ever since.[29]

The Quiet Revolution has also come to be seen as a psychological turning point in Québec's collective identity, whose history has been read as analogous to an individual's life phases. As Fernand Dumont recounts Québec's development in *Genèse de la société québécoise*, there was "une enfance à la société québécoise (jusqu'en 1837), une adolescence qui correspondrait à la révolution tranquille (après la longue interruption, sorte de sommeil de la Belle au bois dormant, que représenterait la survivance) et l'espoir d'un âge adulte avec le passage de la nation au pays" (Lamoureux, *L'amère patrie* 114).[30] While such a reading of over 200 years of history is obviously reductive, and scholars have argued for a more nuanced interpretation, the metaphor nonetheless holds considerable sway in Québec, and the Quiet Revolution can thus be seen in the popular collective imaginary as a growth spurt during which an adolescent Québec awakened to its own potential and savoir-faire, giving it the confidence to envision political independence as the final step in a natural development towards the autonomy associated with adulthood.

It was also during this revolutionary decade that the sovereignist Parti Québécois (PQ) was formed. Other sovereignist parties already existed, such as the Action socialiste pour l'indépendance du Québec (ASIQ), founded in 1960, and the Ralliement national (RN), which was created in 1966 out of the fusion of the Regroupement national and Ralliement créditiste, but the most important early sovereignist party was the Rassemblement pour l'indépendance nationale (RIN), which became a political party in 1963 and was led by Pierre Bourgault in 1964. In 1967, René Lévesque left the Liberal party and founded the Mouvement Souveraineté-Association (MSA). Less than a year later, the Parti Québécois was formed from the fusion of the MSA and the RN, and, later, members of the dissolved RIN. René Lévesque was the PQ's leader from its inception – through four general election campaigns, two government mandates, and one referendum – until his resignation in 1985. The PQ remains the primary sovereignist party in Québec provincial politics today and has been accompanied since 1991 by the Bloc Québécois (BQ), its homologue on the federal front.

The marked difference between the pre- and post-Quiet Revolution periods is particularly evident in the history of women's rights and queer rights in Québec. Before the Quiet Revolution, the conservative ideologies of the Catholic Church dominated social discourse, notably on the question of women's suffrage, which caused a twenty-two-year discrepancy between federal and provincial rights. In Québec, women first acquired the right to vote in 1791 when the Constitutional Act left open the possibility in decreeing that eligible voters were "such persons as shall severally be possessed, for their own use and benefit, of lands or tenements" (section XX). While few women were landowners, those who were did not think to exclude themselves from the term "person," as was the case in other British colonies where the absence of a formal exclusion of women was never interpreted as an authorization to vote. Women stopped voting in practice in 1834 following a revision to the law that was subsequently disclaimed for other reasons, and their official right to vote was removed in 1849. Québécois women did not gain suffrage until 1918 at the federal level, 1940 at the provincial level, and 1974 in all municipalities.[31] The twenty-two-year gap between federal and provincial suffrage can largely be attributed to the strong influence of the Catholic Church in Québec politics. Pressure from several women's groups, led by such notable figures as Marie Gérin-Lajoie, Idola St-Jean, and Thérèse Casgrain, was no match for the influence the church carried with the government. Shortly after Adélard Godbout's Liberal party temporarily took power away from Duplessis in 1939, Godbout faced strong opposition from the Catholic Church in his attempts to pass women's suffrage. Only by threatening to resign, which would have resulted in the anti-clerical Télesphore-Damien Bouchard replacing him as premier, was he successful. The bishops relented on the issue of women's suffrage only to preserve their own power.

Following the wane of the church's power during the Quiet Revolution, women's groups in Québec were able to pass progressive legislation, resulting in greater social protections than in other parts of Canada, although some of the legal progress also involved redressing gross injustices in women's legal status dating back to the ultramontane period. For instance, in 1964, Bill 16 ended the judicial incapacity of married women that had been in place since 1866 when married women were deemed little better than children, illegals, and the mentally disabled, belonging to their husbands rather that existing as autonomous persons. Québec's feminist movement was particularly strong in the 1970s, a time that saw the creation of the activist group Front de libération des femmes du Québec (FLF; 1969–71), the publications *Québécoises deboutte!* (1971–4) and *Les têtes de pioche* (1976–9), and the governmental Conseil du statut de la femme (CSF; 1973–present), which has been orienting government policy ever since on issues such as daycare, abortion, and women's fiscal and judicial equality. In 1978, for instance, the

PQ government evaded federal restrictions on abortion by creating family-planning clinics providing "therapeutic" abortion services that were commonly called "cliniques Lazure," named after Denis Lazure, the minister of social affairs at the time.[32] That same year also saw the institution of eighteen weeks of paid maternity leave.

Post-Quiet Revolution Québec has also been fertile ground for advances in rights for queer people. While the federal government decriminalized homosexuality between two consenting adults as part of the omnibus Criminal Law Amendment Act, 1968–9 – in reference to which then Justice Minister Pierre Trudeau famously declared that "there's no place for the state in the bedrooms of the nation" – Québec became the first provincial or national jurisdiction in the world to prohibit discrimination on the basis of "sexual orientation" via the Québec Charter of Human Rights and Freedoms. Adopted by the Liberal government on 27 June 1975 and effective as of 28 June 1976, the Québec Charter was amended by the PQ government on 15 December 1977 to include sexual orientation after two thousand activists protested the brutal simultaneous police raids at the Truxx and Le Mystique gay bars in Montréal on the night of 21–2 October 1977. In contrast, the Canadian Charter of Rights and Freedoms, which was adopted in 1982, did not explicitly include sexual orientation as protected grounds from discrimination, and it was not until 1995, in *Egan v. Canada*, that the Supreme Court ruled that it should be read into section 15 of the Charter. In 1999, the Québec government, once again under the PQ, passed the omnibus Bill 32 which changed the definition of "spouse" to include same-sex partners, making Québec the first province to treat same-sex spouses equally with common law heterosexual couples. The bill made changes to 39 other laws and regulations in areas such as taxes, pension benefits and retirement plans, car insurance, social assistance, and the workplace. Then, in June 2002, still under the PQ government, Québec passed Bill 84 which legalized civil unions between same-sex couples, becoming the first province, after the slightly more restrictive domestic partnerships enacted in Nova Scotia in 2001, to offer all the same rights as marriage, including the adoption of children. In September that same year, the Québec Superior Court ruled in *Hendricks and Leboeuf v. Québec* that the federal opposite-sex definition of marriage was discriminatory under section 1 of the Canadian Charter, declaring that federal restrictions against same-sex marriage would become inoperative in Québec in two years time, thus obliging the federal government to take action. Michael Hendricks and René Leboeuf appealed the delay, which the

Québec Court of Appeal struck down in March 2004 because same-sex marriage had since become law in Ontario and British Columbia, allowing the couple to be married legally on 1 April 2004, over a year before the federal Civil Marriage Act became law on 20 July 2005, which made Canada the fourth country to approve same-sex marriage nationwide, behind Belgium, the Netherlands, and Spain. In all of these legal struggles for equal rights for queers, then, the Québec government was a leader in the broader Canadian context, and significant gains were accomplished primarily when the PQ was in power, which conferred "une aura pro-féministe et pros-gais" upon the sovereignist party (Lamoureux, *L'amère patrie* 120).[33]

If advances for women's and queer rights were largely accomplished in Québec under sovereignist PQ governments, this does not mean that the relationship between the nationalist movement and the women's and queer rights movements was unproblematic. Rather, tension existed between the two as women resisted allowing the nationalist cause to overshadow their demands, calling instead for solidarity between the nationalist movement and the feminist movement. In fact, a popular feminist slogan from the 1970s by the Front de libération des femmes (FLF) (whose name plays off that of the Front de libération du Québec [FLQ]) suggests that inter-group solidarity is not just desirable but required if each is to achieve its goals: "Pas de Québec libre sans libération des femmes! Pas de femmes libres sans libération du Québec!" (Collectif Clio 483).[34] As Québécois feminists pointed out, the nation cannot achieve freedom without women also achieving greater freedom and a larger role in its political affairs. Robert Gurik's question in *Hamlet, prince du Québec*, "To be or not to be free," cannot be answered without first asking who exactly shall achieve this freedom, for in this scenario the freedom of one social group is contingent upon that of another.

In "Féminisme et nationalisme au Québec, une alliance inattendue," Micheline de Sève describes how, in the early 1970s, the Front de libération des femmes – a movement of radical feminist, Québécois nationalists – was formed by "quelques étudiantes anglophones de McGill, adeptes du *Women's Lib* et converties à la légitimité de la lutte de libération sociale et nationale du Québec" (161).[35] According to de Sève, "ces radicales nationalistes ne réclamaient rien moins que le renversement du patriarcat et de l'impérialisme anglo-américain" (161).[36] The FLF activists link together the feminist and nationalist causes, arguing that "[l]e Québec étant un pays colonisé, la Québécoise est donc doublement exploitée" (FLF qtd. in de Sève 161).[37] As de Sève points out, anglophone

McGill students, mostly of American origin, had more access to the writings of American radical feminists, but soon the francophone feminists in the group felt oppressed by their anglophone sisters. In a letter to the Women's Lib movement in New York, the FLF explicitly renounce Marlene Dixon, an American sociology professor at McGill with a PhD from UCLA, "et ses amies" [and her friends, presumably referring to the students de Sève mentions] on the basis that "elle vit ici depuis un an et demi et elle n'a jamais pu communiquer directement avec nous car elle ne parle toujours pas français. Elle ne peut donc en aucune façon parler en notre nom ni en celui d'aucune Québécoise" (O'Leary and Toupin 80).[38]

De Sève does not tackle the question, however, of why anglo-American women would adopt a joint nationalist-feminist political position in the first place. I would posit that, already having their own national identity firmly in hand, the American women were free to take up gender issues as their cause; Québec feminists, on the other hand, were too caught up in the birthing of a national identity and the decolonization of their nation – as the eventual feelings of double oppression on this front testify – to take on a feminist agenda to a full, radical extent without dividing their energies. As the FLF slogan demands, the freedom of Québec and the freedom of women must necessarily happen conjointly in order for Québécois women not to feel doubly oppressed, but fighting both battles at once, without the collaboration of male nationalists, would make it difficult for either nationalists or feminists to achieve their goals. The American women, on the other hand, would not consider linking the two causes as emotionally divisive since they would be less personally interpellated by the Québec nationalist cause. They were not colonized doubly by their subject position as both nationalists and feminists since they had not internalized the Québécois *complexe de colonisé*, as seen in the fact they were quickly perceived as the colonizer themselves.

Political scientist Diane Lamoureux, in *L'amère patrie*,[39] suggests that it is "possible de s'y tailler une place comme féministe et de lier émancipation nationale et émancipation sexuelle" and adds that it is "significatif que, pour illustrer l'extranéité de l'Alliance canadienne par rapport aux 'valeurs québécoises,' Gilles Duceppe, le chef du Bloc québécois, ait essentiellement fait référence au droit des femmes à l'avortement et à la défense des droits des gaies et lesbiennes" (112).[40] She posits that Québec nationalism is based upon "la promesse de l'émancipation, ce qui permet de lier la cause nationale à toute une série de causes sociales et d'investir le discours national de l'espoir des lendemains qui chantent," but she also cautions that while this national consciousness helped unify diverse social causes "il a aussi servi de frein à l'expression de la diversité sociale" (112).[41] Québécois adaptations of Shakespeare align with this problematic assumption that national liberation will solve other social problems; diverse social causes do not appear in these texts until the 1990s because playwrights focus their attention instead on the overarching cause of national emancipation in keeping with the promise that it will resolve other issues as well. Lamoureux does, however, identify three important points of convergence between feminism and nationalism in Québec:

> Premièrement, une volonté de détraditionalisation complète (puisque ce travail était déjà largement entamé au moment de la révolution tranquille) de la société québécoise. [...] Deuxièmement, un travail commun de construction de l'État providence national comme modalité de constitution de la solidarité sociale et condition de possibilité de la nation civique pour les nationalistes alors que pour les féministes, l'État providence permet de politiser certaines injustices qui passaient autrefois pour privées et de parvenir à une régulation politique des rapports sociaux de sexe. Troisièmement, une convergence dans la politisation de l'identité, même si les deux mouvements privilégient des formes différentes d'affiliation identitaire. (178–9)[42]

Feminism, she argues, played off the polysemic application of the nationalist terms "égalité ou indépendance" – which was the title of a book published by Daniel Johnson (*père*) in 1965 and his slogan in the next year's general election (163). As a potent demand for liberation made by nationalists and feminists, the applicability of "equality or independence" to both movements reveals their potential interdependence.

Differentiating Discourses

Despite the positive influence nationalism has had in advancing the social agenda of women and queers, outside Québec nationalism has gotten a bad reputation in contemporary scholarship, even among some postcolonialists who, rather than associating nationalism with decolonization and liberation movements achieved through democratic means, tend to paint it with the same brush as violent revolutions and terrorism, slandering all nationalism as tribalist, xenophobic, inward-looking, reactionary isolationism.[43] Common to all these criticisms is the implication, and sometimes the direct accusation, of "essentialism." Martha Nussbaum observes that often "the opponents of essentialism use the word polemically as a term of abuse and with a certain air of superiority" (205). The charge of "essentialism" as it is commonly employed, however, is often a vulgarization of a complex philosophical position within debates about metaphysical realism or internalist conceptions of the human being. Nussbaum argues that essentialism can actually promote social justice through an identification of basic human functions; for instance, it is usually better to be alive than dead, to have food than to starve, to feel emotionally fulfilled than dissatisfied, and to be free from violence than to be violated. Forms of cultural relativism that ignore these essential human needs under the guise of respect for the rights of foreign cultures are not synonymous with respect for the rights of individuals, especially when the moral high ground of non-interference is taken by those in positions of privilege as a justification for ignoring their duty to attend to the basic needs of others (216–21, 203–5). Essentialism, then, can be a rallying cry to ensure that basic human needs are met, especially the needs of socially marginalized others, and nationalism can be employed tactically as an appropriation of the power necessary to secure the fulfilment of those needs when they are not already met. The greater social justice the nationalist PQ government created not only for working-class francophones but also for women and queers testifies that we need not fear the "essentialist" bogeyman with which nationalism is associated.

One of nationalism's most famous detractors is Eric Hobsbawm who asserts in *Nations and Nationalism since 1780* that "nationalism is historically less important" in the twentieth century than in the nineteenth century, and twentieth century world history "can no longer be contained within the limits of 'nations' and 'nation-states' as these used to be defined, either politically, or economically, or culturally, or even linguistically" (181, 182). In attempting to argue that nationalism is dying, Hobsbawm mischaracterizes several aspects of Québec's history and social policies. For instance, he claims the French language "seems safe enough" because of "the official bilingualism of the federation" (165). He incorrectly attributes the protection of French to Canadian federal policy rather than the nationalist *Loi 101* instituted by the PQ in 1977, and he fails to acknowledge that official bilingualism in the rest of Canada rarely lives up in practice to its promises on paper.[44] Hobsbawm denigrates Québécois nationalism as motivated by "fear and insecurity" based on his perception that Québécois (whom he incorrectly identifies as *Canadiens*, a term not applicable since Confederation) believe that "Canada's now official 'multiculturalism' is simply a plot aimed at 'crushing *Francophonie*'s special needs under the political weight of multiculture'" (166). Relying primarily on work by federalists Léon Dion, Gérard Pelletier, and R.F. Harney, all of which appeared in the same issue of the same journal (*Daedalus* 117/4, fall 1988), Hobsbawm demonizes historically situated analyses of Trudeau's implementation of multiculturalism as conspiracy theories. In so doing, he ignores scholarship in Québec and even in English Canada that does indeed see multiculturalism as an assimilation strategy, and he makes no mention of Québec's official adoption of a policy of "interculturalism," which I discuss in my conclusion. He further demonstrates his misunderstanding of the ties between language laws and immigration policy when he claims "the threat of immigration is less in francophone than in anglophone Canada" (166), even though the Office de la langue française (OLF) has traced the decline of French in Montréal and the corresponding rise of other mother tongues. Given that francophones constituted only 48.8 per cent of the population of Montréal in 2006, while "allophones" whose mother tongue is neither French nor English made up 31.7 per cent, the threat immigration poses to the number of francophones in Québec's largest metropolitan city is difficult to deny.[45] In denigrating Québec's efforts to educate immigrants' children in the language of the majority (a normal practice in any nation that does have sovereignty), and in characterizing such social policies as "ethnic/nationalist reactions" that he ties to "the recent rise in 'fundamentalism' in many parts of the globe" (167), Hobsbawm reveals his profound misunderstanding of the specifics of the Québec context. As we shall see, "ethnic nationalism" is only a small facet of a range of nationalist discourses at work in Québec.

Despite Hobsbawm's desire to see nationalism die out, this is far from the case. As the PQ reminds Québec voters, thirty-eight new countries have joined the United Nations since Québec's first referendum in 1980.[46] Many of these new countries have been born through entirely democratic processes and have prospered since their independence. The Slovak Republic, for instance, whose economic and cultural situation vis-à-vis the Czech Republic resembles Québec's vis-à-vis English Canada, became independent peacefully on 1 January 1993 and subsequently saw its gross domestic product increase by 4.8 per cent in 1994, 7.0 per cent in 1995, and 6.9 per cent in 1996.[47] More recently, the

Organisation for Economic Co-operation and Development (OECD) reports that Slovakia's GDP grew by 8.5 per cent in 2006, by 10.6 per cent in 2007, the highest of all member countries, and by an impressive 6.2 per cent in 2008 despite the U.S.-provoked global economic crisis.[48] According to former PQ Member of the National Assembly (MNA) François Legault, economics, which is frequently cited as a reason why Québec sovereignty would not be viable, is not an issue at all. Rather, in the 49-page comprehensive Year 1 budget he produced in May 2005, which accounts for federal assets and liabilities in order to calculate Québec's share of the federal debt, Legault demonstrated that a sovereign Québec's economy would reap gains of $1.3 billion in the first year alone, culminating in a $13.8 billion surplus after only five years, compared to a deficit of $3 billion in the current year under the current financial arrangement with the federal government (Legault 41). After taking over the leadership of the PQ in 2007, Pauline Marois reminded voters that, as minister of finance from 2002 to 2003, she created public investment initiatives that resulted in Québec's economic growth surpassing that of the rest of Canada and the United States in the wake of the economic difficulties caused by the 11 September 2001 terrorist attacks, proof that Québec's economic stability can weather political storms, and in fact do so better than its neighbours.[49]

Not only, then, must fear-mongering about sovereignty's supposed economic consequences be assessed with a highly critical eye, but nationalist discourses must also be judged from a nuanced perspective. As described earlier, nationalism was very productive in provoking important social change during the Quiet Revolution, but nationalist discourses prior to that time varied in response to shifting historical contexts, as they have since as well. It would be inaccurate to talk about "Québec nationalism" as a static, singular entity; rather, we need to think in terms of multiple nationalist discourses at work simultaneously since the Quiet Revolution. Within the Québécois nationalist movement there are proponents whose views range from socialism to neoliberalism as well as disagreements about how best to advance the nation. Many members of the Parti libéral du Québec (PLQ) and the Coalition Avenir Québec (CAQ) identify as nationalists; while few members of the former identify as sovereignists, many of the latter do. The PQ is notorious for in-fighting among its members precisely because it characterizes itself as a "parti d'idées."[50] Although it is primarily social democratic and leftist, it remains a big tent for all sovereignists in which arduous debate is encouraged and all viewpoints are valid until the majority of members vote to adopt a particular position within the institutional structures.

Québécois political scientist Denis Monière divides the various forms of nationalism into two typological groups. Monière's first typology opposes ethnic versus civic nationalism. Ethnic nationalism, often associated with a German tradition, is rooted in bloodlines and genealogical admission criteria. In Canada, Mohawk nationalism can be seen as ethnic since non-aboriginals do not have the same political rights as aboriginals on aboriginal lands. Conversely, civic, or political, nationalism, often associated with a French tradition, is rooted in minimum residency requirements, knowledge of the national language and history, and a voluntary conformity to social norms, values, and institutions. The second typology, more nuanced than the traditional ethnic versus civic dichotomy, comprises four kinds of nationalisms: nationalisms of domination, liberation, conservation, and recognition. Nationalism of domination, whose most extreme forms are associated with Naziism and fascism, is rooted in the specific characteristics of one group whose hegemonic belief in its biological or cultural superiority justifies its conquest of other groups or territories. Nationalism of domination can also include imperialism, colonialism, and a "civilizing" mission rooted in discourses of supposed progress and democracy. Nationalism of liberation, associated with the decolonization movement after the Second World War and based on the liberal principle of equality, rejects domination by foreign powers and seeks to establish political sovereignty through the creation of a nation-state. Nationalism of conservation, or official nationalism, describes the patriotism of existing nation-states and manifests itself through the glorification of national symbols in order to preserve and maintain national identity and collective unity. Nationalism of recognition, such as French Canadian nationalism or some versions of Québécois renewed federalism, refers to the political claims made by minority ethnic groups for particular rights without questioning membership within a multiethnic or multinational state. In any society, there may be various combinations of these four types of nationalism, as is the case in Québec where tensions between groups identifying as Québécois, French Canadian, or Canadian produce conflicting nationalist discourses of liberation, recognition, and conservation in circulation simultaneously (*Pour* 11–14).

The Québécois sovereignist movement has frequently been charged with ethnic nationalism, but such an ideology would apply to only a small minority of fringe groups within the broader movement, such as the Mouvement de Libération National du Québec (MLNQ) led by Raymond Villeneuve (formerly a member of the FLQ). With the notable exception of Jacques Parizeau's famous statement on the night of the 1995 referendum attributing the loss to "l'argent puis des votes ethniques," which was later proven to point to material and statistical facts,[51] the movement as a whole, and particularly the PQ which, in conjunction with the BQ, is the movement's primary vehicle, advocates a form of nationalism that can best be classified as a civic nationalism of liberation partially based on recognition. Other critics have called this cultural nationalism because many elements of the PQ's agenda seek to create an "intercultural" nation founded on common principles, as seen in its latest *proposition principale*. Adopted by 2000 delegates at its sixteenth *Congrès national* on 15–17 April 2012, the PQ's proposal for the future shape of the Québec nation includes a constitution establishing its common values, a *Charte de la laïcité* asserting the government's neutral secularism and reaffirming the equality of men and women, the creation of Québécois citizenship to make all citizens feel a welcome part of the nation, and an extension of *Loi 101* to the CÉGEP level to reinforce French as the common language of education and the workforce. Because it rests upon the principles of maintaining a liberal and democratic society, it respects the minority rights of anglophones to receive education and government services in their language (often better than francophones receive in the rest of Canada), and it is based on sharing common values, Québécois nationalism, in the words of Kai Nielson's aptly titled essay, is "a cultural nationalism, neither ethnic nor civic" (143, 157).

For these reasons, critics of nationalism are incorrect in demonizing nationalism itself, as if all atrocities driven by nationalism were provoked by the same kind of nationalism, or even in assuming that only one nationalist discourse exists within a particular national context. Rather, nationalisms are rich, ever evolving, and constantly adapting to the social changes they incite. As we shall see in chapters 3, 4, 5, and 6, nationalist discourses in Québécois adaptations of Shakespeare evolve in parallel to their ever changing articulations in the socio-political sphere, such that there is no single nationalism in Québécois Shakespeares but a series of nationalist discourses that reflect the political concerns of each time period.

Québec's unique social history thus makes it a stimulating case study of how Shakespeare's big-time status works in a nation that has complex colonial, postcolonial, and neocolonial relationships with France,

Britain, and English Canada. Because of these multiple, overlapping relationships to colonialism, Québécois adaptations of Shakespeare exhibit different traits than Canadian adaptations, yet we shall see that they show similar traits to Shakespeares in Australia, New Zealand, Scotland, and Catalonia. The tension between nationalism and feminism further makes Québec an intriguing site of inquiry into Shakespearean adaptation compared to other Western contexts where the national question has already been resolved since there is the potential here for the adapters either to replicate the tension of the political sphere in the literary sphere or to overcome this tension in their art. As I argue in the chapters that follow, these adaptations tend to mirror closely the nationalist discourses of their corresponding historical periods, but gender and sexuality do not figure prominently despite the gains for women and queers under Québec's nationalist government – a contradiction I attempt to explain in the conclusion. In examining Shakespeare's cultural influence through the lens of an ongoing political debate, the following chapters take up the challenge issued by Terence Hawkes and Hugh Grady in *Shakespeare in the Present* and *Presentist Shakespeares* to talk with the living instead of yearning to speak with the dead.

Chapter Two

A Theory of Shakespearean Adaptation

This book is about Québécois adaptations of Shakespeare, yet none of these three key terms – Québécois; adaptation; Shakespeare – is particularly stable. What exactly makes a play "Québécois"? What kind of cultural product counts or does not count as an "adaptation"? What is the relationship between "adaptation" and other terms, such as "appropriation," with which it is often paired or substituted? How directly must an adaptation evoke, cite, reference, rewrite, or appropriate Shakespeare's texts (or imagined aspects of his personal life?), and how much Shakespearean-related content must it contain to be considered an adaptation "of Shakespeare"? This chapter will attempt to define some parameters for these terms, particularly Shakespearean adaptation, parameters which serve my own purposes and which I hope other scholars will be convinced to adopt as well.

"Adaptation" is a term that many Shakespeareans bandy about, few define, and upon which no one agrees. I begin by tracing some of the more popular, recent attempts to define, categorize, and theorize adaptations and appropriations, including how such terms are embedded in the self-other dialectic and Michel Foucault's notion of the author function. Since adaptation involves an adapter deliberately choosing to rewrite Shakespeare, I argue that adaptation involves authorial intention, but this intention is not incompatible with the concept of the death of the author; rather, adapters are participating in what Foucault would call Shakespeare's transdiscursivity. In the case of appropriation, the adapter's intention is to advance a socio-political agenda. Acknowledging authorial intention requires us to acknowledge that adaptations and appropriations exist in a linear relationship to their sources since an adapter chooses to write back to a particular version of a story, or, to employ Gérard Genette's terminology, to a particular layer of the intertextual palimpsest, but nothing prevents such a palimpsestuous layer from acting as both source and adaptation vis-à-vis other layers. Theorists who argue against linearity do so out of concerns about fidelity and the perceived devaluation of new media, but I argue that such concerns are unfounded and fail to account for the real reason some adaptations are disparaged vis-à-vis their sources, which is their aesthetic quality as independent works of art. Instead of attempting to rehabilitate genres and media deemed secondary, I propose acknowledging them for what they are – adaptations that undergo a dual level of transformation. Such an acknowledgment of the different kinds of adaptations, which heretofore have often been lumped together by an umbrella usage of the term "adaptation" itself, can easily be achieved, I suggest, by employing an open-ended system of adjectives that would distinguish different kinds of adaptations without limiting our ability to describe them coherently and consistently. Such adjectives would allow us to distinguish adaptations on the level of genre and media, as well as on the sublevel of characters, plots, and narratives, thereby providing the tools to compare similar types of adaptations without succumbing to the current trend of calling all cultural products "adaptations" in a move that dilutes the term of critical usefulness. I illustrate this practice by applying such an adjectival system to the Québécois adaptations that compose this corpus, and I end the chapter with my definition of what constitutes a "Québécois adaptation of Shakespeare."

Adaptation and Appropriation, or, Self, Other, and Authors

In the general introduction to their anthology *Adaptations of Shakespeare*, Daniel Fischlin and Mark Fortier develop the most nuanced theory of specifically Shakespearean adaptation to date. They point out that the "notion of adaptation (from the Latin *adaptare*, to fit, to make suitable) implies a way of making Shakespeare fit a particular historical moment or social requirement" (17) – hence the witty title of Sandra Clark's anthology of Restoration adaptations, *Shakespeare Made Fit*. But adaptation is also a way of making Shakespeare fit a particular subjectivity. In this sense, adaptation resembles national liberation movements in terms of the drive to make otherness correspond to selfhood. Adaptation involves making a Shakespeare that is foreign, alien, and other fit a particular conception of the self – just as Québec nationalism involves discarding a distorted vision of Québec's collective identity as a conquered people and fashioning a new self-identity built upon the successes of the Quiet Revolution. This definition of adaptation rooted in the self-other dynamic shares some of the properties of "appropriation," a term that Fischlin and Fortier reject because they claim it "suggests a hostile takeover, a seizure of authority over the original in a way that appeals to contemporary sensibilities steeped in a politicized understanding of culture" which might not do "justice to other, more respectful, aspects of the practice" (3). However, "appropriation" can also imply a more holistic practice, a process of making oneness or creating wholeness by merging self and other. Appropriation may involve hostility, but it need not be limited to this sentiment; appropriation can also be a way of making love to Shakespeare, of integrating his foreignness into one's own self identity.[1] This potential bonding is especially probable in a postcolonial context in which Shakespeare is always already foreign, if not linguistically then at least culturally and historically. Appropriation then becomes a means of reducing the gap between a contemporary postcolonial context and the early modern England that informs Shakespeare's texts. Appropriation need not, therefore, connote solely the negative aspects of adaptation; rather, appropriation can be seen as a motivation already implicit in the desire to engage via adaptation with a particular text or author.

Unlike Fischlin and Fortier, I do not settle for "adaptation" "for lack of a better term" but choose it deliberately as the most appropriate word for both the particular Québécois texts under discussion here and other adaptations worldwide (3). Fischlin and Fortier "fall back on adaptation [...] to take advantage of its general currency" because the term's common use renders it "capable of minimizing confusion" (3). This ambivalent adoption of "adaptation" does the term a disservice by underappreciating its most common meaning rooted in the notion of change, a concept to which value judgments cannot be easily attached. They define adaptations as works that "radically alter the shape and significance of another work so as to invoke that work and yet be different from it – so that any adaptation is, and is not, Shakespeare" (3–4). Adaptation finds its most powerful meaning in this notion of an alteration that creates something that is both new and not new to which no predetermined judgment is attached independent of the evaluation of the creation itself. As a signifier, "adaptation" carries neither positive nor negative connotations; rather, it leaves the question of value in the hands of the reader.

To argue that the signifier "adaptation" is free from value judgments does not imply, however, that contemporary adaptations do not try to manipulate the value attached to Shakespeare's text for their own purposes. Indeed, they do, and it is here that appropriation re-enters the equation. Etymologically, adaptation is not value-laden, but contemporary adaptations, especially those written in postcolonial contexts such as Québec, engage in a dialogue with Shakespeare's canonicity. Adapters choose how much weight they want to allot to, and attempt to appropriate from, that canon. Whereas adaptation asks us to examine *how* Shakespeare is rewritten, appropriation forces us to examine *why* Shakespeare is rewritten, or, in other words, for what agenda is Shakespeare rewritten and whose interests does his appropriation serve.

Interests imply intent. Although post-Barthes and post-Foucault critics tend to evacuate the question of authorial intentional, in discussions of adaptation it is difficult to relegate authors to the scholarly dustbin. An adapter chooses to rewrite the text of another author. The intention to change the source author's text is a given; only the degree of motivation varies from one adapter to another. The author's intention is, I would argue, the crucial difference between an "adaptation" and an "appropriation." Since appropriation means making another's text one's own, the author must have a purpose beyond poetic greed, that is, a message to propagate via the adapted text, in short, an agenda, which, forcibly, is socio-political. An "appropriation," then, is an adaptation in which the author uses the source text in order to advance a socio-political agenda, to make the source author's text her own for a particular purpose. As such, all appropriations are de facto adaptations, but all adaptations are not necessarily appropriations since some adaptations may be concerned with making aesthetic, contextual, poetic, or structural "improvements" to a text (such as Nahum Tate's *King Lear*, in which Tate seeks to "rectifie what was wanting in the Regularity and Probability of the Tale" according to his dedicatory epistle) rather than overtly championing a cause (such as Jean-Pierre Ronfard's *Lear*, which will be discussed in chapter 5).[2]

Since authorial intention is crucial in distinguishing a politically motivated appropriation from an aesthetically motivated adaptation, Roland Barthes's notion of the "death of the author" and Michel Foucault's theory of the "author function" become central to adaptation theory. Arguing that a text could have multiple meanings unknown even to the author, Barthes claims that "the birth of the reader must be at the cost of the death of the Author" (1326). Foucault's author function, however, does not so much call for the erasure of authors as it opens up the concept of the author to include followers who participate in the author's "transdiscursivity"; that is, the author function links Shakespeare with his adapters. Foucault's final characteristic of the author function is plurivocality: "it does not refer purely and simply to a real individual, since it can give rise simultaneously to several selves, to several subjects – positions that can be occupied by different classes of individuals" (113). Describing "transdiscursive" authors such as Homer and Aristotle, Foucault argues that "in the sphere of discourse one can be the author of much more than a book – one can be the author of a theory, tradition, or discipline in which other books and authors will in their turn find a place" (113). Adapters find their place in Shakespeare's works and thus participate in the transdiscursivity of the author function "Shakespeare." Foucault groups "'great' literary authors" like Homer with "founders of science" like Aristotle and Hippocrates in a category of transdiscursivity distinct from "founders of discursivity" like Freud and Marx (114). Unlike Homer or Dickens or any other great author, Shakespeare has generated adaptations across many historical periods, geographical contexts, and languages. Shakespeare could arguably be considered a founder of discursivity like Freud or Marx insofar as his plays lend themselves through adaptation to an endless possibility of discourse. Foucault argues that founders of discursivity have "made possible not only a certain number of analogies, but also (and equally important) a certain number of differences. They have created a possibility for something other than their discourse, yet something belonging to what they founded" (114). Foucault's idea of discourses that are other than yet belonging to their founders corresponds remarkably well to Fischlin and Fortier's assertion that "any adaptation is, and is not, Shakespeare" (4). Because his texts are so open and malleable to different contexts, Shakespeare made possible a number of discursive divergences. Adaptations both are and are not Shakespeare. Foucault's argument that "reexamining Freud's texts modifies psychoanalysis itself, just as a reexamination of Marx's would modify Marxism" also applies to Shakespeare (116). Adapting Shakespeare causes us to see Shakespeare differently: after reading Jane Smiley's novel *A Thousand Acres*, one cannot easily reread *King Lear* in the same light as before. Foucault ends his essay with a series of questions we would ask if we were no longer "limited by the figure of the author" (119): "What are the modes of existence of this discourse? Where has it been used, how can it circulate, and who can appropriate it for himself? What are the places in it where there is room for possible subjects? Who can assume these various subject functions?" (120). We often ask the same questions about Shakespearean adaptations.

Shakespeare, then, is a transdiscursive author function and arguably also a founder of discursivity in a Foucauldian sense. His adapters are contributing to the transdiscursivity of his works while simultaneously occupying other author functions that produce new discourses that would be inconceivable within Shakespeare, hence the need to adapt. As author functions themselves, adapters participate in and contribute to a plurality of other discourses – such as Québécois nationalism or contemporary feminism – which exist outside of Shakespeare's discursivity. But while founders of discursivity have great cultural authority, not all author functions are created equal. Shakespeare's author function carries more cultural weight than that of his adapters. The adapter's relationship to Shakespeare as author function is complicated by the adapter's desire both to profit from and to repudiate Shakespeare's cultural authority. It is also complicated by the notion of adapter-as-author. As creators of their own works of art, adapters cannot subscribe fully to the notion of Shakespeare as an author function without also releasing their own works to be rewritten by others. Thus, although the notion of the author function facilitates adaptation, it also comports risks for the adapters. Why should authors write or adapters adapt if their own texts are subject to processes of reinscription, transformation, and reinterpretation that far exceed their intentions?

In the case of Québécois adapters, especially appropriators, the payoff is the conversion of Shakespeare's cultural authority into their own socio-political capital. Shakespearean adaptation thus involves a "power play" (a decidedly Canadian and Québécois metaphor), in which a text unabashedly profits from the cultural strength of Shakespeare's text while simultaneously struggling with it in an aggressive *rapport des forces*, always fighting against its own erasure by the so-called original text whence it is born. We must, as Christy Desmet cautions, "at once challenge the idea that Shakespeare must always already be co-opted by the dominant culture and caution against the easy assumption that Shakespeare can set us free" (3). The assumptions of Shakespeare-as-colonizer or Shakespeare-as-liberator are equally binding upon the adapter. Even as postcolonial writers may feel trapped under the weight of Shakespeare's canonical presence, the act of adaptation (using the master's tools to deconstruct the master's house in Audrey

Lorde's terms) carries with it the risk of contamination, assimilation, or effacement of their own cultural distinctiveness. This risk, however, need not be actualized to the same extent in all postcolonial contexts. In Québec, Shakespearean adaptation is a precarious tight-rope walk for adapters who simultaneously profit from and repudiate Shakespeare's canonicity, risking assimilation of their own cultural identity and authorial vision in the hope of gaining collective political capital.

Québécois adaptations, and especially overt appropriations, are thus what Desmet calls "'small-time Shakespeare,' individual acts of 're-vision' that arise from love or rage, or simply a desire to play with Shakespeare" (2) – a concept she develops from Marianne Novy's and Adrienne Rich's work on "re-visions" and Michael Bristol's concept of "big-time" Shakespeare. As opposed to big-time Shakespeare which "serves corporate goals, entrenched power structures, and conservative cultural ideologies," small-time Shakespeare, Desmet proposes, "emerges from local, more pointed responses to the Bard, [and] satisfies motives ranging from play, to political commitment, to agnostic gamesmanship" (2–3). Various small-time Shakespeares may arise from "the cultural prestige he confers on [a] devalued genre," "the sheer fun of playing 'identify that quotation,'" or a "personal urgency for their creators" to produce "acts of survival" (2). Québécois adaptations are small-time Shakespeare because of the minority status of Québécois culture both internationally and within the rest of Canada. These local adaptations at times play with and at times attack the Bard, and they testify to a political commitment by their authors to seek a currently denied social power within Canada and internationally in order to shore up the survival of Québécois culture.

Fidelity and Palimpsestuous Intertextual Linearity

Since adapters decide intentionally to write back to a particular version of a story, often choosing to engage with Shakespeare's version rather than the many sources and adaptations that came before and after his in order to benefit from his cultural authority, adaptation works within a linear relationship between source(s) and subsequent adaptation(s). Some critics, however, reject the logic of the linear relationship between the adaptation and the source to which it writes back because, like Imelda Whelehan, they are concerned about the "pitfalls created by the demands of 'authenticity and fidelity,'" particularly "the tendency to believe that the origin text is of primary importance" (3). Whelehan does not, however, offer any proof that judgments about the quality of two works of art are based on an assumption of authenticity of an origin text. Fischlin and Fortier argue that adaptation has been misrepresented in the past due to false notions of "originality in creation and fidelity in interpretation" (4), but if "we think outside the distortion caused by the high regard in which our culture has held Shakespeare's plays, it becomes clear there is no necessary relation of value between original and adaptation" (3). They remind us that "cultural reworking [is] taken to be basic to cultural production in general" and "Shakespeare in his own work was not original in the way these judgements [about originality and fidelity] seem to presume" (4). As the eight volumes of Geoffrey Bullough's *Narrative and Dramatic Sources of Shakespeare* testify, Shakespeare was as much an adapter as a writer of original material. Readers and audiences tend to compare subsequent adaptations to Shakespeare not because his works constitute the origin text but because they have been deemed better by generations of critics, as a result of which his works carry more cultural authority than those that precede them. If judgments were based on linear order rather than quality, we would compare adaptations of *King Lear* to *The True Chronicle Historie of King Leir* and adaptations of *Othello* or *Measure for Measure* to Cinthio's *Hecatommithi*. Shakespeare's texts are the baseline for comparison not because they came first – they did not – but because they are richer and therefore confer more cultural authority on the adaptation. An adaptation of Cinthio or Tate would not be imbued by osmosis with the same cultural authority as an adaptation of Shakespeare; it would repudiate the source but would not profit from its connection to it.

Linda Hutcheon's concerns about fidelity in *A Theory of Adaptation* are also unjustified. "Of more interest to me," she writes, "is the fact that the morally loaded discourse of fidelity is based on the implied assumption that adapters aim simply to reproduce the adapted text" (7). This implied assumption that adaptations must faithfully reproduce the source does not strike me as widespread as she implies. I would like to believe that readers and spectators are capable of understanding that if, say, 90 per cent of a text is faithful to the source, then the 10 per cent that is unfaithful stands out all the more provocatively, providing a commentary on the source text and the current context of the adaptation to which the reader or spectator is attuned. She proceeds to argue that the aim of adapters "might well be to economically and artistically supplant their prior works. They are just as likely to want to contest the aesthetic or political values of the adapted text as to pay homage. This, of course, is one of the reasons why the rhetoric of 'fidelity' is less than adequate to discuss the process of adaptation" (20). But without a rhetoric of fidelity, how can attentive readers and spectators assess infidelity? Fidelity is an essential point of critical analysis precisely because the points of infidelity are where we are most likely to find moments of aesthetic or political contestation. Without a concept of and attention to fidelity, we would have no means of assessing infidelity and hence the very contestation Hutcheon values. In allowing us to identify moments of infidelity (the adapter's intended rupture from the source text) or, sometimes equally telling, moments when the adapter chooses not to break away from the source, attention to fidelity is essential to interpreting the adapter's message. Attention to fidelity is not the real problem; rather, the problem lies in the assumption that infidelity equates with inferiority, which is not always the case. Hutcheon sidesteps addressing this faulty assumption when she suggests that "one way to think about unsuccessful adaptations is not in terms of infidelity to a prior text, but in terms of a lack of the creativity and skill to make the text one's own and thus autonomous" (20). Adaptations that do not say anything new about contemporary society are not interesting *as adaptations* and therefore not as worthy of critical study as texts whose creative strength lies in their infidelity.

Autonomy alone is not the answer, however. The adaptation must also be *good* as an independent work of art. The real issue against which Whelehan and Hutcheon are struggling is the subjective judgment of the quality of an adaptation, which has nothing to do with infidelity to the source but has everything to do with its aesthetic value. Some adaptations may convey an important message that has merit in a particular context (as many Québécois adaptations do). But when other adaptations are devalued by critics it is because not all adaptations are of the nuanced richness of a Pulitzer-winning novel, an Oscar-winning film, or Shakespeare. Often such criticism is levied at cinematic adaptations through the popular sentiment that "the movie is not as good as the book." A two-hour film cannot capture every detail of a Dickensian novel or a Shakespearean play, which may be one reason why Kenneth Branagh made a four-hour long *Hamlet* that, contrary to Olivier's (1948) and Zeffirelli's (1990) heavily cut cinematic productions, preserves the full text of the play, to which it adds visual layers that exceed the text. Quality takes time, but long, textually rich, drawn-out films are often deemed tedious by movie-goers and therefore are discouraged by capitalist production companies and marketers. "Movies and radio need no longer pretend to be art," Theodor Adorno and Max Horkheimer argue, because the "truth that they are just business" is evident in the fact "they call themselves industries" (121), and a four-hour long Shakespearean play does not lend itself easily to the mass production and consumption of the culture industry. Judging a cinematic adaptation as inferior to the play or novel upon which it is based derives not from its infidelity to an original; rather, such judgments are based on the richness and nuance of the final product. If a cinematic adaptation cuts some of the richness of a prior novel, the film is not devalued because it was produced after its source but because it lacks depth known to exist in the previous work. Some cuts, such as novelistic descriptions of setting, may be necessary because of the differences in medium, such that a long descriptive passage is rendered instantly in a visual image of a location, but other cuts often reduce elements of the plot or fail to convey the interior thoughts and motivations of a character through voice-overs. The Pulitzer Prize-winning novel *A Thousand Acres* is a nuanced work of art; as such, critics do not devalue it as "secondary" to Shakespeare's text but tend to treat it both as a rich engagement with Shakespeare and as an important text in its own right. The cinematic production of *A Thousand Acres*, however, is not as rich as the novel; the film may be considered inferior not because its production is secondary to the novel but rather because it is abridged and substantially less nuanced. When cinematic productions or adaptations are devalued vis-à-vis their theatrical or novelistic counterparts, those assessments are not about privileging the source text over the adaptation on the basis of primary origin; instead they come down to valuing the more aesthetically rich version of two similar stories, as subjective as such judgments may be.

All texts could arguably be called intertexts, as Barthes claims, but if adapters seek to convey their own vision through their changes to a source text then some texts are more deliberately in dialogue than others. The "task of a careful reader," Fischlin and Fortier assert, "is to see exactly how an adaptation functions in any particular situation, and what effects it has or may have on the literary politics of author and canon, as well as on larger social and political questions" (7). One cannot study the effects of an adaptation without comparing it to its source; adaptation studies are forcibly comparative and therefore involve a linear relationship between source and adaptation. Recognizing this direct link between prior source text and subsequent adapted text goes against Julie Sanders's desire for us to see "intertextual webs of signifying fields, rather than simplistic one-way lines of influence from source to adaptation" (24). Even if multiple texts are in dialogue – say, *The True Chronicle Historie of King Leir*, Shakespeare's *King Lear*, Peter Brook's cinematic production, and Jane Smiley's novelistic appropriation – the temporality by which some were written before others casts us in a linear mode of influence, each on the others, not a web, as Sanders proposes and as M.J. Kidnie takes up in *Shakespeare and the Problem of Adaptation* (4). While Smiley's novel may speak to both Brook's film and Shakespeare's play at the same time, we cannot say reciprocally that Shakespeare wrote his play with the intent of speaking to Brook or Smiley, although he may well have been in dialogue artistically with the anonymous author of *The True Chronicle Historie of King Leir*. Accounting for the historicity of a series of adaptations does not "equate 'derivation' and 'derivative'" as Hutcheon (9) and Kidnie (3) fear. Few would suggest that Shakespeare's play might be "secondary or inferior" because he borrowed and adapted ideas from a variety of sources (Hutcheon xiii). Accounting for the linearity of the production of texts is crucial, however, to acknowledging the author's potential intentions in composing an adaptation that is intertextually in dialogue with prior texts. Readers can appreciate some adaptations, such as *A Thousand Acres*, as independent works of art without knowledge of their intertextual connections. Such texts obviously become more rich and multilayered if the reader is attuned to the source text and the author's divergences from it, but the text is not artistically poor for readers unaware of such intertextual connections. The fact that an adaptation may exhibit such aesthetic and textual richness independent of a connection with its source so as to win a Pulitzer Prize provides confirmation that we need not fear an equation between second and secondary.

A linear rather than rhizoid web of influence corresponds to Gérard Genette's theory of adaptation in *Palimpsestes: La littérature au second degré*. Genette describes five types of "relations transtextuelles": "*intertextualité*" (with the subcategories of "*citation*," "*plagiat*," and "*allusion*"); "paratextualité" (consisting of titles, illustrations "et bien d'autres types de signaux accessoires [...] qui procurent au texte un entourage (variable) et parfois commentaire"); "*métatextualité*" (which constitutes "la relation *critique*"); "*architextualité*" (in which "la perception générique [...] oriente et détermine dans une large mesure l''horizon d'attente' du lecteur, et donc la réception de l'œuvre"); and finally "*hypertextualité*" (8–11). The latter, which we could call adaptation in English, consists of a "relation unissant un texte B ([...] *hypertexte*) à un texte antérieur A

([...] *hypotexte*) sur lequel il se greffe d'une manière qui n'est pas celle du commentaire" (11–12, italics in original).[3] Using the example of Homer's *Odyssey*, he shows how both Virgil's *Aeneid* and Joyce's *Ulysses* can each be considered hypertexts deriving from the same hypotext:

> Elle peut être d'un autre ordre, tel que B ne parle nullement de A, mais ne pourrait cependant exister tel quel sans A, dont il résulte au terme d'une opération que je qualifierai, provisoirement encore, de *transformation*, et qu'en conséquence il évoque plus ou moins manifestement, sans nécessairement parler de lui et le citer. L'*Énéide* et *Ulysse* sont sans doute, à des degrés et certainement à des titres divers, deux (parmi d'autres) hypertextes d'un même hypotexte: l'*Odyssée*, bien sûr. (12)[4]

That *Ulysses* adapts *The Odyssey* before or after *The Aeneid* does not impugn upon its value as a literary work. There is not necessarily a web of influence; rather, each occupies a different point on the linear trajectory of hypertexts related to Homer's hypotext. Applied to Shakespeare, we could say that Tate and Smiley have produced hypertexts vis-à-vis Shakespeare's *King Lear*. Shakespeare's *Lear* may be simultaneously a hypotext of these adaptations but itself a hypertext of *The True Chronicle Historie of King Leir* and Geoffrey of Monmouth's *Historia Regum Britanniae*. Nothing prohibits a text from being both source and adaptation simultaneously; hence, we need not reject a linear relationship for fear of privileging the source over the adaptation. Many texts are both, but not all texts are necessarily interconnected. Hutcheon rightly points out that "[p]alimpsests make for permanent change" (29). Once a reader knows another version of a story, its influence on her interpretation of a prior version cannot be erased from her mind, but not all texts exert such influence on all others. Some do, but others might not be intended by their authors to participate with each and every layer of the palimpsestuous conversation.

Genres and Media

Concerns about fidelity and secondariness also underlie critical attempts to rehabilitate supposedly undervalued genres and media. As in the case of intertextual linearity, such concerns are unfounded but lead some critics to reject important categorical distinctions between different types of adaptations in their zeal not to exclude anything from the term "adaptation" itself. Rather than argue, however, that "everything counts," thereby discarding critical frameworks in the name of inclusivity, developing those critical categories in greater detail would allow a more nuanced analysis of the very cultural products critics are trying to defend. Such categories would allow us to analyse literary texts as literature, performances as performances, and films within the critical discourses native to film studies, rather than confounding different genres and media in a mish-mash that ignores the specific characteristics of each.

As Fischlin and Fortier's use of the adjective "theatrical" implies (1), adaptation can take many forms and therefore it interpolates questions of genre. The term "adaptation" is often applied to cinematic productions of Shakespeare as well as to some innovative stage productions. Adaptation can also work across literary genres, for example from dramatic play text to novel or to poetry. Some critics, such as Hutcheon, apply the term even more broadly to include video games, publicity, and various forms of parody and intertextuality. I would argue, however, that the term quickly loses its usefulness as a categorical tool when it carries such broad signification. If the term becomes a catch-all, it becomes difficult to compare adaptations accurately on their own terms. Just as film studies has evolved within academia into its own discipline, video games cannot be analysed in the same terms as literary play texts because their signifying processes are so radically different on a structural level.[5] Rather than conflating commercial products of the Shakespeare industry with adaptation, developing a new typological framework in which to study different types of adaptations would be a more fruitful enterprise.

Even dramatic play texts do not remain untouched by the problem of medium since they inhabit two media simultaneously, the page and the stage. Fischlin and Fortier claim that "every drama text is an incomplete entity that must be 'translated' by being put on stage. Adaptation is, therefore, only an extreme version of the reworking that takes place in any theatrical production" (7). Like Hutcheon's desire to include video games and theme park rides as "adaptations," I find Fischlin and Fortier's comparison of "translation" and "adaptation" a counterproductive stretching of the term "adaptation." To "translate" a play from page to stage differs drastically from the conventional understanding of translation involving rendering a text in one language with relative accuracy in another.[6] Producing a text on stage does not involve linguistic translation but rather a move from textual to verbal and gestural sign systems, and since, with the exception of closet drama, most plays are written specifically with this transposition in mind, this intended next step in the process is not a "translation," no matter how much latitude the director might take in producing the text on stage. Every "theatrical production" of a play is one reading among many potentialities – the director's and the actors' – but is no more or less legitimate than the multiple readings envisioned each time a reader engages with the text and "sees" a performance in her mind's eye. If a reader's critical interpretation and imaginary staging is not an "adaptation," why should a particular director's or actor's vision of the play be credited as such? When the author's text has not been significantly rewritten during the already assumed move from page to stage, it remains more accurate to speak of "theatrical productions." Otherwise, to include "theatrical productions" in the category of "adaptations" makes the term all inclusive and therefore less useful as a classifying system. If everything counts, what matters?

The tendency to conflate "production" and "adaptation" happens most frequently among performance scholars who begin with the premise of privileging, or trying to rehabilitate, performance over text. M.J. Kidnie privileges production and audience reception but in the process devalues the role of the author whose intentions are crucial to identifying adaptations as such. "Instead of 'the text itself' coming to stand in place of the work, with performance assuming a second-order, adaptive relation as a performance of the text," Kidnie argues, "performance and text are both, in their different ways, instances of the work" (28). But a performance really is "a performance of" the text, just like a reading is "a reading of" the text. Unlike film which produces a final director's cut and fixes the work as the finished product of an auteur, there are multiple, ongoing, overlapping performances of plays, so any performance is always only one "performance of" the text among many. Kidnie wants "to propose a more flexible account of the criteria by which one distinguishes one work from another, locating them not *prior* to the work's instances of production, for example in the mind of the artist, but *subsequent* to production, in users' perceptions of sameness and difference among the many variants found in distinct production instances" (29). But taking intention away from the author and leaving the determination of the play's status up to the audience's interpretation would effectively turn a particular performance into "the work," separate from the text from which it derives. To replace the intentions of the author with hundreds or even thousands of audience members' subjective impressions would make it nearly impossible to conclude whether a play is a "production" or an "adaptation." In focusing on audience reception, which can change from one evening to the next, Kidnie blurs the line between "production" and "adaptation" and complicates the very problem she sets out to solve. She claims that a play is "a form of art that circulates in two distinct media, performance and text, neither of which is controlled finally (or even arguably at first) by the author" (30). It is not true, however, that the author does not control the text at the stage of conceptualization and composition, even in Shakespeare's day, and certainly today with the advent of copyright law, which allows, for instance, the Beckett estate to exert a strong influence over the production of the author's texts and to veto performances it believes may contradict the author's intentions. That Shakespeare's texts exist in multiple versions, and that publishing and copyright did not exist in their current form then as they do now, which allowed other people to modify his texts when they went to print, does not mean that Shakespeare did not seek to control what words he wrote or what he intended to say, that he had no intentions at all.[7] It also does not mean that contemporary adapters do not seek to write against the grain of what they perceive, rightly or wrongly, Shakespeare's intentions to have been. While text and performance are indeed both components of the work, privileging performance equally with text, rather than seeing performance as a single interpretation of the text, as a reading in the mind's eye transposed on stage, blurs the line between production and adaptation that could otherwise be easily established by comparing differences between a source text and an adapted text.[8]

"Everything counts" constitutes the underlying premise in Linda Hutcheon's *A Theory of Adaptation*. "Videogames, theme park rides, Web sites, graphic novels, song covers, operas, musicals, ballets, and radio and stage plays," she claims, "are thus as important to this theorizing as are the more commonly discussed movies and novels" (xiv). While she correctly acknowledges that "some media and genres are used to *tell* stories (for example, novels, short stories); others *show* them (for instance, all performance media); and still others allow us to interact physically and kinesthetically with them (as in videogames or theme park rides)" (xiv), to consider all of these creative works under the umbrella term "adaptation" without subcategories or distinctions between telling, showing, and interaction would erase the very differences between the modes of production and consumption of these cultural products that she points out. If *The Lion King* is a (cinematic) adaptation of *Hamlet*, and if, as Hutcheon argues, theme parks can be adaptations of movies too, then is a *Lion King* ride at Disney World also an adaptation of Shakespeare's *Hamlet*? What about *Lion King* plush toy animals? If so, where does it end? Taken to its logical conclusion, Hutcheon's argument suggests that all of Western civilization is an adaptation of something. Why, then, even bother using the term at all? This "everything counts" logic renders the term "adaptation" too indistinct to be meaningfully functional. If we acknowledge that "adaptation" can occur across genres and media, why not account for these differences in our theorization of the term? Distinguishing between the "novelistic" and "cinematic" versions of *A Thousand Acres* situates a discussion of either one in the genre or medium from which it derives inherent characteristics of telling versus showing that influence a host of other elements upon which an analysis of the adaptation depends. Adding "prosaic," "theatrical," "novelistic," or "cinematic" before the noun "adaptation" does not detract from an analysis of the text, but it does serve to remind us of the specific features of each genre and medium that circumscribe *how* an adapter produces an adaptation.

Characters, Plots, and Narratives

To trace, in Fischlin and Fortier's words, "how an adaptation functions in any particular situation," we must first consider differences in diction, style, plot, and characters, which usually reveal deeper differences in motif and theme that speak to "larger social and political questions." Douglas Lanier, in *Shakespeare and Modern Popular Culture*, is the only Shakespeare scholar to date who attempts to categorize different types of adaptations according to their formal characteristics. He breaks down adaptation into six categories based on the transformation of the Shakespearean narrative:

- *extrapolated narrative*, in which plot material is generated from events mentioned but not developed in the "master" narrative; often this takes the form of filling in gaps of motive or event within the original narrative, or of imagining the next frame out of a plot line or motive;
- *interpolated narrative*, in which plot material is dovetailed with the plot of the source;
- *remotivated narrative*, in which the new narrative retains the basic plot line or situation of the source but changes the motivations of the characters;
- *revisionary narrative*, in which the new narrative begins with the characters and situation of the source but changes the plot;

- *reoriented narrative,* in which the narrative is told from a different point of view;
- *hybrid narrative,* in which narrative elements or characters from two or more Shakespearean plays are combined. (83)

In various combinations and permutations, these categories may cover a range of adaptations and helpfully distinguish among them. Prequels such as Djanet Sears's *Harlem Duet* may fall under the category of extrapolated narrative; Tom Stoppard's *Rosencrantz and Guildenstern Are Dead* is an interpolated narrative; a reworking such as Charles Marowitz's *Measure for Measure* may be deemed a remotivated narrative; the different ending in Marco Micone's *La mégère de Padova* makes it a revisionary narrative; some of the monologues in the *38* event could be seen as reoriented narrative; Jean-Pierre Ronfard's combination of *1 Henry IV*, *2 Henry IV*, and *The Merry Wives of Windsor* in *Falstaff* makes it a hybrid narrative.

Yet, this classifying system does not encompass all types of adaptations. What does one do, for instance, with plays that are not adapted from Shakespeare's texts but rather from aspects, true or speculative, of his personal life? Often, Shakespeare may be either a subject for discussion in a play or he may appear as a character, thereby producing a play that is more *about* Shakespeare than an adaptation *of* Shakespeare depending on the proportion of references to his work that compose the content. What about an embedded narrative in which the characters both enact the play within the narrative frame while also, knowingly or unknowingly, living it out in their "real lives," that is, a dual-level narrative, such as Yves Sioui Durand and Jean-Frédéric Messier's *Hamlet-le-Malécite* or André Forcier's cinematic adaptation *Une histoire inventée*?[9] What about Michel Garneau's "tradaptations" that follow Shakespeare's text very closely – changing neither character, plot, nor narrative – but subtly substitute synonyms that resonate differently in another context in order to imbue the text with palimpsestuous levels of meaning, remaining loyal to Shakespeare while also becoming more than Shakespeare? What about so-called adaptations that have nothing to do with Shakespeare's narratives at all but borrow one of his famous titles? I propose below a more flexible system of classification.

An Apology for Adjectives

"Everything counts" crops up yet again in Mark Fortier's theory of Canadian adaptation "Wild Shakespeare." Claiming to "have long been drawn to Marshall McLuhan's aphorism, 'Art is anything you can get away with'" (2), Fortier shifts omni-inclusivity from art to adaptation: "'Adaptation is anything you can get away with' means that adaptation is what actually exists, what has been done, what becomes, what survives, rather than what does or does not fit an abstract schema or set of rules" (2). Neglecting the important difference between the role of the artist and the role of the critic, this approach serves to locate potential adaptations but not to analyse them comparatively. While we accord artists liberty in the hope they will surprise us with experimental and audacious works, we expect critics to bring meaning to bear upon those works by classifying, categorizing, and making sense of art so that not only art speaks to us but also we can speak to others about art. While he begins by asserting that "[s]ophisticated analysis of adaptation must entail both systems of categorization and an openness to that which doesn't fit in these systems" (1),[10] in concluding that adaptation is "quite literally, anything you can get away with" (7), Fortier's characterization of adaptation as "wild" ultimately drops the systems of categorization, privileging openness but leaving us with no analytical tools to describe the many types of adaptations to which we should be open.

Wary that "[d]efinitions and taxonomies, useful in organizing bodies of knowledge and ways of thinking into fields and disciplines, are also ways of policing the generic borders around bodies of work that might otherwise get out of hand" (v), in the introduction to *The Shakespeare's Mine: Adapting Shakespeare in Anglophone Canada* Ric Knowles takes recourse to Fortier's case for wild adaptation. But just because a corpus of plays "includes work that for various reasons would not be considered to be adaptations by the definitions of Linda Hutcheon" does not mean we must give up on classification (vi). Instead, we could posit a new, more workable definition that accounts for the pieces of the puzzle that do not fit. In fact, although he eschews definition, Knowles hints at categories for the plays in his anthology that, unlike Ken Gass's *Claudius*, do not meet Hutcheon's definitions. For instance, Knowles explains that a play like "*Cruel Tears*, by Ken Mitchell with Humphrey and the Dumptrucks, does not announce itself as an adaptation unless one recognizes the two-word title or, late in the play, an adapted 'Willow Song,' as deriving from *Othello*" (vi–vii). Similarly, Djanet Sears's *Harlem Duet* is a prequel rather than an adaptation of Shakespeare's plot, Vern Thiessen's *Shakespeare's Will* "adapts the life rather than the work of Shakespeare," and Michael O'Brien's *Mad Boy Chronicle* achieves its effect by "adapting Shakespeare's *own* sources for *Hamlet*" (vii). Rather than throwing all of these plays into a hodgepodge of "wild adaptation," might it not be better to flesh out a taxonomy that could usefully be applied to other adaptations – perhaps along the lines of "unacknowledged adaptations"; "prequels" (and "sequels"); "biographical adaptations"; and "primary source adaptations"? In our desire to be as inclusive as possible of the range of creative works available for study, is it really necessary to adopt umbrella terms – such as Fortier's "wild" and Hutcheon's expansion of "adaptation" from literary texts to video games and theme parks – that dilute our analysis?

To resolve the ambiguity that I have identified in the work of these scholars, I propose a rather simple solution: precision or, more precisely, adjectives. The range of plays, poems, novels, films, musicals, operas, and other creative works that get lumped together as "adaptations" is indeed large, but we are not condemned to catch-all categories. If we describe all of these creative works with more care and attentiveness, we may begin to compare apples to apples and oranges to oranges instead of throwing everything into a hodgepodge.

As we have seen, the adaptation hodgepodge varies greatly by degree, influenced by authorial intent, media, genre, and language. There are "theatrical productions," such as Robert Lepage's *Elseneur*, which do not alter significantly Shakespeare's text but which are staged in innovative, even spectacular, ways. Likewise, there are "cinematic productions," such as Peter Brook's *King Lear*, which certainly appear innovative on screen and may illuminate new readings of the text (such as the violent, unpredictable threat posed to the daughters by Lear and his rowdy knights), but which, again, do not actually rewrite Shakespeare's text. There are "theatrical adaptations," or one may say unqualified "adaptations," such as Nahum Tate's *King Lear*, which remain within the same genre and media, following Shakespeare's trajectory from page to stage, rewriting significant aspects of the text, but largely for aesthetic or contextual reasons to please period sensibilities, rather than to advance overtly a socio-political agenda. Likewise, there are "theatrical appropriations," or unqualified "appropriations," such as Robert Gurik's *Hamlet, prince du Québec* (which associates each Shakespearean character with a contemporary political figure, adding a second level of meaning to each character's words), in which the obvious political agenda cannot be denied. We may have "poetic adaptations" or "poetic appropriations" (such as Heinrich Heine's narrative poems *Germany: A Winter's Tale* and *Atta Troll: A Midsummer Night's Dream*), "cinematic adaptations" (such as Akira Kurosawa's *Ran*, which follows Shakespeare's plot while adapting the gender of the protagonists and the socio-historical context) or "cinematic appropriations" (such as Tom Magill's *Mickey B*, which appropriates *Macbeth* to create awareness of prison life and give prisoners an artistic outlet), as well as "novelistic adaptations" (such as Leon Rooke's *Shakespeare's Dog*, a biographical adaptation from the dog's perspective) or "novelistic appropriations" (such as Jane Smiley's *A Thousand Acres*, which follows closely the plot of *King Lear* while commenting on and radically transforming its gender politics). Identifying adaptations or appropriations according to the genre or media to which they belong distinguishes the apples from the oranges and allows us to analyse the differences between adaptations and their sources not only based on their content but also in regard to genre- or media-specific conventions that circumscribe how the content can be rendered.

Translation further complicates matters in Québec. Nearly every Québécois adaptation of Shakespeare is written in French, but literal translations are not adaptations. Fidelity and authorial intention are again key indicators of how to distinguish such works. Translations demonstrate the translator's attempted fidelity to render the text accurately, notwithstanding idioms, problematic or difficult-to-translate words and concepts, and the potential pitfalls that translation theorists acknowledge as inherent to the practice. Literal word-for-word translations rarely, if ever, represent a source text with one hundred per cent accuracy. As the Italian expression succinctly puts it, *traduttore, traditore*. Nonetheless, we can distinguish between a translator's intention towards fidelity in contrast to an adapter's intention to rewrite the text at critical moments in order to convey a message that runs against the grain of the source text. For example, Normand Chaurette has translated many plays following closely the source text (*AYL*, *MWW*, *RJ*, *TN*, among others, for Montréal's Théâtre du Nouveau Monde and Québec City's Théâtre Trident, which tend to stage classic texts conservatively), whereas the content of his play *Les Reines* is entirely of his own invention. An intention towards fidelity is clearly demonstrated in the first instance in contrast to an intention towards adaptive creativity in the latter. Less obvious is the case of Marco Micone's *La mégère de Padova*, first performed under the less adaptive title *La mégère apprivoisée*, which translates Shakespeare's text loyally throughout, until the final few pages in which the ending is rewritten, initially giving the appearance of a translation but surprising the reader as an adaptation. Another less than clear-cut example is the case posed by Michel Garneau's three "tradaptations," the neologism he coined to describe his *Macbeth de William Shakespeare: Traduit en québécois* (1978), *La tempête* (1989), and *Coriolan* (1989). Each text translates Shakespeare into a different linguistic register – *Macbeth* approximates an imaginative eighteenth-century New France dialect; *Coriolan* sounds like standard French; *La tempête* is in between the two and has different registers within the text itself – but subtle changes to the text also change radically the meaning, making *Macbeth* and *La tempête* adaptations, as we shall see in chapter 4, although *Coriolan* is not textually adapted.

Other terms are sometimes used akin to adaptation – Ruby Cohn says "offshoots," Marianne Novy prefers "re-visions," and more recently critics have offered up "spin-offs," "mash-ups," or "memes" – but "adaptation" remains the most encompassing term. Some of these terms though – such as spin-off and mash-up, or even other terms such as prequel and sequel – could be seen as types of adaptations. The Women's Theatre Group and Elaine Feinstein's *Lear's Daughters* is a prequel adaptation while John Fletcher's *The Woman's Prize* is a sequel adaptation – or both could be seen as spin-offs. Antonine Maillet's *William S* could be a revisionary, hybrid narrative in Lanier's terms or could equally be described as a mash-up of *Hamlet, Macbeth, Romeo and Juliet, King Lear, 1–2 Henry IV, The Merchant of Venice*, and *The Taming of the Shrew*. While it would be difficult to persuade all critics to agree to any one set of terms, we can at least agree to be more descriptive since an imperfect system of classification would be more critically useful than none at all.

In the spirit of taking a stab at taming the wild, I propose the following adjectival categories for the Québécois adaptations of Shakespeare examined closely in this book. *Hamlet, prince du Québec*, by Robert Gurik, is a theatrical adaptation of *Hamlet*. This play was then adapted into *Hamlet, Prince of Quebec*, by Marc Gélinas, producing an adaptation of the original adaptation. Michel Garneau's neologism "tradaptation" strikes me as an apt characterization of his *Macbeth, La tempête*, and, to a lesser degree, *Coriolan*. Jean-Pierre Ronfard's *Lear* is a carnivalesque adaptation, while his *Vie et mort du Roi Boiteux* is a carnivalesque, hybrid adaptation of Shakespeare's first tetralogy and non-Shakespearean texts such as Homer's *Odyssey*. Pierre-Yves Lemieux's *À propos de Roméo et Juliette* is an extrapolated adaptation in Lanier's terms. Normand Chaurette's *Les Reines* is a remotivated, revisionary, hybrid adaptation of the first tetralogy. Antonine Maillet's *William S* could be described as a mash-up or revisionary, hybrid adaptation, and, more importantly, is also a biographical adaptation in which the Bard figures as a character. *Hamlet-le-Malécite* is a parallel narrative adaptation in which the main character both acts and lives out elements of Shakespeare's plot. Finally, *Henry. Octobre. 1970.* is, to employ Lanier's terms again, an interpolated, remotivated, reoriented adaptation, in which contemporary poetry and the letters and speeches of contemporary politicians are dovetailed into Shakespeare's plot, while characters' motivations are changed by reorienting speeches from each side of the English-French divide to the other.

Other types of Québécois adaptations not discussed at length in this book include meta-adaptations, such as René-Daniel Dubois's *Pericles, Prince of Tyre, by William Shakespeare*, Reynald Bouchard's *Touchez pas à ma paroisse*, Jean-Frédéric Messier's *Le* Making of *de Macbeth*, and Alexis Martin's *Dave veut jouer Richard III*, all plays about characters struggling to act in Shakespeare's plays themselves. Michel Garneau's children's play *Shakespeare: un monde qu'on peut apprendre par cœur*, which does not feature Shakespeare as a character but consists of a discussion of his most famous plays, could be called an analytic adaptation. *Sous l'empire de Iago* by Kader Mansour is a postcolonial adaptation. Applying the term feminist to Daphné Thompson's *Sauvée des eaux: Texte dramatique sur Ophélie* remains disputable, as I explain in chapter 6.

Analytic, biographical, carnivalesque, extrapolated, feminist, hybrid, interpolated, mashed-up, meta, parallel, postcolonial, prequel, primary source, remotivated, reoriented, revisionary, sequel, spin-off, tradapted, unacknowledged adaptations... this list of adjectives is not exhaustive. It could not be exhaustive because there are undoubtedly many adaptations of Shakespeare yet to be written that might not fit tidily into these categories. If not exhaustive, this categorization is, however, expansive. In this, I agree with Fortier's concern about the openness of any system of classification and the dangers of policing too strictly to the point of excluding radical and exciting works of art. The simplicity of an adjectival-based system of classification is that one can always add a new adjective to the list, remaining open to newness while refusing to throw out analytic tools in the quest for inclusivity. Like open-source software – always editable, expandable, upgradeable, and subject to tweaking by multiple users – an open, adjectival system of classification can tame "wild" adaptation without locking it in a cage.

To sum up, then, I define adaptations as additions (although not reductions for the purpose of playing time), transpositions, rewritings, or translations that alter significantly the content or meaning of the source text. I exclude innovative stage productions, and I limit the unqualified use of "adaptation" to dramatic playtexts whose trajectory from page to stage (and in some cases commercialized text) mirrors the production pattern of their Shakespearean counterparts. Cross-generic adaptations, such as plays to novels, and cross-media adaptations, such as plays to films (or even poems to plays as in some recent stagings of *The Rape of Lucrece*), necessarily involve a double process of adaptation resulting from norms and constraints of the new genre or medium, distinct from the process of adaptation rooted in a playwright's deliberate literary choices. Applying qualifying adjectives to cross-generic and cross-media adaptations prevents the loss of the term's theoretical usefulness. If a textual definition of adaptation seems reductive, the fact remains that the text is all the ephemeral theatre leaves behind. Even in the age of video, Fischlin and Fortier's *Adaptations of Shakespeare* prints texts, as does Fischlin's *Canadian Adaptations of Shakespeare Project* website. When scholars rely on performance rather than textual difference, "adaptation" slides down a slippery slope on which all stage productions are considered adaptations, thereby erasing important distinctions between performance and text and between the different contributions made by actors and authors. For this reason, following Hutcheon's caveat that adaptations be "acknowledged as adaptations *of a specific text*" (21), I would define an adaptation as an "acknowledged intertext," emphasis on *text*. An appropriation is an adaptation with a clear political agenda; it deliberately "writes back" to make a point about the source, rather than adapting the text solely for the pleasure of reading something similar but more palatable. As such, all appropriations are adaptations, but not all adaptations are appropriations. Nahum Tate's *The History of King Lear* is an adaptation, while the Woman's Theatre Group and Elaine Feinstein's *Lear's Daughters* is a feminist appropriation, as is Jane Smiley's novelistic feminist appropriation.

Situating "adaptation" at the level of the text – whether the text of a play, novel, screenplay, or graphic novel – brings us back to the notion of authorial intention in determining what counts as an adaptation. Playwrights write plays, screenwriters write film scripts, and while their end products may be the result of collaborative work and the collaborative vision of actors, directors, producers, and a host of other people, a textual definition of adaptation reminds us that someone, somewhere, probably sitting all alone, conceptualized a vision and put words on a page before those words were spoken by an actor or shot by a filmmaker. The author's vision, her intent, gives birth to the characters and the plot prior to interpretations by other collaborators. Even in film, there is an author before there is an auteur.[11] Kidnie attempts to exaggerate textual problems in order to rehabilitate performance by conflating "Shakespeare Made Easy" "translations" in "plain everyday English," the closing Sly frame of the anonymous *Taming of A Shrew*, and textual variants in *Hamlet* or *Othello* (24). Despite the problems textual scholars have correctly identified in Shakespeare's texts (corruptions, variants, printing errors, editorial interventions, etc.), we can nonetheless recognize the difference between texts Shakespeare wrote and those he did not. *Hamlet* and *Othello* are Shakespeare; *Taming of A Shrew* and "Shakespeare Made Easy" are not. The former bear four hundred years of cultural authority and have made what Bristol calls the "big-time"; student study guides designed to make Shakespeare "easy" market themselves precisely as "not Shakespeare" by exploiting the assumption that his works are "hard." Distinguishing "Shakespeare" from "not Shakespeare" is not as difficult as Kidnie would have us believe and therefore not a valid basis for discrediting the text in favour of performance.

How, though, do we define what counts as "significantly" or "radically" altering the source text? Inevitably such judgments involve subjective interpretation but also common sense. By intelligently speculating about the author's intent, we can distinguish changes that do not affect our interpretation of the text from more radical changes. Cutting some obscure lines in order to shorten the play's running time or combining minor characters in order to facilitate audience comprehension (as Shakespeare himself did in his history plays) constitute minor changes compared to, for example, Marowitz's redistribution of character lines in his *Measure for Measure*. Without adding any non-Shakespearean text (the only addition is the Jailer's Daughter's green-sickness-induced soliloquy from Shakespeare and Fletcher's *The Two Noble Kinsmen*), Marowitz's rearrangements radically change the characters and plot of Shakespeare's play in a way that time-motivated cuts to an otherwise unaltered production do not.

Québécois Shakespeare?

In addition to "adaptation" and "appropriation," two other key terms in this project deserve careful consideration: "Québécois" and "Shakespeare." What counts as a Québécois text and who counts as a Québécois author? Likewise, how much Shakespeare must an adaptation contain before it becomes an adaptation "of Shakespeare"? Should aspects of his life be included as related to Shakespeare or not? Should some plays be more suspect for exclusion than others?

First, who or what is "Québécois"? The legal definition of Québécois according to most ministerial departments, such as education or health care, is any person born in Québec or any resident living permanently on the territory of Québec. Supportive of Québec's intercultural approach to immigration and conscious of the need to integrate immigrants cohesively into Québec society, the nationalist Parti Québécois and Bloc Québécois often include as Québécois anyone who embraces Québécois culture and adheres to its civic values (including immigrants and emigrants), for neither newcomers nor those living in exile can claim citizenship in a nation lacking sovereignty and therefore passports. In this book, I define a Québécois playwright as any person born in Québec or living in Québec at the time of the composition of his or her play. I define a Québécois adaptation as any adaptation written by a Québécois playwright whether or not it was first published or produced in Québec. This broad definition permits the inclusion, therefore, of the English version of *Hamlet, prince du Québec*, which was written by the Québec-born playwright Marc Gélinas but first performed in Ontario, as was also the case of Québec-born playwright René-Daniel Dubois's *Pericles, Prince of Tyre, by William Shakespeare*. Similarly, this definition encompasses *William S*, which was written by Acadian-born playwright Antonine Maillet while she was living in Québec and was first performed in Montréal, as well as the 1995 play *Songe d'une nuit*, which was written by the Franco-Ontarian-born playwright Michel Ouellette who moved to Gatineau, Québec, in 1994. Although it may be considered a French Canadian adaptation, Tibor Egarvari's *Le Marchand de Venise de Shakespeare à Auschwitz* does not meet this definition of Québécois since Egarvari was born in Hungary, wrote the play while living in France, and it was first performed in 1977 at the University of Ottawa before its more mediatized performance in 1993 in Montréal.

Second, how much of a connection to the Bard must a text have to become an adaptation "of Shakespeare"? I would suggest we should be most resistant to attribute adaptive status to the one Shakespeare play that gets adapted the most frequently and often the most tangentially: *Romeo and Juliet*. The names of Shakespeare's two lovers have become so synonymous with "true love" as to become cliché, often to the point that the attribution of "star-crossed" does not apply to the lovers anymore. Two such plays only tangentially related to Shakespeare's text through their titles exist in Québec: *Rodéo et Juliette* by Jean-Claude Germain and *Roméo et Julien* by Jacques Girard and Reynald Robinson. The former is a Western musical set in the small village of St-Tite, which is famous for its Western Festival and rodeo, and features a mostly absent love interest named Juliette who shares no specific traits linking her to Shakespeare's character. The latter play initially leads the audience to believe they are witnessing two men dealing with a complicated relationship, but in a final twist they turn out to be two aspects of the same man's personality. There is no direct link to Shakespeare beyond the title. Such works, and Western culture produces many of them, ought to be considered titular "allusions" to Shakespeare rather than "adaptations" of his works since they ride Shakespeare's popularity and cultural authority rather than engaging critically or aesthetically with the content of Shakespeare's plays. In contrast to such passing references, plays that engage substantially with Shakespeare as a topic of discussion or that transform him into a fictional character contribute more substantially to the types of dialogues about the author's works that adaptations usually engender.

How, then, do we define a Québécois adaptation of Shakespeare? I would suggest that such a work must be a play, written by an author born or living in Québec, that rewrites significantly Shakespeare's text yet retains sufficient ties to Shakespeare to constitute more than a passing allusion to his titles or characters.

Chapter Three

The Quiet Revolution: *Passer à l'action*

Thought versus action: Hamlet's dilemma is also Québec's. Robert Gurik's *Hamlet, prince du Québec* (1968) allegorically aligns Québec's quest for sovereignty with Hamlet's problem of ceaseless thought versus the need to take immediate action and suggests Québécois must throw off their Hamlet complex, an imperative in keeping with nationalist discourses during the Quiet Revolution. In the late 1960s and early 1970s, Québécois nationalism was expressed largely in terms of taking action, *passer à l'action*,[1] and throwing off the defeatism of a *né pour un petit pain* attitude of self-deprecation.[2] This type of nationalism was manifested through anti-ecclesiasticism, neo-Marxism, and parallels with African decolonization, and it was articulated in terms of Québec's socio-political, linguistic, and economic inequality within the framework of Canadian federalism. Since women occupied little space in the political sphere in 1968, they are absent from the adaptation. Instead, Shakespeare's female characters correspond to male politicians. Gender issues manifest only through the Conquest/rape trope and the fear of federasty.

Gurik's choice of *Hamlet* as the first ever adaptation of Shakespeare in Québec is uncanny since the independence movement's trajectory shows remarkable parallels to many elements of Shakespeare's play. The sovereignist movement's different groups have positioned their various strategies along a spectrum of thought versus action. On one end, radical groups such as the Front de Libération du Québec have embodied the philosophy of direct action as the only means to liberate a nation considered occupied by a foreign power. Inspired by Frantz Fanon and the decolonization movement that was changing the political map of Africa, the direct action elements of the sovereignist movement never struggled with a Hamletian impasse and were already resolved from the moment of their inception to free their nation from those considered Claudius-like usurpers. On the other end of the spectrum, however, the majority of sovereignists valued the democratic process above their freedom and, like Hamlet, chose a route that delays the accomplishment of their goals until the proposed action can be legitimated. Since its foundation in 1968, the Parti Québécois (PQ), which represents the largest number of sovereignists, has defined itself as a "party of ideas," and since November 1974 its governing strategy has been *étapisme*.[3] Like Hamlet who refuses to kill Claudius while he is praying, to martyr the enemy, and to damn his own soul in order to achieve his goal, the PQ is sometimes accused by impatient sovereignists of delaying attaining its raison d'être in its desire to remain above moral or democratic reproach. Retrospectively, the PQ's history parallels the plot of Hamlet, but even without the luxury of over forty years of hindsight Gurik's play teased out the nation's Hamlet complex ten months before the PQ's founding on 11 October 1968.

Composed in November 1967, *Hamlet, prince du Québec* was first performed in Montréal on 17 January 1968 on the boat theatre L'Escale and then adapted into English by Marc Gélinas for performance at the London Little Theatre in Ontario in November of the same year. The English version of *Hamlet, Prince of Quebec* presents so many significant changes from the French version as to constitute an adaptation of the adaptation rather than a translation since its destination for an English Canadian stage provided the translator with the opportunity to address directly an audience who could be considered the colonizer. The shift in audience necessitated changes to cultural references that would be "too Québécois" for a "foreign" audience to understand. It also allows the English version of the text to drive home its satire at the perceived colonizer and Canadian federalism in general, messages that would be redundant for a Québécois audience already more sympathetic to the cause. In both the French and English versions, the changes to *Hamlet* include its setting within the Québec political scene of 1967–8, the association of Shakespeare's characters with Québécois politicians, the addition of a second gravedigger (as opposed to *Hamlet*'s rustic clown who quickly exits), two extra scenes of dialogue between the working-class gravediggers, five short radio broadcasts of current events, the elimination of Fortibras and his invading army, and numerous references to Québécois history and current affairs. Nearly every line of text functions simultaneously on the level of Shakespeare's narrative and that of the Québécois political situation. The adaptation is a remarkably accurate political satire, but it also signifies as an allegory of the hesitation that marks Québec's collective consciousness. Gurik's play is a thinly veiled national allegory in Fredric Jameson's sense of the term; that is, for Gurik's protagonist the "story of the private individual destiny is always an allegory of the embattled structure of the public [...] culture and society" (Jameson 67). Gurik's Hamlet is identified as a representation of the Québec nation itself in parenthesis after the speech prefix in the text, by his fleur-de-lys-covered cape on stage, and by the play's title itself.

Each character in Gurik's *Hamlet* is similarly identified with a symbolic collectivity or a well-known politician. Except for Hamlet, all the characters wear white masks that mark them as their political counterpart, and all are also identified in speech prefixes. Le Roi, King Claudius, is "L'anglophonie," at once the English-speaking world in the broadest sense, the British army of General Wolfe during the Conquest, the English-dominated Canadian federal government, and encroaching American capitalism. La Reine, Queen Gertrude, is "L'église," the Catholic Church that controlled nearly every aspect of Québec society from the failure of the Patriots' Rebellion in 1837–8 until the Quiet Revolution, particularly during the period dominated by ultramontanism. Polonius is Lester B. Pearson, prime minister of Canada from 18 June 1962 until 20 April 1968 (when Trudeau was sworn in after winning the Liberal party leadership). Pearson was responsible in February 1965 for endowing Canada with its flag, which, like "O Canada" originally composed for French Canadians in celebration of Saint-Jean-Baptiste Day, appropriates the symbol of the maple leaf found primarily in Québec.[4] Laerte is Pierre Elliott Trudeau who, in January 1968, though well positioned for the role of prime minister, was still the federal minister of justice and known as an intellectual for his writings in *Cité libre*. Laerte's sister, Ophélie, is Jean Lesage, leader of the provincial Parti libéral du Québec (PLQ) and father of the Quiet Revolution in his role as premier of Québec from June 1960 until June 1966 when he lost the provincial election to Daniel Johnson of the Union nationale. Hamlet's loyal companion, Horatio, is René Lévesque, known as a journalist and host of the television program *Point de mire*, as the instigator of the nationalization of Québec's various electricity companies under the banner of Hydro-Québec (whose insignia appears on his costume), and as the MNA who sparked a series of resignations from the PLQ on 14 October 1967. His impromptu departure from the PLQ resulted in the foundation of the Mouvement Souveraineté-Association in November 1967, which became the Parti Québécois in October 1968. L'Officier du Rhin, the leader of the watch, is Pierre Bourgault, the leader of the Rassemblement pour l'indépendance nationale, an intellectual and a politician considered more radical and leftist than Lévesque. Rosencrantz and Guildenstern are Gérard Pelletier and Jean Marchand, a federal member of parliament (MP) and the minister of citizenship and immigration respectively, co-founders and contributors with Trudeau to *Cité libre* for which they were known collectively as "les trois colombes" [doves] in French and the "Three Wise Men" in English. As a sign of their duplicity, Rosencrantz-Gérard Pelletier and Guildenstern-Jean Marchand wear reversible capes that are federalist red with Canadian maple leaves on one side and nationalist blue with Québécois fleurs-de-lys on the other. Finally, Le Spectre, the ghost of Hamlet's father, is General Charles de Gaulle, the French president whose famous cry of "Vive le Québec libre" from the balcony of Montréal's city hall on 24 July 1967 caused considerable controversy in Québec and especially in English Canada.

Hamlet, prince du Québec is an allegory in the primary sense that the characters represent more than their individual identity, particularly in the case of Hamlet-Québec, Le Roi-L'anglophonie, and La Reine-L'église. It is also a national allegory because the plot exposes the collective consciousness of the nation, ending with a moral imperative to resolve the nation's principal character flaw, its inaction, as articulated in the opening line of the play's introduction: "Hamlet c'est le Québec avec toutes ses hésitations, avec sa soif d'action et de liberté, corseté par cents ans d'inaction" (5).[5] Hamlet-Québec's problem is its hesitation, and only by throwing off the corset of inaction can it finally quench its thirst for freedom. The necessity for Québec to resolve its Hamlet complex is a matter of life and death, made clear by the play's opening scene of two "fossoyeurs" digging a "tombe [qui] peut très bien être celle d'Hamlet" (5).[6] Failing to throw off the restraints of hesitation and ceaseless contemplation will have fatal consequences. Given that the two gravediggers represent respectively the older and younger generations of poor, francophone workers, the nation is literally digging its own grave and burying itself alive. Philosophical debate is more than just a caprice; it creates stagnancy and a slow, self-inflicted death. As Hamlet-Québec realizes with his dying breath at the end of the play, the people are trapped in "la fange des compromis, de l'esclavage" by "les chaînes qu'hypocritement [ils ont eux]-mêmes forgées" (95).[7] The allegory's moral imperative could not be clearer: in order to break free from the chains it has placed on its own freedom, the nation must renounce its Hamlet complex, cease its self-introspection, and "take arms against a sea of troubles" (3.1.59), or *passer à l'action*.

While this portrait of Québec's collective hesitation constitutes the adaptation's driving force, just as Hamlet's hesitation paradoxically drives Shakespeare's plot, the satire derived from the association of each character with a political figure substantiates the allegory. Laurent Mailhot and Melanie Stevenson have applauded the neat parallels between Shakespeare's characters and the political personalities with whom they are associated, rightly attributing the play's satire to these conjunctions, but political satire pierces Gurik's adaptation more profoundly than previous critics have acknowledged. The allusions to socio-historical situations embedded in the association of literary characters with their corresponding political stand-ins and the subtle social critiques conveyed through anti-ecclesiastic and neo-Marxist discourses are essential to the adaptation's appropriation of Shakespeare in service of Québécois nationalism.

Of all the social changes that took place during the Quiet Revolution, secularization was the most far-reaching and abrupt. Most Catholics broke free from the church over the course of only a few years, particularly in the urban centres. The play opens with a discussion between gravediggers who typify the changing attitudes towards the church's stranglehold over everyday life. The 1er Fossoyeur, representative of the older, obedient generation, tells his work companion, the 2ième Fossoyeur, that he has six children, and his family size places an economic strain on domestic life (although six children was not abnormal during this period when families with fifteen to twenty children were relatively common). The 2ième Fossoyeur, from the more liberated generation that participated actively in the changes instituted during the Quiet Revolution, deplores, "Et y en a qui disent que c'est fini la revanche des berceaux… pourquoi tu essaies pas la pilule?" to which the first replies, "Avec le salaire que je fais, j'ai pas les moyens de m'acheter des bonbons. Et puis ma femme voudrait pas… à cause du curé" (10).[8] Critical of the "revenge of the cradles," that is, the church's insistence that the survival of the French language and Catholicism in North America, and hence the fate of the nation, rested on a numbers game of producing as many children as possible (regardless of the burden on individual families), the younger generation adopted a counter-discursive position to the effect that the church has no place in the bedrooms of the nation (before Trudeau made his famous declaration in 1967 about the state). This anti-ecclesiastic discussion about birth control portrays the slippage of the church's social and moral authority over its parishioners, its rule destined to die out as Québécois youth categorically refute its dominance.

Later in the play, La Reine-L'église, upset with Hamlet-Québec's rejection of her, asks, "Avez-vous oublié qui je suis? J'ai guidé vos premiers pas," and Hamlet-Québec defies, "Et vous m'avez brouillé la vue" (67).[9] Hamlet-Québec's retort marks a heightened self-awareness compared to his earlier response to La Reine-L'église which ends in reluctant submission: "Vous avez guidé sagement mes pas alors que mes jambes étaient trop frêles pour me porter. Aujourd'hui, encore, je vous écoute et vous obéis" (13).[10] In both statements, Hamlet-Québec exposes the colonizing paradigm within which Québec has been trapped by both the church and Canadian federalism. Under the pretence of guiding timid first steps, colonization creates a dependence that prevents the colonized from walking alone by blurring their vision of the final destination and the path to travel. The helping hand creates a disability where one did not previously exist. This metaphor of stunted growth describes both the church's overwhelming control of daily life until the Quiet Revolution as well as Canadian federalism which, while supposedly guiding Québec's socio-economic development, also hinders it with obscured tactics that many nationalists of the period, influenced by African decolonization, arguably describe as neocolonial domination.

Several changes to the English version of the adaptation highlight further this critique of the church's long-standing but quickly diminishing surveillance of Québec's francophone majority. In criticizing Le Roi-L'anglophonie's hasty marriage to La Reine-L'église, Hamlet-Québec comments that he built her "des résidences à travers le pays, toutes plus somptueuses les unes que les autres" (14).[11] To the end of this claim, the English text tags on the observation "and now empty…" (4), a jab at the desolation of Québec's churches. The people's rapid abandonment of the church is further reinforced by the addition of the qualifier "and yet within not even a day, but one poor hour in history" (4), a comment not found in the French text that differs from Shakespeare both in time (a month) and the object it modifies (Gertrude's affections rather than the empty palaces). Moreover, Hamlet's condemnation of Gertrude – "frailty, thy name is woman" (1.2.146) – becomes "Fragilité, ton nom est robe" (14) in French but "frailty thy name is cassock" (4) in

Gélinas's English translation.[12] While the French version is ambiguous, "robe" potentially signifying both the priest's robes as well as a woman's dress, in the English adaptation this pun is eliminated in order to transform the criticism of women's sexual infidelity into an outright accusation against the Catholic Church.

The English version adds two other criticisms of the church that are absent from the French text but allow Hamlet/Quebec to assert him-/itself in the face of Canadian federalism with which the Queen/The Church is associated by virtue of her/its complicity with the King/The English.[13] More than insults mocking the church's sudden loss of power, these insertions testify to an underlying resentment about the church's manipulation. In questioning whether or not Rosencrantz and Guildenstern attempted to assay Hamlet with a pastime, the Queen/The Church confesses, "'Tis a proven way to occupy the mind, bind and bend it. I myself held Hamlet chained to his ignorance, by games of 'beads', 'rhythm', 'follow the cross', 'suffer, suffer', and 'do it now or you'll burn forever'. But he plays no more… How children go!" (25). Later, in the bedchamber scene, Hamlet/Quebec rhetorically asks the Queen/The Church, "Have you consented to barter away your freedom in this land to which you have given love and mountainous labour against security, status and the trinkets of power but without this power, really" (38). These two additions to the English version accuse the church of manipulating Québec's francophone, Catholic majority with games of guilt and punishment, of stunting Québec's development by keeping it unaware of its full, adult potential, and of privileging the church's self-interested desire for the illusion of control. The pun on "mountainous" and "ultramontanism" takes aim at the late nineteenth-century period when the church appealed to the people's patriotism with a defensive nationalist discourse oriented towards a solidification of the church's political influence rather than the betterment of the nation, a protectionist discourse that privileged immobility over social advancement. In each accusation, bitterness fades into the stark reality that the church's power exists no more. The repeated use of ellipses at the end of these anti-ecclesiastical reminiscences points past the fall of the Queen/The Church to the fall of the King/The English. Not only do the unfinished sentences signal other unfinished tasks left to be accomplished, but Québec's liberation from the church serves as a model of liberation from English Canadian domination. The realization that the Queen/The Church has blurred his/its sight endows Hamlet/Quebec with the awareness to avoid the dangling beads of his/its other adversaries and to regain the vision required to achieve his/its other goals, such as economic wealth and political sovereignty.

Similar to its anti-ecclesiasticism, the play's neo-Marxism is also tied to nationalism. Neo-Marxism was becoming increasingly popular in Québec in the late 1960s, largely due to a collective recognition by francophones of their economic disenfranchisement compared to the wealth of their anglophone bosses and overseers. Neo-Marxist consciousness-raising occurred in conjunction with African discourses of decolonization, rooted in a similar disentitlement, and reached its peak in 1970 with the October Crisis (as we shall see in *Henry. Octobre. 1970.* in chapter 6). The connection between neo-Marxism, African decolonization, and Québécois nationalism manifests itself in the play through a radio broadcast announcing anniversaries of historic events: "Il y a cinq ans jour pour jour éclatait la première bombe séparatiste dans une boîte à lettres. Ce même jour en 1959 le Congo se rebellait pour accéder à son indépen..." (24–5).[14] The English version adds the specific target of the FLQ bombs, "the English Montreal suburb of Westmount," as well as the origin of the Congo rebellion "in Leopoldville, Africa" (9–10). Evoking King Leopold of Belgium's conquest and exploitation of the Congo associates African decolonization with the FLQ's struggle for national liberation. Evoking Westmount, a metonym for the socio-economic disparity between wealthy anglophone bosses and poor francophone workers, reinforces the neo-Marxist discourse. Specifying the anglophone town of Westmount is a biting addition to the English version of the play because it directly implicates the Ontarian audience in the colonizing mission of Canadian federalism and it antagonizes the audience by making them experience indirectly the fear of attack with which their fellow English Canadians were living. Westmount draws in the audience as vicarious victims of terrorism and associates them with the English Canadian exploitation of Québec.

The play's comparison of Québec to Africa, and hence of Westmount to imperial Europe, is not reductive, nor does it lend itself to the common accusation that Québécois nationalism is motivated by a *repli sur soi* or xenophobic inward turn. On the contrary, the parallel testifies to a passionate concern about global affairs and solidarity with "Third World" countries. The radio announcement refers to the United States's "rôle de pacification" in Vietnam (19),[15] suggested to be colonization, if not war-mongering. The radio's subsequent anniversary date describes the imprisonment of Montréal mayor Camillien Houde in 1941 for protesting conscription, with the trailing reminder that a year later the battle of Dieppe took place in which many Québécois soldiers conscripted by the Canadian government were killed. The valorization of the Québécois pacifist who predicted the slaughter of his people on the front lines in the Second World War aligns the Québécois in solidarity with the slaughtered Vietnamese. The English version also aligns Hamlet/Quebec with the Gabonese (4), and, through the satiric addition of a black slave vocative, "boy come" (13), it figures Horatio/Lévesque as an associate member of the African negritude movement as a "nègre blanc d'Amérique."[16] Far from the navel-gazing of Shakespeare's Hamlet, Gurik's Hamlet-Quebec, who greets Horatio-Lévesque in Spanish with "Holà" (30), is in tune with world affairs. The parallels between African decolonization and Québécois nationalism strengthen the play's neo-Marxist argument for independence because the exploitation of workers by imperial conquerors turned global capitalists creates a bond of solidarity between all those who feel enslaved, encouraging those who have not yet broken free from their (neo-)colonial masters to emulate those who already have.

The two gravediggers make explicit the neo-Marxist link between colonization and poverty. In the opening scene, the 1er Fossoyeur explains why he is poor and dissatisfied with his job but unable to change his lot in life: "j'ai pas d'instruction et puis j'parle pas anglais..." (10).[17] As a result of the Conquest and the colonization of New France by England, Québec's francophone majority has become trapped in a cycle whereby linguistic difference prevents access to education and well-paying jobs, and the poverty caused by low-level employment prevents workers' children from furthering their education through which they could erase their linguistic, and hence economic, difference. Without education and a mastery of the English language, poor francophone workers cannot even rise up socially and economically to the class of *contremaîtres*, that is, foremen who were typically seen as colonial mimic men because they lorded power over their own people in an unsuccessful attempt to join the ranks of their anglophone bosses (as we shall see in the text's construction of Laerte-Trudeau). In the play's English version, the criticism of this situation is accentuated by the First Digger's accent, broken English syntax, and a pun on a common nickname for anglophones derived from their swearing habits, "des goddamns": "I never go to dhe school and me goddamn I no spick Ingliss..." (2). The Second Digger also evokes indirectly the linguistic colonization of Québec when he consoles the First by telling him to listen to the radio because "de hit parade is good" (2), a comment that does not appear in the French version but points to the encroaching assimilation of francophones through (mostly American) anglophone mass culture since Canadian Radio-television and Telecommunications Commission (CRTC) rules establishing a minimum level of French content (set at 65 per cent by the Broadcasting Act of 1991) did not yet exist to protect Québécois culture.[18]

The discursive overlap between Québécois neo-Marxism and nationalism is further developed in the Patriots scene that Gurik adds between the equivalent of 3.4 and 4.5 in Shakespeare's play. Midway through Gurik's 2.7, the gravediggers experience a transition in time and come out of their grave wearing clothes from the 1837–8 Patriots' Rebellion.[19] The 2ième Fossoyeur complains that "la dîme a été augmentée et tout cet argent s'en va vers d'autres contrées, celles-là même qui ont aidé le nouveau roi à monter sur le trône" (72).[20] His Patriot-era recognition of the people's colonization – taxation by their own religious authorities, functioning as *compradors*, which is being used to reinforce the wealth and power of foreign conquerors – merges neo-Marxism and nationalism in a discourse of decolonization. The gravedigger's complaint rejoins his earlier, contemporary-era frustration at exploitation and desire for liberation: "Tant qu'à manger de la *scrap* j'aime autant la manger à ma table et pas à celle d'un autre" (70).[21] Here the 2ième Fossoyeur combines a neo-Marxist discourse on poverty with the nationalist discourse of "maîtres chez nous" into the idea of eating scraps at one's own table, prioritizing national liberation above wealth. The Patriot scene is instigated by a conversation between the two gravediggers about René Lévesque's resignation from the paradoxical Québec-nationalist-Canadian-federalist PLQ and his plans to found a new "parti pour l'indépendance," the MSA (70).[22] The second gravedigger links Lévesque to the Patriots, wishing for him to lead a new rebellion (democratic this time) to finish the task the Patriots failed to complete the first time: "Moi avec un gars comme ça, je marche. [...] Si on avait tenu notre bout en ce temps-là [des patriotes de '37]... on n'en serait pas là. Je suis sûr qu'on aurait pu" (70).[23] Gurik's addition of the Patriots scene thus functions both as a warning against repeating the mistakes of the past (failing to finish the revolution for independence) and as an exposition of how little the socio-economic condition of francophone workers has changed in 130 years, thereby suggesting that independence is the only solution to poverty.

While the play's nationalist discourse depends on neo-Marxism, the opposing discourse of Canadian federalism propagated by Le Roi-L'anglophonie, Polonius-Pearson, and Laerte-Trudeau ignores the presence, let alone the plight, of Québec's working class. Instead, the federalist discourse is rooted in a Foucauldian paradigm of power relations focused on discipline and punishment. Le Roi-L'anglophonie, for instance, describes Hamlet-Québec as "une plaie brûlante dans mon flanc" and writes to England requesting "une aide armée pour raffermir notre autorité dans ce pays" (64).[24] Taken in conjunction with Rosencrantz-Pelletier's subsequent observation that "il suffit d'une étincelle pour faire exploser la poudre" (64),[25] Gurik not only alludes to FLQ bombs that had already exploded but also predicts the federal government's response to the October Crisis two years later when the Canadian army occupied the streets of Montréal to re-establish its authority over the territory of Québec. Le Roi-L'anglophonie then warns La Reine-L'église, "Il faut que votre fils se soumette totalement" (65), an absolutist position consistent with the King's decision to "mettre des gants de fer" as related by the Patriot-era 2ième Fossoyeur: "'À partir d'aujourd'hui, la seule langue tolérée sera celle en usage à la cour. Tout contrevenant sera puni sévèrement'" (71).[26] This portrait of English Canada's hard-line approach to Québec is not inconsistent with federal tactics, such as Stéphane Dion's "Plan B."[27] Domination is Le Roi-L'anglophonie's position from the outset when he tells Hamlet-Québec, "Il faut faire face aux réalités… ce qui était n'est plus" (13),[28] reminding him of the Conquest of Old Hamlet-New France and encouraging him to accept his defeat with obedient submission.

As Hamlet-Québec becomes increasingly conscious of his domination by Le Roi-L'anglophonie and of La Reine-L'église's complicity, Le Roi-L'anglophonie becomes more preoccupied with his project to "les mâter, et lui et le peuple" (78).[29] His desire to quell Hamlet-Québec's and the people's uprising reveals not only his obsession with suppressing Hamlet-Québec's quest to understand the murder-Conquest of Old Hamlet-New France but also the myth common in English Canada that all Québécois nationalists are radicals, and hence terrorists, who must be stomped out by force. This generalization conflates the myriad political positions espoused by the population of Québec, including those of conservative federalist-nationalists (such as Duplessis), progressive federalist-nationalists (such as Lesage and the PLQ), conditional sovereignists (Johnson and the Union nationale with "Égalité ou Indépendance"), partnership-oriented sovereignists (Lévesque and the MSA), left-wing sovereignists (Bourgault and the RIN), and radical, action-oriented sovereignists (such as the FLQ). Le Roi-L'anglophonie's fixation on suppressing all the people aligned with Hamlet-Québec, regardless of ideological differences within the collective "peuple," belies his incomprehension of the underlying causes of the uprising he is determined to wipe out. Le Roi-L'anglophonie's totalitarian discourse derives from his desire to secure his dominance through the enactment of the ritualistic violence characteristic of an early modern revenge tragedy rather than a rational assessment of the social conditions, such as poverty, that motivate the allegiance of various factions of the population to Hamlet-Québec.

Laerte-Trudeau fully supports Le Roi-L'anglophonie's strategy of punishment and ritualistic violence in his dealings with Hamlet-Québec. Following Hamlet-Québec's accidental stabbing of Polonius-Pearson behind the arras, Laerte-Trudeau ignores his father's earlier advice that "la patience fait souvent triompher les causes, mêmes les plus faibles" (23).[30] Polonius-Pearson advocates the slow assimilation of Québec into English-Canada while simultaneously admitting the moral illegitimacy of such a strategy, an ironic deviation from Shakespeare's Polonius's imperative "to thine own self be true" (1.3.78). Laerte-Trudeau, on the other hand, wants to be Le Roi-L'anglophonie's instrument in Hamlet-Québec's murder and says that he "l'égorger[ait] au pied de l'autel que sa mort serve d'exemple aux têtes brûlées du pays" (80).[31] No longer motivated by grief over his sister's and father's deaths, as in Shakespeare, Laerte-Trudeau wants to slit Hamlet-Québec's throat in order to repress all of Québec's radicals, that is, its sovereignists and neo-Marxists. The adaptation reveals, however, that Laerte-Trudeau has also been caught in Le Roi-L'anglophonie's trap. With his dying breath Laerte-Trudeau confesses to Hamlet-Québec, "Je t'aimais, maintenant, je le sais, mais le miroitement des honneurs, les malheurs qui se sont abattus sur moi, la langue perfide du grand responsable de notre tragédie ont obscurci ma raison…" (94).[32] Gurik could have omitted Laerte-Trudeau's attempted reconciliation with Hamlet-Québec, just as he cuts Fortinbras's invasion and many other lines, but Laerte-Trudeau's apology enriches the adaptation by figuring him as a colonized subject who recognizes too late his role as *comprador* in Ashcroft, Griffiths, and Tiffin's sense of the term. Gurik's adaptation constructs Laerte-Trudeau, like the bourgeois in V.S. Naipaul's novel, as a "mimic man," a subject who is oblivious to his own colonization because of his desire to identify with the colonizer and who enacts his self-hatred on his own people in order to earn the colonizer's praise.

Since the Ontario production provided the opportunity to mock an audience representative of Canadian federalism, the Laertes/Trudeau character changes in the English version, as does the King/The English's political strategy. Le Roi-L'anglophonie's phrase "Mais j'ai su les mâter, et lui et le peuple" becomes "But I have him bewildered, both he and the people also, and thou, dearest Laertes, art part of the show" (78, 44). The shift from "mâter" (meaning to quell or suppress a rebellion or terrorists) to "bewildered" signals a transformation of the King/The English's tactics in dealing with Hamlet/Quebec. Instead of forcefully inflicting punishments, the King/The English approaches Québec more strategically, in keeping with the policy of assimilation, and he purposefully employs his mimic man to create the illusion the Québécois population may voice its positions through its democratic representative, but in reality this representative speaks in service of the colonizer. Laertes/Trudeau is no more than a talking head, full of sound and fury but signifying nothing, and he does not know that he is a puppet in the King/The English's "show" until he is explicitly told so. While the English version tones down the physical violence of colonization by omitting the reference to suppressing rebellion, it highlights the more insidious colonial strategy of using artifice to confuse the people so that, like Laertes/Trudeau, they fail to recognize their colonized state.

The English version of the adaptation further undercuts the Laertes/Trudeau character by adding several references to flowers. When Laertes/Trudeau returns from his voyage to Ottawa to study law, he enters "clenching raggedly-looking flowers which he swings like a club" (43), and when the King/The English recounts the plan of the poisoned sword, he charges with his flowers crying, "I will do it! Ha! Ha!" (45). As Stevenson suggests, the heightened parody of Trudeau may be attributed to his increased public profile following his swearing in as prime minister (76). I would argue, though, that the additional mockery of Trudeau in the English version has less to do with public familiarity with his real-life antics and can instead be attributed to a Québécois fear of federasty, as described in chapter 1. Wielding flowers in lieu of a sword makes Laertes/Trudeau a laughing stock by parodying the characteristic red rose in Trudeau's lapel and constructs the character as an effeminate "fédéraste" by replacing a virile, penetrating rapier with a traditionally feminine symbol that wilts when picked. By disarming Laertes/Trudeau in an Ontarian context, the English version is more subversive than the French since English Canadians revered Trudeau as a "wise man," a cultural icon of Shakespeare's grandeur, more than Québécois whose opinion of him was often divided. Undercutting the character on the English Canadian turf to which Trudeau "defected" from Québec attacks the unified Canadian nation that Trudeau defended.

The English version also mocks Trudeau's crusade for bilingualism coast to coast. The messenger who announces Laertes/Trudeau's return recounts how he "rambles on and on going without pause or warning from well hewn words to senseless jargon; a foreign language […] unknown to most, and he rambles on and on, then back to sense, till this folly strikes again and then flowers again" (43). The messenger's description effeminizes Trudeau by attributing to him Ophelia's flower-strewing in Shakespeare, and it makes bilingualism a fit of folly that strikes its victim at random. Laertes/Trudeau's ability to switch effortlessly between well-hewn words in English and French, which is experienced as a foreign language unknown to many in English Canada, does not garner respect in an Ontarian context; instead, Laertes/Trudeau's bilingualism characterizes him as schizophrenic since French is nonsense to English Canadian ears. Trudeau's argument for bilingualism on the grounds of civil liberties is further undercut when Laertes/Trudeau threatens his father's killer with his "bilingual wrath, one of snarl, the other of spit," claiming, "For 'tis my right, I will use it, no one can take this from me. I have the 'right to free spit…oh…'" (43). By transforming the right to free speech into "free spit," the English version suggests the bilingual speaker does not speak effectively in two languages. Rather than eloquent words, only hot air and spit leave his mouth. Bilingualism is transformed from a right to a caprice with which the speaker attempts to impress his interlocutor but produces nothing of substance except a projection of his own internal processes, bodily or otherwise. This mockery of bilingualism, which was supposed to heal the divide between the English and French and unify Canada, is more effective when addressed to an English Canadian audience who, while probably reticent about the idea, might nonetheless see bilingualism as a way to avert the threat of "separatism." While this argument would be redundant to a Québécois audience, in the English version it satirically undercuts the audience's ambivalent belief in this magical solution to national unity.

The federal government's use of bilingualism to colonize Québec is made explicit in the English version through the Rosencrantz and Guildenstern characters who are transformed from Pelletier and Marchand to the "B & B Commission," that is, the Royal Commission on Bilingualism and Biculturalism led by André Laurendeau and Davidson Dunton whose preliminary report was submitted in 1965.[33] Contrary to the French version in which no English is spoken, the English version contains occasional incursions of French, such as the B & B Commission's repetition of every line, one member saying the line in English while the other simultaneously says the same thing in French. Stevenson points out this difference between the two versions of the adaptation (81), but she does not propose its significance. I would argue that the double-speak of the B & B Commission alludes to several sovereignist arguments. First, the repetition of Rosencrantz's and Guildenstern's sentences in both languages underscores the redundancy of bilingualism, especially in a unilingual anglophone context where the audience is unlikely to understand the French sentences. The simultaneity of the bilingual sentences further obscures the French, drowning it out with the English that would enter the ears of anglophone audience members more easily. Second, the redundant double-speak illustrates the sovereignist argument that Québec's independence will usher in administrative efficiency by reducing two levels of government to only one. Since the increased cost to taxpayers has traditionally been an argument against bilingualism in English Canada, highlighting bilingualism's redundancy likewise evokes the anglophone audience's disavowal of it on the grounds of administrative efficiency. Third, Gélinas's English adaptation of Gurik's adaptation stages its redundancy because in the Canadian context bilingualism generally means francophones who speak English, rather than vice-versa, as portrayed by Hamlet/Quebec's anxious yet effortless switch from French to English under the policing gaze of the anglophone audience.[34] Finally, by staging the redundancy of a policy to which a southern Ontarian audience in 1968 would be unsympathetically predisposed,[35] the English version of the play creates favourable conditions for another sovereignist argument: the refusal of English Canada to acquiesce to Québec's demands for the respect of French language and culture.

The duplicity of double-speak and English Canada's refusal to respect French culture are verbalized by the King/The English when he praises Rosencrantz and Guildenstern/B & B Commission for their bilingualism. As Stevenson describes, the King/The English "note que ceux-là sont très chanceux d'être bilingues, car ils peuvent profiter des avantages des deux cultures; puis il se livre à une courte autocritique ayant trait à sa propre incapacité d'apprendre le français" (82),[36] but the King/The English's speech exceeds self-criticism. He reveals his duplicity, telling the Commission, "I know some words: 'Je vous aime', but have no feeling for them" (16). The King/The English confesses that the political strategy underlying bilingualism is to appease Québec superficially without transforming English Canada's disinterest in its concerns. English Canada's profession of love for Québec is false, a duplicitous discourse in which the words mask its true disdain.[37] The King/The English's praise of the B & B Commission's biculturalism is also insincere, motivated by envy and a resigned acceptance of his own inadequacies: "You have two cultures; I wish I had even one" (16). Here, the play justifies its translation from French to English: Gurik's play must be presented to an anglophone audience, even at the risk of assimilation by English Canada's political hegemony, because Québec is the heart of Canada's cultural production. The English version of the adaptation argues that English Canada, being devoid of any distinct culture of its own, depends on Québec artists to provide meaning, even if English Canada's identity must be formed counter-discursively to Québécois culture.

The B & B Commission alludes repeatedly to the dangers of assimilation. As Stevenson notes (82), B & B state their mission twice, first when they confess "with time we assimilate" (21), and again when they explain their "golden rule": "Homogenize, unify, bleach the brains so that all will come to the same pot, and melt within" (24). The assimilation of francophones by English Canada's linguistic hegemony takes place onstage subtly, however. When Hamlet/Quebec first greets Rosencrantz and Guildenstern/ B & B Commission, he begins in French, stops, looks at the audience, makes Rosencrantz/B anxious by this pause, and then begins his welcome again in English. Stevenson explains Hamlet/ Quebec's awkward switch as a reminder that the play takes place in London rather than Montréal (81). More than a nod to the play's relocation, however, Hamlet/Quebec's switch from French to English reenacts the quotidian phenomenon in Québec, prevalent in 1968 and still common today, of a group of francophones who switch from speaking French to English as soon as an anglophone becomes part of their conversation. The play dramatizes the anglophone audience's complicity in English Canada's assimilation of Québec; it appropriates their silent, policing gaze in order to critique both anglophone linguistic hegemony and francophones' own colonized mentality. Although linguistic assimilation stems from English Canada's superior demographic and political weight, the play acknowledges francophones' complicity in their own assimilation due to the neocolonial inferiority complex that causes them to capitulate to the presence of English in their daily lives. This attitude is also dramatized by the Queen/The Church's reply to Rosencrantz/B of "Thank you, 'merci'" followed by a laugh (16). The nervous discomfort of her laughter following her pitiful attempt at bilingualism betrays her assimilation by the King/The English's and the B & B Commission's political agenda. The B & B Commission also reveals its assimilation to the King/The English's agenda when it reports back on its conversation with Hamlet/Quebec: "Words, torrents from a drunken babbling babe, come forth but I know not, hear not, what he wants" (25). B & B acknowledge bilingualism's pitfalls; it does not increase linguistic or cultural comprehension but incapacitates it. Linguistically, the B & B Commission cannot make sense of Hamlet/Quebec's words, and, culturally, it is complicit with the King/The English.

The nationalist discourses articulated through anti-ecclesiasticism, neo-Marxism, and a critique of linguistic and cultural imperialism provide a catalogue of reasons for Québec's sovereignty in both versions of *Hamlet, prince du Québec*. Rooted in concrete socio-political arguments, these nationalist discourses reinforce the adaptation's national allegory that Hamlet-Québec must take action. Hamlet-Québec's hesitation is voiced through self-criticism, making Gurik's Hamlet initially more timid than Shakespeare's, but awareness of his flaws is essential to his awakening. Whereas Shakespeare's Hamlet begins the play with sufficient self-assurance to attack Claudius through the pun that he is "too much in the sun" (1.2.67), Gurik's Hamlet-Québec turns that critique inward on himself: "je vois peu la lumière" (12).[38] Hamlet-Québec criticizes the nation's lack of insight into its own colonization. His hesitation also manifests itself in his inability to resist Le Roi-L'anglophonie's colonial power. Unable to speak up against injustices around him, he recognizes he is "forcé d'enchaîner [s]a langue" (14).[39] Hamlet-Québec realizes the only escape from his colonized state is through direct action, but he is unable to put this strategy into practice: "De nos jours, Horatio, l'homme qui veut survivre ne rend pas les armes, il se bat. Mais je suis bien mal placé pour te dicter ta conduite" (16).[40]

Despite knowing he must *passer à l'action*, Hamlet-Québec cannot do so without a response to the questions of what action and why: "Que faire? Pourquoi faire?" (14).[41] The Spectre-De Gaulle awakens him with the revelation of the murder/Conquest of Old Hamlet-New France. Hamlet-Québec laments that Le Roi-L'anglophonie "foule cette terre où il est un étranger" (30),[42] thereby evoking the Conquest of New France, which, as explained in chapter 1, is experienced as a national rape.

"La terre," an image associated with the mother, recurs frequently in Québécois poetry (by Nelligan, Garneau, Chamberland, Miron, etc.) as a metonymy for the nation, as we shall see in chapter 4, so the violation of the land by a foreigner symbolizes the rape of the mother. The murder/Conquest of Old Hamlet-New France and the rape of the symbolic mother/land scars Hamlet-Québec psychologically as a victim of this murder/rape/Conquest too.[43] Recognition of this trauma precipitates Hamlet-Québec's *prise de conscience* of what he knew instinctively but could not articulate, allowing him to rise up from being *à genoux*.[44] Historical knowledge "vient confirmer toutes [ses] présomptions, tout ce [qu'il sentait] sans oser [se] l'avouer ouvertement" and breaks him free from denial in order to experience the repressed feelings associated with this trauma, "toute cette angoisse, ce ressentiment d'oppression, d'esclavage, d'abaissement," buried inside him (30).[45] Rather than a reactionary motivation for decolonization, however, this trauma acts as a catalyst in acquiring rational arguments, such as the workers' poverty and desire to be free from the "tyrant" as Hamlet-Québec discovers in his conversation with the 2ième Fossoyeur (84). Hamlet-Québec's feelings of anxiety and oppression do not justify his plan to overthrow the usurper, but they do endow him with the self-confidence to trust what he suspected and to defend his convictions. The knowledge of past trauma puts an end to Hamlet-Québec's *né pour un petit pain* defeatism ("Je n'attache pas grand prix à ma vie" [27]), and it allows him to see clearly the duplicity of Le Roi-L'anglophonie whom the Spectre-De Gaulle describes as a "profiteur qui pourrait [le] laisser croire qu'il [le] comprend et qu'il [l]'aime" (30).[46]

Even after his *prise de conscience*, Hamlet-Québec delays, like Shakespeare's Hamlet, by pondering the nature of hesitation. He tells Horatio, "Ceux qui disent demain, pensent jamais..." implying with trailing ellipses *qu'il ne viendra pas* (27).[47] Despite recognizing the price of hesitation is death, Hamlet-Québec struggles to throw off the habit that has laced him in a "corset d'immobilité pour engourdir en [lui] le sentiment de la vengeance et de la libération," so like Shakespeare's rogue and peasant slave he opts for "encore demain..." (47).[48] Hamlet-Québec takes a significant detour from Shakespeare, however, in the "To be or not to be" speech (3.1.56–88), which Gurik rewrites as "Être ou ne pas être libre!" (51). The word "libre" [free] transforms Hamlet-Québec's soliloquy from a deliberation about suicide to a plan of action for national independence. A series of cuts and additions shift the speech's focus from a hopeless present to a hopeful future and from the "undiscover'd country" of death to "l'espoir de quelque avenir" (3.1.79, 51).[49] Significantly, Gurik's Hamlet-Québec ends the soliloquy by resolutely refusing sleep in order to "se battre!" for "[des] projets enfantés avec le plus d'énergie et d'audace" (51).[50] The exclamation mark ending the soliloquy after "fight" signals Hamlet-Québec's conquest of his hesitation.

Overcoming hesitation is thus a complex psychological process for Hamlet-Québec that requires a *prise de conscience* predicated on learning his own history, a confrontation of denial, the release of repressed feelings, and the self-confidence to fight for his convictions. Hamlet-Québec's trajectory differs from Shakespeare's Hamlet's introspection, as seen in the graveyard scene. Whereas Shakespeare's Hamlet gives latitude to his melancholy through his reminiscence of his youth with poor Yorick, Gurik's Hamlet-Québec refuses to dialogue with death, focusing instead on avoiding the grave in order to ensure the nation's future well-being. He points out to the 2ième Fossoyeur, "Si tu te couches dans la fosse, cela n'aidera pas tes fils" (86),[51] who replies that a *patriote* who dies fighting for his country will remain living after death. Hamlet-Québec is ready to *passer à l'action*, but the question of what kind of action remains unanswered until his conversation with the 2ième Fossoyeur: a popular revolution first requires a dialogue with the people in order to educate them and awaken them from their colonial mindset. The 2ième Fossoyeur reveals that "beaucoup d'hommes" are ready to imitate the *patriote* lying in the grave, but they are waiting for a new leader, such as Papineau and De Lorimier who led the rebellion: "un crâne... un chef..." (86).[52] Despite Hamlet-Québec's assurance that a leader will come, this waiting, emphasized by the multiple ellipses, hides two dangers. First, waiting for a leader can slip into waiting for a messiah to deliver the people magically from their oppression, and no political leader can live up to such expectations and single-handedly liberate the nation without the contribution of the people themselves, not even Horatio-Lévesque to whom the bald skull refers. Second, waiting is an inaction that does not hold the people responsible for confronting their colonization head-on; rather, waiting creates a psychological dependence on a forthcoming leader that leaves them open to neocolonial exploitation equal to, if not worse than, that of the current colonial regime.

This tension between the people's need for a leader to mobilize their energy and for them to rise up and lead themselves to independence is at the heart of Hamlet-Québec's dying speech:

> Je meurs… qui viendra nous conduire vers la lumière, car il ne suffit pas de tuer le serpent mais il faut aussi détruire son nid pour que sur cette terre pousse librement ce qui doit s'épanouir. Vous sentirez-vous assez fort pour le faire, assez courageux pour le vouloir? Il est tellement plus facile de pourrir dans l'habitude. Manger… dormir… mourir… et ne jamais rêver… ne jamais rire. Qui… qui… nous sortira de la fange des compromis, de l'esclavage, qui brisera les chaînes qu'hypocritement nous avons nous-mêmes forgées. Il faut que ma mort serve aux autres. Il faut… que vive… un… Qué… bec… libre. (95)[53]

Although Hamlet-Québec addresses Horatio-Lévesque (and in some stage performances L'Officier du Rhin-Bourgault),[54] the question posed in "vous" form, which can be read in both its polite, singular and its plural meaning, also calls upon the audience. The speech addresses the collective nation through its references to the people's daily life – eating, sleeping, dying – and the possibility of improving that life by dreaming and laughing. The adaptation suggests the people are stuck in life's repetitive trance, waiting for their leader, but they need to open their eyes as Hamlet-Québec has done. Although Le Roi-L'anglophonie's treachery causes Hamlet-Québec to follow the fate of Shakespeare's Hamlet, if his death sets an example and teaches the people to break free from the chains they have placed on themselves, then his death will have served its purpose of saving future *patriotes* from dying in the fight for freedom and will let live a free Québec.

Hamlet-Québec's plight functions as a national allegory, then, because, as Jameson explains, the "telling of the individual story and the individual experience cannot but ultimately involve the whole laborious telling of the experience of the collectivity itself" (85–6). In living out Hamlet's struggles in a Québécois context, surrounded by the political figures who work with and against the nation's development, Gurik's Hamlet cannot help but reveal the concerns with which the nation is preoccupied. What Jameson calls the "radical split between the private and the public, between the poetic and the political" is brought closer together in this play where Hamlet's "private individual destiny" aligns neatly with the "embattled situation of the public […] culture and society" in Quiet Revolution Québec (69). The distinction between Hamlet's hesitation to overthrow his usurping uncle in Shakespeare becomes blurred with Québec's hesitation to achieve its decolonization from English Canada in the adaptation. Hamlet's story parallels Québec's so closely that the reader cannot determine with certainty to what extent the narrative is driven by Shakespeare's text or by the political situation upon which Gurik draws.

As the first ever Québécois adaptation of Shakespeare, *Hamlet, prince du Québec* is a profoundly nationalist play that articulates a clear *prise de position* in favour of sovereignty. In such a nationalist play, however, gender issues are largely absent, except where they intersect theoretically with nation through Conquest/rape and federasty. Since there were no women politicians in the national spotlight in 1968, even the female roles of the Queen and Ophelia are adapted into male characters, the male-dominated Catholic Church and Premier Jean Lesage, resulting in an entirely male cast of actors. There are "many men" ready to follow a new leader towards freedom, but the possibility of female *patriotes* joining the cause does not occur to Hamlet-Québec. *Hamlet, prince du Québec* thus articulates a masculinist vision of how a Québec *libre* should develop.

Chapter Four

Tyrants and Usurpers: Tradapting the Conquest

The use, quality, and even existence of the Québécois language was a key debate during the 1970s to which Michel Garneau contributed with his "tradaptations," to use his own neologism, of *Macbeth* (1978) and *La tempête* (1973/1989). Without changing Shakespeare's plot or characters, Garneau exposes the semiotic richness of the Québécois language by translating the text into an approximation of an eighteenth-century dialect spoken in New France prior to the Conquest while he subtly adapts geographical and historical details in order to conflate the action within the world of Shakespeare's plays with the Conquest and contemporary neocolonialism. The overlapping spatio-temporal markers produce a palimpsest, simultaneously locating the play in either medieval Scotland or on Caliban's island, in eighteenth-century New France, and in contemporary Québec. The palimpsest's layers are blurred because the three spatio-temporal contexts are linked by a single nationalist discourse centred on the country's usurpation by a tyrant and its need for liberation.[1] This nation excludes the contributions of women, however, except as a means to ensure the continuation of patriarchal kinship. While the plays' nationalism transcends the spatio-temporal gap between Shakespeare's England and contemporary Québec, their treatment of women perpetuate early modern gender norms. As in the case of *Hamlet, prince du Québec,* the exclusion of women from important roles in the nation-building process can partially be attributed to the tradaptations' setting since women in New France were circumscribed to the roles of wife, mother, nun, nurse, or *fille de joie;* however, for Garneau, as for Gurik, nationalism, not gender issues, remains the primary motivation for appropriating Shakespeare's cultural authority.

In 1973, Michèle Lalonde wrote "La deffence et illustration de la langue quebecquoyse,"[2] a manifesto for the defence and promotion of the Québécois language modelled after Joachim du Bellay's 1549 *Deffence et illustration de la langue françoyse.*[3] Du Bellay defends the aesthetic beauty of vernacular French and pleads for the use of French, rather than Greek or Latin, in the composition of poetry. He begins his argument with the concept of language as a living tree whose branches are in constant growth; he then discredits the idea of vernacular French as "barbarous," qualifying it as "as rich as" its classical predecessors. In his pride in the local language and in the populism underlying his high culture defence of the *vox populi*, du Bellay inflects his essay with nationalism. Lalonde picks up these elements of du Bellay's text and expands the argument, first by situating the notion of the living tree in the historical context of Québec's linguistic isolation from France in the aftermath of the Conquest, and then by explaining how Québécois is not only as rich as *français de France* but also less corrupted by anglicisms. Although she imitates several of his arguments, follows the structure of his text, and even adopts his sixteenth-century orthography, Lalonde adapts du Bellay by adding two related arguments, one psychoanalytic and the other postcolonial.

Lalonde identifies the two most common views of the Québécois language: the first ensconces the virtues of *français de France* while maligning Québec's working-class *joual*; the other, vice versa, extols *joual* to the detriment of grammar. Lalonde frames her psychoanalytic reading of the first discourse as the "difficulté de s'exprimer dans la langue à-sa-mére" (12), which she characterizes as an inferiority complex for certain people, still tied by the umbilical cord to France, whose "langue maternelle [...] les humilie personnellement si fort" (13).[4] This "aliénation" and renunciation of one's mother tongue is also a rejection of the nation since those who practice this linguistic snobbery "insultent [sa] famille et qu'à trop admirer le Bon Parler, ils en viennent à mépriser inconsciemment les bonnes gens qui parlent..." (13, 12).[5] Lalonde's psychoanalytic reading of the inferiority complex underlying this high culture versus low culture linguistic dichotomy thus translates into a postcolonial analysis since she exposes the symptoms of this *complexe de colonisé*. She claims that both the pro-French and the pro-*joual* groups have adopted "sous le coup de l'angoisse la conduite de l'autruche" (17), burying their heads in the sand rather than admitting their colonization.[6] Pro-French advocates, "refusant d'admettre la présence d'un Conquérant & Occupant étranger, qui les dépossède chaque jour un peu plus de la richesse de leur culture & leur langue," prefer to take themselves for "l'agresseur à abattre" and see only the Québécois people's blindness, ignorance, and supposed collective impotence to improve their vocabulary and correct their grammar (17).[7] They are content to "prendre leur trou" (a Québécois idiom expressing the colonial mindset) where they find their enemy "au fond de leur propre humiliation" (17).[8] In contrast, pro-*joual* advocates, in their "fierté de parler Kébecway," believe that by speaking less and less French they are "moins en moins colonisés" and that from the bottom of their hole they see that "anyway l'ennemi c'est la France!" (17).[9] By mocking both discourses, Lalonde illustrates the position of double colonization in which Québec finds itself relative to imperialist France and to neocolonial cultural and capital imperialism of anglophone nations.

These psychological responses to Québec's colonization, rooted in a recognizable reality for the reader of the period, lend credibility to Lalonde's political claims about Québec sovereignty earlier into the same chapter. She explains the contextual difference between du Bellay's text and hers, namely that sixteenth-century France was already independent from the ancient Roman Empire against whose Latin du Bellay was writing. Lalonde does not see herself or the "vulgaire Québécois" she is defending as "réunis sous un sceptre audacieux capable de les mener très très loin" (15).[10] Unlike du Bellay's French compatriots, the Québécois are not united under a bold sceptre that will lead them into the future because they are not a sovereign nation. Rather, the Québécois are colonized because they are "cernés de toutes parts par des puissances estrangières tantôt Anglaise, tantôt Américaine, voire, récemment, Italienne, qui [...] les soumettent à leurs lois, privilèges ou droits acquis de plus ou moins longue date sur ce territoire" (15).[11] While recognizing that some Québécois already feel "independent" in their interiority, she ironizes that she does not know yet that "cette excellente disposition psychologique soit bel et bien reconnue par aucune disposition de nos lois ou proclamation d'Indépendance très réelle et claire, entendue des Nations-Unies" (16).[12] Lalonde brings together the logical connection between language and the psychology of colonization in her stark observation that celebrating the autonomy of the Québécois language is pre-emptive when "la nation qui veut la parler ne parvient mesme pas au jour d'huy à conjuguer ses forces au premier temps de l'indicatif…" (16).[13] Like Gurik, Lalonde decries the Québécois nation's inability to *passer à l'action* through the linguistic metaphor of its inability to conjugate its strengths in the present indicative tense.

Lalonde is not alone in linking language and nationalism in order to construct a strategic discourse of literary, and potentially even political, decolonization. In 1977, after ten years of reflection on the subject, the internationally known Kenyan writer Ngũgĩ wa Thiong'o, whose novel *A Grain of Wheat* chronicles his country's struggle for independence, decided despite the success of his novels in English to write exclusively in his mother tongue of Gĩkũyũ, thereby making his texts available to international readers in translation only. In *Moving the Centre,* Ngũgĩ describes the critical moment of consciousness that provoked his decision:

> I came to realise only too painfully that the novel in which I had so carefully painted the struggle of the Kenya peasantry against colonial oppression would never be read by them. In an interview shortly afterwards in the *Union News* [...] in 1967, I said I did not think that I would continue writing in English: that I knew *about* whom I was writing, but *for* whom was I writing? (9–10, italics in original)

Ngũgĩ's recognition of the futility of recounting a national liberation movement's struggle in a language inaccessible to the people for whom he was writing exposes the cultural imperialism underlying literature and translation in neocolonial and postcolonial contexts. Rather than bolstering the cultural preponderance of the colonizer's language, Ngũgĩ's decision to privilege his mother tongue disempowers the colonizer and constructs Kenyan readers as the dominant cultural presence in their nation. Likewise, Garneau deploys language's cultural power to turn the tables on the colonizer, but Garneau's strategy is more subversive because he appropriates the colonizer's own texts and re-signifies through them an inaccessible language and cultural context.

Just four years after Lalonde's "Deffence" and in the same year as Ngũgĩ's exclusive adoption of Gĩkũyũ, Garneau undertook the task of translating and adapting *Macbeth* at the request of the Montréal-based École nationale de théâtre du Canada. *Macbeth de William Shakespeare: Traduit en québécois* was performed by the Théâtre de la Manufacture at Montréal's Cinéma Parallèle from 31 October to 2 December 1978, at which time the text was published. Prior to *Macbeth,* Garneau tradapted *La tempête* in 1973 for the École nationale de théâtre, but, as Denis Salter points out, "Garneau came to *re*write *Garneau's Tempest* in the early 1980's" ("Between" 63). The 1989 published version analysed in this chapter is different from his 1973 ur-*Tempête,* but without the earlier text I am unable to determine the extent of the changes. In 1989, Garneau also published *Coriolan*. Of his three Shakespearean tradaptations, *Coriolan* is written in the most standardized French and diverges little from the source text, so it is excluded from this chapter's analysis.[14] All three plays were re-staged by Robert Lepage in 1993 for the Festival de théâtre des Amériques.

Garneau's tradaptations are neither literal translations of Shakespeare nor adaptations that largely modify the content of the source text. Tradaptation, as the word implies, involves both translation and adaptation in such a way that it defies distinctions between the two practices. As Lieblein observes, tradaptation challenges Québec's double colonization by French-language purists and by British hegemony through its resistance to "standard" French translations and its appropriation of Shakespeare's cultural authority ("Cette" 255). Almost all translation in a postcolonial context involves a form of cultural adaptation of the text, according to Maria Tymoczko, for whom translation "reflects the literary system of the post-colonial or minority culture itself," which may involve introducing "various forms of indigenous formalism to the dominant culture" (34). For this reason, Salter asserts that tradaptation "is close to being oxymoronic, as it discloses the kind of prodigious doubling to which the translator's identity [...] is necessarily subjected" as he seeks to preserve the linguistic heritage of the past and assert cultural autonomy in the present ("Between" 63). Garneau thus uses the methods of both the translator and the adapter to create hybrid plays that articulate the need for Québec's decolonization. Like Gurik, Garneau encourages the reader to draw parallels between the world of the play and the political and socio-historical context of Québec, and his nationalism is marked by anti-ecclesiasticism and the imperative to *passer à l'action*. In addition, Garneau subtly integrates nationalism into the Shakespearean text through metonymy, intertextuality, and archaisms.

Macbeth is Garneau's most nationalist tradaptation,[15] and Annie Brisset, who has documented in *Sociocritique de la traduction* his use of metonymy, concludes that Garneau appropriates the text foremost by consistently replacing the word "Scotland" with either "chez-nous" or "pays."[16] The repetition of this simple substitution throughout the play transforms its setting. Although Garneau's *Macbeth* still takes place in Shakespeare's Great Britain, near the centre of the canon, it simultaneously takes place on the margins of the British Empire with geographical and natural traits characteristic of Québec. This shift in context then allows for a shift in theme and the introduction of a nationalist discourse.

In the published text of his tradaptation, Garneau both draws attention to and attempts to disguise his most nationalist speeches.[17] In Act 3, scene 6, he intervenes in the text and writes, *"J'saute du vers 38 au vers 47 parc'c'est melé, mêlant"* (3.6.97, italics in original as for stage directions).[18] This scene stands out for readers because it is one of only two instances of acknowledged authorial intervention in this play, and there are no such cases in the other two plays of the trilogy. The cut results in Ross's account of all that is wrong in the country being followed by Lennox's longing plea, "Ça s'ra't eune bénidiction pis eune sainte justice/Si not'pays s'ra't libéré d'la main damnée qui l'opprime" (3.6.97).[19] While, as Oxford editor Nicolas Brooke explains in his introduction (1989), 3.6 is "perfectly coherent until l. 37, and thereafter it becomes confusing" (52), Arden 2 editor Kenneth Muir explains in his introduction to the 1984 reissue of the edition that the passage could be made more logical by simply transposing the line order (xxxiv n.2).[20] Although Garneau is correct in noting the confusion associated with the passage, the Shakespearean text is not so incoherent that he could not have included a logical version of it. His authorial intervention thus seems more motivated by a desire to draw attention to the nationalism in Lennox's two concluding lines, as well as to prepare the reader for his second textual incursion in 4.3 by invoking here the argument of textual interpolation that scholars of *Macbeth* would be likely to accept at face value.

The second authorial intervention occurs in Act 4, scene 3 when Garneau writes, *"J'traduis pas du vers 139 au vers 161* (Édition Oxford University Press) *parc'c'est la scène avec le docteur où on parle du don de guérisseur du roi d'Angleterre, une scène de ventilation comme on dit au cinéma, qui n'a rien à faire avec l'action dramatique pis qui sonne même pas très Shakespeare"* (4.3.120–1, italics in original).[21] This textual incursion stands out more than the first because Garneau's reason is unjustified. There is no indication that these lines are not Shakespearean or that they are meaningless filler. Although the authorship of several scenes in *Macbeth* has been contested and this passage has been included in that debate, both Muir and Brooke have judged it consistent with Shakespeare's pen. Muir contends that 4.3.140–6 "contains examples of Shakespeare's characteristic imagery and is certainly his" (xxxii). He also argues that even if the passage on the King's Evil is an interpolation Shakespeare may have inserted while revising for the stage "it can still be justified on dramatic grounds" (n.4.3.140–59). Brooke concurs with Muir that the passage's "dramatic function is evident – and the text we have is itself coherent" (51). The lines cut by Garneau recount how the king of England, who is preparing to help Macduff defeat Macbeth, has special healing powers. As Muir points out, the passage relates thematically to many aspects of the play: the opposition between the king's good supernatural powers and the evil powers of the witches; the contrast between the holy Edward the Confessor of England and the unholy Macbeth of Scotland; and the disease imagery in Act 5 (n.4.3.140–59). In addition, Ross's entrance with tragic news is heightened dramatically by its placement after this factual passage. From a socio-historical perspective, the passage may have functioned as flattery of King James I who occasionally "touched" to heal the sick and who had a well-known interest in the supernatural (Brooke 72).

Rather than eliminating confusion in the text, Garneau is attempting to disguise the fact that, as Brisset has convincingly argued (220–2), these lines interrupt the most nationalist speech of the play. By omitting them, the scene becomes a poignant discussion about the imperative to liberate the nation before it is too late. Malcolm laments how Macbeth is destroying his country and then encourages Macduff to join him in overthrowing the tyrant: "Ensemble, on va y aller!/Not'cause peut pas ête plus jusse! La victoére nous attend/Au boutte d'la route!" (4.3.120).[22] Not only is Malcolm's cause just, but so too is the cause of Québécois to imitate him and throw off the reins of oppression by usurping the usurper. The word "notre" in Malcolm's battle cry conscripts the Québécois audience into the army that will defeat tyranny at the end of the play. Without the interruption about the wonders of the king of England, Malcolm's rally is followed by Ross's eulogy for the country:

> Not'pauv'pays a quaisiment d'la misére à se r'connaîte lui-même.
> Not'mére-patrie, on peut quaisiment pus la nommer mére, faudra't
> Ben proche dire tombeau, fosse commune. Y'a ben jusse les innocents
> Qui savent arien su rien qu'y'ont l'coeur d'sourire cheuz-nous.
> [...]
> La seule extase que l'rêgne nous parmet
> C'est d'avoér toute la peine du monde. (4.3.121)[23]

This mournful account of the pitiful state of the country convinces Macduff of the urgency to act and is designed to encourage the audience to fight for national liberation as well. The suggestion that Québécois should emulate Macduff and *passer à l'action* situates Garneau's nationalist discourse in the same current of thought as Gurik's.

Garneau draws attention to the history of the Conquest and to Québec's alterity from Britain through subtle geographical differences. In *La tempête*, Garneau marks Caliban's island as Québec by replacing foreign wildlife with "oies blanches," white geese, also known as "oies de neige" or snow geese, whose regional specificity and twice annual migration along the St Lawrence River (particularly at Cap-Tourmente, Baie-du-Febvre, and Montmagny) are well known to a Québécois reader (4.1.108). In *Macbeth*, the metonymic substitution of "Birnam wood" by "la forêt," or the forest, and "Dunsinan" by "la colline," or the hill, as well as a reversal in the direction in which the forest moves, notably locates the play's final battle on the Plains of Abraham, the site of the 1759 Conquest.[24] In Shakespeare's *Macbeth*, the movement of Birnam wood is mentioned seven times, and in each case Garneau consistently translates this movement with the verb "descendre," to descend, contrary to the upward direction in the source text. The first indication of the relation of Birnam to Dunsinan makes clear that the wood is below the hill on which the castle sits. The Third Apparition predicts, "Macbeth shall never vanquished be, until/Great Birnam Wood to high Dunsinan Hill/Shall come against him" (4.1.107–9).[25] Yet, in the tradaptation, the apparition prophesizes, "Macbeth s'ra pas vaincu tant qu'la forêt descendra pas d'la colline" (4.1.106).[26] To follow Shakespeare, the correct verb should be "monter," to go up or to climb, since the castle is "high" atop the hill. The tradaptation insists on the verb "descendre" in each instance the forest is evoked, even when the Shakespearean text varies the expression, from "remove" (5.2.2) to "come" (5.3.59, 5.5.45–6, 5.7.60). In order for the forest in Garneau's version to descend the hill, the trees must be situated on top or on the side of it. I would argue that relocating the forest serves to evoke the Battle of the Plains of Abraham on 13 September 1759 and the Conquest of New France by the British.

Two other changes to Shakespeare's text support this reference to the Conquest – the generalization of proper names and the addition of a notion of surprise attack. In Garneau, Birnam wood is consistently referred to as an unnamed forest, removing its geographical situatedness from Scotland, and two mentions are cut (5.2.5, 5.2.31), thereby reducing a reader's potential disjuncture between the narrative location of Scotland and the symbolic location of New France. Similarly, Dunsinan is translated vaguely as "la colline," which evokes the fortified city of Québec on its hilltop as well as the "colline parlementaire" now located in the upper city near both the hilltop fort and the Plains of Abraham.

An addition to Malcolm's explanation of why they should adopt the tree branches as a disguise evokes the surprise attack on Québec City during the night of 12–13 September 1759. Shakespeare's Malcolm orders, "Let every soldier hew him down a bough/And bear't before him, thereby shall we shadow/The numbers of our host, and make discovery/Err in report of us" (5.4.4–7), using the tree branches to hide the number of soldiers as they approach and make reconnaissance. He does not evoke the notion of a surprise attack, which would be pointless because Macbeth has already received report from a servant of the approach of ten thousand soldiers and begun to make battle preparations (5.2.13). These facts remain unchanged in the tradaptation, but the notion of a surprise attack is added contrary to the plot's logic: "Tu vas dire à chaque soldat d's'arracher un buisson, un arbuste,/Ou ben un p'tit âbre pour s'cacher aveuc, comme çâ, y'a'ront pas/Idée du nombre qu'on est pis c't'eune erreur qui va nous parmette/D'es surprende" (5.4.139).[27] The surprise arrival of English soldiers up the hill to the Plains of Abraham is the error that changed the face of New France. The French were taken by surprise because access to the Plains of Abraham was believed to be impossible as long as the trees remained on the hill as a source of protection, barring any path to the top. The Plains would only be accessible were the trees to fall or be cut down, *d'être descendus*. In fact, just as it is possible for Birnam wood to move, it was possible for the trees to provide the traction and the cover necessary for the English to climb a narrow goat path unnoticed. The metonymy that dislocates Birnam from Scotland and the re-creation of the Battle of the Plains of Abraham both align the reader's sympathy temporarily with Macbeth. Although Macbeth becomes the tyrant from whom the nation must liberate itself by the end of the play, he begins as the hero and a defender of Scotland (a nation whose quest for freedom mirrors Québec's). Since the colonization of Scotland arrives at the hands of the English army under Edward the Conqueror, the defeat of Dunsinan maps smoothly onto the Conquest on the Plains of Abraham.

Intertextuality is Garneau's second means of tradapting Shakespeare's text. Just as metonymy serves to Québécize the text, so too does the insertion of typically Québécois motifs found in the poetry of his contemporaries. Brisset's detailed study of Garneau's use of intertextuality demonstrates how he reproduces motifs and themes common to the poetry of Paul Chamberland, Gérald Godin, and Gaston Miron, among others (236–51). For example, Garneau's *Macbeth* contains many characteristics found in Chamberland's *L'afficheur hurle*: the same apocalyptic vision of society, the same resistance to dominant power, the same discourse of despair, of exile, of dispossession, the same subjectivity of a collective destiny, the same tone of eulogy, the same images of wounds and blood, the same incantic structure, in other words, all the traits of Québécois poetry in the 1960s and 1970s (246).

Garneau's third tradaptive technique is the use of archaisms.[28] To some extent the language of *Macbeth* resembles the contemporary *joual* of Michel Tremblay's Plateau Mont-Royal, but it is best described as an approximation of French spoken in eighteenth-century New France under the *ancien régime*. Regional and historical variations aside, the language is Québécois in *pure laine* form.[29] While *La tempête* and *Coriolan* use Québécois words and expressions, *Macbeth* also transcribes the accent and the rhythm with which the words are pronounced. *Macbeth*'s linguistic *québécité* is significant in the play's literary and political context, arriving on the heels of Lalonde's manifesto and in the midst of the debate surrounding the implementation in 1977 of *Loi 101*, the Charter of the French Language that seeks to make French "the normal and everyday language of work, instruction, communication, commerce and business." In response to Lalonde's challenge, Garneau defends and illustrates the Québécois language, demonstrating it to be "as rich as" not only Shakespearean English but also "standard" *français de France*. Garneau's *Macbeth* dispels the myth that Shakespeare can only be represented in French in the style of François-Victor Hugo whose nineteenth-century translations of the complete works had a major impact on French and Québécois stage productions and are still used today. The Québécois text valorizes the poetry and beauty of the Québécois language and, by extension, Québécois culture. *Macbeth*'s title specifies "traduit en québécois," announcing that Garneau foregrounds the local language and disregards the rules of the Académie française in Paris. Garneau's decision to represent Shakespeare in archaic Québécois could be compared to Ngũgĩ's decision to write in Gĩkũyũ. Garneau provides textual proof that his language is on a par with those of colonial Britain and France, thereby destabilizing the hierarchy between "proper" metropolitan speech from the centre and "degenerate" colonial dialects spoken on the margins of those former empires.

In addition to the ways metonymy, intertextuality, and archaism shape the form, the content of Garneau's tradaptations is made Québécois by the nationalist themes of anti-ecclesiasticism and the urgency to *passer à l'action* to liberate the usurped nation from tyranny. In keeping with Gurik's work, Garneau eliminates a crucial moment in the text when characters fail to take action – Malcolm and Donalbain's inability to claim the throne that is rightfully theirs upon the murder of their father. Like Hamlet, Malcolm allows his birthright to be usurped by his father's conqueror, putting melancholy before action. Shakespeare's Donalbain urges Malcolm, "Let's away, our tears are not yet brewed," and Malcolm completes his idea, "Nor our strong sorrow upon the foot of motion" (2.3.125–6). Garneau redirects attention from Malcolm and Donalbain's flight to their suffering and the loss of their birthright. Donalbain laments, "On s'rait mieux d'déguarpir nous-autes; d'autant plusse/Qu'on sait pas 'xact'ment sur quoé pleurer," and Malcolm adds, "Chu comme engourdi d'vant l'malheur, la douleur m'vient lent'ment" (2.3.66).[30] By compounding "malheur" with "douleur" and adding Malcolm's feeling of "numbness," the tradaptation shifts the focus from the inaction provoked by sorrow to the emotional experience of sorrow itself. Rather than sorrow slowing his charge to action, Malcolm experiences his sorrow slowly, as if it must be savoured and appreciated in the moment in contrast to Shakespeare's metaphor of brewing sorrow that quickens or ferments for a specific purpose, as the witches brew trouble. The transformation of Malcolm's sorrow complements Donalbain's leading remark that they are so upset that they are incapable of understanding rationally the cause of their sorrow, an addition that could be interpreted as much in terms of their emotional excess as in terms of their lack of reliable knowledge about their father's murder. The tradaptation's emphasis on sorrow and its removal of the yet unbrewed "foot of motion" construct Malcolm and Donalbain as post-Conquest mourners, more concerned with navel-gazing than the rational course of action required to reclaim their loss. The loss of the Father, symbolized by the loss of language to describe the reason for their tears, corresponds to the rape of the Mother/nation for the Québécois in the wake of the Conquest.

Like Gurik's *Hamlet*, Garneau's *Macbeth* is anti-ecclesiastical, but Garneau treats the relationship between nation and religion with subtlety and social inclusivity. Garneau's tradaptation is concerned with freeing Québécois from the reign of the church, but his anti-ecclesiasticism also attends to the secularization of society at large through the elimination of religious prejudice. In the porter scene, Garneau replaces every occurrence of the noun "equivocator" and the verb "equivocate" (2.3.8–33) with "jésuite" as both a noun and a verb (2.3.56–7). While the equivocator in Shakespeare's *Macbeth* is considered an allusion to the Jesuit Superior Father Henry Garnet found guilty of perjury about his role in the gunpowder plot (Brooke 59), there is no semantic impediment in French preventing Garneau from using Shakespeare's term in one of its many derivative forms (the verb "équivoquer," the noun "équivocation," or the adjective "équivoque"), which all share the same Latin etymological origin of *aequivocus* as the English term. Garneau's metonymic substitution must therefore serve a larger discursive purpose, and I would argue that the emphatic association of liars with Jesuits functions in the play's *ancien régime* context as a critique of the role Jesuit priests played in the colonial development of New France that resulted in the near genocide of aboriginals. Recounted most famously by Jean de Brébeuf in *Les relations jésuites*, New France's establishment involved the religious conversion of aboriginals, especially the Hurons. Importing devastating diseases along with their "civilizing" mission and fuelling strife among aboriginal peoples, such missionaries were untrustworthy equivocators. By metonymically replacing "equivocator" with "jésuite," Garneau's *Macbeth* accepts responsibility for the Jesuit mission's cultural and biological imperialism, thus encouraging Québécois to perceive themselves as not only the victims of colonialism but also its perpetrators.

Religious and ethno-cultural tolerance reappears later in the tradaptation through Garneau's deletion of anti-Semitism from Shakespeare's text. Whereas Shakespeare's third witch throws into the cauldron "Liver of blaspheming Jew" (4.1.26), associating Judaism with blasphemy of a supposedly higher and implicitly Christian religion, in the tradaptation she speaks of "foé d'blasphémateur" unqualified by any specific religious practice (4.1.102).[31] The removal of anti-Semitism and resulting egalitarianism by which anyone may be considered a blasphemer, regardless of religious affiliation or lack thereof, points to a concern about social inclusivity. This sensitivity to a plurality of ethno-cultural and religious identities in the composition of the nation anticipates the immigrants and aboriginals who appear in Ronfard's *Vie et mort du Roi Boiteux* discussed in chapter 5 and in the adaptations since 1990 discussed in chapter 6.

The move towards social inclusivity regardless of religious or ethnic origins – that is, interculturalism, which is discussed in this book's conclusion – is rooted here within a larger movement of secularization stemming from the same anti-ecclesiasticism found in Gurik's *Hamlet*. The duplicity of religious discourse is established early in the play when Garneau's Macbeth and Macduff refer to the late Duncan with the collective possessive pronoun "our" as opposed to Shakespeare's use of "your" to refer to Malcolm and Donalbain's father. Immediately after the murder, Macbeth tells Duncan's sons, "la source, la riviére d'not'sang,/La vra'e r'source de nos vies, toute s'assèche" (2.3.63).[32] Macduff picks up on Macbeth's "notre" and adds, "Not'pére le roé a subi l'meurte" (2.3.63).[33] The words "notre père" resonate with the beginning of a religious prayer well known to every Québécois: "Notre Père, qui êtes aux cieux…"[34] With the words "our blood" and "our life," Macbeth appropriates the sanctity embodied in Duncan as holy father, mixing his blood and his life with the life he has just taken, thereby revealing the ease with which religious discourse can be fraudulent. Yet, by killing the holy father figure, Macbeth also symbolically eradicates the church. In this moment the character represents the secularization that took place in Québec in the 1960s and 1970s as the priest-ridden province liberated itself from the holy fathers who had heretofore dominated its cultural and political life.

Macbeth later exposes the urgency for Québécois to free themselves from the grasp of Catholicism in order to devote energy to national liberation in his conversation with the hired murderers. Shakespeare's Macbeth asks the first murderer, "Are you so gospelled to pray for this good man" (3.1.88), but Garneau's Macbeth chastises the church more pointedly: "J'voudra's savoér si les prêtes/Vous ont assez endormis qu'vous allez continuer d'prier/Pour l'âme de c'te brave homme" (3.1.76–7).[35] "Gospelled" implies that the first murderer has been indoctrinated, but he still possesses the potential for independent thought. A "sleeping" subject, however, lacks consciousness and free will over his thoughts and actions. The substitution of "endormis" for "gospelled" indicates that, lulled to sleep by priests, Québécois lack the capacity to question religious discourse. The Québécois murderers should challenge Macbeth's orders for the sake of national liberation because Macbeth, as the hypnotizing priest he himself condemns, is responsible for the nation's destruction through his plot to murder Banquo and Fleance, the first of a long line of sovereign kings. Through their sleepy inability to analyse the situation presented by a duplicitous voice of authority, the murderers allow themselves to be coerced into an attack on sovereignty. The tradaptation implies that Québécois who allow themselves to be lulled asleep by priests without questioning their authority are participating in the murder of the nation.

While Shakespeare's *Macbeth* provides Garneau with the opportunity to produce a nationalist tradaptation by focusing on liberating Scotland from a usurping tyrant, *The Tempest* could have served for an analysis of the Hegelian master-slave dialectic, which postcolonial adaptations such as Aimé Césaire's *Une tempête* attempt to subvert by focusing on the Prospero-Caliban relationship, but by choosing to preserve the structure of colonial power relations on the island Garneau diverges from the formula adopted by other postcolonial playwrights. Continuing with the theme of usurpation found in *Macbeth, La tempête* emphasizes Prospero's deportation from Milan, a form of colonial violence that could evoke empathy in Québécois since many today are descendants of deported Acadians.[36] In *Macbeth,* "chez-nous" transforms Scotland into Québec. In *La tempête,* "chez-nous" never refers to Caliban's island but rather indicates Prospero's lost dukedom of Milan, replacing metonymically "thence" whence they came (1.2.62). Associated with "pays" in *Macbeth,* in *La tempête* "chez nous" is synonymous with Prospero's "seigneurie" (1.2.18), a term that evokes the semi-feudal land distribution in New France prior to the Conquest where some Acadians resettled following the violent deportation of 1755.

Garneau's *La tempête* encourages the reader to identify with Prospero, whose rightful dukedom has been usurped, first by exaggerating his suffering and second by softening his interactions with the other characters on the island. In describing his exile from "[sa] ville" (1.2.20), a nameless city metonymically disassociated from Milan, the Québécois Prospero repeatedly relives his betrayal. The words "foul play" (1.2.60, 62) are translated as "trahis" and "vilaine trahaison" (1.2.17), while "treacherous army" (1.2.128) becomes "belle armée d'hypocrites et de traîtres" (1.2.20), modified by three adjectives instead of one, and Shakespeare's vague "ministers for th' purpose" (1.2.131) concretely becomes "bande de visages à deux faces" (1.2.20).[37] Qualifying the traitors as "two-faced" links Prospero's usurpers to Gurik's Rosencrantz and Guildenstern and their federalist/nationalist reversible capes. In the poetry of the period, the recurring "je" expresses an emerging selfhood and sense of independence, and in *La tempête* the first person takes an inordinate place in order to remind the audience of their belonging to the suffering nation. In telling his story of exile, Prospero repeats the collective pronoun "our." Garneau translates "Under my burden groaned" (1.2.156) as "grandement écrasé par nos misères" (1.2.21) and transforms "wrings mine eyes to't" (1.2.135) into "notre histoire me crève le coeur" (1.2.20).[38] Playing on its double meaning as both "our story" and "our history," Prospero's collective tale evokes a series of historical incidents – the Conquest, the crushed Patriots' Rebellion and subsequent executions, the conscription crises of 1917 and 1944, and the October Crisis, among others – intended to pierce the reader's heart as they do Miranda's.

To keep the reader's empathy, Prospero's relationship with Miranda is less authoritarian than in Shakespeare, and their treatment of Caliban and Ariel is less deplorable. Rather than addressing Caliban as "Abhorred slave" (1.2.352), Garneau's Prospero simply says "toi" (1.2.33). Rather than accusing, "Thou liest malignant thing" (1.2.257), he more comically says "tu mens comme un notaire" (1.2.28).[39] Prospero does not unnecessarily taunt the others on the island with his magic. The banquet scene, in which Shakespeare's Prospero tortures the starving shipwreck survivors with disappearing food, is omitted from Garneau's tradaptation (3.3.18–51), as is his sadistic pledge towards Caliban, Stephano, and Triculo to "plague them all,/Even to roaring" (4.1.192–3). No longer undercut by his moments of sadism, this kinder, gentler Prospero becomes more worthy of the restoration of his kingdom at the end of the play.

In the final act, Garneau omits Prospero's gratitude to Gonzalo for helping him during the coup d'état and most other references to this assistance, painting Prospero's deportation as more violent and unanimous than in Shakespeare. By essentializing this plot incident, Garneau heightens sympathy for Prospero with this unmitigated betrayal. In Shakespeare, Antonio's coup d'état is merely an "act" (5.1.73), but in Garneau's text it becomes a "saloperie" (5.1.114).[40] Significantly, Garneau cuts Prospero's forgiveness of Antonio: "I do forgive/Thy rankest fault" (5.1.131–2). The Québécois Prospero also rejects the romantic notion that fate separated him from his crown so Miranda would marry Ferdinand to end the brothers' strife. In Garneau's *La tempête,* no excuse justifies the violent territorial dispossession by which Prospero's *seigneurie* was stolen from him, and he commits no wrongs that mitigate the usurper's treachery. Unlike Shakespeare's Prospero who tells Alonso, "Let us not burden our remembrances with/A heaviness that's gone" (5.1.199–200), for the Québécois Prospero the past is neither forgiven nor forgotten. There is no statute of limitations for rectifying past wrongs, that is, for reclaiming the rule usurped long ago during the Conquest.

In addition to the Conquest, Antonio's usurpation of Prospero's power represents English Canada's neocolonial rule over Québec. Prospero's description of Antonio's insidious takeover alludes to the Union of Upper and Lower Canada in 1840:

> et mon propre frère s'est laissé tenter
> par le diable et ma confiance en lui
> a rencontré une grande malhonnêteté

et il est devenu maître
non seulement de mes revenus
mais de ma puissance même
à force de mentir
il a fini par croire à ses accraires
les voir légitimes (1.2.19)[41]

First, Prospero's brother, that is, one who grew up alongside him yet is a distinct entity, succumbs to the devil. Not following the same religious leader, Antonio's and Prospero's opposing religious beliefs echo the divide between English Canadian Protestants and Québec's francophone Catholic majority. Second, Antonio confiscates not only Prospero's political power but also his finances, an accusation evoking the financial losses accrued by Union. Lower Canada was significantly wealthier than Upper Canada, but Union allowed Upper Canada to pay its debts with the revenues of Lower Canada and become the more affluent of the two. Third, Antonio's growing belief in the legitimacy of his lies corresponds to the increased power over Québec that English Canada gained in Union and then the Confederation of 1867, reinforcing its neocolonial economic and political rule by sheer force of numbers, just as Lord Durham advocated in his *Report on the Affairs of British North America*. Antonio/English Canada's belief in his lies corresponds to the rewriting of history by the victors that usually occurs in the context of colonization. Such historical revisionism applies not only to the Conquest but also to the Union and Confederation, which, although considered democratic by English Canada, has arguably been deemed undemocratic in Québec because it was decided not by the people's voice in a referendum but rather by the voices of a few members of Parliament at a time when the election of MPs was democratically questionable due to *bras de fer* strongmen outside polls who intimidated voters in favour of particular candidates. Prospero/Québec's bitterness in retelling his tale derives not only from his political and financial losses but also from the arrogance of his brother/English Canada who should have been an equal partner but whose usurpation belies a legitimacy to which he/it is not entitled. The play thus advocates Québec sovereignty since the restoration of Prospero's kingdom corresponds to a rectification of both the Conquest and the Union leading to Confederation.

Although thus far I have attempted to describe the incursion of nationalism into the texts as a consistent imposition onto the Shakespearean plot structure, the constraints of working with a predetermined source text do not always make this possible within the subtle genre of tradaptation. While it is possible to impose a nationalist discourse onto the plot, this is not the only means by which Garneau Québécizes the text. Since it would be impossible for the Shakespearean text to correspond completely to Québec's historical or contemporary political situation, rather than try to make the structure fit his nationalist agenda, as Gurik does, Garneau exploits the most vulnerable points in the source, regardless of plot or character constraints, unifying the nationalism discursively rather than structurally. At times, Québécois nationalism is voiced by characters from the other side of the plot-imposed hero/enemy binary, by Macbeth or the shipwrecked sailors, because the elimination of proper nouns blurs the self/other dichotomy and allows the nationalist discourse to enter the text wherever it can best be articulated. For example, when asked at the beginning of the play whence he comes, Ross replies, "Du plein coeur d'la bataille/Ousqu' les drapeaux des étranges insultent/Not' beau ciel" (1.2.16),[42] a phrase that evokes the battle of the Plains of Abraham and continues to resonate today as Québec-Canada flag wars rage on.[43] This early scene casts Macbeth as the hero, yet later he becomes the "main damnée qui opprime" from whom Lennox seeks liberation. In the final battle, Macbeth shifts again into the role of hero, fighting single-handedly to hold off Scottish traitors who ought to defect to the invading English army: "Vous pouvez sacrer vot'camp, mes p'tits seigneurs manqués, allez-vous en/Gloutonner ac'les Angla's" (5.3.136).[44] Garneau does not limit nationalist discourses to certain characters, which testifies to the plurivocality of the text and refutes the common charge that Québécois nationalism is exclusionist. Everyone is welcome to join the battle for national liberation regardless of political allegiances within the world of the play. In this respect, Garneau's writing is more progressive than that of Lalonde who figures Italian immigrants as a source of anxiety and as potential agents of linguistic assimilation. *Macbeth* encourages outsiders to adopt a nationalist discourse without fear that they may recuperate it or evacuate it of its strength.

Nationalist discourses in Québec in the late 1970s were not homogenous and thus not always sovereignist, but even nationalists who did not advocate independence agreed that Québec formed a distinct nation with a distinct culture. Garneau's valorization of the Québécois language, particularly in *Macbeth*, makes the play nationalist even in instances when the text does not call for liberation. The use of a *langue québécoise* confirms the existence of a *peuple québécois*. Since the first ontological criterion of a language is to express whatever reality it encounters, translating Shakespeare into Québécois proves it is a language distinct from *français de France*. Refusing to qualify Québécois as a subsidiary dialect of *français de France* eradicates what Brisset calls an "internal bilingualism" in which local orality is subconsciously "policed" by an overseas empire whose language cannot properly convey that local experience (269–70). Since, however, *Macbeth* is in eighteenth-century Québécois, Brisset proposes that Garneau's tradaptation does not seek to endow readers with a new orality but rather a sense of their history and ancestral attachments (240).

Brisset argues that readers of Garneau's *Macbeth* will have the impression that the Shakespearean tragedy admirably symbolizes the Québécois condition, thereby endowing Québec's destiny with a universality that legitimizes its nationalist struggle mythically beyond spatio-temporal borders (253). As theoretically problematic as "universality" may be for postcolonialists, the concept does legitimize a people's quest for freedom, which is why the current sovereignist discourse relies on universality to remind us that all over the world, from the Czech Republic to East Timor, more and more nations are acquiring full political statehood through democratic referenda. Since the composition of Garneau's plays, globalization has made universality a more important concept in response to the accusation that nationalists cannot see beyond Québec's own borders. "Universality" transforms the notion of separatism as a *repli sur soi* into the argument that a nation requires political independence in order to participate in dialogues at the table of international organizations (such as the United Nations, World Trade Organization, World Health Organization, etc.); therefore, Brisset is correct to assert that Garneau's tradaptations attempt to appropriate not only the Shakespearean text but also his so-called universality. By minimizing the British text's alterity with distinctly Québécois geographical and linguistic markers while still telling the same story, the tradaptations attempt to ascend to Shakespeare's level on the ladder of "universality" and carve a niche for themselves in the elite space of the Western canon. The Québécois tradaptations acquire authority through their association with Shakespeare, and the nation of Québec, represented by the *langue québécoise*, moves beyond its status as marginal other to become a legitimate cultural entity worthy of sovereignty like other nations across the globe. Unlike more radical Québécois adaptations, such as *Henry. Octobre. 1970.*, Garneau's tradaptations do not subvert the Eurocentrism that lends authority to the Shakespearean canon and they do not deconstruct the centre/margin dichotomy, but they do displace the centre and appropriate its authority in order to legitimize Québec's nationalist aspirations.

The project of national liberation in these tradaptations ushers in a partial emancipation of Shakespeare's women characters marked by an ambivalent support for gender equality. Lady Macbeth and Miranda are the main women characters who appear in these two plays, and the latter role is adapted more progressively, undoubtedly due to the decade of social reforms between the publication of the two tradaptations. Gender norms governing men's behaviour are challenged as well, but Conquest/rape imagery and the fear of federasty continue to manifest themselves, which is in keeping with the tradaptations' frequent allusions to the Conquest as one of the palimpsestuous layers in which the plays' action takes place.

Due to its nostalgia for eighteenth-century New France, Garneau's *Macbeth* occasionally introduces sexism into the play where none exists in Shakespeare's text, relegating Lady Macbeth to a domestic role. Rather than being Macbeth's "dearest partner of greatness" (1.5.10), occupying an equal role in their enterprises, Lady Macbeth is transformed into Macbeth's moral support system: "eune femme comme y s'en fa't pus comme/Eune compagne encourageante à plein" (1.5.33).[45] Macbeth's back-handed compliment about his wife's support of his goals constructs her as a traditional symbol of "Woman," that is, the type of woman in danger of extinction by the rising militant feminism of the 1970s. As a dutiful woman like those that "aren't made anymore," Lady Macbeth is circumscribed within the domestic sphere and relieved of the ambition and agency she demonstrates in Shakespeare.

Lady Macbeth's "unsex me here" speech epitomizes the tradaptation's ambivalence about gender, which is also highlighted in the ambiguity of the word "sexe" which means both "sex" and "gender" in French (1.5.39–53).[46] In Shakespeare, Lady Macbeth utters a performative speech act in order to perform masculinity instead of femininity. In the tradaptation, her determined plea to be unsexed by spirits is transformed into a paradoxically wistful rejection of what may be either her sex or her gender: "J'veux pus rien savoér d'mon beau sexe doux, j'veux pus rien savoér/D'mon beau sexe tendre" (1.5.34).[47] Garneau's Lady Macbeth praises her sex/gender as soft, tender, and beautiful, thereby performing femininity even as she renounces it and undermining the performative gesture of unsexing accomplished by Shakespeare's Lady

Macbeth. The tradapted text also introduces the possibility of homoeroticism and autoeroticism. Lady Macbeth's praise of her sex/gender as beautiful, soft, and tender could apply to all members of the female sex, indicating homoerotic desire. Since "sexe" in French also refers to genitals, Lady Macbeth's praise of her beautiful, tender "sexe" can also be read as an autoerotic infatuation with her own body.

This ambivalent adaptation of Lady Macbeth's plea to be unsexed evacuates from the text what could otherwise have been an effective moment for Garneau to allude to radical feminism and the deconstruction of gender norms beginning to occur in the late 1970s in Québec, as in the rest of the Western world. Lady Macbeth's desire to be unsexed can be read as a renunciation of what Judith Butler would call the heterosexual matrix of sex/gender/desire as well as a celebration of how the strategic manipulation of gender performativity may effect sociopolitical change. As I have argued elsewhere, in Shakespeare Lady Macbeth's sexual and gender identity may be read as "stone butch" lesbian masculinity,[48] but Garneau's Lady Macbeth surrenders her potential to disrupt the matrix of sex/gender/desire. On one hand, her homoerotic desire for the female body signals her potential to remove herself from the masculinist warrior culture of medieval Scotland, or even the Seven Years War between France and England, because her longing for the soft tenderness of her own sex/gender implies lesbian, and perhaps separatist, tendencies. On the other hand, her hyper-feminization of the female body undercuts her potential to embody physically the masculine strength she seeks to assist her in accomplishing her goals.

Although Lady Macbeth's hyper-feminization fails to disrupt traditional gender norms, the tradaptation's representation of men challenges the dichotomy by eliminating sexual difference from key passages that reinforce the men's virility. To prepare for crowning the new king, Macbeth tells Banquo, Macduff, Malcolm, and Donalbain that they should "put on manly readiness" (2.3.135), that is, clothes and armour as well as a masculine temperament appropriate for the occasion. Garneau's Macbeth, however, says that they should "s'habiller comme du monde" (2.3.66),[49] a gender-neutral phrase that degenders the clothes, removes the implication of armour, and erases the requirement of a bellicose temperament. This elimination of a gendered discourse of virility recurs when Garneau translates Lady Macbeth's taunting question to Macbeth "What, quite unmanned in folly?" (3.4.74) as "T'es-tu en train de toute t'laisser envahir par la folie?" (3.4.88).[50] The tradaptation disrupts Shakespearean gender relations in two ways, first, by disassociating Macbeth's madness from a loss of manliness, and, second, by introducing a more disturbing image, his penetrability. While Shakespeare's Macbeth surrenders his manhood to madness, as if putting down his virile weapons after losing a battle, Garneau's Lady Macbeth accuses her husband of allowing himself to be "invaded," that is, penetrated or raped by madness. To man up and complete his task, the Québécois Macbeth must therefore conquer the fear of federasty, the potential that like the conquered nation he too may be raped by *fédéraste* traitors. Rather than adapting Lady Macbeth to correspond to the values of 1970s feminism, the tradaptation thus participates instead in the propagation of a *complexe de colonisé* in which the masculine is posited as always potentially penetrable, vulnerable, and conquerable.

Published eleven years later, *La tempête* focuses more than *Macbeth* on the role of women in Prospero's soon to be reclaimed nation. From the outset, this tradaptation eliminates Shakespeare's most sexist language, such as Gonzalo's comparison of the sinking ship to "an unstanched wench" (1.1.46–7), which Gail Kern Paster has identified as a representation of women as "leaky vessels" (25). The exorcism of the early modern anxiety about women's lack of containment also applies to Prospero's relationship with Miranda, which is less focused on controlling her speech. The tradaptation cuts Prospero's order for Miranda to "[o]bey and be attentive" (1.2.38), retaining only the idea of "ope thine ear" (1.2.37), which is translated by the gentle phrase "sois toutes oreilles" (1.2.16).[51] The increased mutuality of the father-daughter relationship in Garneau's tradaptation carries over to two key scenes regarding Miranda's marriage to Ferdinand and, consequently, the relationship between nation and gender.

Prospero does not have a dynastic project to regain his kingdom through Miranda's marriage to Ferdinand in the tradaptation. Shakespeare's Prospero stages a court masque in celebration of Miranda's betrothal to Ferdinand (4.1.60–142), and he insists on the couple's sexual abstinence until their marriage rites have been properly performed, that is, until Alonso has also sanctioned the marriage, thereby ensuring his grandchildren will inherit both Milan and Naples. Garneau's tradaptation omits the masque with the goddesses of light, marriage, and the harvest because the restoration of Prospero's usurped *seigneurie* does not pass through his daughter's reproductive capacity as it does in

Shakespeare. To suggest in 1989 that national liberation is dependent on marriage and women's wombs would offend Québécois men and women for whom the *revanche des berceaux* ended with the advent of the Quiet Revolution.

Likewise, Garneau disentangles nationalism from women's bodies by cutting Gonzalo's romantic notion that "Milan [was] thrust from Milan that his issue/Should become kings of Naples" (5.1.205–6). Gonzalo's sentimental reliance on Fate would deprive Prospero of any agency in the reclamation of his usurped kingdom, thereby compromising the tradaptation's nationalism. Gonzalo's naive trust in a higher power to provide a happy ending runs counter to Garneau's anti-ecclesiasticism and would lessen the responsibility of Québécois to *passer à l'action* to reclaim the usurped nation. Including this speech would also be problematic due to the implication that the new utopian nation will not be ruled by those, like Prospero, who seek it in the present but rather by their children, deferring the nation's restoration until a tomorrow that may never come. Moreover, this reclamation would be conditional on women collectively dedicating their bodies to biological reproduction, thereby tying the success of national liberation to their compulsory heterosexuality and domesticity. Like many post-Quiet Revolution Québécois women for whom liberation from the church also meant access to birth control for the first time (as the second gravedigger tells the first in Gurik's *Hamlet*), Garneau's Miranda escapes this fate. In keeping with the Quiet Revolution's anti-ecclesiastic social reforms, the tradaptation rejects the *revanche des berceaux* and the exploitation of women's bodies for nation-building.

Garneau's Miranda also escapes sacrificing her independence. In Shakespeare, Miranda accuses Ferdinand of playing false, but she then withdraws her accusation, denying her perception of reality in order to remain an object of his heterosexual desire: "Yes, for a score of kingdoms you should wrangle,/And I would call it fair play" (5.1.174–5). The tradaptation preserves the game of chess and Miranda's accusation of cheating, but it omits Miranda's final line that sanctions future cheating. Accepting Ferdinand's cheating would entail a sacrifice of Miranda's autonomy and create a gender-based hierarchy within their relationship contrary to the ideals of late 1980s feminism. Moreover, were Miranda to accept Ferdinand's falsehoods she would be complicit in the perpetuation of the nation's colonization since to excuse unfair acts is to participate in one's own subjugation. As the young heir to the soon-to-be-restored nation, Miranda represents a new generation of

Québécois who diligently defend against false moves and liberate the nation from the colonial mindset of accepting the treachery of others. Miranda and Ferdinand's game of chess thus writes back to the game of chess of provincial-federal negotiations on a host of political matters, such as *la nuit des longs couteaux*.[52] While writing back cannot undo false moves, that is, omitting Miranda's complicity does not negate Ferdinand's cheating, Miranda's refusal to sanction duplicity functions as a model of steadfastness for the next generation of Québécois when negotiating with those who refuse to play by the rules of the game.

Michel Garneau's tradaptations of Shakespeare thus subtly manipulate the Québécois language in order to advocate the liberation of the usurped nation from the rule of tyrants. Unlike other adaptations, Garneau's plays do not change Shakespeare's plot structure or attribution of lines, but rather they create a palimpsest that situates the action simultaneously within the historical context of the Conquest as well as the 1970s political context of neocolonialism believed to have resulted from it. Minor cuts, the use of words that both convey the same message as the source and radically alter it, and the valorization of a distinctly Québécois language, history, geography, and hence culture all combine to add new meaning to Malcolm's disposition of the tyrant who usurps his throne and to Prospero's reclamation of his usurped kingdom from his treacherous brother. Garneau then supplements the nationalism that does map onto the plot with discursive incursions of nationalism even at points where the plot structure does not allow it. The tradaptations thus defend the Québécois language because they recount Shakespeare's narrative with little change, demonstrating the capacity to reproduce his so-called genius and gain access to his "universality." Garneau chooses, however, to tradapt patriarchal plays almost devoid of women characters, leaving little room for women to contribute to the process of national liberation. While Miranda exhibits greater independence than in the Shakespearean source, Garneau's Lady Macbeth loses her drive and ambition, and the male characters are subjected to the trauma of the Conquest/rape of the nation and the fear of federasty. In Jean-Pierre Ronfard's adaptations in the next chapter, we will see a greater contribution by women characters to the reconstruction of the nation, especially after the trauma of the Conquest is replaced by the trauma of the first failed referendum.

Chapter Five

The First Referendum: Daughters of the Carnivalized Nation

Jean-Pierre Ronfard's *Lear* (1977) and *Vie et mort du Roi Boiteux* [*Life and Death of the Limping King*] (1981), adaptations of Shakespeare's *King Lear* and *Richard III* respectively, employ carnival and magic realism to parody the bastardized state of the nation whose corruption and decay can be eliminated only by the rise to power of strong-willed women.[1] Rabelaisian carnival dominates every aspect of these two adaptations;[2] food, drinking, rampant sexuality, and references to the grotesque lower body abound, but, since it is temporary, the result of carnival must ultimately be the reinstatement of social order.[3] For Mikhail Bakhtin, carnival is also about "death as renewal" (51), a regeneration of the social order which Ronfard locates in a generation of heirs both genealogically tied to the past and oriented towards the future. When the collapse of the nation precipitated by absentee male rulers finally reaches its nadir at the close of both plays, that is, when there is no old order left for the carnivalesque to reverse, only the daughters of the former rulers remain to take responsibility for the fate of the nation and lead it to a brighter future. Ronfard's plays thus highlight the interdependence of nation and gender, and the different relative weights accorded to nation and gender in each play reflect the evolving social and political importance of these issues on the eve and in the aftermath of the first referendum on sovereignty. In addition, Ronfard's carnivalesque approach to adaptation illustrates the artificiality of the signifier "Shakespeare" as the embodiment of high culture, simultaneously appropriating and undercutting *le grand Will*'s claim to cultural authority.

Ronfard's two Shakespearean adaptations straddle a crucial turning point in Québec's history, the 1980 referendum on sovereignty-association in which the "No" side won 59.6 per cent to 40.4 per cent over the "Yes." The Québécois population's struggle for political independence (the momentum for which was at a high point on the heels of the surprisingly strong, and first ever, Parti Québécois electoral victory in 1976), followed by their subsequent rejection of it, marks both of these plays. Whereas in the pre-referendum *Lear* the declining state of the nation and the need to rescue it figure prominently, in the post-referendum *Vie et mort du Roi Boiteux* the obvious degeneration of the nation is relegated to the background in favour of a focus on gender relations and sexuality until the nation finally acquires a new ruler at the play's end. The later play's inquiry into women's independence in marriage and their political role in society corresponds to the rise of the feminist movement in Québec in the 1970s and the increased social presence of women's issues following the temporary decline of the national question after the referendum.

Lear was performed at the Théâtre expérimental de Montréal (TEM) in January 1977 – just two months after the historic election of the PQ to power on 15 November 1976 – and published in the TEM's own journal, *TRAC*, in April of the same year – shortly before the instauration of *Loi 101*, the *Charte de la langue française*, on 26 August 1977. The play's truncated title immediately informs the reader that it is an adaptation, devoid of the regal decorum of Shakespeare's *King Lear*. The adaptation conserves the basics of Shakespeare's main plot but very little of the text. The cast of characters is also trimmed to the bare minimum, but the parallels to Shakespeare are obvious: Le roi (who, unnamed, is only addressed as king or father) is King Lear; Josette is Goneril; Violette is Regan; Laurette/Le fou is Cordelia/The Fool; Corneille, a woman, assumes the parts of Kent and Gloucester while her son, Hector, is the adaptation's Edmund figure. Ronfard adds two new characters: two "Shakespeares" work the stage lighting while drinking half-pint mugs of beer in the play's technical booth-*cum*-tavern. The drunken Shakespeares signal from the outset the adaptation's parodic undercutting of the Bard's authority and set the tone for the carnivalesque debauchery that ensues.

Ronfard's *Vie et mort du Roi Boiteux*, subtitled as "une épopée sanglant et grotesque en six pièces et un épilogue," was first published in two volumes in 1981.[4] The epic's six plays were gradually performed between July 1981 and June 1982, and the entire fifteen-hour drama was performed from morning to night at the Expo-Théâtre at Montréal's Cité du Havre on 24 June and 26 June, as well as at Bishop's University in Lennoxville on 3 July, and in Ottawa on 11 July 1982. The adaptation sprang from a collective initiative by the Nouveau Théâtre Expérimental to create a play entitled *Shakespeare Follies* following a study of Shakespeare's complete works with the four other permanent group members (Robert Claing, Robert Gravel, Pol Pelletier, and Pierre Pesant); they conferred the writing of this project on Ronfard who created *Roi Boiteux* instead. The epic is a hybrid, feminist adaptation of Shakespeare's War of the Roses tetralogy (*1–3 Henry VI, Richard III*) in which the male characters from the York and Lancaster families are replaced by warring women of the Ragone and Roberge families. Like the absent King Edward III underlying Shakespeare's history plays, the warring families have a common ancestor, Le vieux père Roberge, Roi de l'Abitibi, but a split occurred prior to the play when his oldest daughter, Angela Roberge (married to the supposedly insane Filippo Ragone), committed suicide by driving into a brick wall, for which the other Roberge sisters blame their Ragone in-laws. The adaptation's dramatic action takes place in a fictional working-class neighbourhood of Montréal named l'Arsenal that the characters also imagine as a royal kingdom.

The parallels between the plots of Shakespeare's tetralogy and Ronfard's six-play epic are too extensive to enumerate,[5] and the associations between Ronfard's characters and their Shakespearean counterparts are frequently in flux; however, several correspondences stand out between the characters of both authors' works. Richard Premier (Premier being his surname, not a regal designation), who limps in an orthopaedic shoe, is Richard III. Marie-Jeanne Larose, who is seduced by Richard in the presence of the body of her dead husband, Alcide Premier, corresponds to Lady Anne. Richard's older brother Alcide evokes both Edward IV and Clarence, with Alcide's death from thirst on a mountaintop ironically parodying Clarence's dream of drowning. Shakespeare's Queen Margaret resembles most closely Madame Emma Roberge, a widow with a biting tongue, but Margaret also manifests herself in Filippo Ragone *dit le Débile* whose crippled body and crazy persona mask his wisdom and perceptiveness, as well as in Lou Birkanian, a magical witch who dies when nobody listens to her fanciful tales anymore. Peter Williams, a pastor who dies at the hands of cannibals, evokes Henry VI, the religious king who is metaphorically eaten alive by the blood-thirsty nobles surrounding him. His wife Judith drowns her madness with mud and flowers in a nod to Ophelia. Their son, Roy Williams, a businessman who prostitutes his own sister to Richard and then leads a mafia that controls the butchery industry and the local police, embodies the most violent traits of Richard III and functions in the plays as Richard Premier's doppelgänger. Their mutual friend Freddy Dubois, who follows Richard loyally at first, resembles Buckingham. Finally, Moïse, whose far-removed, bastard lineage makes him an unlikely candidate to be king, who is largely absent throughout the play, and who leads his horde across the sea and kills Richard with an arrow, resembles Richmond, later Henry VII. For the fifth and sixth plays of *Roi Boiteux*, Ronfard creates a new character with no Shakespearean counterpart, Claire Premier, Richard's daughter. Like her counterpart Laurette in *Lear*, Claire inherits a decaying nation that only a woman can save.

Lear opens with the first Shakespeare's consternation, "Notre pays est malade, profondément malade" (6); here and throughout the abstract term "country" evokes Québec.[6] The accuracy of his assessment is immediately confirmed when the king emerges from behind crumpled newspapers to divide up the nation he wishes to bestow on his daughters and the reasons for the nation's sickness are revealed: the king lacks agency; as such, the nation is in a survivalist mode and consuming itself in order to remain barely alive. The nation is represented, rather than by a map, by a pizza that the first two daughters begin to eat, literally acting out their self-interested consumption of the nation's resources in disregard of the needs of its people. The nation's decline is also signalled by the king's unwitting revelation that his regal power is no more than an empty signifier devoid of authority. He pitifully requests that his daughters profess their love for him "dans cette belle langue qui nous reste encore, signe et symbole de notre pouvoir ancestral" (7).[7] Language is one of the only remnants of the nation's historical strength, but, since the king never uses it performatively, even the national language is nothing more than a symbol; the former power of the nation's ancestors now lacks agency. While language is frequently a signifier of cultural difference, culture itself has been reduced to no more than an ineffective life-support system for the nation's heritage: "La culture [...] nous relie au souffle et au sang des ancêtres comme les tuyaux de toutes les couleurs entretiennent à l'hôpital l'existence du moribond momifié dans ses bandelettes" (28).[8] As little more than artificial respiration for a terminally ill nation, culture can only prolong survival, but it cannot heal the nation's sickness or endow it with agency. In this brief moment of clarity, the king recognizes that survival is not progress. From its outset, then, Ronfard's adaptation adopts a nationalist, perhaps even sovereignist, stance through its assertion that the nation should not content itself with the status quo.

The king's self-inflicted disempowerment, which represents the nation's collective loss of agency, results in a national lack of direction since the king's approach is survivalist. The striking image of culture on life support as a futile prolongation of death works as a criticism of the survivalist approach to Québécois nationalism common in the late 1970s. The adaptation denounces a colonized attitude towards independence – that the priority of nationalism is to preserve the dying remains of the past rather than to build a better future. When Corneille seeks reassurance about the ability of the king's daughters to run the country (one of whom is writing to a nuclear power plant while the other masturbates loudly in the corner), the king replies, "Les charges de pouvoir, je connais ça. Bien content d'en être débarassé [*sic*]" (16).[9] By throwing away his responsibility to maintain and exercise authority, the king strips his subjects of the agency necessary to heal the wounded nation. The king's lack of direction (in the sense of leadership) causes the collectivity to lack direction (in the sense of goals). The nation needs to reclaim agency to achieve goals oriented towards the future; that is, it must stop conceiving of political power, and by extension sovereignty, as a responsibility that is too heavy to carry, a burden to be happily surrendered. Rather, the nation must see kingship/sovereignty as a privileged opportunity to create something enduring that goes beyond individualist, masturbatory pleasures, such as those Josette and Violette seek.

In justification of his abdication of sovereignty, the king claims that the new order inaugurated by his daughters is completely "normal" (16), but what is really normalized by his abdication is disorder. The nation has entered into a prolonged state of carnival-like topsy-turvyness. Carnival, in Bakhtin's terms, normally celebrates a "temporary liberation from the prevailing truth and from the established order," marking "the suspension of all hierarchical rank, privileges, norms, and prohibitions" (10), and it creates a parallel "second-world" (11). However, at the beginning of *Lear* the established order has been replaced by disorder because the daughters were already carnivalesque before they were consecrated as the new national rulers, so this "second-world" shows no signs of being "temporary." Michael Bristol argues that carnival has "*both* a social and an antisocial tendency" (*Carnival* 25). In *Lear*, Josette and Violette embody carnival's antisocial elements since their self-gratification is antithetical to the strengthening of the community that ought to emerge from carnivalesque disorder. Carnival does not serve its intended purpose of creating a free-for-all zone alongside order; rather, it replaces order for the duration of the play.

Josette recognizes near the end of the play that disorder reigns, but it is then too late for her to reinstate the order that existed prior to the king's abdication. Although she derives personal pleasure from specific carnivalesque elements, carnival is "not an individual reaction" but for "all the people" (Bakhtin 11). When Josette realizes that carnival is a collective event encompassing the entire community, she becomes critical of it because she understands that it endows the people with liberty to subvert her authority:

> Il faut que ça change! [...] Des folles excitées, seins au vent, bourrent le crâne de leur [*sic*] leurs congénères et commencent à nous casser les oreilles avec leurs slogans démagogiques: 'le vieux pouvoir est mort!', 'vive le droit des peuples à disposer de tout!', 'le jour se lève...la couleur du ciel change...saluons la naissance d'un nouvel ordre!'. Et c'est moi, (*gémissements de Violette dans son lit.*) enfin moi et ma sœur, c'est nous qu'on attend pour le réaliser ce fameux nouvel ordre. Imbéciles! L'ordre est l'ordre. Il n'a pas à être nouveau ou ancien. L'ordre n'a pas de couleur. (54)[10]

The half-naked women demand that the nation embody the true spirit of carnival, which is democracy, since one of its principal features is the equality of everyone through the temporary abolition of socially constructed rank, class, age, and gender norms. The people's slogans, which Josette qualifies as demagogic, sum up the democratic principles that underlie carnival, that is, the rule of the people by the people rather than social superiors, and the new, second-world order that is born out of the death of the established order. Josette's futile protest that order is order lacks credibility due to the hypocrisy of the sudden rejection of her own carnivalesque nature and due to her reluctant acknowledgment that her sister, who is fully engaged in carnivalesque sexuality at that moment, shares her social authority. Everything around her confirms the difference between carnivalesque democracy and the authoritarian control that she seeks to impose. Moreover, her claim that order has no colour resonates strongly in a Québécois context where order is often symbolized by "flag wars" in which the differences between red, federalist order and blue, nationalist order affect most aspects of democratic life. In the context of the recent PQ election and a pending referendum on independence, Josette's reactionary response to a new order becomes a parodic criticism of those who fail to see the differences, and the advantages, of a new order in which the people have the right to control their own affairs.

The carnivalization of the nation and the creation of a new order are embodied in the character of Hector. A bastard, and thus the personification of illegitimacy's triumph over order, Hector is significantly "baser" than his Shakespearean counterpart Edmund. Edmund questions the socially constructed nature of an order that categorizes humans as either base or legitimate, but he nonetheless strives to ascend within that order through the acquisition of his father's lands and titles. Edmund criticizes the system for excluding him, but he does not seek to topple it. Hector, on the other hand, relishes bastardry and strives to reverse the social order so baseness may mark the nation. Hector literalizes his valorization of baseness when, after entering pulling a "*seau de merde*" (18), "*il se met à lancer des boules de marde partout, particulièrement sur le trône, sur la cage des shakespeares-techniciens et au plafond*" (20).[11] This scatological scattering of the abject incites Hector to invoke the "temps dénaturé" in a soliloquy reminiscent of Edmund's plea to Nature (1.2.1–22), but rather than attempting to elevate the base to a status equal with the legitimate, Hector praises the ability of the base to soil and overthrow social order entirely: "Vive la bâtardise/Qui bouleverse les lois/Qui souille les églises/Et détrône les rois" (20–1).[12] His concluding cry of "Les bâtards au pouvoir!" provokes the uprising of a horde of protesters who take up his slogan (21).[13] The facility with which Hector creates a popular uprising confirms that the reversal of social order he champions has already begun. Bastards can be in power because the king has renounced the responsibility of sovereignty, thereby allowing them to instate a new carnivalesque and democratic social order. The play thus advocates a popular uprising in which bastards, that is, oppressed working-class Québécois,[14] could rule themselves according to their own will. Yet, written only six years after the October Crisis, the play also cautions against such a popular uprising getting out of control, turning to violence, and destroying the nation even as it seeks to heal it. Through its invocation of carnival, and thus a notion of cyclical chaos and order, the adaptation calls for a necessary return to an order that is strengthened by the democratic principles underlying carnival itself.

This state of carnival also affects the gender relations in *Lear*. Carnival typically subverts gender hierarchies and permits a fluid exchange whereby sexed bodies may temporarily occupy their opposite gender role, most notably by adopting drag, which Judith Butler argues parodies heterosexuality by exposing the social constructedness of gender itself (*Gender Trouble* 174, 187). Ronfard's adaptation uses carnival both to reverse gender roles and to reveal the performativity of gender. The reversal of gender roles already occurs in Shakespeare's *King Lear*; Lear is emasculated by Goneril and Regan's appropriation of the phallus when they begin to exercise his regal authority. Ronfard's adaptation literalizes this theme with a crudeness typical of carnivalesque sexuality when the king soliloquizes upon his downtrodden state: "je suis fourré, jusqu'à l'os. [...] Violette, par dérision, a fait rajouter aux armoiries royales un pénis de sinople sur fond de gueules qu'elle prétend m'avoir dérobé à jamais. C'est dur" (24).[15] The term "dérision" occurs frequently in Ronfard's Shakespearean adaptations, especially in *Roi Boiteux*, and it captures the carnivalesque spirit found in the tone of the texts themselves, as evidenced here by the pun on "hard" that can refer to both the king's difficulty in accepting his emasculation and the firmness of Violette's appropriated phallic symbol. Ronfard's delight in "dérision" is akin to the larrikinism characteristic of Australian Shakespeares, as discussed in chapter 1.

The performativity of gender is highlighted in Shakespearean comedy by characters who pass successfully as the opposite sex, notably Cesario in *Twelfth Night* and Ganymede in *As You Like It*. In Ronfard's *Lear* though, the carnivalization of gender and the exposure of its performativity take a sinister twist in the course of a long dialogue between the king and Corneille. As in Shakespeare when Lear does not recognize Kent, the king asks who Corneille is, to which she replies that she is a woman, which the king then surmises "n'est pas grand chose," that is, not much of anything (32), or, in a throw-back to Shakespeare, nothing more than a "nothing" or a vagina (1.1.90).[16] When Corneille adds that she is the king's old accomplice, he ignores her gender so that she might fulfil his desire to reminisce "[e]ntre hommes" about their last exploit: "*(D'un seul coup elle prend une voix avinée, une attitude de corps de garde, une face de salaud. Elle replace des couilles imaginaires.)* [...] On s'est dit: '[...] on en a dans la culotte, oui ou non? Bien sûr qu'on en a. Deux belles grosses comme grand-père'" (33).[17] On one hand, the king's assertion that a woman is nothing makes the category of "woman" an empty signifier, thereby reaffirming "man" as the only gender that can lay claim to meaning. On the other hand, Corneille's effortless transition from the materiality of *zir* female sexed body to the performance of a male one, that is, *zir* adoption of a transgendered identity through the growth of imaginary balls, demonstrates the fluidity and social constructedness of gender.[18] Corneille's gesture of grabbing *zir* balls like a man confirms both *zir* masculine gender identity and *zir* entrance into the boy's club of male homosociality of which the king is the guardian, thus confirming that all gender is a simulacrum of social norms.

The sinister twist to the adaptation's carnivalization of gender comes at the climax of Corneille's story about their conquest of a village and arson of abandoned warehouses in which local women were hiding:

> Elles arrachaient leurs vêtements qui les brûlaient la peau. Nues, elles sautaient sur place comme des sauterelles estropiées. Elles se sont groupées en un tas au milieu des nôtres qui rigolaient de leur bon coup. 'Heïe! C'est moi le roi!' Tu as crié. 'À moi la fleur!' Tu as tombé culotte et toute l'armée a vu. Toute l'armée t'a vu dans toute ta puissance. Elles y ont passé l'une après l'autre. Écartelées par quatre soldats qui se relayaient. Tu étais infatiguable [*sic*]. Tu riais de plaisir. Tu hurlais de rage et de fureur. Et ça y allait. Et ça y allait. Tu as enfourché la dernière en bâillant à te décrocher la mâchoire. Et tu t'es écrasé au sol, endormi tout d'un coup. Je t'ai recouvert de mon manteau. Quand tu t'es réveillé, au petit matin de la victoire, la fille sous toi était morte.
>
> (*Pendant tout le récit, Corneille et le roi se taponnent, se frottent, s'excitent l'un l'autre. Corneille chevauche le roi et l'épuise. Ils finissent écrasés à terre.*) (35)[19]

Corneille's fluid transition from biological woman to performative man leaves *zir* in a problematic position (much like that experienced by contemporary FTMs) because *zir* gender identity is unfixed, floating in a liminal space between the material body that the audience sees before them and the "almost but not quite" mimicry of masculinity (to adapt Bhabha) which fails to mask it (86).[20] The reader is thus forced to question where Corneille's gender allegiances lie in this brutal gang rape with which *zie* was complicit. The text (and its accompanying photographs of the original performance in which *zie* is smiling) implies that *zie* has fully adopted the identity of a male soldier and that *zie* derives pleasure from the king's and, by association, *zir* own show of virility. *Zie* shows no sympathy for the raped women or even for the one who dies under the king. *Zir* transition across gender lines and initiation into male homosociality, with the sexual privilege of potential rape it confers, appears to be complete.

Yet, Corneille's entry into the world of male homosocial bonding is complicated and undercut by the image of *zir* female body sexually straddling the king in a re-enactment of heterosexuality. The mutuality of the sexual exchange in which they excite each other indicates that

Corneille's masculine identity does not interfere with *zir* female body's ability to derive pleasure from heterosexual interaction. However, *zir* re-enactment of heterosexual intercourse further complicates an interpretation of the story. On the one hand, *zie* occupies the role of the story's women, making the tale itself a rape fantasy from which *zie* derives excitement. On the other hand, *zir* physical position astride the king that ends with them lying together exhausted on the ground (presumably with *zir* still on top) re-enacts the king's crushing of the girl underneath him at the same moment that *zie* recounts that part of the story. This reading constitutes another gender role reversal by which Corneille becomes the king and the king becomes the dead girl that he had raped. Alternatively, if the king continues to ignore Corneille's female body and interacts solely with the masculine gender identity that *zie* performs, then their mutual sexual excitement is no longer heterosexual at all; instead it is a homoerotic slippage from the homosocial bond of soldiers into the realm of physicality. I would argue that all these multiple and contradictory levels of interpretation are in fact at work in the scene simultaneously. The scene thus performs the performativity of gender itself by highlighting the impossibility of fixity in a scene whose disturbing textual content is undercut by the carnivalesque reversal of all gender norms.

Roi Boiteux gives even greater attention than *Lear* to gender issues but instead of carnivalizing gender it focuses on the harsh social reality of widowhood through the play's matriarchs – Madame Emma Roberge, Catherine Ragone, Judith Williams née Roberge, and Lou Birkanian – who are referred to as "les quatre reines" (2.6.125). All four queens become widows, and their diverse reactions to this marital status, and sexuality in general, speaks to the overall complexity of gender relations and possible roles for women within the world of the play, as well as the different competing constructions of "woman" in circulation in Québec at the time of the adaptation's composition, ranging from the bitter, radical separatist to the emotionally detached, power-hungry businesswoman to the traditionally passive Yvette who resurged during the referendum campaign.

Emma Roberge articulates a gynocentric, separatist discourse, rejecting free sexuality in favour of another kind of liberty, the social power enjoyed by men. Like Shakespeare's Queen Margaret, Emma's anti-male rants are as much born out of a protectionist necessity as they are from her bitterness at having been wronged. Catherine Ragone, after being called "une coque vide, un nom sans répondant" in her widowhood (2.6.128),[21] decides to use her sexual body to manipulate men for social and political power, transforming her status as an empty shell into a form of agency. Judith's self-sacrificing complacency to a disempowered domesticity figures her as an "Yvette": that is, one of the women, named after a dutiful, young girl from Québécois schoolbooks, who celebrated their own domesticity and protested against sovereignty on the eve of the 1980 referendum in reaction to Lise Payette's comparison of Québécois women to "Yvettes" because their education made them docile and afraid of change.[22] Judith's vulnerability also locates her as a site for colonial desire, that is, a colonial man's desire for the white woman upon which he can enact symbolic violence against his colonizer through miscegenation. As the site of the ritualized violence of decolonization, Judith signifies only insofar as she is a symbol of her husband Peter's colonizing mission. Lou Birkanian, the queen most closely associated with carnival, extols the advantages of a separatist, homosocial community of women, but rather than seeking to overthrow patriarchal rule the women of Lou's homosocial community subvert it with carnivalesque heterosexuality and achieve mutually satisfying results for both sexes. Lou's story of her childhood exposure to sexuality and the adventure of her wedding night are both marked by carnivalesque laughter, which she locates as the source of her liberty but which is absent in the nation around which the epic is centred (3.6.174).

Lou's embrace of carnivalesque sexuality affords her, of the four matriarchal, widowed queens, the most personal liberty to operate outside the bounds of socially constructed order. The adaptation thus valorizes free sexuality, both for the purpose of carnivalesque laughter and pleasure and for personal power and strength. This dual valorization of unfettered sexuality for both pleasure and power manifests itself in the incestuous homosexuality of the Nelson twins and of Claire Premier in whom the adaptation situates hope, rebirth, and liberty.

Sandy Sparks and Nelson Trapp, fraternal twins in Lou's care, resemble the double beings described by Aristophanes in Plato's *Symposium* who were split asunder by the gods and constantly seek their other half because they are incomplete without it. During their childhood, they compose a hermaphroditic being on the playground (2.3.118), and in their youth they have an incestuous sexual relationship that neither can live without (3.4.165). In the fifth play, the twins are trapped with their friend Freddy Dubois on a raft in the middle of the Pacific Ocean for eighteen days in an adaptation of the story of Noah's ark. Freddy tells them that he would like to marry them and wants the three of them to all make love together. Both Sandy and Nelson accept, express their love for him, and, as the three unite to form "une figure à trois," a dove approaches and drops an olive branch (5.11.172). Freddy claims that the olive branch is a sign of the beginning of a new world, and, indeed, when they open their eyes they discover land. In rewriting biblical myth, the adaptation posits unrestrained sexuality, including the homosexuality between Nelson and Freddy and the incest between Sandy and Nelson, as a source of salvation rather than destruction. In fact, the love between Sandy, Nelson, and Freddy is the most enduring relationship of the epic, for, even after Nelson is killed, Sandy and Freddy carry Nelson's body with them everywhere they go. Nelson's pointless death to save a father whose own unrestrained sexuality was fickle and loveless serves to heighten the reader's sympathy for this trio whose incestuous and homosexual desire belies a love that endures beyond the grave, the only such love of the epic. As Freddy points out, the trio's love, blessed by the heavens, embodies the potential for a new world order. The breakdown of the socially constructed norms of traditional sexuality through its greatest taboos creates a free space for the construction of a new national order. In fact, their new world is a paradise until confronted by an old world order dominated by taboos and superstition that falsely locates the trio's potential for regeneration in their material bodies (i.e., Nelson's blood) instead of in their transcendent love.

Moreover, the Sandy-Nelson-Freddy relationship, and later Catherine-Claire's, directly contradicts Jean-Cléo Godin and Pierre Lavoie's assertion in the epic's introductory essay of "l'absence, dans l'œuvre de Ronfard, de l'homosexualité, très présente dans la littérature québécoise contemporaine" (20n12).[23] There are several additional episodes of homoeroticism in the epic, such as Annie's desire for Swedish women with honey breasts, Amazons, and Marie-Jeanne Larose (2.3.111–13), Annie's desire for Circe reminiscent of Helena and Hermia in *A Midsummer Night's Dream* (5.9.159), and Richard's boast that no man could help being seduced by a picture of his naked body (4.3.36). Godin and Lavoie's claim may stem from knowledge of authorial intention (nine years later, Ronfard published a critical article denying the existence of a specific homosexual identity and its relevance to theatre),[24] but homoeroticism pervades the text of *Roi Boiteux*, as it does in *Lear* between Corneille and the king.

Sexual liberty, including incestuous homosexuality, as the source of national regeneration is equally embodied by Claire Premier, one of the nation's two rightful, female heirs. The power to rule the nation is transmitted sexually to Claire by her grandmother, Catherine, thus bypassing the male heir, Richard, who is ruled by his mother but unable to exercise political agency himself. This matrilineal transfer of power takes place in a photography session in which every click of Claire's camera intensifies the sexual exchange of power from her grandmother to herself. Claire symbolically captures Catherine who willingly surrenders, emotionally and sexually, for the only time in the epic:

> *D'un seul coup, Catherine se lève et joue avec un abattage extraordinaire le rôle de mannequin photographique. Elle prend toutes les poses possibles, depuis celle de la grande dame contemplant l'univers jusqu'à celle de la putain de bas étage. Elle et Claire font un numéro éblouissant. Elles s'amusent, rirent, courent, tournent sur elles-mêmes, se pressent l'une contre l'autre. Claire fait vraiment l'amour avec son appareil-photo. En poussant des gémissements de chattes en chaleur, elles finissent par rouler à terre. Claire, sexe contre sexe, les jambes de Catherine nouées dans son dos, prend un dernier cliché de la tête de Catherine extasiée. Entre Richard Premier qui voit le tableau.* [...] *Catherine pousse un immense gémissement d'orgasme.* (6.10.294)[25]

Thus, when Claire exits and Richard finally kills his mother in a futile attempt to appropriate her power to rule the nation, it is too late because Catherine has already abdicated it to Claire through their incestuous, homosexual bonding.

The epic's conclusion revels in an ambiguity that presents the reader/audience with two legitimate daughters surviving to claim the nation's throne, depending, oddly enough, on the epic's performance schedule. According to authorial, prefatory instructions in the published text, the epic's epilogue is only supposed to be performed when the epic as a whole has been played in one day, but the epilogue should be omitted when each play is performed on a different day. Thus, performed as "théâtre-feuilleton" or leaflet theatre (1.36), Claire Premier emerges as the new leader of the nation following Catherine's and Richard's deaths because, despite Leïla's daughter holding the dying Richard in the second last snapshot of the play, Leïla's daughter mysteriously disappears from the final shot. The final snapshot of Richard's dead body, with the blind monk who represents Fortune behind him, indicates that nobody else remains to lead the nation except for Claire who took the picture. Her omniscient position above the carnage of the horde signals her objective perspective and ability to rule rationally over the collectivity, in contrast to the self-interested narcissism that drove Richard to seek his mother's power. Claire emerges as the rightful ruler of the nation both through matrilineal descent and through a concerned interest in the needs and suffering of others (her grandmother's need for release and Richard's painful death) that inspires collective empathy (the photographs are transmitted to the audience). Since concern for others is precisely what has been lacking in the largely narcissistic and capitalist world of the play, Claire represents hope for a better future for the nation. She has received the right to rule from Catherine and Richard, but unlike them she has remained innocent and uncorrupted by the knowledge that she is heir to power.

If, however, the epilogue is included in the performance of the epic, then Leïla's daughter emerges as the new, legitimate ruler of the devastated nation. As the daughter of Leïla and Alcide Premier, Richard's older half-brother and first son of François Premier, Leïla's daughter's claim to the throne takes precedence over Claire's (in a situation that echoes the disputing genealogical claims traced back to Edward III in Shakespeare's tetralogy). The reader has no prior knowledge of Leïla's daughter before she appears in the closing scene as a snake charmer leading Moïse's horde against Richard, but in the epilogue she magically destroys the entire neighbourhood, including Claire's pictures and Moïse's café. Moïse's destruction by Leïla's daughter aligns with the carnivalesque spirit that permeates the play. As the bastard and thus underdog hero of the epic (in echo of Hector in *Lear*, Lou sings the praises of bastards [4.5.107]), Moïse can lead a popular revolution that topples the despotic old order of Richard, but he cannot lead the nation because he cannot create the new order to which carnival is supposed to return. Leïla's daughter, on the other hand, symbolizes new order because she is descended through Alcide from François Premier and his first wife, Augustine Labelle, both of whom are outsiders to the genealogical feud between the Ragone and Roberge families. She thus descends from a line of immigrants external to the epic's power struggle over the rule of the neighbourhood/kingdom. Leïla's daughter is further marked as immigrant other by her birth in Azerbaijan and her exoticism as a snake charmer. Like Claire, Leïla's daughter embodies hope for a new social order through the contribution of her exotic otherness and through her obliteration of a stale patriarchal power struggle by wiping out the male heads of each family, Richard for the Ragones and Moïse for the Roberges. Even her name, or lack thereof, as "Leïla's daughter" marks her as the representative of a new order, since her genealogy emphasizes the matrilineal.

In a Québécois context, Leïla's daughter's conquest speaks to a greater social acceptance of otherness in light of the losing referendum that pitted francophone sovereignists (such as René Lévesque) against francophone federalists (such as Claude Ryan, Robert Bourassa, and Pierre Elliott Trudeau), both of whom descended from the same *pure laine* roots. In this way, the referendum parallels the family feud around which *Roi Boiteux* is based with the Roberge family, represented by Moïse, the abandoned son who leads a horde of bastards, as the sovereignists, and the Ragone family, represented by Catherine, epitomizing colonial mimicry through her denial of her roots, as the Québécois federalists. Catherine describes the Roberge family as a "sale race" [dirty race], despite the fact that her mother was a Roberge, which makes her a Roberge by blood if not by name (2.3.119). The denial of her maternal roots through her assertions that she is purely Ragone, which she considers superior, belies her colonial mimicry; she is "almost but not quite" Ragone, in Bhabha's terms, and her frequent outbursts against the Roberge family expose her own self-hatred. Her rule over the court is merely that of a *comprador*, a derivative stand-in for the outside colonizing force of the Ragone family that acquired the Roberge gold mines by conquest of her mother Angela. In this, Catherine Roberge-Ragone evokes the ruling Québécois federalist elite that holds its own people in tutelage in the interests of the exploitation of its resources by an outside neocolonial force, the Canadian federal government. Catherine Roberge-Ragone denies her Roberge heritage in the name of Ragone, thus resembling *pure laine* Québécois federalists who deny the heritage of their birth in order to extol the ideal of a federal Canadian identity. However, as neither Roberge nor Ragone, Leïla's daughter transcends this feud and illuminates the ridiculousness of such debates on ethnic origin. Leïla's daughter's unexpected conquest represents, then, the arrival of immigrants and international culture and the explosion of the Roberge-Ragone/sovereignist-federalist binary that dominates the genealogical table prefacing both volumes of the epic. The literal explosion of the neighbourhood/kingdom provoked by Leïla's daughter in the epilogue creates a third space and opens possibilities for a new social order based on the contributions of a plurality of ethnic identities. This emphasis on an internationalist perspective is in keeping with the entire fifth play of the epic with its intertextual nods to Homer's *Odyssey* and to Captain James Cook's exploration of the South Pacific. *Roi Boiteux* explores international cultural exchange as a contribution that may enrich national identity without threatening or destroying it. The explosion caused by Leïla's daughter does not destroy the national community (as the continuing radio broadcast proves), only the rigid identity paradigms that were perpetuating rancour. This conclusion to the play does not discount national identity or sovereignty, but it speaks to the need for exterior influences to renew the debate.

The ambiguous conclusion thus produces two very different readings of the adaptation, but one constant remains: both Claire and Leïla's daughter are daughters of the nation's legitimate rulers. (The inheritance of the nation by these two women also explains why Richard is never able to govern alone the nation to which he thinks he is entitled: his attempts at rule are both profoundly colonialist and misogynist, as parodied when he "discovers" Circé's island, addresses her as "poupée" [doll], and unsuccessfully attempts to dominate her into a master-slave dialectic [5.9.156].) Thus, in one of the epic's two conclusions, women carry the potential for national renewal through uninhibited homosexuality, and, in the other, women bring the potential for national renewal through increased internationalism and cultural openness; in either case men cannot rule without recognition of women's strength and contribution to national development. The six-play conclusion favouring Claire's rule carries greater weight, however, for several reasons. The Claire-ending connects strongly to the Sandy-Nelson-Freddy relationship through the valorization of homosexual desire in loving relationships. Moreover, the epic's predominant emphasis on carnivalesque sexuality throughout, rather than the more limited treatment of international exploration, favours the six-play conclusion and Claire's succession. As François Premier observes, "Partout Éros triomphe, le sexe, le cul" (3.10.188).[26] Internationalism is primarily contained within the fifth play and relegated elsewhere to subplot characters. While sexuality is a function of carnival, internationalism is a function of magic realism, and the entire Odyssey of the fifth play is undercut when, upon the characters' return, the reader learns that their global voyages were merely an illusion (5.21.216).

Ronfard's *Lear* also concludes with a daughter's inheritance of national rule, although less ambiguously than in *Roi Boiteux*. Whereas in Shakespeare the responsibility of rebuilding the nation falls to Albany who offers it to Edgar,[27] in Ronfard's adaptation no counterparts exist for these two characters, and the only character still alive at the end is Laurette, the Cordelia figure:

> *Tout le monde est donc mort sauf Laurette. Elle arrive revêtue d'une grande chemise blanche, pieds nus, cheveux dénoués; elle n'a plus son maquillage de fou. Elle passe au milieu du charnier et se dirige vers le trône, au bout du tapis rouge. Elle*

y monte, s'y installe et d'un beau geste tranquille, elle tire la langue et la tient entre le pouce et l'index. Elle s'immobilise. (70)[28]

The only rebuilder of the destroyed nation is a pure woman (as symbolized by her large, white shirt), but she has been silenced and rendered immobile by the men and her own sisters. The nation lacks solidarity, as do the gender relations typified by her sisters; therefore, she is unable to speak or to act on behalf of a community (either national or sororal) that does not recognize her participation. In their own self-destruction, the rest of the characters destroy the possibility of rebirth that is normally the outcome of carnival. Within the confines of the play, there is no return from the carnivalesque second-world to another new social order. Yet, despite her silence, as the lone survivor and an angelic figure, Laurette represents hope since she escapes the fate of both of her Shakespearean counterparts, Cordelia who dies and the Fool who inexplicably disappears. Although the final scene is desolate, the image of Laurette's purity stands out in contrast to the death/ absence of her Shakespearean counterparts. She symbolizes the potential for rebirth which may be actualized beyond the limits of the play.

The reader can find hope for change and regeneration in Laurette's character at the end of the play because it is located in her from the beginning through her steadfast surveillance of the affairs of the nation and refusal to accept an unjustified exile (contrary to Shakespeare's Cordelia). When the king banishes her for failing to speak during the love test, Laurette tells herself that it is out of the question to "faire du tourisme africain quand c'est ici que ça se passe" (13).[29] In opposition to the references to African decolonization in Gurik's *Hamlet, prince du Québec*, Laurette's statement marks a turn in nationalist discourse. Whereas Gurik's adaptation valorizes African decolonization, in keeping with a 1960s trend of Fanonism-inspired Québécois nationalism drawing parallels with Africa, Ronfard's adaptation emphasizes that it is here, in Québec, that things are happening. It is no longer the time to study quietly international events from the outside like a tourist; it is now time to be in the centre of the action, and Laurette accepts the challenge by refusing exile. In an adaptation about the destruction of the nation due to the patriarchal ruler's divestiture of power to women, it is telling that Ronfard's ending figures a woman as the only potential healer of a sick nation in need of rebirth. Contrary to the church doctrine of *la revanche des berceaux*, or the comic closure typical in Shakespeare, Laurette's contribution is not located in her womb. Rather, by adopting a disguise as the fool and overseeing the affairs of the nation from her safe space perched above "toute la scène agrippé au haut d'une colonne" (38),[30] Laurette demonstrates her wit, her strategic intelligence to survive dire situations, and her recognition of the need to rebuild the nation once the horde has passed.

Laurette's adoption of this progressive, action-oriented attitude from the outset supports reading her as a source of regeneration. Even the silence with which she ends the play cannot diminish the potential she embodies since she held her tongue in the same manner during the love test, that is, at a moment of resistance to the king's capriciousness when silence may represent inner strength. Once the king and her sisters are dead at her feet, the closing image of her in her self-imposed silence is imbued with uncertainty, and the reader may envision that her liberation from the conditions leading up to her silence will free her from it. Her potential to *passer à l'action* to rebuild the nation remains unconstrained, like her flowing shirt. While Lieblein claims that the king's dying words, "Le reste est silence" (68) from *Hamlet* (5.2.363), indicate that "the father (Lear? Shakespeare?) proves unable to empower his child's speech" ("Shakespeare" 274), I would argue that Lear's dying words strengthen the reading of Laurette as a national leader. Neither Hamlet's death nor Lear's indicates that everything is silent or that the dramatic action has come to a close. Like the soon-to-be silent Hamlet, who implores his trusted friend Horatio to "[r]eport [him] and [his] cause aright/To the unsatisfied" (5.2.344–5), here Lear emphasizes his silence in order to encourage that his tale be told by someone close to him whom he can trust to oversee the rebirth of the state after his death. Liberated from the king's patriarchal rule that was responsible for her initial silence, at the end of the adaptation Laurette has leave, like Horatio, to "speak to th'yet unknowing world/[...]/Of carnal, bloody, and unnatural acts,/Of accidental judgments, [and] casual slaughters" and thus instate a new order in the aftermath of the carnivalesque chaos that has just ensued (5.2.384–7). She embodies the potential to return from carnival's "second-world" and to breathe new life into the nation now that its baser elements have been both celebrated and expunged.

Lear's conclusion is also marked by an unexpected, if not parodic, regeneration of another sort, one that dramatizes the theory of the death of the author. After all the other characters have died (except Laurette who is still offstage), the two Shakespeares mysteriously decide to engage in a sword fight punctuated with the typically British, decorous words exchanged by Hamlet and Laertes. The duel consists of four brief exchanges taken from Laertes and Hamlet, which are the only words in the text reproduced in English. The reproduction of the "original" English text lends more authenticity to these lines than that accrued upon the two Shakespeares' previous scenes in French translation. The fact that both Shakespeares slide interchangeably into the role of *Hamlet*'s heroic title character compounds this authenticity while blurring any distinction between the two author-characters.

The stage directions indicate that they stab each other and both fall down dead, but after Laurette returns onstage the adaptation ends on a note of magic realism with Shakespeare's return from the dead: "*Coup de théâtre: l'un des Shakespeares, en gémissant se redresse, arrache l'épée qui le perforait, se traine* [*sic*], *agonisant, vers la cabine d'éclairage et dans un dernier élan de vie, éteint les lumières, en disant:*/2: Calvaire!" (70).[31] The death of Shakespeare by Shakespeare and his spontaneous regeneration function as a metaphor for both the ambivalence inherent in the theory of the death of the author and the ambivalent status of Shakespeare in Québécois adaptations. On one level, this scene reinscribes the Bard's canonical authority through the implication that nobody can kill off Shakespeare entirely, not even Shakespeare himself; he will continue to pop up when we least expect it, if not in one incarnation then in another. On another level though, this scene undercuts that same authority by highlighting how easily Shakespeare can be appropriated by Québécois playwrights. Shakespeare's pronunciation of a typically Québécois blasphemy with his dying breath, in contrast to the Elizabethan English spoken during the preceding duel and the "standard" French of the opening scene, confers on Shakespeare an "authentic" Québécois identity, that of the *pure laine*, francophone, beer-drinking, working class. Rather than being crushed by the weight of Shakespeare's canonical authority, Québécois popular culture has turned the tables on him and forced Shakespeare to adopt its own discourse. While Shakespeare as both historical author and fictional author-character gets the final word in the adaptation, his blasphemy is a sort of baptism that culturally marks the signifier "Shakespeare" as distinctly Québécois – vulnerable to appropriation and hence "dead" as an author, despite his continual regeneration.

The tenuous balance between so-called authentic Shakespeare and his appropriation within the Québécois context is the subject of several other intertextual moments in the adaptation. During the equivalent of Shakespeare's storm scene, the fool hides in the rafters and pours water down onto the two Shakespeares who, huddled together under "*un parapluie typiquement 'british,'" "se lancent, avec verve et conscience historique* [...] *dans la grande narration du rêve de Clarence (authentiquement tirée de* RICHARD III *du grand William)"* (46–8).[32] The excerpt from Shakespeare's *Richard III* is "authentic" insofar as it is a literal translation with no additions or cuts that alter the meaning of the source text (1.4.1–33), and the authenticity of the translation, which renders the passage recognizable with or without the above stage directions, permits the passage, and the adaptation as a whole, to lay claim to a certain amount of Shakespeare's canonical authority. Nonetheless, the authority of this "authentic" text is undercut by the informal reference to Shakespeare by his first name, by the mocking jab at the stereotype of the British weather, and by the two Shakespeares' ironic obliviousness to the fact that they are being drowned, like Clarence, by water that the fool describes as "pipi de chat" (50).[33] This carnivalesque association of Shakespeare with the grotesque lower body also takes place at the end of the horde's protest when *"le roi contemple une boule de merde qu'il tient dans sa main, dans une posture qui rappelle Michel-Ange, Rodin, l'Hamlet traditionnel"* (21).[34] In both cases, the reduction of Shakespeare from cerebral philosopher to a target of the products of the grotesque lower body serves to undercut the popular conception of his "greatness" within a false high culture/low culture hierarchy.

The grotesque body is, of course, a dominant feature in Shakespeare's works, as Bakhtin points out (11), but in the popular imaginary Shakespeare's name tends to be associated with high culture to the convenient exclusion of the bawdy and carnivalesque elements of his plays. In fact, Ronfard's *Lear* plays upon, even as it subverts, the popularity of this false perception of a high culture/low culture binary with "Shakespeare" as signifier of "universal human greatness" (and other hyperboles of the like) in contrast to the carnivalesque and the grotesque of low culture. The protest by the horde of pro-bastard supporters culminates in the opposition collapsing in on itself: *"Sur leur trajet, ils rencontrent les deux shakespeares sorties de leur cage par curiosité. Deux mondes sont confrontés. Silence. Immobilité. Question: Qu'est que nous faisons tous ici? Chacun s'abîme dans ce vide théâtral plein d'angoisse métaphysique"* (21).[35] The confrontation of Shakespeare and carnival as two diametrically opposed worlds that collapse when they come into contact with each other strengthens the high culture/low culture binary. Yet, it is precisely this event that provokes the king to adopt the persona of Hamlet in his contemplation of the ball of shit. The onstage confrontation of Shakespeare and carnival can thus be interpreted as an invitation for the reader to examine more closely the carnivalesque that is already part of Shakespeare and the grotesque that lurks behind the high culture image of "*Hamlet*" as signifier of literary greatness.

Both Ronfard's *Lear* and *Vie et mort du Roi Boiteux*, then, figure daughters as the survivors, inheritors, and sources of regeneration for fictional, bastard nations that pass through the disorder of carnival and then hover on the precipice of a new social order which will be more inclusive of women, and to some extent immigrants, that is, of the "others" to whom carnival gives leave to rule. Both adaptations employ carnival, and to a lesser extent magic realism, to parody the diseased state of the nation and the fixity of traditional gender roles, ultimately suggesting that the rule of women, or at least a greater social recognition of their potential, is the only way to heal the nation's ills. By positing that national development is dependent on the instauration of gender equity, and thus highlighting the interdependence of issues of nation and gender, the adaptations participate in a crucial social and political debate of their time, as the first referendum's Yvette scandal brought forcefully to the fore. As well, Ronfard's adaptations take *le grand Will* down a peg in order to expose the carnivalesque that has always been present in his "high culture" plays, while also baptizing "Shakespeare" as distinctly Québécois.

Chapter Six

The Second Referendum: Plurality without Pluralism

Since 1990, Québec has seen an explosion of adaptations of Shakespeare by a range of playwrights from various sociocultural backgrounds, including the first Québécois adaptations written by women, queers, and aboriginals. No fewer than twenty-seven adaptations have been written and produced since then, and the number continues to grow (see the appendix). With such a wide range of texts, one would not expect to find much commonality among them. What unites these texts is their plurality, not only as a trait embodied by the diversity of the corpus itself but also in the emergence of a cacophony of other voices speaking up for the first time. In this respect, each of the diverse adaptations from this period, whether its focus is on the social roles of women, queers, aboriginals, or immigrants, falls in line with the Western postmodernist tendency to recognize the existence of fragmented subject positions and to embrace pluralistic identities more openly, even when such multiple subject positions may be in conflict with one another, a problem third-wave feminists sought to address with the notion of intersectionality. This new generation of adapters engages in a dialogue with Shakespeare about a range of issues not seen in adaptations of the previous three decades, but the plurality of identity positions they bring to the forefront does not erase the strong bent towards nationalism seen in earlier adaptations nor does this plurality of voices signal a turn towards pluralism as it operates within Canadian multiculturalism. Rather, this proliferation of texts provides a snippet view of issues dealing with various forms of alterity, of others who join the national collective and add their voices to the intercultural mix, but the nationalist drive remains an important component of Québécois adaptations in this time period as well. While female playwrights finally begin to contribute to this corpus of texts, few of these plays focusing on women's experiences are arguably feminist.

The 1990s began in Québec with a violent shock. On 6 December 1989, Marc Lépine entered l'École Polytechnique in Montréal with a semi-automatic rifle and a hunting knife, went into a classroom, and separated the male students from the female students. After the approximately fifty men had left, he told the remaining nine women, "Je combats le féminisme," and added, "Vous êtes des femmes, vous allez devenir ingénieures. Vous n'êtes toutes qu'un tas de féministes, je hais les féministes."[1] He then opened fire, killing six of them, and continued his rampage throughout other floors of the building, killing a total of fourteen women, wounding fourteen other people, including two men, before finally committing suicide. The Montréal Massacre was a pan-Canadian tragedy, but its after-effects were felt particularly strongly by women in Québec since the target of the attack, clearly identified in Lépine's suicide note, was "les féministes qui [l]'ont toujours gaché [*sic*] la vie" [feminists who have always ruined [his] life]. The Massacre was a wake-up call that drew attention to the latent sexism, misogyny, and backlash against feminism still present in Québec society. As Nicole Brossard argued shortly after the attack in an article entitled "Le tueur n'était pas un jeune homme," Lépine "était aussi vieux que tous les proverbes sexistes et misogynes, aussi vieux que tous les pères de l'Église qui ont douté que les femmes avaient une âme. Il avait l'âge des tous les législateurs qui ont interdit l'université, le droit de vote, l'accès à la place publique aux femmes [...] aussi vieux que l'Homme et son mépris pour les femmes," while the murdered women "étaient jeunes, aussi jeunes que les acquis du féminisme [...] aussi jeunes que la vie recommencée d'espoir par chaque génération de femmes."[2] The first Shakespearean adaptations by women authors emerge shortly after this tragedy, perhaps as part of a larger social awakening to how the political gains feminists had made to date were subject to a backlash that required further cultural dissemination before equality could become entrenched as a common social value.[3]

Just prior to the Massacre, Pierre-Yves Lemieux's 1989 play *À propos de Roméo et Juliette* alluded to another tragedy that was claiming the lives of a gendered minority, queers ravaged by the AIDS epidemic. The Prologue immediately establishes the AIDS analogy by situating the play "EN TEMPS DE PESTE" and then constructs Shakespeare as queer by telling the audience "L'ADAPTEUR A PRIS BEAUCOUP DE LIBERTÉ" and that they will understand "POURQUOI SHAKESPEARE

AIMAIT TANT MERCUTIO," who is portrayed as a campy gay in the opening dialogue through a discussion about the "lion" he's waiting to meet and "suce[r]" [give a blow job] (2, 3, 5). After Romeo flirtatiously teases Mercutio with gentle kisses on his cheek and neck, Mercutio says Romeo has "La douceur des lèvres de Vénus… Le souffle d'Adonis…," telling him "tu aimes que je t'aime" but that Romeo is "trop lâche pour un plongeon si vertigineux" (6).[4] His queerness firmly established, Mercutio reveals he has been a muse for "Le seul être [qu'il a] aimé" before quoting part of Sonnet 104 and sighing "William…" (8, 9).[5] Unable to have Shakespeare anymore, Mercutio is promiscuous, sleeping with the prince from whom he receives an invitation to the ball, which he attends in drag (31–2, 54). Prior to their fight, Mercutio also flirts with Tybalt (89). The allusions to AIDS emerge in Laurence's reference early in the play to "ces temps de peste" [these times of plague] (24), as well as in Mercutio's use of the word "peste" five times in his dying curse compared to the three times it appears in Shakespeare's text (91, 92). Although there is no indication that Mercutio or any other characters are actually infected with this omnipresent plague, Mercutio is unable to escape his Shakespearean destiny, dying by Tybalt's sword. He does so, though, of his own accord, deliberately throwing himself with wide-open arms upon Tybalt's weapon and offering up his blood to seal Romeo and Juliette's marriage. Contrary to Shakespeare's Mercutio who gets stabbed accidentally under Romeo's intervening arm, Lemieux's Mercutio welcomes death by penetration because he will not grow old and it frees him from his unrequited love for Romeo (92). Mercutio is the first openly homosexual character to appear in a Québécois adaptation of Shakespeare. He is, however, also the *only* homosexual character to appear in a full-length play within this corpus in which representations of queerness are strangely absent.[6]

The absence of queerness in this corpus, with the exception of Lemieux's play, is in keeping with the relative absence of feminism in post-1990s plays despite the emergence of female and gay male authors and plays containing female characters. During this period there are four plays by or primarily about women, yet only one can be categorically described as feminist. These women-oriented plays are Normand Chaurette's *Les Reines* (1991), Antonine Maillet's *William S* (1991), Jean-Frédéric Messier and Paula de Vasconcelos's *Le* Making of *de Macbeth* (1996), and Daphné Thompson's *Sauvée des eaux: Texte dramatique sur Ophélie* (2000).[7] In the readings that follow, I demonstrate how *Les Reines* attempts to give voice to Shakespeare's queens but ultimately reinscribes early modern norms while *William S* allows Shakespeare's Shrew to voice her grievances more freely. *Le* Making of *de Macbeth* and *Sauvée des eaux: Texte dramatique sur Ophélie* are more problematic texts. Neither strikes me as feminist, although both could be described as "feminine" works in their subject matter and stylistic composition.[8]

Le Making of *de Macbeth*, written by Messier based on an idea by de Vasconcelos, turns around the question of whether Elizabeth, a theatre director, should continue her career or sacrifice it to have a baby. For the majority of the play, she puts her career first and is reticent about the idea of motherhood, often pressured towards it by others. Elizabeth only begins to change her mind at the very end of the play as she is about to learn she is pregnant. Ultimately, she decides partway through the rehearsal process to abandon putting on *Macbeth*, leaving the other actors in the lurch as she gives up her career to become a mother. Never is the option to have both a career and a baby presented as viable – a double burden for women that often causes supermom burn-out, but nonetheless the default for men who, with the help of a child-rearing partner at home, rarely face such a dilemma. In fact, the play includes a single father, Pierre, who does continue his career as an actor, often taking his four-year-old daughter to the theatre. Yet for Elizabeth career and motherhood are presented as an either-or choice, and social pressures force her into the latter, which the play represents as a "happy ending." In an interview with Denis Salter, de Vasconcelos states that her main character's name "evokes Elizabeth I, who was also powerful and childless" (77), yet she does not allow her heroine to remain childless, even though she also alludes to another powerful virgin queen in her representation of Lady Macbeth as an "evocation of Diana, the Amazon, the woman warrior" (77). Despite its valorization of femininity and women's reproductive capacities, feminists who remain childless by choice, who see challenging careers as more fulfilling than a social but not biological imperative, or who want and do achieve both career and a satisfying family life would likely disagree with the play's representation of motherhood.

Similarly, Thompson's *Sauvée des eaux* falls short of the libratory potential with which it teases the reader. The play consists of text generated in WordPerfect by an early 1990s style computer, including the commands that make the computer function in response to an unknown author character ("l'écrivain," gendered as male). Although the title promises the reader that Ophelia will be saved from drowning, the author character, while sympathetic to her plight, fails to save her from her Shakespearean fate. Leanore Lieblein argues that by the end of

Sauvée des eaux "it is clear that Ophelia's death does not proceed from madness but is a lucid choice. The play does not save Ophelia from drowning. But through an act of imagination and empathy it dismantles the process by which generations of Ophelias have been written and releases her from her victimization" (*A Certain William* 188). She admits, however, that "Thompson's text does not give Ophelia many words of her own, and does not change her destiny" (188). Lieblein presents an illuminating reading of Ophelia's "dead and absent presence" ("Ghost" 13), but the script does not make clear that the character's choice of suicide necessarily releases the character from her victimization. Rather, the text emphasizes the patriarchal norms in which Ophelia is caught, unable to escape despite the author character's affirmation, "Je suis le spectre d'Ophélie et je demande paix pour son âme" (11).[9] The play affirms that an adapter may inhabit the spirit of Shakespeare's characters who have been victims of early modern gender norms, but the author character cannot rewrite Ophelia's fate or save her from death. The most the adapter can do is to bring peace to a troubled soul after the fact. This postmodern metatextual work calls attention to the potential of adaptation to rewrite Shakespeare from a feminist standpoint only to end by reaffirming misogyny and death as inescapable for his women characters.

Compared to Ann-Marie MacDonald's Canadian play *Goodnight Desdemona (Good Morning Juliet)* (1990), Margaret Clarke's Canadian play *Gertrude and Ophelia* (1993), or Jean Betts's Australian play *Ophelia Thinks Harder* (1993), neither *Le* Making of *de Macbeth* nor *Sauvée des eaux* takes a resolutely feminist stand. MacDonald's heroine Constance Ledbelly, a graduate student at Queen's, saves Desdemona and Juliet from death and discovers that she herself is Shakespeare's "Wise Fool" who prevents comedies from turning into tragedies, that is, an adapter. Clarke's Ophelia tells Gertrude how Hamlet raped her and Gertrude sings to Ophelia, helps her through a miscarriage, and loves her like her own daughter. Betts's heroine fights back against the beauty myth, female passivity, male duplicity, organized religion, a discriminatory educational system, and the sexual double standard. In contrast, the main characters in these two Québécois adaptations are circumscribed by social and authorial forces represented as inevitable and unbreakable, and the plays do not tap into feminist adaptation's potential to show readers different visions of women's social roles.

Normand Chaurette's 1991 play *Les Reines*, which has been translated as *The Queens*,[10] also sets up the reader to expect a libratory adaptation only to see instead the reinscription of early modern gender norms.

This adaptation showcases the offstage lives of five of Shakespeare's matriarchs from *1–3 Henry VI* and *Richard III*, creating a parallel world in which we see what they are doing while Shakespeare's "main" characters are engaged in the plot with which the reader is already familiar – much like Tom Stoppard's *Rosencrantz and Guildenstern Are Dead* constructs a parallel world set against the plot of *Hamlet*. To the past or aspiring queens found in Shakespeare – Queen Margaret (wife of Henry VI and former mother-in-law of Lady Anne Warwick), Queen Elizabeth (wife of Edward IV), the Duchess of York (Edward's mother), Lady Anne (wife of Richard III), and Isabelle Warwick (wife of George, Duke of Clarence) – Chaurette adds a character of his own creation – Anne Dexter – who is Edward, George, and Richard's sister. Limited to these six women characters, the play focuses on their pettiness and manipulation as each one, except for Anne Dexter, reminisces and revels in the glory of past power or dreams about and plots to achieve future rule of England on the eve of Edward's death and George's murder.

The viciousness with which these women lie to, spy on, and manipulate each other in their jostle for power plays into stereotypes about both straight women and queer men. As Lois Sherlow observes, the word "reine" in French, like its English counterpart "queen," has a double meaning that alludes not only to female royalty but also to gay men (358). I would add that it particularly evokes those who exhibit excessive femininity, either drag queens or "flaming fags." Sherlow relies on biographical information to support a queer reading of the play's title when she claims that the play is "cryptically signed as the work of a homosexual playwright" by the date of the play's action, 20 January, which is the feast of Saint Sebastian,[11] adding that such "a use of significant dates is characteristic of Chaurette's writing" (369–70n3). While any reading of the play could arguably interpret the queens' performance of gender simultaneously in terms of early modern women, contemporary women, and contemporary gay men, the queens never succeed in escaping the early modern context, so the wordplay and the potential multiple levels of meaning implied by the title are not actualized. The queens are "bitchy" with each other, but nothing in the text marks them as stand-ins for contemporary gay men; rather, the queens are women firmly trapped within early modern gender norms.

The adaptation's inability to rewrite early modern norms is represented through images of the nation's frozen immobility and grotesque decay that are symptomatic of the queens' marginalization from political power. Sherlow claims that Chaurette's play is "post-nationalist" theatre (358), a work that foregrounds poetry over politics. While *Les Reines* is not *théâtre engagé*, this supposedly "post-nationalist" play does in fact say a lot about the Québec nation. Like Macbeth's Scotland or Caliban's island in Garneau's tradaptations, the nation in Chaurette's adaptation is marked geographically as Québéc, thereby turning the world of the play into a palimpsest of both England in 1483 and Québec in 1991. Rather than alluding to the Plains of Abraham or local wildlife as Garneau does, *Les Reines* marks the nation as Québec by invoking its climate. On the particular day during which the play takes place, it is snowing so hard that the queens describe the snow as a flood that is causing the city of London to disappear (46). As Sherlow points out (356), the snow evokes the "winter of discontent" that opens *Richard III* (1.1.1), but she does not pursue its significance. I would posit that the mysterious snow pervading the backdrop of the play marks the nation as Québec first because it rarely snows in London and second because snow and frost are frequent themes in Québécois poetry, especially in poetry of the 1920s–1950s. The most famous example of the image of winter in popular, nationalist discourse is Gilles Vigneault's song "Mon pays, ce n'est pas un pays, c'est l'hiver" (1964) in which the nation must awaken from the cold so that it can, in the equally famous words of sovereignist songwriter Paul Piché, be "Heureux d'un printemps" (1977) when it gives birth to itself.[12] The snow overshadowing the play is thus both a poignant spatial marker and an indication of the distress of the yet unborn nation. In Québécois poetry, such as that of Hector de Saint-Denys Garneau, Paul Chamberland, and Pierre Châtillon, winter is associated with immobility and sleep whereas fire signals the awakening of the nation and the energy needed to accomplish sovereignty. The adaptation's snow is a sign of frozen immobility and symptomatic of the nation's inability to accept change, such as the contributions of women to its political life.

As a reference to Shakespeare's "winter of our discontent," the adaptation's snowy backdrop is equally problematic because in *Richard III* "now" is not at all the winter of discontent but winter "[m]ade glorious summer by this son of York" (1.1.2). In Shakespeare's text, the winter of discontent refers, for Richard on the one hand, to the rule of the Lancasters that ends with Edward IV's ascension to the throne and, for the audience on the other hand, to the War of the Roses that has reached a ceasefire at the beginning of the play and will, ironically for Richard, reach its final conclusion by the end. In the adaptation, Shakespeare's "winter of our discontent" is never "[m]ade glorious summer"; rather, civil strife opens the first scene of the play in the form of the queens' babble and continues as they bicker among themselves for the entire play. In 1991, the nation was also in a state of discontent, caught between the failed Meech Lake Accord of 1990 and negotiations leading towards the rejected Charlottetown Accord of 1992. These civil debates were not only dividing Québécois between sovereignists and federalists but also dividing English Canada where a babble of marginalized voices – women, aboriginals, francophones outside of Québec – was heard emanating from the hallways of power louder than ever before.

The nation's decay is symbolized though the death of its monarch. In *Les Reines*, Edward IV is dying; in fact, according to Anne Dexter, he has been in a constant state of dying since his birth (63). The grotesque description of his death by Queen Margaret constitutes an entire scene of the play in which the reader learns how first he lost one of his hands which rolled to the foot of his bed, then his left eye fell out and rolled down his cheek, his mouth died and sealed his lips forever only to open again and spit out foamy potions from his esophagus and stomach, his blood poisoned his veins one by one, his forehead blackened, and his hair fell out of his head (25–7). The grotesque decay of Edward's body is a powerful description of the pitiful state of the nation that ties Chaurette's adaptation to those of Jean-Pierre Ronfard. The dying Edward is more grotesque than Ronfard's Lear or his limping King Richard, signalling an even greater decline of the Québécois nation, upon which the play focuses more than the women who inhabit it. Politically, the queens have no voices; they produce only a senseless cacophony like the babble that opens the play in which none of their words can be properly identified. Since they cannot participate directly in state affairs, the queens attempt to engage in covert manipulation of men, but their unsuccessful manoeuvres only corrupt them further. Operating within a masculinist culture characterized by backstabbing in the hallways of power, the women, except Anne Dexter, are all complicit in contributing to the nation's downfall through their malicious yet futile quest for power. While the nation suffers under a literal blanket of snow, the queens' attempts to "make glorious summer" involve trips to a basement furnace room where they devise murder plots that reveal them to be just as violent as Richard.

One might expect an adaptation written by an openly gay author about the lives of six women to explode the patriarchal structures responsible for their marginalization and to rescue them from their fate. Instead the play reinscribes early modern gender norms since the queens are endowed with ineffective voices and are unable to transcend the limits imposed by the Shakespearean source text. *Les Reines* could have been written as a feminist adaptation, but it falls short. Notably, the queens are all bad mothers and disciplined for their lack of femininity. Queen Elizabeth is constantly searching for her children who are always being tended by someone else, and her lack of personal care for them is responsible for their murder when the Duchess of York gives them, at the end of the play, to Anne Warwick (who will deliver them to Richard) in exchange for wearing her crown for ten seconds. Queen Elizabeth is obsessed with patriarchal lineage and the fact that the "Woodville, [elle] la première/Sont en train d'hériter/Le trésor d'Angleterre" (33).[13] She is punished for her attempted incursion into patriarchal affairs of wealth and lineage through the death of her children. Her punishment is enacted via primogeniture since her only claim to power is through the reproduction of her husband's lineage. The loss of a stake in the political game upsets her more than the actual loss of her sons. The play thereby suggests that at the risk of punishment women ought to be loving child-rearers, and it fails to offer an alternative option of life in the public sphere.

The Duchess of York's motherhood is more troubling than Queen Elizabeth's insofar as she has given birth to Richard's villainy yet she refuses to acknowledge her daughter. The conversation between the Duchess and her supposedly mute daughter Anne Dexter, the longest scene in the play, articulates the conflict between the Duchess's masculinity and her children's femininity which is encoded in early modern notions of women's silence. Anne and George have both been silent since childhood, speaking only when alone with their mother who commanded their silence in reaction to discovering their incestuous love for each other, a crime for which she also ordered Richard to cut off Anne's hands. Anne reminds her mother, "George était un sphère d'amour/Mais je régnais dans son coeur/Ah ce devait être souffrant/De t'incliner devant sa reine!" (61).[14] She charges that her hands were cut off because her mother was consumed by jealousy that Anne's hands had touched George. Anne Dexter, then, is, or at least was, a queen too, the queen of George's heart. Because she challenged her mother, whose one dream in life is to be a queen as well, if only for ten seconds, Anne's punishment for usurping her mother's place in her brother's heart must exceed mere silence or a dismemberment evocative of Lavinia's in *Titus Andronicus*; she must cease to exist. In her heartless mother's eyes, Anne is "nothing" at all (66).

Anne's and George's punishments are indicative of the other women's gender trouble: Anne is a womanly non-presence while George's speech is effeminized. Anne confirms that George speaks only at the Duchess's command, but the sounds are not really language at all: "Des râlements, des cris/Des sons mis bout à bout/Des mots qui n'ont de place/En aucun dictionnaire" (60).[15] As a language controlled by his mother, the "langue à-sa-mère" to which Lalonde refers, George's "speech" is feminine. He has been feminized by his mother in terms of the feminine language he speaks, which the Duchess claims only she can understand, and in terms of his silence towards everyone else, a characteristic of "good" early modern women. Yet, George's feminization is not only a result of the Duchess's manipulation but something to which he was already in tune through his incestuous love for Anne. Anne says their love for each other was "avant le temps/Tu as compris que nous avions été là d'abord/Et que le monde était venu ensuite/Tu n'étais que notre mère/Mais engendrée après nous – " (61).[16] Existing before time and before the world, George and Anne's love precedes the construction of social norms, conventions, and taboos. Their incestuous love is embedded with a purity experienced temporarily by the other characters as a peace that they are unable to understand or endure because they have been indoctrinated by violent masculinist norms. Before silencing them both, the Duchess was moved by their happiness and taught Richard by their example: "Qui mieux que nous pouvait illustrer/La paix dans notre maison?/Et pourtant au bout de six mois/Cette paix avait trop duré" (62).[17] Anne concludes that their feminine love and peace could not survive in this masculinist realm because it was incomprehensible to everyone else, including the Duchess who subscribes to the realm's norms.

Anne confronts her mother about her attempts to erase her existence because she was born the wrong sex in a masculinist realm: "On m'a parlé aussi/D'une fille parmi ces frères./[...]/Il te faut des heures/Pour expliquer que cette enfant-là/N'est jamais née" (58).[18] The Duchess is successful in transforming Anne into "nothing," but she pays the price for her rejection of the feminine with her own living death. One hundred years old, but unable to die because she has prevented her children from living, the Duchess will soon fade into oblivion: "À défaut d'avoir mis au monde/Une sœur pour tes fils/Une fille qui aurait peut-être pu/Regretter sa mère," nobody will remember or mourn her (65).[19] She retorts that she would have liked to have had a daughter, but she could not give birth to the feminine element inside her: "Pour qu'elle naisse/Je lui promettais tout ce qu'elle désirerait/Pourvu qu'elle arrive en moi/Rien n'y faisait/Elle n'était pas en moi" (65).[20] The Duchess has not actively subscribed to patriarchal kinship but is a product of it against her will. She wanted to produce the feminine and set it free in the world, but the social constraints were too strong. Since the feminine cannot exist within the world of the play, Anne is "nothing." The Duchess tells Anne that "elle est à notre langue/Ce que zéro est à nos nombres," and then adds paradoxically, confirming Anne's existence in the same breath that denies it, "Aussi vrai que toi tu existes/Aussi vrai que tu es devant mes yeux/Elle n'est rien./Rien. Nothing" (66).[21]

Anne's status as "nothing," as that which does not signify, is in fact full of signification. First, although her mother equates her with the number zero, zero is an essential mathematical placeholder without which most equations could not be solved, and Anne too is the key to this puzzling play. Anne both is and is not a queen; she is the incestuous queen of her brother George's heart, but she is also an inversion of a queen, since the word "rien" is an anagram of "reine." Yet she is not a queen in the royalist sense, so within this world she is nothing. Second, because she is a daughter rather than a son, her silent invisibility as an early modern woman also makes her nothing. Anne embodies the silence of all the queens since everything they say is a cacophony that fails to signify. Third, since she is called "Nothing" in English in the original French text, she is tied intertextually to Shakespeare's most famous representation of nothingness, Cordelia, and Lear's warning that "Nothing will come of nothing" (1.1.90). Like Mariana in *Measure for Measure,* who as "neither maid, widow, nor wife" is nothing (5.1.177–8), Anne thus becomes "a punk" or a used vagina; she represents the transgressive female sexuality that cannot be expressed in the world of the play. Fourth, Anne is nothing because she does not exist in Shakespeare's *Richard III*; she is outside of history as the audience knows it since the cultural weight of Shakespeare's history plays has replaced History itself. Queen Margaret, Queen Elizabeth, the Duchess of York, and Lady Anne all appear onstage in Shakespeare, and although Clarence's wife Isabel does not, she is presumed to exist by virtue of her reproductive capacity as the mother of Clarence's children who do appear. Only Anne Dexter, sister to two kings but mother to none, does not exist in Shakespeare and thus not at all. She is nothing because she has not fulfilled a reproductive capacity, through the use of her vaginal "nothing," to perpetuate patriarchal kinship.

As nothing, then, Anne Dexter literalizes the condition of the other women who do not think that they are nothing but are because their only real power is the use of their "nothings" to produce male heirs. They do not exist either, except by virtue of their husbands and their sons. In this respect, the queens echo the widows in the other Québécois adaptation of *Richard III*, Ronfard's *Roi Boiteux*. Much like Judith Roberge who tells Catherine Ragone that she is nothing once she becomes a widow, a name with no guarantor, so too are these queens nothing more than reproductive vessels for a patriarchal system that, despite all their cunning, they are unable to control. Their non-presence in the affairs of the nation, and the lack of a feminine element represented by George, whom Anne calls purity, causes its decay: "la pureté va bientôt mourir/Noyée dans un tonneau/Cette maison n'est plus qu'un entonnoir/Où tout se mélange et s'écoule/Dans la bouche pourrie de la mort" (63).[22] The nation is rotten because it lacks the purity of George and Anne's unconventional love and a feminine influence to counterbalance Richard's violence.

Les Reines reproduces early modern gender norms about women's silence and patriarchal kinship as well as contemporary stereotypes about the perceived masculinity and lack of maternal tenderness of women who seek political power. It is thus a play about gender but not feminist. Even at the play's end, feminine elements continue to be misrecognized as "nothing" – as something that must be eliminated just as the Duchess ordered Richard to chop off Anne's hands – and there is no indication that the nation will cure itself of its decay – which is both a cause and an effect of the marginalization of women from its political process. In ignoring women's potential political and cultural contribution to the nation, exemplified in the failure to recognize Anne's very existence, Chaurette's play suggests that women and the nation will continue to be buried in a perpetual snowy winter.

Anne's nothingness ties *Les Reines* intertextually to Antonine Maillet's play *William S.*[23] Anne is an analogue to Lear's Fool, first as an analogue to Cordelia, given Shakespeare's association of the two characters, and second through the Fool's frequent references to Lear's state of nothingness following the loss of his kingdom. Sherlow also ties Anne to the Fool, but only in relation to the Tarot (361). I would argue that Anne functions as the Fool in a more Shakespearean sense, as the character who observes everything and understands the most. She is the only character who appears to speak the truth amidst the lies of the five other women. Yet, Anne does not speak for the last three scenes of the play.

She may be onstage or she may not; the stage directions do not indicate whether she is still present observing the others or whether, like Lear's Fool in 3.6, she has mysteriously disappeared. In reaction to the last words she does speak, Queen Elizabeth replies, "Voyez comme tout me rend folle" (70),[24] accusing her of creating folly. If, by virtue of her similarities to Lear's Fool, Anne is the fool of *Les Reines*, then she is also the most Shakespearean character, at least according to Maillet whose Fool is Shakespeare himself. Since Maillet's *William S* was first produced in April 1991, only four months after *Les Reines*, the connection between the two plays is more likely to be intertexual than coincidental.

Antonine Maillet's *William S* articulates a clear feminist discourse, taking issue with early modern gender norms more directly than *Les Reines*. The play gives voices to some of Shakespeare's most famous women characters – Lady Macbeth, the Shrew, Juliet, and her Nurse. Maillet's characters literally speak to Shakespeare himself, charging him with the crimes that were their fate in his texts – silence, domestic violence, and death. In attempting to justify the misogyny of his plots, the character of Shakespeare, personified as his own Fool, cannot help but acknowledge the violence to which he has subjected his women characters and the futility of attempting to fix textual meaning transhistorically.

The adaptation intertwines questions of gender and ethnicity with authorial intention and canonical authority. Shakespeare, feeling god-like,[25] descends from the sky into the theatre to spy on how his characters are doing after 400 years, but he rudely discovers that they are not pleased with the roles written for them and they do not regard their author as the benevolent creator he thinks himself to be. The fictional Shakespeare's descent from the sky, balancing on a cable, immediately posits the author as god, a comparison that is evoked textually several times in the play and also intertextually by the historical Shakespeare's use of this theatrical device for the god Jupiter in *Cymbeline* and the spirit Ariel in *The Tempest*.

The fictional Shakespeare's opening monologue to the audience establishes his disinterested god-like possession of his characters that he "a créés, sortis de rien, pour [le] distraire" (23).[26] He then explains his reason for writing his plays: "J'ai voulu, comme tant d'autres, avoir le dernier mot dans mon dialogue avec [… le Temps]" (23).[27] Shakespeare's confessions raise two important questions about authorship and authority. First, are characters "real" people, and, second, can the author fix transhistorically the meaning of his work? The fictional Shakespeare's view of his characters as amusing playthings suggests they are objects rather than thinking subjects; however, their encounter forces him to re-evaluate his position since they are self-aware and conscious of their role as characters. Shakespeare's characters are endowed with agency and able to rebel against and exceed their prescribed roles. The characters' independence from their author confirms that the author cannot have the last word on his work after all, that Time will indeed give new life to his characters and allow them to develop in unexpected directions beyond his intentions.

The adaptation appears, then, to extol Barthes's theory of the death of the author since the subversion of authorial intention by the characters themselves prevents any fixity of the text's meaning. In fact, a dialogue between Shakespeare-as-Fool and Hamlet explicitly connects Nietzsche's death of god with Barthes's death of the author, a problematic association for the fictional Shakespeare as author-god:

SHYLOCK: Nous réclamons l'auteur.
FOU: L'auteur est introuvable.
HAMLET: Le créateur est introuvable. Dieu est introuvable!
FALSTAFF: Dieu est mort et enterré. (59)[28]

An absurdist, Beckettian exasperation with the absence of god becomes a Barthes-like assertion of the death of the author through an implied syllogism that if both the author and god are absent, and god is dead and buried, then the author must also be dead and buried. Shakespeare-as-Fool is confronted with his own characters' claim that he does not exist, that is, that he can claim neither authorship nor authority. Their agency to debate the topic proves they have "lives of their own"; that is, they are not only subject to interpretations beyond his intentions but are also active subjects. This debate on the nature of authorship is paradoxical since it depends on the interaction of the author with his characters who must expose his motivations, thereby endowing his intentions with a certain authority as if they were indeed the word of god. Shakespeare's intentions *define* the characters despite failing to *circumscribe* them. Ironically, Maillet's staging of the death of the author depends on his presence (it is in fact Shakespeare-as-Fool who claims the author is absent) and the explicit confession of his intentions.

This deconstructive absent-presence of the author does nothing, however, to resolve the characters' concerns about their gendered or religious oppression. Juliet's Nurse categorically rejects any debate about an author-god, asserting, "Personne ne m'a faite, moi, hormis mon père et ma mère. Pour les autres… auteurs, créateurs, Dieu… bouillie pour les chats. Parlons de choses sérieuses" (73).[29] In her blissful disdain for existential angst, the Nurse exposes the debate as irrelevant because she cannot change the nature of an author-god, only her own condition. The conditions of her existence are the only serious topic of discussion, and for the women characters who compose the majority of the play's dramatis personae their existence is defined by a misogyny that limits the "life" of their character. The Shrew, for instance, wears heavy chains throughout the play even though there is no stage direction to this effect in *The Taming of the Shrew*. She is in a constant struggle between the destiny her nature demands of her and the circumstances preventing her from achieving it: "Conçue mégère, puis mise au monde apprivoisée. […] Je suis mon propre contraire. Un paradoxe ambulant" (44).[30] In reference to postcolonial criticisms of Caliban's relationship to Prospero, the Shrew claims, "nous sommes tous ses esclaves" (45),[31] evoking a discourse of decolonization from the early modern gender norms responsible for her chains.

The Shrew's interaction with Juliet furthers her exposé on the slavery tied up in these norms, particularly through primogeniture. She asks Juliet, "Depuis quatre siècles, ma fille, depuis le début du monde que nous nous trouvons, femmes, en position de faiblesse. Et qu'a-t-on fait de nous?" (64).[32] Juliet responds, "On nous a aimées," provoking the Shrew to retort sarcastically, "Oh! oh!! Entendez roucouler le gentil pigeon! Aimées, dit-elle, aimées dans les chaînes, aimées esclaves, courtisanes, machines à leur fabriquer une progéniture, progéniture de mâles pour hériter de leurs biens et titres, et de quelques femelles pour assurer la lignée. Et vous appelez ça aimer, Juliette?" (64).[33] Katherine's exasperation at the custom of primogeniture is nothing new for Shakespeareans – Edmund criticizes it eloquently, if self-contradictingly, in *King Lear* (1.2.1–22) – but her frustrated outburst prepares Shakespeare-as-Fool to receive the more nuanced complaints of other female characters.

Maillet's Lady Macbeth, for instance, plays on the gender fluidity that characterizes Shakespeare's Lady Macbeth and expresses a transgendered identity. She asks the fictional Shakespeare why he made her a woman when she was better equipped than her husband to be king: "Moi seule de nous deux possédais la tête, l'âme, le coeur d'un roi… mais dans un corps de femme. Pourquoi?" (78).[34] Lady Macbeth claims that Shakespeare's complicity with early modern gender norms is responsible for her downfall. Had her character been free to act unconstrained, she would have proven a better ruler than her husband:

> Mais moi dans tout ça, moi votre créature, aiguillonnée par l'ambition, tentée par le pouvoir, que vous avez doté d'une âme d'acier pour venir ensuite l'enfermer dans une enveloppe de conventions et de lois à l'usage des mâles, qu'avez-vous fait de moi, la femme? Vous m'avez faite femme, justement, avec tout ce que cette condition entraîne de misères et de limitations. La femme qui ne saurait porter l'épée, ni commander à son homme, ni transgresser les lois de son sexe. (79)[35]

Her demand for rectification – "Que le roi mâle remette aux femmes le pouvoir usurpé" (67)[36] – interpolates not only her husband the king but also Shakespeare, the author-god who is king of her fictional universe. She specifically blames Shakespeare for attributing a female body to her masculine gender identity. Yet, rather than negating that body, she rejects instead the early modern norms that circumscribe it, calling for a social paradigm shift rather than for Shakespeare to issue her a male body. Lady Macbeth's proposed reordering of social hierarchy draws upon what Judith Butler calls working the variation in the norm in order to expose the social constructedness and lack of transhistoricity of early modern gender relations (*Gender Trouble* 185).

The potential disruption of social hierarchy is, according to Maillet's Shrew, the reason why Shakespeare refused to let her character live out her natural life:

> Quand il s'est rendu compte qu'il avait créé une femme si forte, si libre, si indépendante, l'homme en lui a tremblé pour sa suprématie. Je risquais de bouleverser l'ordre des choses. Et pour me couler dans sa vision misogyne du monde, il m'a pliée en quatre et m'a rompu l'échine. Puis il m'a mis en bouche, à moi qui fus douée d'un si splendide franc-parler, le discours le plus plat, insipide et moralisateur de la littérature universelle. (100–1)[37]

The Shakespearean Katherine's final speech is problematic for contemporary audiences precisely because the gender norms it espouses have not passed the test of time, such as the wife placing her hand under her husband's foot, a ritual removed from the Book of Common Prayer in 1549 and thus already forty years outdated at the time of the play (Boose 182–3). As Maillet's Shrew points out, this discursive shift between dramatic action and religious ordinance is possibly the most awkward theatrical moment in the Shakespearean canon because the socially constructed norms do not correspond to what the audience expects based on past knowledge of the "life of the character." The jolt in the dramatic action signals a potential point of disruption of the early modern social hierarchy that Shakespeare fails to smooth over sufficiently, thereby highlighting the precise point in his play where the introduction of a variation in social norms could wreak the most havoc. Maillet's Shrew describes Shakespeare's unexpected turn in her character's behaviour as "pas un très bel exemple de son prétendu génie. S'il avait fait avec elle comme avec vous, Falstaff, Hamlet, ou Lear, s'il avait donné à la Mégère ses coudées franches et l'avait laissée vivre jusqu'au bout son personnage, vous pensez qu'elle se serait laissé apprivoiser, domestiquer, réduire à l'état de paillasson de son homme?" (99)[38]

In analysing not only her character's lot in life but also the dramatic and aesthetic qualities of the Shakespearean text's narrative continuity, Maillet's Shrew becomes a literary critic of her own author-god, employing the same critical techniques required of contemporary adapters to write back to the canon. She compares the well-roundedness of Shakespeare's Shylock and the two-sided balance of *The Merchant of Venice* to the sudden break in the action of *The Taming of the Shrew*: "au Juif au moins il a fourni l'occasion de se défendre. Pas à la Mégère" (97); "avec moi, il s'est révélé un piètre auteur. Car en apprivoisant la Mégère, il a raté sa pièce" (99).[39] The fictional Shakespeare agrees with this assessment of his early comedy compared to Shylock's later "Hath not a Jew eyes" speech: "Hé oui! brave Juif. Vous venez de prononcer le plus beau discours de toute mon oeuvre. Dans la bouche d'aucun autre n'ai-je mis paroles plus sublimes. C'est à vous que j'ai confié l'éloquent plaidoyer à la défense de tout un peuple, et vous vous plaignez de moi?" (97).[40] However, as with much of the rest of the play, Maillet's fictional Shakespeare provides a pat answer that does not get to the heart of the issue. Shylock's character defends himself while the Shrew cannot, but this superficial distinction between the two fails to account for the social construction of anti-Semitism. Rather than uniting the causes of gender and religious oppression by bringing the Shrew and Shylock together as allies, the play's conclusion is a cop-out that represents early modern gender norms as inherently "worse" than early modern religious and ethnic stereotypes, failing to acknowledge the constructedness of all norms, gender, religious, ethnic, or otherwise. By recognizing the social construction of one norm but not another, the adaptation does not acknowledge the potential for disruption of the supposed transhistoricity of such norms through strategic actions, such as Butler's suggestion of introducing a variation into the norm, and the potential alliances that can be forged by social activists of different oppressed groups.

This easy dismissal of Shylock's cause that results in a division between gendered and religious oppression typifies how *William S* smoothes over opportunities for a more in-depth criticism of Shakespeare's texts. In two other instances, Maillet's adapted characters perpetuate rather than challenge gendered readings. When a confused and slightly senile King Lear meets Juliet, he states, "Je n'ai engendré nulle Juliette. Un ange, deux démons, mais aucune Juliette" (60).[41] Upholding the misogynist representation of Goneril and Regan found in traditional criticism, the adaptation does not engage with contemporary feminist interpretations, such as Peter Brook's production depicting Goneril and Regan as victims rather than villains or the Women's Theatre Group and Elaine Feinstein's *Lear's Daughters* (1987), performed a few years earlier. Similarly, Falstaff perpetuates norms about female loquacity by introducing the Shrew to Lear as "la Mégère, Sire, la Commère, le Tonnerre..." (61).[42] While the description of Katherine as a "commère" links her to *The Merry Wives of Windsor* whose standard French title is *Les Joyeuses commères de Windsor*, this noun misrepresents Shakespeare's Shrew. According to *Le Petit Robert*, "commère" designates a "femme qui sait et colporte toutes les nouvelles," that is, a "bavard," and "commérage" signifies "bavardage indiscret" or "ragot" or "médisance."[43] Yet, Shakespeare's Katherine cannot be classified as a gossip in the same sense as the women in Thomas Middleton's *A Chaste Maid in Cheapside*. Maillet's Shrew attributes her verbosity to self-defence, not idle gossip, and she claims that by criticizing domestic violence her loquacity posed a threat to social order. The discursive inconsistency created by Falstaff's characterization of the Shrew as a merry gossip undermines her plea to be free from her chains, positing her loquacity as trivial and immoral rather than legitimate and necessary.

Despite these inconsistencies, *William S*'s overall attempt to challenge early modern gender norms and Shakespeare's transhistorical canonical authority achieves a certain success. By staging characters who literally talk back to an absent yet present author-god and who give voice to their ethnic, religious, and gender diversity, the adaptation endorses the Shrew's loquacity and proposes that a wide range of clamorous voices may be a strategy for challenging a dead author's authority.

While Maillet's Shrew is the most outspoken feminist in this corpus of adaptations, a cacophony of other voices emerged on the political and literary scene at the same time. The early 1990s were marked by the voices of aboriginals who spoke up more publicly than before during debates about the Meech Lake and Charlottetown Accords. Elijah Harper, a Cree from Red Sucker Lake First Nation in northern Manitoba, effectively killed the Meech Lake Accord by raising an eagle feather to signal his dissension from the unanimity needed for the Manitoba legislature to ratify the accord. In so doing, he stopped a constitutional amendment that would have brought Québec under the still unsigned 1982 Constitutional Act by recognizing it as a "distinct society." Working in consultation with Phil Fontaine, another Manitoban First Nations leader, Harper opposed the notion of "two founding nations" and the exclusion of First Nations from the negotiations leading to the Accord, but not special status for Québec per se (CBC Digital Archives). The Charlottetown Accord, which followed close on the heels of the failure of Meech, focused more strongly on aboriginal concerns, including them in section I.A.2.(1).(b), section 2, section 9, section 24, and section IV.A.41, which would have strengthened aboriginal rights under the Charter of Rights and Freedoms, guaranteed aboriginal representation in the Senate in addition to seats attributed to the provinces and territories, and guaranteed the right to self-government. While the Meech Lake Accord died in June 1990 because it was not approved by all the provinces, the Charlottetown Accord was subjected instead to a national referendum in October 1992. 54.3 per cent of Canadians voted against it overall. The attribution of "distinct society" status to Québec angered many English Canadians. Conversely, 56.7 per cent of Québécois voted against the Accord, which was perceived as not giving Québec enough powers. English Canadians' unwillingness to grant Québec even less powers in the Charlottetown Accord than those approved in the Meech Lake Accord led to a rise in support for sovereignty, the election of the Parti Québécois led by Jacques Parizeau in 1994, and the referendum on sovereignty in 1995, culminating in the narrow margin attributed to the "No" side and Parizeau's famous statement on "l'argent puis des votes ethniques," as discussed in chapter 1. In this sense, Meech and Charlottetown are part of a discursive trajectory in which diversity was often on the political forefront during the first half of the 1990s. Aboriginal rights received greater media attention in Québec in particular due to the Oka Crisis, which occurred less than a month after the failure of Meech. The Oka Crisis was a seventy-eight-day standoff between the Mohawk community of Kanesatake and the town of Oka, just outside Montréal, who called in the provincial police, the RCMP, and eventually the Canadian army to try to get the Mohawks to stop blocking the Mercier bridge and to tear down the barricade designed to stop construction of a golf course on their ancestral burial grounds. While this crisis was resolved peacefully, it was no longer possible for Québécois or English Canadians to ignore the concerns of aboriginals to the extent they had before.

Before Oka, the aboriginal theatre troupe Ondinnok had already produced two plays. Founded in Montréal in 1985 by Yves Sioui Durand, Catherine Joncas, and John Blondin, Ondinnok is the first and only professional aboriginal theatre group in Québec. The troupe focused primarily on using traditional aboriginal theatrical forms to discuss contemporary issues – preservation of myths and traditions, alcoholism, domestic violence – before later turning to Shakespearean adaptation as a vehicle for tackling these same issues. The group created five plays between 1985 and 1995 followed by five more between 1995 and 1999, a period it describes as its "théâtre de guérison" [healing theatre]. Ondinnok is a Huron word for a theatrical healing ritual that reveals the secret desire of the soul. Sioui Durand considers Ondinnok's work a "théâtre de résistance parce qu'il est une tentative de décolonisation culturelle" through the performance of "[des] cérémonie[s] pour se guérir de la violence et échapper à l'abîme du suicide."[44] In 1996–7, Ondinnok produced *Sakipitcikan*, which the company describes as the story of *Romeo and Juliet*:

> Le drame de Sakipitcikan est celui d'une histoire d'amour, celle de Roméo et Juliette de Shakespeare bien sur, mais surtout celle de cette histoire d'amour que nous avons tous souhaitée pour nous-même et qui, ici, nous est racontée sur fond de chaos, de promesses trahies, de déchirements familiaux et collectifs que fonde la perte des racines. Ce travail est fait par des gens pour qui cette histoire coule dans leurs veines.[45]

Although two families come between teenage lovers, this play does not demonstrate any direct connection to Shakespeare in the body of the text or even constitute a titular allusion to Shakespeare as I have defined such plays in chapter 2. Ondinnok's next, and more direct, engagement with Shakespeare occurs in 2004 with the play *Hamlet-le-Malécite*, a remarkable work of hybridity created by interpreting Shakespeare's text through the lens of aboriginal culture.

Written by Yves Sioui Durand and Jean-Frédéric Messier (the author of *Le* Making of *de Macbeth*), *Hamlet-le-Malécite* was produced in Montréal in June 2004. Directed by Messier, the performance was staged at American Can, an old warehouse with a spectacular view over the working-class Hochelaga-Maisonneuve district of Montréal where the climactic final scenes of the play are set even though the main action takes place in the fictional, rural village of Kinogamish.[46] In this parallel narrative adaptation, the main character, Dave, wants to play Hamlet but fails to see how he is actually living out Hamlet's story in his real-life relationships. Like Ondinnok's earlier healing theatre work, medicine and suicide are important themes in the play: while Dave calls out for his father to give him medicine (58), ironically the acts of this same father provoke Ophélie to commit suicide. Failing to escape from the fate of her Shakespearean namesake, Ophélie exposes how many First Nations communities are plagued by the problem of suicide, especially among youth.[47]

Hamlet-le-Malécite is primarily concerned with First Nations issues, not only those that typically make headlines for their shock value, such as suicide and alcoholism, but also problems that do not, such as racism between different aboriginal peoples. Sioui Durand points out that there exists "parmi les Amérindiens, un racisme interne face aux Malécites, nation méconnue originaire de la rivière Saint-Jean, au Nouveau-Brunswick" (qtd. in Lévesque, *Le Devoir*).[48] The Malécites (also known as Malecite or Maliseet in English), who are part of the Algonquian linguistic family, have a population of only 712 people in Québec (only two of whom live on reserve) and are located in the region near Rivière-du-Loup. The adaptation exposes this internal racism though the numerous insults brought to bear on the protagonist Dave. Because his father was "rien qu'un Malécite" (71), other aboriginals consider Dave "trop blanc pour jouer un indien" (10).[49]

The denigration of Malécite culture is also critiqued in the play through telling associations with Shakespeare. Claudius says that the name "Shakespeare" sounds so strange to his ears that it must forcibly be Malécite (42). Granted, this same Claudius is also ignorant as to who is French president "Jacques Chieriac" (with a pun on "chier" meaning "to shit") (17), takes Hamlet for "Femellette?," and considers all theatre to be "des projets d'homosexualité" by "des gars en collants" (30),[50] but his association of the Malécite people with a Shakespeare who is foreign, alien, and other to his own culture testifies nonetheless to a discrimination towards a fellow aboriginal people that he also qualifies as other. Laerte similarly evokes Shakespeare in order to underscore the otherness of the Malécites both in regard to the British canon and the local Québécois culture in which they are immersed. Taunting Dave's Shakespearean aspirations, Laerte suggests, "*Hamlet*? Dave, come on…

Tu pourrais peut-être commencer par *Les Belles-sœurs* en Attikamek, c'est à peu près la seule langue dans laquelle ça pas été traduit" (30).[51] Doubting Dave's abilities as a Malécite to perform Shakespeare, Laerte also points out that Dave's language of Attikamek is under erasure even by Québécois,[52] which is itself a minority language whose erasure has been slowed to some extent only by the cultural recognition it has acquired internationally through the work of Michel Tremblay.

As an adaptation of Shakespeare, *Hamlet-le-Malécite* works within a mise-en-abyme. Dave, who wants desperately to play Hamlet, is both the character Dave, the actor Dave Jenniss, and a Hamlet figure who does not recognize the parallels between his life and the plot of Shakespeare's play. Like Hamlet, he returns home from his studies when his mother Gertrude marries the new great chief Claudius following the murder of his absent father, the former chief Tony Bear. He falls in love with Ophélie whose brother Laerte has always harboured an incestuous desire for her. In his quest to learn what it means to be an aboriginal person and who can claim this identity, Dave meets paternal ghosts. The spirit of Tony Bear seems to manifest itself in Claudius's backyard in the form of a bear carcass whose rotting smell signals the decrepitude of the community's new beer-swilling, porn-obsessed chief. Dave also finds among his late father's belongings a video of Leonard Peltier, an aboriginal leader from North Dakota who has been wrongfully imprisoned since a tragic shoot-out in 1975 between the American Indian Movement (AIM) and the FBI. Dave's real father, Tony Bear, fails however to provide the spiritual leadership that Dave finds in Peltier's example of aboriginal resistance to colonialist violence. Although subversive, Tony Bear's strategy – to attempt to father 500 children in response to 500 years of colonization, and to resist assimilation through sheer force of numbers – was ultimately conceived by a "méchant malade" [real sicko] (70).

Hamlet-le-Malécite is thus marked throughout by a cynical dark humour that resists the colonization of aboriginal peoples by critiquing defeatism yet exposes the sombre reality underlying that defeatism. This double position of recognizing and seeking to overcome one's own colonized status while tacitly accepting one's place within the structures of power is embodied most forcefully in the character of Laerte. Laerte, who has a penchant for fine French wine but becomes sick from eating foie gras, is what Bhabha would call a colonial mimic man; he is "almost but not quite" right or white (or in this case *français de France*). Dave's desperate quest for his paternal origins leads him only to the disastrous discovery that his genealogy – and the history of consanguinity and incest of some aboriginal communities – is much darker than he could have imagined. Laerte, on the other hand, rejects as futile any such dwelling on the past. Laerte's cynical acceptance of the social construction of his identity by colonization harbours a critique but does not consume him to the point of immobility characteristic of Hamlet:

> Moi, j'ai jamais su c'était qui mon père. Pis je veux pas le savoir, i peut rien faire pour moi. Quand je veux savoir qui je suis, je sort [*sic*] mon portefeuille... *Laerte sort son portefeuille.* ...pis dedans y'a une carte que le gouvernement du Canada m'a donné [*sic*], avec ma photo dessus, qui dit que je fais partie des premières nations, ce qui me confère le même statut que les poteaux de téléphones et les parc [*sic*] nationaux. (78)[53]

While the dark realization that aboriginal peoples are little more than government property resounds with defeatism, Laerte refuses to be paralysed by the system and attempts to exploit it as best he can: "Moi, je payes pas de taxes pis je suis ben content" (78).[54]

Although Laerte's espousal of neoliberal values – such as his support for Dave's theatrical endeavour insofar as an evening cultural production will force tourists to reserve hotel rooms (33) – may construct his character as a figure for the audience to distrust, his attempts to take on capitalism and reap profits for other members of his community nonetheless resonate loudly in the context of recent political agreements between First Nations and the Québec government, in particular the *Paix des braves*.[55] In *Hamlet-le-Malécite*, Laerte wants to make his community rich by selling pure drinking water to France after having used "cultural autonomy" as an excuse to get rid of Hydro-Québec (52). Dave finds himself forced to concede that the future economic development of aboriginal communities is dependent on the exploitation of the environment:

> C'est vrai que les indiens d'aujourd'hui, on a compris: quand les colons sont arrivés, on leur a dit qu'on pouvait pas vendre notre territoire, fait qu'ils l'ont eu gratis. On s'est fait fourrer avec la terre, mais astheure check-nous ben faire la passe avec l'eau. On est lents, mais on comprend. (28)[56]

Although more resistant, Dave too must subscribe to some extent to Laerte's observation that since colonization has already ravaged the land and its peoples, the only way to survive and prosper is through a cautious manipulation of the system in which they find themselves.

Despite this sombre reality, Dave persists in his desire to play Hamlet, even abandoning Ophélie's dead body so that the opening night show may go on. Sioui Durand explains that "Dave veut jouer *Hamlet* et pour lui, c'est une question de vie et de mort. Il lutte en nous plaçant devant son déchirement; c'est sa façon de résister à l'écroulement d'un monde factice et c'est pour cela qu'il veut faire du théâtre" (program notes).[57] Faced with death, art is all that remains; without it, Dave has no reason to go on. Through Dave's final commitment to perform Hamlet after Ophélie's death, the adaptation suggests that art may indeed be a healing medicine against suicide and what Sioui Durand calls "l'asphyxie culturelle" [cultural asphyxiation]. Preoccupied with the question "c'est quoi que je suis?" [what am I?] (48), Dave seems to find his identity through theatrical art.

Sioui Durand and Messier's adaptation tackles, then, a complex range of issues. What constitutes aboriginal identity and who can claim it? What is Québécois identity and can aboriginals lay claim to it? Can multiple national and ethnic identities co-exist peacefully in a single individual (given that Dave's own mother accuses him of being too Québécois [21])? The play explores not only cultural questions, such as the nature and purpose of artistic creation, but also sociological questions, such as incest and suicide, as well as the history and economic impact of colonialism. *Hamlet-le-Malécite* thus exemplifies the enormous potential of contemporary adaptation to exploit Shakespeare's canonical authority in the most positive way – in order to draw attention to the pressing social issues of a marginalized community and to give voices to all those for whom theatre may become a survival strategy.

While Ondinnok has successfully appropriated Shakespeare to draw attention to aboriginal issues, *Hamlet-le-Malécite* is the exception rather than the rule in terms of aboriginal contributions to the larger corpus of Québécois adaptations of Shakespeare. Despite the increased focus on aboriginal concerns in the public sphere following Meech, Oka, and Charlottetown, aboriginal theatre exists separately from broad-scale Québécois theatre within this corpus. Following the second referendum – prompted by the individualism inherent to the failure of the collective dream – the emphasis on plurality can be seen in the *38* event (1996), a series of thirty-eight monologues about each of Shakespeare's plays written and performed individually by thirty-eight different playwrights or actors under the age of thirty-eight. Each monologue is a personal, even intimate, interpretation of a play by a particular individual with no intertextual or thematic exchange among the thirty-eight texts.[58] The monologues reflect larger social debates of the period, but only to the extent that the individual writer feels personally interpolated by them. For instance, "38 métiers 38 mégères" by Yvan Bienvenue, inspired by *The Taming of the Shrew*, quite unexpectedly disregards the character of Katherine completely; instead, his monologue is an apology for patriarchy through the lens of new masculinity as the character of a washed-up actor laments having to choose between playing the role of Petruchio against his conscience or losing his girlfriend because of his chronic "loserdom" (to employ a term coined by Richard Burt). Martin Doyon's "Richard III, pauvre chou,"[59] based on *Richard III*, also neglects the opportunity to explore the play's women characters and chooses instead to parody the "psycho-pop" discourse emerging at the time by analysing Richard's character in terms of his childhood development – complete with the politically correct technobabble of educators, psychologists, and juvenile rehabilitators – thereby recreating another 1990s emblem of individualism gone awry, the phenomenon of *l'enfant-roi* (the spoiled child-king, now known as the Millennial generation). Of the thirty-eight authors, none is aboriginal. Only one text references queerness, yet it does so from a self-loathing perspective. The *38* event embodies plurality, but it does not embrace pluralism, multiculturalism, or diversity. The texts are highly individualist, several of them side-stepping the assigned source text and focusing instead on the author's struggle to understand or feel inspired by Shakespeare.[60] Many monologues are thus typical of a post-referendum move away from the collective nation to which everyone belongs to the navel-gazing typical of individualism. Two other plays from this post-referendum period, however – *Dave veut jouer Richard III* (2001) by Alexis Martin, in which an actor with cerebral palsy plays Richard III,[61] and *Sous l'empire de Iago* (2002) by Kadar Mansour, in which the ghosts of Othello and Desdemona return for revenge on an "imperialist" Iago – do, unlike the *38* event, attempt to generate recognition of Québec's social "others."

The dip in the support for sovereignty following the second referendum was only temporary. By the next decade it became clear that support for sovereignty, which has hovered at a level similar to that before the 1995 referendum campaign was launched, has remained relatively consistent.[62] The inseparability of nationalism from Québécois adaptations of Shakespeare becomes evident when such sentiment returns forcefully in 2002 with *Henry. Octobre. 1970.*, Madd Harold and Anthony Kokx's bilingual adaptation of *Henry V* transposed into the context of Québec's 1970 October Crisis – a national drama that began on 5 October with the kidnapping of British Trade Commissioner James Cross by the Libération cell of the Front de Libération du Québec and lasted until 28 December when the members of the Chénier cell, who had kidnapped Québec Minister of Labour Pierre Laporte on 10 October, were found and arrested. Like *William S*, the play is invested in subverting the authority of a man who has acquired god-like sociocultural status, not Shakespeare but rather Pierre Elliott Trudeau, prime minister of Canada from 1968 to 1979 and from 1980 to 1984. Harold and Kokx appropriate Shakespeare's version of the fifteenth-century British invasion of France in order to highlight the anti-democratic nature of the Canadian government's military occupation of Québec and Trudeau's invocation of the War Measures Act in peacetime. By setting Shakespeare's play during the only twentieth-century military operation to take place on Canadian soil, Harold and Kokx draw attention to the persistence of the linguistic and sociocultural cleavage imported to Canada by both French and English European colonialism. Further, this setting subverts traditional readings of Shakespeare's text as a supposedly rousing elegy to English imperialism,[63] highlighting the moral uncertainty underlying Henry/Trudeau's actions and illustrating the legitimacy of the FLQ's socio-political concerns and Québec's aspirations for independence.[64] In this return to nationalist discourses reflective of the 1970s context, including traditional French-English cleavages, the adaptation forecloses an examination of the contributions of immigrants, queers, and women to the nation, except in the case of the latter two as victims of symbolic violence.

The play was directed largely in English by Harold with additional French text by Kokx. It employs Shakespeare's text so deftly as to appear initially to be composed mostly from original material, but upon close textual examination it becomes clear that, except for Kokx's FLQ scenes, most of the text does derive from Shakespeare. Rather than rewriting the source text, the adaptation achieves its originality through the redistribution of roles, often attributing the speeches of the English forces to the FLQ and its supporters, or speeches of the French army to the federalists, thereby distributing more evenly than Shakespeare the play's aggression to both sides of the conflict. Following the precedent set by Gurik's *Hamlet, prince du Québec*, the play contemporizes its characters within the political context of 1970. The character of René

Lévesque corresponds variously to Shakespeare's French King or the Dauphin. The French army is the FLQ, anonymously identified as P'tit Jeune, P'tit Grand, and P'tit Gros rather than the real names of Francis Simard, Bernard Lortie, Jacques Rose, and Paul Rose who made up the Chénier cell that kidnapped Laporte. Katherine, Shakespeare's French princess, is a student protester. The English noblemen are Québec Premier Robert Bourassa, a minister from Ontario, and a minister from Alberta. The central character of Henry V, simply named "Prime Minister" in the performance program and "Henry" in the play script, is never directly referred to as Pierre Trudeau despite being undeniably portrayed onstage as such, complete with a red rose in his lapel and his famous dancing twirl.

Five significant additions further contextualize the play geographically and historically: (1) an abridged reading of the FLQ manifesto in English translation; (2) Michèle Lalonde's poem "Speak White," first read at the *Nuit de la poésie* on 27 March 1970 in Montréal; (3) scenes recreating the hostage situation, including an English translation of the letter Laporte wrote to Bourassa on 11 October begging him to save his life for his family's sake; (4) video projections on the theatre's upstage wall of black-and-white newsreel footage of the October Crisis, including images of police finding Laporte's body in the trunk of a car near the Saint-Hubert military base and the long police-escorted drive from downtown Montréal to Dorval airport taken by the dynamite-rigged kidnappers of James Cross who flew to Cuba in exchange for his release; and (5) live streaming video projections recreating parts of Trudeau's speech on national television on 16 October informing the population that War Measures had been declared at 4:00 am that morning, as well as a nearly exact recreation of the six-minute-long conversation between a reporter and Trudeau on the steps of Parliament on the morning of 13 October that concluded with Trudeau's famous "Just watch me" statement.

The issue at the heart of the FLQ manifesto, class equality across linguistic lines, opens the play, thus situating the adaptation in socio-political terms and connecting it intertextually to the neo-Marxism underlying Gurik's *Hamlet*. The audience is introduced to Mafoie and Majoie (who later corresponds to Shakespeare's Montjoy as the French messenger to Henry), two francophone janitors disillusioned with the current political state of affairs. Alone together, they employ homophobic insults to describe Trudeau and Bourassa as loud-mouthed but ultimately weak, effeminate politicians who, unlike the FLQ, do nothing to enact social change. As the francophone janitors sweep silently the corridors of power along the margins of the stage, Henry/Trudeau and his cabinet take centre stage and make important political decisions while ignoring protests uttered by Bourassa in a disempowered English with a clumsy accent. By the time a messenger arrives to read the FLQ manifesto to Henry/Trudeau, the audience has had the opportunity to witness first-hand that the manifesto's frequent references to the impoverished, lower-class, francophone workers of Québec are not simply rhetorical flourishes or unreasonable pleas for sympathy; rather, the FLQ demands are poignantly validated by the image of the slow, steady sweeping of the janitors whose blue working-class overalls contrast sharply with Henry/Trudeau's elegant business suit. Although the play reduces considerably the length of the FLQ manifesto, which took eleven minutes when read by Gaétan Montreuil on all media outlets on 8 October 1970, its central argument nonetheless pervades the rest of the play: the FLQ does not consider itself to be a terrorist group; its principal concern is to incite the government to instil social reforms that would efface the inequality enjoyed by privileged anglophones from Westmount profiting on the backs of francophone workers.

This neo-Marxist discourse is reiterated later in the student protest scene. The protest ties together the neo-Marxism of the FLQ manifesto, the language issues that provoked the McGill Français protests (and eventually led to equal rights for both francophone and anglophone students), and the explosion of arrests without warrants that followed the proclamation of the War Measures Act and its suspension of the Canadian Bill of Rights. The scene begins with Lévesque proclaiming to a crowd of students, "Thus come the English with full power upon us,/ And more than carefully it us concerns/To answer honourably in our defenses" (17, 2.4.1–3).[65] This initial uprising is followed by the arrival of a messenger with Laporte's letter to Bourassa pleading for Bourassa to negotiate with the FLQ, then an onstage recreation of Trudeau's declaration of the War Measures Act using a live video feed projected in real time onto the upstage wall of the theatre. Immediately after this historical declaration, the camera zooms from a wide shot to just Henry/Trudeau's face as he recites Henry's "Once more unto the breach, dear friends" speech (21, 3.1.1–34); however, Henry/Trudeau speaks aloud only the first and last lines of the monologue, mouthing the rest silently, while Lévesque stands in front of the video projection and simultaneously delivers aloud the same speech in French. Lévesque's speech rouses the students, but the French leader is overshadowed by the wide-eyed, obsessed look of Henry/Trudeau's giant head behind him which creates an image chillingly evocative of George Orwell's Big Brother in *Nineteen Eighty-Four*. This rapid sequence of events sparks the scene's concluding rally that consists principally of Katherine waving a Québec flag and passionately reciting Lalonde's "Speak White" to a crowd of enthusiastic students.

Lalonde's "Speak White" integrates seamlessly into the text of *Henry. Octobre. 1970.* because it both alludes to Shakespeare and articulates the same socio-political and economic concerns as the FLQ manifesto. Twice the poem evokes Shakespeare as the epitome of "proper" English. First, the image of Shakespeare's English opens the poem ironically as a tongue-in-cheek critique of linguistic and cultural imperialism:

> Speak white
> il est si beau de vous entendre
> parler de Paradise Lost
> ou du profil gracieux et anonyme qui tremble dans les sonnets de
> Shakespeare. (1–4)[66]

Shakespeare is later associated in the poem with the atrocities of war:

> dans la langue douce de Shakespeare
> avec l'accent de Longfellow
> parlez un français pur et atrocement blanc
> comme au Viêt-Nam au Congo (73–6)[67]

While, as a text with a strong emphasis on linguistic and cultural imperialism, "Speak White" articulates a protectionist discourse about the Québécois language, the protest scene as a whole foregrounds the presence among the students of an Italian immigrant who does not speak English but rather the language of the francophone majority and who embraces the nationalist and neo-Marxist struggles of his *pure laine* friends. Named Rodolpho in the script, the Italian immigrant may be a wink to the audience indicating that although the scene is set in the context of 1970 when the poem "Speak White" was a legitimate response to the widespread use of English, especially in the workplace, a more relevant poem in 2002 might be Italian author Marco Micone's "Speak What" about the need for *pure laine* nationalists to be more welcoming of immigrants, especially *enfants de la loi 101* [children of Bill 101] who have integrated into the francophone majority and are willing to join the sovereignist movement.[68] Identified by a heavy accent that makes him stand out as he shouts protests alongside his *pure laine* companions, Rodolpho has only one designated line in the script – "Apaise ton courroux!" which means "Calm your wrath!" (23) – but this brief interjection characterizes him as a potential peacemaker. Rodolpho's role as a builder of bridges ties him to Micone's "Speak What" which validates Québec's protectionist approach to language in the face of assimilation ("nous dirons notre trépas avec vos mots/pour que vous ne mouriez pas") and ends with a plea for immigrants to be included in the sovereignist project ("nous sommes cent peuples venus de loin/ pour vous dire que vous n'êtes pas seuls").[69]

In addition to focusing on the linguistic assimilation of the Québécois people in a 1970s context, "Speak White" also emphasizes the need to "raconter/une vie de peuple-concierge" (58–9),[70] an image that ties the poem to Mafoie and Majoie's janitorial duties. Like the FLQ manifesto, "Speak White" is a rallying cry to the effect of "workers of Québec unite!":

mais quand vous really speak white
quand vous get down to brass tacks
pour parler du gracious living
et parler du standard de vie
et de la Grande Société
un peu plus fort alors speak white
haussez vos voix de contremaîtres
nous sommes un peu durs d'oreille
nous vivons trop près des machines
et n'entendons que notre souffle au-dessus des outils (23–32)[71]

By linking the neo-Marxist discourse of the FLQ manifesto to Lalonde's famous poem, the play de-terrorizes the FLQ. Rather than being portrayed as radical terrorists, as is often the case in English Canadian historical accounts, they appear as one facet of a larger social movement, also comprised of well-educated students and respected poets, that represents the views of a large portion of Québec's francophone population.

The protest scene also alludes to historical events preceding and during the October Crisis. By staging "Speak White" as a protest, the play recalls the McGill Français demonstration of 28 March 1969 as well as the protest in Québec City on 31 October 1969 against the government's Bill 63 linguistic policy. Katherine's onstage arrest at the end of the next scene evokes Montréal Mayor Jean Drapeau's anti-demonstration legislation of 12 November 1969 that resulted in a series of violent arrests. The subsequent scene in which Katherine and all the students are shown in jail recreates the 500 arrests without warrants that took place in the days and weeks following Trudeau's invocation of the War Measures Act despite a lack of "conclusive evidence that war, invasion, or insurrection, real or apprehended exists and has existed for any period of time therein stated, and of its continuance."[72] As a result of the suspension of civil liberties, including habeas corpus, approximately 500 people – many poets and artists, including Pauline Julien, Gérald Godin, Michel Garneau, Gaston Miron, and Denise Boucher, as well as political activists – were arrested without warrants in the following days and weeks, the first 450 persons being taken in a mass operation during the night of 16 October 1970. The armed soldier standing watch over the prisoners from the corner of the stage is a perfect copy of those seen patrolling the streets of Montréal in news clips of the period that later appear along with documentary footage of army trucks and helicopters in the funeral scene video projections.

The professionalism of the well-trained soldier who refuses to flinch in response to Katherine's aggressive assertion that he is a "con" [idiot] is contrasted with the bumbling confusion that pervades the FLQ hostage scenes. In most respects, *Henry. Octobre. 1970.* follows closely the details provided by Francis Simard in *Pour en finir avec Octobre*, his personal account of events leading up to, during, and after the October Crisis. This is the only public account by someone who was actually present during these events since there was no need for testimony at trial because the Chénier cell pleaded "responsible" in court (rather than "guilty"). Simard's narrative, published in 1982 about the same time he was released from prison, was adapted into Pierre Falardeau's 1994 film *Octobre*. The play follows Simard's and Falardeau's demystification of the events by giving the audience a privileged peek into the *huis clos*. The audience witnesses a relatively accurate dramatization of Simard's account of the tense waiting period after the kidnapping until the moment of Laporte's death. Through the characters of P'tit Gros, P'tit Grand, and P'tit Jeune, *Henry. Octobre. 1970.* emphasizes that the FLQ were young men holed up in a house with little food for Laporte or themselves and with no plan for what to do with Laporte after kidnapping him.

The FLQ's youth and ineptitude is comically portrayed through the difficult challenge of writing a ransom note that requires a group effort to complete. This task echoes the collective writing of the FLQ manifesto;

however, the adaptation diverges from real-life accounts to heighten the comic effect. Whereas the FLQ manifesto testifies to the young men's education through its proper use of grammar and its skilful use of rhetorical convention to appeal to the emotions of the working-class population who would hear it broadcast on radio and television, the play's ransom note falls far short of this eloquence. The two attempts to write the communiqué become comic releases of the onstage tension. P'tit Gros's attempt ironically gives voice to the "langue à jurons/[...] pas très propre" mocked by Lalonde (64–5):[73]

> Communiqué.
> À Robert Bourassa.
> Ont [*sic*] a Pierre Laporte.
> Va te faire foutre par une vielle [*sic*] marmotte.
> Va chier.
> On t'aime pas.
> Tu sent [*sic*] la crotte.
> De chaval.
> Dans une grotte.
> De vielle [*sic*] marmotte? [...]
> Merci beaucoup, P'tit Gros, P'tit Grand et P'tit Jeune.
> Et Pierre Laporte.
> Front de Libération du Québec.
> Nous vaincrons! Nous vaincrons! (12)[74]

P'tit Grand's subsequent attempt is even less articulate and borders on the absurd:

> Communiqué.
> Robert,
> C'est nous autres.
> Devine qui?
> Pas capable?
> Essaye don't [*sic*]?
> Peur?
> Peureux?
> Va chier, salté [*sic*].
> Nous vaincrons! Nous vaincrons! (15)[75]

Important in making the hostage situation more palatable for the audience, the comedic manifesto-writing episodes also heighten the contrast between the FLQ and the powerful figures of political authority. While Henry/Trudeau and even the neocolonial Bourassa both master Shakespeare's English and articulate some of the most eloquent monologues in his canon, the FLQ scenes are written almost exclusively in a *joual* that emphasizes their working-class background. The politicians are estranged from their Québécois roots and from the linguistic and cultural discourses through which the common people express their reality.

There is one exception to the *joual*-only rule in the FLQ scenes. For the final speech of their final scene, P'tit Jeune appropriates Henry V's famous St Crispian Day speech (40, 4.3.18–67). Delivered in French, the speech is neither Shakespeare's language nor that of the FLQ but transformed into a case of cultural hybridity typical of postcolonial appropriation. No longer are fair cousin Westmorland and the English army encouraged to fight for the honour of being remembered each year at the feast of St Crispian; instead, P'tit Jeune spurs on his two lone companions "to make a stand" (the only English words inserted into the speech) so that tomorrow may finally be declared "la Journée de la Liberté" [the Day of Freedom] (40). *Henry. Octobre. 1970.* thus constitutes a discursive shift from Gurik's *Hamlet, prince du Québec*. Rather than emphasizing Québec's perpetual inability to choose its destiny and *passer à l'action*, as Gurik's adaptation implies, *Henry. Octobre. 1970.* revolves around the FLQ's choice to move from deliberation to action. By associating that decisive action with a speech pronounced on the eve of victory, the adaptation constructs the FLQ's stand as an important moment necessary to win the struggle for independence. To the end of Shakespeare's rousing testimony to the soldiers' strength and courage, the adaptation adds a passionate cry of "Vive le Québec; vive le Québec libre!" (40). At this moment, the emotion of the speech culminates in P'tit Jeune's strangulation of Laporte using a Québec flag. Dramatically, this is the strongest moment of the play, but it is not achieved without compromising an important detail from the historical account. Laporte attempted to escape by jumping through a window, but he was unsuccessful because, despite being free from his handcuffs, in his panic he did not remove his blindfold and got stuck in the broken window. He severely cut his wrists and chest on the broken glass, and the ensuing panic caused by this unexpected turn of events precipitated his unpremeditated murder. Unable to stop his bleeding but unwilling to risk leaving the house and being apprehended while taking him to a hospital, the FLQ members strangled Laporte with the chain he was wearing around his neck; it was a perverse, spontaneous *coup de grace.* The governmental inquest ruled his death accidental. In omitting this sequence of events, the adaptation constructs Laporte's death as a well-planned act of liberation rather than a confused act of desperation.

The victorious movement towards national liberation suggested by the association of Laporte's death with Henry V's St Crispian's day speech is undercut by the adaptation's treatment of gender and sexuality. Its recurring undercurrent of homophobia – including Henry/Trudeau's gay pornography magazine and staging Shakespeare's camp scene in a gay sauna – could be interpreted as a representation of what Schwartzwald calls the "false feminine" found in nationalist discourses of colonized peoples. Henry/Trudeau is called a "tapette" (2), a "pansy" (16), and a "queer" (17), and Bourassa is described as a "momoune" who "fait yainque tèté [*sic*] la queue du Boss" (2, 16),[76] insults that may derive from a slur calling Trudeau a "tapette" in the historical FLQ manifesto or from the homoeroticism in Shakespeare's play between Henry V and his former bedfellow Lord Scroop (2.2.8–11).[77] Inappropriate in 2002, these homophobic incursions contextualize the play more convincingly in 1970 when such insults went largely unchallenged.[78] Since all of the play's homophobic epithets are directed at the federalists to convey scorn, they represent yet another case of the fear of federasty. Given that the popular discourse of impoverished francophone workers often reflected the sentiment of "on s'est fait fourrer,"[79] it is not surprising that they would redirect that demeaning, sexualized violence towards the privileged francophone politicians whom they considered to be *compradors* or sold-out traitors. In the play's 1970 context, the use of homophobic verbal violence constitutes the only means by which disempowered workers could strike back against those who wielded power over the conditions governing their daily lives, short of going on strike. In its 2002 context, however, this fear of federasty undercuts the adaptation's nationalist discourse since it could alienate queer audience members who otherwise would support the sovereignist cause. Federasty's association of queerness with treason no longer resonates for a contemporary audience and therefore is not an effective means of condemning the federalist politicians for abandoning their people.

The scene entitled "Dream" does, however, establish Henry/Trudeau's guilt as a traitor by reversing Henry V's charges against the traitors Cambridge, Scroop, and Grey. Henry/Trudeau is implicated for betraying his nation and for the impending death of Laporte which becomes inevitable once Henry/Trudeau declares War Measures and states his refusal to negotiate with the FLQ. While Shakespeare's Henry's reputation remains untarnished as the victim who offers mercy before he ensnares the traitors with their own words, Henry/Trudeau is far from being, as King Lear claims to be, "a man/More sinned against than sinning" (3.2.59–60), and he becomes the accused rather than the accuser. Lévesque usurps the role of Shakespeare's Henry V, telling Henry/Trudeau:

> You must not dare, for shame, to talk of reason,
> For your own reasons turn in your bosom,
> As dogs upon their masters, worrying you. –
> See you, my princes and my noble peers,
> This English monster! (13–14, 2.2.81–5)

Lévesque's appropriation of these lines is effective because Henry/Trudeau's subsequent announcement of War Measures and his refusal to negotiate with the FLQ (a speech quoted from historical accounts) hinges rhetorically on the notion of "reason" when he pre-emptively absolves himself from criticism by arguing that to blame the federal government as responsible in any way for the outcome of events would be a "most twisted form of logic" (20). At the end of the dream scene, however, despite his brave public persona, Henry/Trudeau's inner demons haunt him. After Lévesque's final accusation, "You have conspired against our sovereign state" (14, 2.2.167), Henry/Trudeau wilts like a sacrificial lamb and discovers that he has lost his tongue, which he pulls from his pocket in a small glass bottle.

Lévesque's appropriation of Henry V's words is not always accusatory. At the end of the gay sauna/camp scene, after Henry/Trudeau has reflected on the burden borne by leaders, Lévesque returns onstage alone to pray:

> O God of battles! steel my people's hearts;
> Possess them not with fear; take from them now
> The sense of reckoning, if the opposed numbers
> Pluck their hearts from them. Not to-day, O Lord,
> O, not to-day, think not upon the fault. (39, 4.1.286–90)

In Shakespeare, the fault is not that of Henry V but that of his father, Henry IV, whose usurpation of the throne leads to the murder of Richard II. When Lévesque usurps Henry's role, he seeks penitence, bearing like a true leader the "fault" of his FLQ subjects (with whom he had no historical association) in contrast to Henry/Trudeau's explicit rejection of responsibility. The soliloquy figures Lévesque as a more honest leader who is in tune with the concerns of his people and who exhibits a genuine care for their emotional and moral well-being.

A final role reversal that contributes to the adaptation's sympathetic treatment of the French over the English is the transfer of arrogant self-obsession from the French King and his forces to the anglophone Ministers from Ontario and Alberta. While in Shakespeare's play the Constable of France, Orleans, and the Dauphin boast about their superior armour and horses, in the adaptation Minister Ontario brags to Minister Alberta about his suit and chauffeured car while sitting on a toilet flipping through Henry/Trudeau's gay pornography magazine (31, 3.7.1–68). This image of excessive indulgence not only ridicules the anglophone politicians but also lends weight to the FLQ claim that many anglophones, and some colonized Québécois mimic men, are living in luxury while the majority of francophone workers suffer in poverty.

Minister Alberta returns in the adaptation's final scene which perverts Shakespeare's heteronormative promise of rebirth and renewal symbolized by Katherine's marriage to Henry V in order to expose the harshness of prison and Canada's unceasing domination of Québec. The last prison scene between Minister Alberta and Katherine evokes Michel Brault's 1974 film *Les Ordres*, a black-and-white docufiction of the October Crisis from the perspective of a few of the 500 ordinary Montréalais who were arrested and imprisoned for months without trial, over 90 per cent of whom were eventually released without explanation and without being charged (Fournier 487). The most moving scene in the film focuses on the character of Richard Lavoie, a "chômeur" [unemployed man] played by Claude Gauthier, who is dragged down to the prison basement in the middle of the night to be executed without charges or trial entirely at the behest of the guards. He is taken to an empty room, told to face the wall, and shot execution style. Hearing the click of the trigger, he falls to the ground – not in death but having fainted in sheer terror – and he wakes up in his cell later as a man broken by the torture of being executed with a gun that he did not know contained only blanks. Brault's portrayal of the torture of October Crisis prisoners is mirrored in *Henry. Octobre. 1970.* when what begins as a courting scene ends with the violent rape of Katherine. The audience hears Katherine's wailing screams during the offstage rape and then sees her return onstage in a torn shirt, fall down writhing and convulsing her hips sexually to simulate the violation, and then curl up pitifully in a fetal position.

The intertextuality of this scene is multilayered. Beyond Brault's film, the scene also recalls Henry's threats in both versions of the play to subject the French's "pure maidens" to "hot and forcing violation" and to "[d]efile the locks of [their] shrill-shrieking daughters" (26, 3.3.20–1, 3.3.35). In Shakespeare these threats do not materialize, but here their actualization symbolizes the rape of Québec by Ottawa.[80] Minister Alberta's ravishing of Katherine's body metaphorically recreates the penetration of Montréal by the truckloads of soldiers and helicopters of the federal Armed Forces, images the audience sees during Laporte's funeral. Although these forces were officially sent in response to a request by Bourassa and Montréal Mayor Drapeau, later evidence has proven that the request itself was orchestrated by Trudeau and the federal government in order to make sending the army into the streets of Montréal appear as aid to a beleaguered Québec government rather than an invasion. Tommy Douglas, the leader of the federal New Democratic Party (NDP) and a rare dissenting voice in Parliament, said at the time that by sending in the army the federal government was "using a sledgehammer to crack a peanut." Finally, the prison rape scene is connected to the sense of futility and the ongoing domination of Québec by Canada that marks the end of Michel Tremblay's *Les Belles-Sœurs*, a play that concludes with "O Canada" as an indication of the protagonist's defeat and the destruction of her dreams of grandeur. With Katherine still crying on the floor, *Henry. Octobre. 1970.* ends with the playing of "O Canada" and the video projection of a test pattern – like that aired nightly at the end of its programing by CBC, the bastion of English Canadian culture. Originally composed as the national anthem of French Canadians for Saint-Jean-Baptiste Day before being appropriated by English Canada, for some Québécois "O Canada" represents English Canadian cultural theft. The music is without lyrics, so it is impossible to determine whether it is intended for anglophones or francophones, but, taken in conjunction with Katherine's rape, "O Canada" signals Canada's conquest of Québec.

Henry. Octobre. 1970., then, appropriates the nationalism inherent in Shakespeare's work in order to legitimize, ironically, the nationalist struggle of a people descended from the antagonists of the source text.

The play's sympathetic treatment of the FLQ's dilemma of weighing individual human life against collective national freedom, its endorsement of the FLQ's socio-political concerns through the janitors and students, its Machiavellian portrayal of Henry/Trudeau, its images of helicopters and armed soldiers invading the streets of Montréal, and the rape of Katherine all combine to undermine the rousing elegy to English imperialism upheld by pro-Henry readings of Shakespeare's play. Instead, the adaptation illustrates the ethical problems inherent in the Canadian federal government's invocation of the War Measures Act without proof of a real or apprehended danger to the general populace. In effect, *Henry. Octobre. 1970.* suggests that Henry/Trudeau's invocation of the War Measures Act constituted a rape of the Québec nation, and it legitimizes Québécois' aspirations of national liberation. However, the adaptation also replicates 1970s nationalist discourses that problematically construct the nation monolithically with minimal attention to the potential contributions of women, queers, and immigrants.

As one of the most recent adaptations in this corpus, *Henry. Octobre. 1970.* demonstrates a return to a more politicized approach to Shakespearean adaptation in Québec, but one in which the politics are focused more strongly on the national question than on the recognition of gendered or ethnic others. While adaptations from the 1990s onward are marked by a plurality of voices and perspectives, few adaptations are overtly feminist or contain positive representations of queerness, and aboriginals and immigrants show up in the corpus only briefly. Still unresolved, the national question remains an inescapable driving force within these adaptations. In the next chapter, I will lay out both the practical and theoretical reasons why the national question continues to dominate issues of gender and sexuality in this corpus, even after the turn towards plurality ushered in by the political events of the 1990s, and how pluralism in Québec is governed by the principle of interculturalism rather than multiculturalism as it is in English Canada.

Conclusion

Québec v. Canada: Interculturalism and the Politics of Recognition

The Québec nation has a recognition problem; so do women. Since they are devalued social groups that constitute a statistical majority but occupy a minority status, one would expect to find evidence of solidarity in each group's struggle for social justice. While the 1970s feminist slogan "Pas de Québec libre sans libération des femmes! Pas de femmes libres sans libération du Québec!" suggests that inter-group solidarity is not just desirable but required if each is to achieve its goals, these ideals have yet to materialize as a political reality. As a corpus of literature, Québécois adaptations of Shakespeare embody this solidarity even less. In the readings provided in the previous four chapters, and across the whole corpus catalogued in the appendix, Québécois adaptations of Shakespeare reveal themselves to be much more concerned with the national question than with issues of gender and sexuality. Of the thirty-seven adaptations I have uncovered, ten deal extensively with nation while eight deal extensively with gender (of which two address both) and twenty-one deal with neither. Of the sixteen that deal with either nation or gender, 63 per cent address the former while 50 per cent examine the latter.[1] Before the 1989 Montréal Massacre, the ratio is even more striking: 85 per cent of the plays deal extensively with the national question while only 28 per cent of these plays deal extensively with gender and sexuality. Among the eight plays that do deal with gender and sexuality, only three strike me as progressively feminist or queer on gender issues.[2] In Québécois adaptations of Shakespeare, nation trumps gender.

Québécois adaptations are thus not Canadian adaptations of Shakespeare. Québécois Shakespeares prioritize the national question whereas Canadian Shakespeares of the past fifty years embrace a diversity of topics, in keeping with the celebration of "diversity" underlying English Canadian multiculturalism – which may itself be considered part of Canada's political nation-building strategy but which also allows feminist and a wider range of Shakespearean adaptations to flourish.[3] By using Shakespeare to work through various stages of national(ist) identity in what sovereignists call *la longue marche vers le pays*,[4] Québécois adapters challenge the fundamental principle underlying modern Canadian nationhood: the belief in one multicultural nation *a mari usque ad mare* united in all of its diversity. In articulating a nationalist, and arguably sovereignist, discourse through the British Bard who has played such a pivotal role in the evolution of British North America into modern Canada, Québécois adapters undercut the success of that particular colonial project and expose its present day composition as a false construct, a case of wishful thinking in which unity in diversity has not been achieved and the age-old divide of "two founding nations" that was prominent at Confederation remains prevalent today.

Daniel Fischlin confirms that Canadian national identity may be nothing more than a false construct when he writes that "[n]ational identity is an imaginary entity, an ideality based on the simultaneous production and eradication of difference through the filter of communal values, in this case, putatively embedded in Shakespeare and the Shakespeare effect" ("Nation" 327). For Fischlin, Canadians have no essential national identity other than that which they socially construct through cultural production, of which Shakespearean adaptation is an important part. This tradition of adaptation "links the iconicity of Shakespeare with the symbolic destiny, however illusory, of nation" (321). However, I would argue that national identity is not imaginary even if the community constituting the nation is imagined. Fischlin agrees with Benedict Anderson that nations are imagined communities, but I would contend that the imaginary composition of that community does not invalidate or render illusory the subjective experience of a national identity by the community's individual citizens. While, as Fischlin observes, the very definition of "communal" values obviously depends on the eradication of difference within the imagined community, in Québec these communal values are not embedded in Shakespeare as they are in English Canada because Québec does not have the same colonial relationship to the Bard, and its citizens possess a collective, subjective, settler/invader experience very different from that of English Canadians. Not being as closely entangled with Shakespeare as

English Canadian settler/invader subjects, Québécois playwrights are freer to manipulate the effect produced by Shakespeare's authority in their call for national freedom.

Fischlin pursues this notion of the nation as a false construct in his claim that "[n]ation assumes assimilation into the authentic bosom of an originary identity, however spurious or illusory such an idea may be" (326). This assertion holds true in that Québécois nationalism claims an originary identity (be it derived from France, l'Île d'Orléans, or the Conquest), but the rest of his argument does not apply to Québec when he adds:

> The authentic, because it is always predicated on a belatedly assimilative effect, signifies an identity crisis by way of a dialectic that presumes and requires the inauthentic (that which is assimilated) in order to give it meaning. Shakespeare's assimilation by state (read "authentic") culture is used as a bulwark against incursions in state culture by its "inauthentic," nomadic margins. (326)

In Québec, the "inauthentic" (or the bastard, in Ronfard's terms) is precisely what characterizes Shakespearean adaptation – the "inauthentic" nation which is not yet a state, and especially the inauthentic, undervalued class, since the use of *joual* inscribes the adapted Shakespearean characters as working class. Inauthentic Québécois adaptations reverse Fischlin's Canadian paradigm and make that which is Québécois a marginal incursion into "authentic" Shakespearean culture.

Unlike Canada, whose history of "Shakespearean adaptation is coincident with its emergence as a nation-state" (321), Québec is a state-less nation whose history of Shakespearean adaptation precedes this political emergence. Shakespearean adaptation in Québec does not coincide with the ascension to full political statehood, although it does coincide with the emergence of renewed and more fervent nationalism because nationalist playwrights may find in Shakespeare's authority validation for their cause – provided they negotiate carefully the power relations inherent in their collaboration with him and avoid drowning out their own voices by the clamour with which Shakespearean authority resounds. Garneau's *Macbeth* typifies this search for balance between manipulating the power of Shakespearean authority and succumbing to it – as the long title of his play suggests, beginning with *"de William Shakespeare"* but ending forcefully with *"Traduit en québécois."* In this case, Fischlin's claims about the nature of adaptation hold true:

"Adaptations work both sides of this coin, whether confirming a myth of authenticity and origin or interrogating such a position through alternative and revisionary definitions of authenticity" (326). Québécois adaptations confirm the authenticity of Shakespeare's authority by relying on his cultural power, but they interrogate the English colonialism that his canon of works helped promulgate.

Fischlin sums up his argument with the assertion that "adaptation questions the essentialist qualities associated with Shakespearean authority, canonicity, and cultural value. In short, adaptations serve multiple positionings with regard to national self-identity as mediated by a cultural icon like Shakespeare" (328). While it is true that Québécois adaptations question authority and canonicity (to the extent that a national group can question a literary canon which is not its own and in which it does not have the invested stakes of those who helped form it), Québécois adaptations do not serve multiple positions within Québécois national self-identity. There are no federalist adaptations of Shakespeare in Québec to construct a unified Canadian identity by anglo-Québécois,[5] and certainly not by franco-Québécois. Instead, Québécois adaptations are largely oriented in the same direction towards the creation and solidification of one national identity, of a sovereign people, which includes women, queers, aboriginals, and immigrants but who are expected in these plays to participate in an overarching national identity. Gender and ethno-religious difference are acknowledged and respected, but that diversity exists within a larger national identity.

In respect to this textually and socially constructed nation, Mark Fortier's astute observation about Canadian identity, which I would agree holds true in that case, does not, however, apply to Québec:

> [T]here is always something un-Canadian about being Canadian, that the from-elsewhere is part of being here. Shakespeare, therefore, is one manifestation of from elsewhere at work in Canada. As such, Canadians confront Shakespeare as the cultural undead, neither dead nor living, not a person but an other forming part of living personalities, if only as part of the sublime personality, the otherness of the past the remains of which reside here. Canadians too, in their specific ways, are the undead, although as *noir* subjects they may not always realize this. (342)

Fortier's underlying premise does not hold true in Québec where the notion of "from-elsewhere" did not consistently appear until after the 1995 referendum campaign, at which point it entered nationalist discourse as damage control after Jacques Parizeau's famous statement on "l'argent puis des votes ethniques" that was considered to be based on a definition of "nous" as *pure laine*.[6] After the referendum, the notion that Québec was *le pays de tous les Québécois* (the country of all Québécois, to borrow the title of a collection by Michel Sarra-Bournet) began to enter academic discourse, but a general mistrust prevailed regarding sovereignists' claims of openness to the inclusion of people of multiple ethnic origins within the national project. Only very recently has the concept of "from-elsewhere" entered public discourse with some popularity,[7] but the celebration of foreign origins was not in circulation at the time the majority of these Shakespearean adaptations were written to the same extent as in the rest of Canada.

The reason that "from-elsewhere" was not current in Québec public discourses is nationalism: Canadian nationalism (i.e., federalism) is disguised by the celebration of "multiculturalism" as a replacement for the discourse of "bilingualism and biculturalism," based on the notion of "two founding nations" (which ignores, of course, all the First Nations) that dominated public discourse until the reign of Pierre Elliott Trudeau.[8] After the 1980 referendum, it became apparent that one way to diminish Québec's claim as a founding nation, on which its claims for greater political autonomy were based, would be to multiply the number of national identities that compose Canada (and indeed many do outside of Québec, although the phenomenon is hardly as widespread as official discourse would have one believe and tends to be confined to the immigration of specific ethnic groups to specific geopolitical locations). Although the 1963 Laurendeau-Dunton Royal Commission on Bilingualism and Biculturalism led to the 1969 Official Languages Act which made Canada a bilingual nation, Trudeau steered the country away from biculturalism to multiculturalism, which was recognized in 1982 under section 27 of the Canadian Charter of Rights and Freedoms (which is part of the repatriated Constitution that Québec still has not signed) and further enshrined in 1988 in the Canadian Multiculturalism Act under Brian Mulroney. Despite these political attempts to reconceptualize Canadian identity as multicultural, the idea of "two founding nations" still pervades popular thought in Québec and until recently has overshadowed references to "from-elsewhere."[9] As Schwartzwald puts it, "Nationalist politicians and intellectuals in Quebec have long expressed hostility toward Canadian multiculturalism. They have seen in it a deliberate effort on the part of Trudeau-fashioned federalism to deny the national status of Quebec within Canada and to 'dilute' the status of *les anciens Canadiens* from a founding people to one ethnic group among many" ("Rush" 122).

Québécois nationalists, though, are not the only critics of Canadian multiculturalism. Even those with the most to gain from multiculturalism – immigrants from non-Western European countries, variously labelled as visible minorities or ethnic minorities among other terms – recognize that official multiculturalism may be nothing more than a political strategy intended to solve the English-French problem rather than a genuine philosophy of good will or true espousal of diversity.[10] In *The Dark Side of the Nation: Essays on Multiculturalism, Nationalism and Gender*, Himani Bannerji describes how multiculturalism is just a tool in English Canada's arsenal against Québécois nationalism. First, multiculturalism serves to obscure Canada's originary bilingualism and biculturalism; second, it serves to stake a claim on the supposed moral high ground:

> "Canada," with its primary inscriptions of "French" or "English," its colonialist and essentialist identity markers, cannot escape a fragmentary framework. Its imagined political geography simplifies into two primary and confrontational possessions, cultural typologies and dominant ideologies. Under the circumstances, all appeals to multiculturalism on the part of "Canada Outside Quebec" becomes no more than an extra weight on the "English" side. Its "difference-studded unity," its "multicultural mosaic," becomes an ideological sleight of hand pitted against Quebec's presumably greater cultural homogeneity. [...] That is why usually undesirable others, consisting of non-white peoples with their ethnic or traditional or underdeveloped cultures, are discursively inserted in the middle of a dialogue on hegemonic rivalry. The discourse of multiculturalism, as distinct from its administrative, practical relations and forms of ruling, serves as a culmination for the ideological construction of "Canada." This places us, on whose actual lives the ideology is evoked, in a peculiar situation. (95–6)

English Canada's espousal of multiculturalism relies on a superficial denial of a homogenous collective identity even as it implicitly acknowledges that same identity in opposition to Québec. Insofar as multiculturalism's duplicitous foundation is relatively apparent to those whose diversity it appropriates for less than noble purposes, it may be deemed a failure, thereby lending credibility to Québec's alternative approach to social diversity and the integration of immigrants.

Québec's approach to social diversity and integration is called "interculturalism." Seeking to integrate immigrants into Québec society, interculturalism exists midway on a spectrum ranging from Canadian multiculturalism (which values differentiation, multilingualism, and insertion into society) to French republicanism (which values dedifferentiation, unilingualism, and assimilation into a universal vision of French society). The Québécois model of interculturalism gives immigrants the liberty to preserve an affiliation with their native ethnic group; however, unlike Canadian multiculturalism which asserts that all cultures within Canada hold equal value and therefore should be promoted and treated equally, Québécois interculturalism insists upon adherence to a common civic culture, that of the francophone majority, with the intent of preventing ghettoization by making immigrants feel fully integrated into their adopted country.[11] The government of Liberal Premier Robert Bourassa adopted interculturalism as an official policy in 1990 in its "Énoncé de politique en matière d'immigration et d'intégration" which states that there is a "moral contract" between Québec as host society and particular cultural groups. Consequently, immigration and integration must be considered "indissociable." Three principles characterize Québec and guide its policies on cultural integration:

- une société dont le français est la langue commune de la vie publique;
- une société démocratique où la participation et la contribution de tous sont attendues et favorisées;
- une société pluraliste ouverte aux multiples apports dans les limites qu'imposent le respect des valeurs démocratiques fondamentales et la nécessitée d'échange intercommunautaire. (16)[12]

These principles establish a common public culture to which everyone participating in the moral contract is bound. The French language acts as the vehicle for this common culture and binds the collectivity together. While these principles do not mean that immigrants must abandon their own cultural heritage upon arrival in Québec, they do mean that they must speak French in the public sphere, become fully integrated members of Québec public life by participating in its democracy, and respect the fundamental values of Québec society (such as the equality of the sexes). Québécois interculturalism focuses more strongly on integration and the reciprocal nature of the moral contract than Canadian multiculturalism which supposes a mosaic of juxtaposed ethno-cultural groups and which puts more emphasis on individual rights than collective social cohesion.[13]

Interculturalism became a hot topic of public debate beginning in 2006 as a series of cases of "reasonable accommodation" hit the media.[14] Prominent examples include a ruling by the Supreme Court of Canada allowing a young Sikh boy to wear a kirpan to school (and subsequent banning of the kirpan from the Québec National Assembly);[15] the YMCA on Avenue du Parc in Montréal covering up its windows so Hassidic Jewish boys would not see women working out in skimpy exercise clothes as they walked by;[16] demands by some Hassidic men not to take driving tests with female examiners of the Société de l'assurance automobile du Québec (SAAQ);[17] and the mayor, André Drouin, of the small town of Hérouxville in the northern part of the Mauricie region writing "des normes de vie" banning niqabs, female genital mutilation, and female immolation (revealed four years later to be a deliberately exaggerated document in order to provoke public debate).[18] Public outcry came down loudly against religiously motivated accommodations deemed unreasonable and also led Québécois to question the vestiges of Christianity left in their largely secular society, such as prayers at some municipal council meetings and whether or not to remove the cross on the wall of the National Assembly (placed there in 1936 by Maurice Duplessis to signal the Union nationale party's alliance with the Catholic Church).[19] That some accommodations, such as the ruling on the kirpan, came from the Canadian federal government via the Supreme Court and the Charter of Rights and Freedoms contained within a Constitution not signed by Québec only furthered Québécois' awareness of the differences between their intercultural approach and Canadian multiculturalism. While multiculturalism would require allowing such accommodations, and in Ontario there was talk of allowing Sharia courts to judge Muslim family matters,[20] Québécois citizens largely agreed that immigrants should espouse the common civic values of the majority, particularly that the equality of the sexes should trump religious freedoms. For many, the incursion of religion into the public sphere harked back to the omnipresence of the Catholic Church prior to the Quiet Revolution and would constitute a step backward for Québec society. In Québec public discourse, there was a wide consensus that gender equality should trump religion. This line of thinking is in keeping with interculturalism's emphasis on collective rights (respect for all women as a social group) in contrast to the way in which multiculturalism puts a greater emphasis on individual rights (the freedom to practise different religions, each person perhaps in his or her own way, a slippery slope recently condemned by some prominent English Canadians on the thirtieth anniversary of the Charter).[21]

The relative absence of feminist and queer adaptations of Shakespeare in Québec can be traced back, to some degree, to interculturalism and to Québec's emphasis on all citizens belonging to a collective entity, regardless of gender or race. This social policy is only part of the equation, though, and a fuller explanation of the relative dearth of feminist and queer adaptations requires both a practical and a theoretical approach. On the practical side of the problem, authorship, education, linguistic difference, and social progress combine to make feminist adaptations of Shakespeare less likely to be written in Québec than in English Canada. From a theoretical standpoint, the politics of recognition privilege nation over gender as the top priority about which authors may be inclined to write.

To begin with the practical, the majority of Québécois adaptations are written by male authors. With the exception of Claude, Maillet, Reyes, Thomas, Thompson, Veilleux, and some of the *38* authors, all of whom wrote after 1990, the authors of 83 per cent of plays in this corpus are men who might have been predisposed to an inherently masculinist approach to adaptation and to consider the national question more important than gender issues (except for Pierre-Yves Lemieux who wrote a queer *À propos de Roméo et Juliette* at the height of the AIDS crisis). Women play crucial roles in the formation of the nation, but the collective survival of the nation takes precedence over the concerns of individual female characters, of which these plays have very few. In this entire corpus, only Maillet's Lady Macbeth and Shrew constitute resolutely feminist characters.

To some degree, the small proportion of female authors in this corpus of plays may be attributed to an overall marginalization of female playwrights in Québécois theatre in general. While the collective Théâtre des Cuisines was founded in 1973, and Pol Pelletier co-created the Théâtre expérimental des femmes in 1979 following a rupture with the Théâtre expérimental de Montréal she had co-founded earlier, feminist theatre remained marginal in Québec. In an article about the 1976 feminist play *La nef des sorcières*, Louise Forsyth laments that "le pourcentage de pièces de femmes créées sur des scènes institutionnelles est nettement inférieur au pourcentage des pièces écrites par des hommes. [...] Les textes des femmes dramaturges qui osent aborder les problèmes encore sérieux de la condition féminine ou qui dramatisent les expériences des lesbiennes ou encore celles des femmes issues des communautés culturelles restent statistiquement insignifiants aujourd'hui au Québec" (53–4n16).[22]

While Québec boasts many renowned queer male authors, such as Michel Tremblay, and feminist authors, such as Nicole Brossard, Louky Bersianik, Anne Hébert, Gabrielle Roy, Marie-Claire Blais, Denise Boucher, Carole Fréchette, Jovette Marchessault, and France Théoret, Shakespeare seems not to have been as suitable a vehicle for women authors to transmit feminist ideas as he was for male authors to transmit nationalist ideas. Nicole Brossard suggests, "Si certaines féministes sont intervenues en anglais (Ann-Marie MacDonald) c'est qu'il leur était tout à fait naturel à cause de la langue et de la référence culturelle de pouvoir intégrer Shakespeare dans leur corpus de références, alors qu'au Québec, il aurait plutôt fallu penser à Racine ou Molière, l'un et l'autre ne prêtant pourtant pas comme Shakespeare à des glissements de sens lesbien ou gay." In response to my question as to whether it ever occurred to her to use Shakespeare as a vehicle to disseminate a feminist worldview, Brossard confirms my hypothesis that it did not: "Non, cela ne m'est jamais venu à l'esprit de passer par l'œuvre de Shakespeare pour élaborer mon analyse du patriarcat ni pour élaborer une autre vision du monde."[23] Since Shakespeare is not part of the secondary school curriculum in Québec, women writers would not have encountered him and experienced frustrations with the misogyny in his works at a young age, the way, say, an anglophone girl reading *The Taming of the Shrew* might. Having no reason to rebel against an objectionable view of women they had not encountered, francophone feminist writers in Québec would see no need to rewrite Shakespeare. Even Molière, who is not officially on the secondary school curriculum either but who tends to get included at the discretion of the teacher, is not much of a target for writing back to the canon since writing back supposes a more prominent presence of canonical works in an author's formative years than is the case in Québec.[24] In practice, Shakespeare simply was not on most francophone feminist authors' radars, so there was little motivation to bother to rewrite him when they could create new styles, original forms, and innovative works of their own, such as *l'écriture au féminin*. In this context, participating in male-dominated theatrical practices, such as adapting the world's most famous male playwright, would be a distraction, or arguably even a waste of time, from the more radical projects they envisioned.

In contrast, Shakespeare's appropriation by male authors concerned with nationalism was, pragmatically, in keeping with the trend in Québécois playwriting at the time to make almost any and all drama nationalist, including Shakespeare whose works were often performed at the Théâtre du Nouveau Monde. As Michel Bélair explains in *Le nouveau théâtre québécois*, a polemical history of Québécois theatre from the end of the Quiet Revolution until the book's publication in 1973, "le théâtre québécois n'existe que depuis cinq ans," that is, since about 1968, the year Michel Tremblay's *Les Belles-Sœurs* was first produced, as well as Gurik's *Hamlet, prince du Québec*, because prior to this "le théâtre d'expression française au Québec a d'abord été canadien" (12).[25] Corresponding to the collective self-confidence emerging from the Quiet Revolution, "partout dans le nouveau théâtre québécois, l'affirmation culturelle va de pair avec l'affirmation de l'identité nationale" (56).[26] In analysing the controversy surrounding the 1978 feminist play *Les fées ont soif*, Yves Jubinville attributes the contradictory discourses within the critical opposition to the play to "une société négociant son passage à l'ère du pluralisme avec des moyens – c'est-à-dire les outils interprétifs – d'une société qui conserve d'elle-même une image d'homogénéité" (68).[27] On the one hand, critics damned the play for being too radical, especially in its portrayal of the Virgin Mary character, while, on the other hand, "on insiste sur le caractère non évolutif et même régressif de l'iconologie féministe dans des termes qui vont du 'les femmes répètent toujours la même chose' au 'il faudra tôt ou tard passer à une autre étape'" (68).[28] The latter vein of criticism suggests that women had already achieved sufficient liberation at the time, as if the play were a redundant contribution to public discourse, even though the ire it produced demonstrates this was not the case. Rather, it seems that there was little room for feminist concerns within this *nouveau théâtre québécois* which was primarily focused on the affirmation of a single, collective national identity, not feminist identities.

Focusing on both national and gendered identities at once is no easy task – for artists or for theorists. In analysing the work of several prominent scholars of Québec studies, Schwartzwald notes the absence of a real engagement with gender issues in their work on the national question. Of Jocelyn Létourneau's embracing of "already-achieved North American normalcy as a way of taking his distance from the topoi and tropes which have been used to explain the Quebec past" in *Passer à l'avenir: Histoire, mémoire, identité dans le Québec d'aujourd'hui* (2000), Schwartzwald ponders:

> [O]ne has to wonder whether this represents an actual acceptance and integration of those sexualized and gendered subject-positions articulated over the past twenty-five years that have posed challenges to the monolithic claims of the *Sujet-Nation*, or whether instead we are witnessing a new instance of their being written out of social discourse? One might object that considering gendered and/or sexualized notions of political participation is a separate issue, and that is unfair to criticize Létourneau on this score because it is not the topic of his book. Yet, that is precisely the point. There seems to be a systematic, general tendency in much revisionist work to believe that such questions are extraneous, or peripheral, to an analysis of the Quebec social formation and the challenges of advanced democracy and citizen participation. ("Rush" 120)

Schwartzwald finds a similar lack of attention to gendered subject positions in Jocelyn Maclure's *Récits identitaires: Le Québec à l'épreuve du pluralisme* (2000):

> Yet no parallel attention is given to the possibility of putting into play multiple identities located *in relation to* the national. This omission underwrites a developmental narrative in which the melancholic, identitarian discourse articulated over time by a lineage of male *penseurs* is transcended exclusively by men themselves in a new leap toward national maturity. Tellingly, Maclure's account contains not a single significant reference to theorists who have written on relations between the *Sujet-Nation* and regimes of gender and sexuality in Quebec over the past two decades. The only two women theorists to be discussed at any length, Sherry Simon and Régine Robin, are included for their work on cultural, i.e. *ethnic and racialized,* hybridity and heterogeneity. Despite claiming that issues of "identitary abnormality" and "ontological insecurity" can no longer encompass the multiple identity positions held by Québécois subjects, Maclure's account in fact returns to the secure home of the *Sujet-Nation* by enacting a curiously disembodied, abstract form of pluralism. (120, italics in original)

Daniel Salée arrives at a similar critique, writing of Maclure's book in a passage quoted by Schwartzwald that "'il manque en définitive un chapitre à cet ouvrage,' a chapter that would take seriously the identitary narratives he has named but failed to analyze – 'immigrantes, autochtones, anglophones, féminines et féministes' (277) – since without them only a very limited redefinition of the Quebec political community can be offered" ("Rush" 121). Playwrights alone, or the artistic sphere writ large, are not to blame for the absence of attention to gender issues when the national question is also on the table; even those scholars who acknowledge the need to examine the intersection of national and gendered identities struggle to do so too.

It would seem that the national question trumps the theorization of gender in Québec, even among well-meaning scholars, by the sheer force of its preponderance, that is, the fact that it remains at the forefront of political debate, always unresolved, while steady political progress continues to be made on feminist and queer issues, as outlined in the brief history presented in chapter 1. In other words, the nation's "misrecognition" seems to be greater than gendered misrecognition. Charles Taylor is perhaps Canada's most respected theorist on the politics of recognition. In his 1992 essay in *Multiculturalism: Examining the Politics of Recognition*, he describes the collective psychological effects of national misrecognition: "The projection of an inferior or demeaning image on another can actually distort and oppress, to the extent that the image is internalized. Not only contemporary feminism but also race relations and discussions of multiculturalism are undergirded by the premise that the withholding of recognition can be a form of oppression" (36). Misrecognition constructs group identity, Taylor claims, along Fanonist lines: "dominant groups tend to entrench their hegemony by inculcating an image of inferiority in the subjugated. The struggle for freedom and equality must therefore pass through a revision of these images" (66). The need to revise a collective self-image of inferiority brings us back to Schwartzwald's assessment of Québécois federasty, described in chapter 1, which seeks to invert a Fanonist trope of effeminizing colonizer and effeminate colonized. Moreover, what makes Québec's demand for recognition complicated – either as a distinct society, as a nation (as surprisingly Stephen Harper's government granted on 27 November 2006), or as a country – is that it puts in opposition two views of liberalism that Taylor finds incompatible: individual and collective rights.

Three problems exist with Taylor's account of the politics of recognition. First, as Susan Wolf has pointed out in her "Comment" in the same collection of essays, Taylor's theory of recognition is primarily concerned with multiculturalism and the relationship between Québec and Canada. Although he claims his theory maps onto gender, he never seriously accounts for women as a collective group that is in need of recognition but is not threatened with extinction, as other cultural groups are (76–7).

Second, Taylor's sympathy for Québécois claims for recognition conflicts with his espousal of multiculturalism, particularly as it has come to be articulated in Canadian liberal thought. This tension became especially clear when Taylor co-chaired the Bouchard-Taylor Commission de consultation sur les pratiques d'accommodement reliées aux différences culturelles. Many Québécois citizens and scholars asserted that Taylor's commitment to multiculturalism was at odds with, and made him fundamentally biased against, Québec's espousal of interculturalism and the francophone majority's right to collective self-affirmation. Jacques Beauchemin, a sociology professor at Université du Québec à Montréal (UQÀM) who was one of fifteen members of the Bouchard-Taylor Commission's advisory committee of experts, stated days before the release of the final report, "'I get the feeling they [Bouchard and Taylor] didn't think they needed public hearings, they didn't need to hear all those people' – more than 3,500 attended the events in 17 towns and cities across the province – 'because in their minds the report was already written.'"[29] He added, "But where they're wrong is to think the solution is to get people from birth to death to incorporate the virtues of multiculturalism into their lives."[30]

Third, many scholars of recognition, including Taylor and German philosopher Axel Honneth, take recognition "to be a matter of self realization," a "necessary condition for attaining full, undistorted subjectivity," thereby construing "misrecognition in terms of impaired subjectivity and damaged self-identity," that is, as an "injury in ethical terms, as stunting the subject's capacity for achieving a 'good life'" (Fraser and Honneth 28). In this sense, Taylor, much like Fanon and Schwartzwald in his analysis of federasty, is engaging in a kind of collective psychoanalysis or group psychology. While their assertions may appear true – that Québec's collective identity has been damaged by conquest and misrecognition – these claims cannot be proven empirically. The majority may indeed share a common culture, including literature, through which that damaged identity is expressed, but any attempt to pinpoint such a national identity would rely on a strategic essentialism that obscures the roles of subgroups, such as women and queers.

The work of American political theorist Nancy Fraser brings us out of the epistemological dead end of speculative group psychology by proposing that recognition is a matter of social justice, thereby treating it as "an issue of *social status*" (Fraser and Honneth 29). In framing recognition as a matter of status, that is, as a matter of "the *relative standing* of social actors" who either are or are not equal (29), Fraser is able to bridge the gap between recognition theory and another important component of social justice – the distribution of resources. Unlike Taylor and Honneth who deal only with recognition, Fraser places recognition at one end of a continuum of social justice, with redistribution of resources at the other. This status model of social justice, encompassing both the recognition of cultural identities and the redistribution of socio-economic resources, is more open to the third-wave feminist theory of intersectionality, in which one's oppression may be the result of multiple identitary factors, not just gender but also race, class, national origin, or sexuality, to name but a few. Some social groups may need redistribution of resources to remedy injustice, others may need cultural recognition, while yet others may require both. The latter are caught in what Fraser calls "the redistribution-recognition dilemma."[31]

Fraser explains the difference between struggles for recognition and redistribution like this: "Recognition claims often take the form of calling attention to, if not performatively creating, the putative specificity of some group and then of affirming its value. Thus, they tend to promote group differentiation. Redistributive claims, in contrast, often call for abolishing economic arrangements that underpin group specificity. (An example would be feminist demands to abolish the gender division of labour.) Thus, they tend to promote group dedifferentiation" (*Interruptus* 16). In the examples of class and queerness, it is easy enough to see how this works. If economically disadvantaged workers achieve social justice through the redistribution of resources, that is, if they successfully dedifferentiate themselves by acquiring equal pay and rising in socio-economic status, they cease to exist as a marginalized group. On the other hand, if gays and lesbians achieve social justice through recognition, that is, if they successfully differentiate themselves as a marginalized group entitled to specifically entrenched rights necessary to guarantee equal treatment, they permanently etch their difference in law. The redistribution-recognition dilemma is that "[p]eople who are subject to both cultural injustice and economic injustice need both recognition and redistribution. They need both to claim and to deny their specificity. How, if at all, is this possible?" (16). For instance, feminists must, on the one hand, demand equal pay for equal work, thereby arguing that women's abilities are not different from men's in the workforce, while, on the other hand, they must demand special provisions, such as pregnancy leave, which are predicated upon the recognition that women are biologically different from men.

Fraser calls collectivities that require both recognition and redistribution, such as those defined by gender or race, "bivalent":

> They are differentiated as collectivities by virtue of *both* the political-economic structure *and* the cultural-valuational structure of society. When oppressed or subordinated, therefore, they suffer injustices that are traceable to both political economy and culture simultaneously. Bivalent collectivities, in sum, may suffer both socioeconomic maldistribution and cultural misrecognition in forms where neither of these injustices is an indirect effect of the other, but where both are primary and co-original. In that case, neither redistributive remedies alone nor recognition remedies alone will suffice. Bivalent collectivities need both. (19)

The problem with Fraser's otherwise astute paradigm is that she does not situate nation anywhere along her continuum of social justice. Her analysis, as she admits in her 2009 book *Scales of Justice,* tends to focus primarily on the United States, that is, a nation-state that has already achieved international recognition as a legitimate country. (Likewise, in analysing gender, she maps the redistribution-recognition dilemma onto the history of US feminism, a trajectory that Québécois feminism did not follow identically.) Since the redistribution-recognition dilemma assumes that marginalized social groups exist within a predefined, internationally recognized nation-state, the case of Québec complicates matters considerably.

Québec can be considered a bivalent collectivity insofar as it is trying to gain political and economic redistribution as well as cultural recognition. Both socio-economic injustice and cultural misrecognition are co-original and need to be remedied, although the degree and form of maldistribution and misrecognition have changed over time. At the beginning of the period corresponding to my corpus of Shakespearean adaptations, maldistribution occurred primarily along linguistic lines within Québec itself. Anglophones earned 35 per cent more than francophones according to the 1965 Laurendeau-Dunton preliminary report on bilingualism and biculturalism, which resulted in a nationalism focused on redistributive remedies, such as the neo-Marxism seen in *Hamlet, prince du Québec*. Likewise, linguistic cleavage played a strong role in misrecognition, which resulted in cultural nationalism, as seen in Garneau's *Macbeth.* These nationalisms of redistribution and recognition coexisted simultaneously and feature prominently in adaptations of Shakespeare prior to the 1995 referendum on sovereignty.

Skipping ahead to the beginning of the twenty-first century, nationalist discourses seeking to rectify both maldistribution and misrecognition have changed in focus and in intended audience. The platforms of both the PQ and the Bloc Québécois have reframed maldistribution in terms of fiscal inequality, that is, the unequal distribution of wealth between the provincial and the federal governments that results in a net loss for the Québec government and undermines its ability to implement social programs as it chooses, particularly in the domains of health and education. Likewise, as a result of growing interculturalism, national discourses about misrecognition have evolved too, particularly since Meech Lake and the 1995 referendum. Many nationalists have shifted from cultural nationalism to civic nationalism, that is, from focusing on the ethno-linguistic differences of individual citizens to the rising threat of globalization and the consequent need for international recognition and a seat at the table of world organizations, such as the WHO, WTO, UNESCO, and post-Kyoto talks.[32] These new themes of fiscal inequality and international affairs do not appear in recent adaptations of Shakespeare, no doubt, in part, due to their inherent unattractiveness from a literary standpoint, that is, their focus on governments rather than individuals who may become compelling characters. However, misrecognition does continue to inform nationalism in the plays at an individual level in terms of Québec's increasingly heterogeneous composition and the role of aboriginals and immigrants in its new intercultural identity.

Québec is also bivalent because it is concerned with both differentiation from the rest of Canada and dedifferentiation of its own immigrants. Unlike Fraser's examples of gender or race though, Québec has two different target audiences for its differentiation and dedifferentiation efforts. Québec must differentiate itself from Canada on the world stage, while at the same time dedifferentiating among its own citizens, especially non-*pure laine* immigrants whom it needs to integrate into the collective national identity in order to win a referendum and achieve sovereignty. During the 2007 Bouchard-Taylor Commission, controversial public hearings often pitted *pure laine* Québécois *de souche* against new immigrants who refused to integrate into the larger Québécois community and espouse certain civic values, most notably around the issue of ostensible signs of religion, thus highlighting that Canadian multiculturalism is incompatible with Québécois interculturalism as a governing value in the social contract. The tricky political tightrope the Québec government must walk, regardless of whether it is led by the Liberals or the PQ, is thus differentiation and dedifferentiation at the same time.

How does a collectivity differentiate and dedifferentiate itself simultaneously? I have not yet found a solution to this conundrum. Neither have any of Québec's political parties, nor its feminist or queer movements, nor the political theorists. The redistribution-recognition dilemma does give us some insight, however, into the case of Québécois adaptations of Shakespeare and why this corpus of plays leans so heavily towards nationalist plays to the exclusion of feminist plays. When two bivalent communities are both caught in the redistribution-recognition dilemma, and one social group, women, is a subset of the other, the Québec nation, it makes sense that the strategic goals of the macro group would preempt or overshadow those of the micro group. Women are deemed part of the nation, and, contrary to the advice provided by feminist nationalists in their "Pas de..." slogan, it is easy enough for predominantly male nationalist leaders and male authors to assume that the liberation of women will happen as a result of, rather than in conjunction with, that of the nation to which they belong. Moreover, since political advances for women are strategically easier to achieve (it takes merely a bill in the National Assembly to give women greater rights and freedoms, not a referendum of 7.7 million people), the focus of attention both in the political sphere and in the cultural sphere (in this case a corpus of Shakespearean adaptations) remains riveted on the larger and more difficult goal for which more support must be drummed up. Shakespeare's cultural authority, his big-time status, is appropriated in service of the cause perceived to need it most – the nation that can be recognized as a country only if the majority of its citizens differentiate themselves enough to mark an X next to "Yes."

The practical reasons (authorship, education, linguistic difference, and social progress) and the theoretical influences (interculturalism, the redistribution-recognition dilemma) associated with the incongruity of nationalism and feminism in Québec's political and literary spheres cannot be fully disentangled. Another part of the equation, according to de Sève in the analysis mentioned in chapter 1, is the relative absence of women in key positions within the nationalist movement:

> Les féministes du Québec confrontées à leur double, triple ou quadruple marginalisation sur la base du genre, de l'identité nationale, de la classe ou de l'orientation sexuelle, sont loin d'avoir résolu l'énigme de la construction d'une stratégie politique adaptée à la fragmentation de l'identité du

> sujet politique post-moderne. Mais au moins ont-elles appris qu'il est inutile de vouloir simplifier l'équation, de quelque côté qu'on l'aborde. Si les tensions qui promettent d'accompagner la tenue d'un troisième référendum sur la souveraineté du Québec sont à craindre, c'est moins parce que le nationalisme recouvre le féminisme québécois de son ombre que parce que les féministes, monopolisées par des dossiers sectoriels sans nombre, délaissent la scène politique centrale, laissant une fois de plus les citoyens décider seuls du genre de la nation, sans les citoyennes. (171)[33]

It is less a question of nation trumping gender, de Sève argues, than feminists being caught in the ever increasing demands of the intersectionality of postmodern identity politics. By spreading out their efforts over a variety of causes, women do not constitute a statistically significant group of actors on the main political stage, which in Québec deals primarily with the national question. In fact, the percentage of women who choose to enter politics in Québec is low. In the 2012 general election, the PQ ran thirty-four female candidates (27 per cent, a drop from 31 per cent in 2008) and the PLQ ran forty-six female candidates (37 per cent, up from 32 per cent in 2008) for the 125 seats available in the National Assembly. The 2012 election resulted in forty-one women being elected as MNAs (32.8 per cent, the most to date).[34] Significantly, Pauline Marois became *la première Première Ministre*, Québec's first ever female premier. In terms of positions of power, when Marois formed her cabinet in September 2012, counting herself, nine of the twenty-four ministers were women (37.5 per cent).[35]

The crisis within the PQ over Pauline Marois's leadership while she was still leader of the official opposition highlights the difficulty for women to assume power on the political stage, even thirty years after Lise Payette's "Yvettes" incident, and thus the ongoing tensions between nation and gender. In June 2011, Marois was criticized by members of her caucus for forcing them to vote for an anti-democratic law that would prohibit legal challenges to a new amphitheatre in order to drum up support in the typically conservative region of Québec City. After PQ MNAs Louise Beaudoin, Pierre Curzi, and Lisette Lapointe resigned collectively on 6 June, she admitted her mistake the next day. Attention to this incident that instigated the crisis surrounding her leadership was short-lived, but the crisis within the party then dragged on until 21 January 2012 with detractors frequently invoking the refrain "elle passe pas,"[36] claiming that the population simply did not like her. Critics often cited her personal wealth, her mansion in the suburbs, and her fancy clothes, which she had been working to "tone down" (i.e., de-feminize) since becoming leader of the party in June 2008 in order to resonate with ordinary voters. As supporters pointed out, however, the very same personal characteristics for which she was often criticized – demonstrating ambition and drive in order to amass personal wealth – were the same for which her long-time rival, ex-PQ minister and founder of the CAQ, François Legault, was praised. The double standard by which Marois was deemed unpopular for exhibiting the same characteristics judged responsible for Legault's popularity confirms gender stereotypes were at work in the minds of detractors who adamantly insisted they were not sexist.[37] After she resisted a potential putsch or contestation of her leadership by former BQ leader Gilles Duceppe and then led her party through a congress characterized by solidarity rather than the in-fighting typical of the previous six and a half months, Marois suddenly became "la dame de béton," or the concrete woman.[38] Insofar as the discourse surrounding Marois changed literally overnight from months of "elle ne passe pas" to "elle est la dame de béton," all the contradictions of the tension between Québécois nationalism and gender were played out on her body. While the personal characteristics for which the nationalist leader was attacked were gendered as masculine – ambition and intransigence – so too were those for which she was ultimately praised – courage, steadfastness, and emotional resilience in a situation which might well have led many a man to resign his position. It is precisely because Québec sees itself as progressive on the gender front, as seen in the many legal advances mentioned in chapter 1, that it refuses to acknowledge latent sexism, particularly within the nationalist movement which must suppress attention to other social causes in order not to detract from its primary goal of independence.

This tension between nation and gender also played out during the crisis surrounding Marois's leadership over the notion of "gouvernance souverainiste," which was adopted at the same convention in April 2011 at which she received 93 per cent approval in a confidence vote by party members. While the actual meaning of "gouvernance souverainiste" is to govern Québec so as to recuperate from Ottawa as many powers as possible, knowing full well that Ottawa will deny those requests (essentially doing what had been called just a few years earlier by another group "des gestes de rupture," but only within provincial domains of competence), the word "gouvernance" disturbed some party members because it raises the question of what the sovereignist party should do when it is not in a position to call a referendum and declare independence. If the party's main objective is to achieve sovereignty, simply governing Québec as a province in the meantime is seen as failing to pursue its goals and abandoning its project. Yet progress – for women, for queers, for aboriginals, for all others, as well as for the *pure laine* majority – happens during these periods of governance, as demonstrated in the progressive social policies mentioned in chapter 1. However, some hard-line sovereignists consider that focusing on governance – or on the social role of these groups for whom progress is made, and to acknowledge that perhaps there is still room for improvement, that is, that collective mentalities have not evolved to the point of eradicating sexism from Québec society – is to detract from independence. This desire in the political sphere to prioritize nationalism above other social causes mirrors the tension between nation and gender found in the literary sphere in adaptations of Shakespeare.

Québécois adaptations of Shakespeare are not Canadian Shakespeares, then, because of the preponderance of Shakespeare's appropriation in service of various nationalist discourses of redistribution and recognition and the consequent relative absence of feminist, queer, or aboriginal adaptations, a phenomenon in keeping with Québec's espousal of interculturalism rather than Canadian multiculturalism. The national question has a totalizing effect that permeates the collective consciousness, so forms of alterity, such as gender, sexuality, and ethnicity, are eclipsed – without, however, being erased. In Québec, the moment of departure from the Shakespearean source text by the adapter imposes a cultural specificity on the text, distinguishing it from the Shakespeare usually performed in either Stratford, Ontario or England. While Canadian adaptations of Shakespeare struggle to wrest authority from an undead author, Québécois adaptations – because they run differently the risk of contamination by that authority, and because Québec has complex colonial, postcolonial, and neocolonial relationships with France, Britain, and English Canada – appropriate it primarily, and often with irreverence, in service of the nation's decolonization.

Appendix

Chronology of Québécois Adaptations of Shakespeare, 1960–2013

This appendix charts chronologically all adaptations of Shakespeare in Québec since 1960 whose publication or production details I have confirmed. This chronology lists the year, title, author, the Shakespearean source text(s) from which a play is adapted, publication details, production details of the earliest performance if known, and any translations if applicable. Since the definition of "adaptation" employed here is text-based, the year is determined (1) by date of publication, or (2) if the text has not been published, by the date of composition on the author's manuscript, or (3) failing that, first production. In keeping with a text-based definition of adaptation, the publication history is privileged over the production history. "CEAD" designates unpublished manuscripts that are available for public consultation at the Centre des auteurs dramatiques in Montréal, originally named the Centre d'essai des auteurs dramatiques. The CEAD website has a searchable database of all of its holdings, which include both published and unpublished plays.

Year:	1968
Title:	*Hamlet, prince du Québec*
Author:	Robert Gurik
Adaptation:	*Hamlet*
Publication:	Montréal: Éditions de l'homme, 1968
Production:	Théâtre de l'Escale, Montréal, 17 January 1968
Re-adapted:	*Hamlet, Prince of Quebec*. Trans. Marc F. Gélinas. Toronto: Playwrights Guild of Canada, 1968. (London Little Theatre, November 1968)

Translation: *Hamlet, Prince of Québec.* Trans. Leanore Lieblein. *A Certain William.* Ed. Leanore Lieblein. Toronto: Playwrights Canada P, 2009. 1–63

Year: 1974
Title: *Elle*
Author: Serge Mercier
Adaptation: *Macbeth*
Publication: Ottawa: Éditions Leméac, 1974 (Version II February 1973)
Production: Coproduction du CEAD et du Secrétariat d'État, 21 March 1973
Notes: First written 18 April 1968–4 June 1969

Year: 1977
Title: *Lear*
Author: Jean-Pierre Ronfard
Adaptation: *King Lear*
Publication: *TRAC* (1977)
Production: Théâtre expérimental de Montréal, January 1977
Translation: *Lear*. Trans. Linda Gaboriau. *A Certain William.* Ed. Leanore Lieblein. Toronto: Playwrights Canada P, 2009. 65–105

Year: 1978
Title: *Macbeth de William Shakespeare: Traduit en québécois*
Author: Michel Garneau
Adaptation: *Macbeth*
Publication: Montréal: VLB Éditeur, 1978
Production: Théâtre de la Manufacture, Cinéma Parallèle, Montréal, 31 October 1978

Year: 1981
Title: *Vie et mort du Roi Boiteux*
Author: Jean-Pierre Ronfard
Adaptation: *1–3 Henry VI, Richard III*
Publication: 2 Vols. Montréal: Leméac, 1981
Production: Théâtre expérimental de Montréal, École nationale de théâtre, Montréal, 20, 21, 22 July 1981

Year: 1986
Title: *Pericles, Prince of Tyre, by William Shakespeare*
Author: René-Daniel Dubois

Adaptation: *Pericles*
Publication: Unpublished manuscript (in English) (December 1986)
Production: Théâtre Passe Muraille, Toronto, 9–19 April 1987

Year: 1986
Title: *Macbean: An Interminable Pseudo-Serious Tragicomedy in Several Acts & Innumerable Scenes With Apologies from William Shakespeare whose* Macbeth *was freely adapted from it*
Author: Terrance Ryan Hughes
Adaptation: *Macbeth*
Publication: Outremont, QC: Ormond House, 1986
Notes: Parody of academia

Year: 1989
Title: *À propos de Roméo et Juliette*
Author: Pierre-Yves Lemieux
Adaptation: *Romeo and Juliet*
Publication: Unpublished manuscript (CEAD 1989)
Production: Théâtre de l'Opsis, February 1989

Year: 1989
Title: *La tempête*
Author: Michel Garneau
Adaptation: *The Tempest*
Publication: Montréal: VLB Éditeur, 1989
Production: Groupe d'animation urbaine de Montréal et École nationale de théâtre, Vieux-Port de Montréal, 25 July 1982
Notes: First tradapted for École nationale de théâtre, Montréal, 1973

Year: 1989
Title: *Coriolan*
Author: Michel Garneau
Adaptation: *Coriolanus*
Publication: Montréal: VLB Éditeur, 1989
Production: Centre national des Arts, L'Atelier, Ottawa, 3–7 December 1991

Year: 1990
Title: *Falstaff*
Author: Jean-Pierre Ronfard
Adaptation: *1–2 Henry IV, The Merry Wives of Windsor*

Publication: Unpublished manuscript (1990)
Production: Théâtre du Trident, Québec, 1990

Year: 1991
Title: *Shakespeare: un monde qu'on peut apprendre par coeur*
Author: Michel Garneau
Adaptation: Shakespeare as subject, *The Tempest*, *Richard III*, *1 Henry IV*, *Hamlet*, *Sonnets*, *The Merry Wives of Windsor*, *Romeo and Juliet*, *King Lear*, *Henry V*, *Macbeth*
Publication: Unpublished manuscript (CEAD January 1991)
Production: Nouvelle Compagnie Théâtrale, salle Denise-Pelletier, Montréal, 15 April 1991
Notes: Children's literature

Year: 1991
Title: *Les Reines*
Author: Normand Chaurette
Adaptation: *1–3 Henry VI*, *Richard III*
Publication: Montréal: Leméac, 1991
Production: Théâtre d'Aujourd'hui, Montréal, 18 January 1991
Translation: *The Queens*. Trans. Linda Gaboriau. Toronto: Coach House P, 1992. (Canadian Stage Company, Toronto, 6 November 1992)

Year: 1991
Title: *William S*
Author: Antonine Maillet
Adaptation: Shakespeare as a character, *Macbeth*, *1–2 Henry IV*, *The Merry Wives of Windsor*, *The Taming of the Shrew*, *King Lear*, *Hamlet*, *Romeo and Juliet*, *The Merchant of Venice*
Publication: Montréal: Leméac, 1991
Production: Théâtre du Rideau Vert, Montréal, 16 April 1991

Year: 1994
Title: *Touchez pas à ma paroisse*
Author: Reynald Bouchard
Adaptation: *Hamlet*
Publication: Unpublished manuscript (CEAD May 1994)

Year: 1995
Title: *La mégère de Padova*

Author: Marco Micone
Adaptation: *The Taming of the Shrew*
Publication: Unpublished manuscript (CEAD 1995)
Production: As *La mégère apprivoisée*, Théâtre du Nouveau Monde, Montréal, 14 March–8 April 1995

Year: 1995
Title: *Songe d'une nuit*
Author: Michel Ouellette
Adaptation: *A Midsummer Night's Dream*
Publication: Unpublished manuscript (CEAD April 1995, revised July 1999)

Year: 1996
Title: *Le* Making of *de Macbeth*
Author: Pigeons International [Jean-Frédéric Messier] d'après une idée originale de Paula de Vasconcelos
Adaptation: *Macbeth*
Publication: Unpublished manuscript (04/03/1996)
Production: Musée d'Art Contemporain de Montréal

Year: 1996
Title: *38 (A, E, I, O, U)*
Author: Thirty-eight individual authors of the following monologues: *38 métiers 38 mégères* by Yvan Bienvenue; *Lady Percy's Grande Traîtrise* by Olivier Choinière; *Henry IV deuxième partie* by Jean Gaudreau; *Macbeth* by Jean Pelletier; *Timon d'Athènes* by Emmanuelle Amoni; *La Mort de Falstaff* by Dominic Champagne; *Martine versus Richard II* by Chantal Cadieux; *Sur deux colonnes* by Emmanuelle Roy; *Le Songe* by Wajdi Mouawad; *Hamlette* by Dominick Parenteau-Lebeuf; *Titus Andronicus* by François Boulay; *Henry V* by Anne Legault; *Erreur* by Isabelle Thivierge; *Taxi Actor* by Michel Monty; *Le Juif* by Jean-Rock Gaudreault; *Les aut' mots* by Claude Champagne; *Souvenirs d'une auteure malade* by Hélène Boissinot; *Le rêve d'Albert Levert* by Pascale Rafie; *Roméo et Juliette tel que (…)* by Michel Duchesne; *Comme Henri* by Raymond Villeneuve; *Milford Haven* by Patrick Leroux; *Richard III, pauvre chou* by Martin Doyon; *La vie inimitable de Cléopâtre* by François Archambault; *Les deux nobles cousins* by Nathalie Boisvert; *Othello* by Jérôme Labbé; *Périclès* by Alexis Martin; *Polyxéna*

	by Benoit Pelletier; *La nuit d'un roi* by Francis Monty; *Le fils amère* by Hélène Ducharme; *Comment vous plairait-il?* by Pascal Brullemans; *Tempête* by François Paré; *Jules César* by Johanna Murphy; *La comédie des méprises* by Isabelle Hubert; *La Vierge* by Christine Germain; *Measure for Measure* by Erik Charpentier; *Anne Boleyn* by Pierre-Yves Lemieux; *Le beau jardin secret de Jean-Stéphane* by Stéphane Laporte; *Peines d'amour perdues* by Josée Plourde
Adaptation:	All 38 of Shakespeare's plays
Publication:	5 Vols. Montréal, Dramaturges Éditeurs, 1996
Production:	Théâtre Urbi et Orbi, Théâtre d'Aujourd'hui, Montréal, 17–21 September 1996

Year:	1997–98
Title:	*Richard moins III*
Author:	Lük Fleury
Adaptation:	*Richard III*
Publication:	Unpublished manuscript (CEAD 1997–98)
Production:	Théâtre Kafala, Théâtre Du Maurier au Monument-National, Montréal, 27 October 1998

Year:	1999
Title:	*Mon royaume pour un cheval*
Author:	Daniel Paquette
Adaptation:	*Richard III*
Production:	Société Richard III, La Petite Licorne, 1999
Notes:	Text by François-Victor Hugo with additions by Daniel Paquette

Year:	1999, 2001, 2006
Title:	*Teaching Shakespeare; Teaching Detroit (Teaching Shakespeare 2); Teaching* As You Like It *(Teaching Shakespeare 3)*
Author:	Keir Cutler
Adaptation:	Shakespeare as subject, *Henry V*, *As You Like It*
Production:	Montréal Fringe Festival, 1999, 2006
Notes:	Parody of academia

Year:	2000
Title:	*Sauvée des eaux: Texte dramatique sur Ophélie*
Author:	Daphné Thompson
Adaptation:	*Hamlet*

Publication: Unpublished manuscript
Production: Théâtre de l'Esquisse, 12–14 May 2000
Translation: *Saved from the Waters*. Trans. Daphné Thompson. *A Certain William*. Ed. Leanore Lieblein. Toronto: Playwrights Canada P, 2009. 185–207

Year: 2000
Title: *Roller*
Author: Larry Tremblay
Adaptation: *Romeo and Juliet*
Publication: Unpublished manuscript (CEAD 2000). Rpt. *Théâtre à lire et à jouer* 4. Manage, Belgium: Éditions Lansman, 2000.
Notes: Very similar to *Guitare Tatou/Burger Love* (2003/2007)

Year: 2000
Title: *L'aventure de Shakespeare au pays des rêves*
Author: Fabien Cloutier
Adaptation: Shakespeare as subject
Publication: Unpublished manuscript (CEAD 2000)
Production: Centre d'art La Maison Jaune, Summer 2000
Notes: Children's literature

Year: 2001
Title: *Dave veut jouer Richard III*
Author: Alexis Martin
Adaptation: *Richard III*
Publication: Unpublished manuscript
Production: Nouveau Théâtre expérimental, L'Auditorium Justine Lacoste-Beaubien de l'Hôpital Ste-Justine, Montréal, 15–27 October 2001

Year: 2002
Title: *La leçon d'Anglaise*
Author: Nathalie Claude
Adaptation: *Romeo and Juliet*
Publication: Unpublished manuscript
Production: *Le Boudoir, cabaret saphique*, Le Lion d'Or, Montréal, 26 June 2002

Year: 2002
Title: *Henry. Octobre. 1970.*

Author: Madd Harold and Anthony Kokx
Adaptation: *Henry V*
Publication: Unpublished manuscript
Production: Gravy Bath, Théâtre Calixa-Lavallée, Montréal, 21–31 August 2002

Year: 2002
Title: *Sous l'empire de Iago*
Author: Kadar Mansour
Adaptation: *Othello*
Publication: Unpublished manuscript (CEAD 2002)

Year: 2002
Title: *Richard III ou la chute du corbeau*
Author: Nancy Thomas
Adaptation: *Richard III*
Publication: Unpublished manuscript (11 December 2002)
Production: Théâtre du Cloître, Festival Fringe, Salle Jean-Claude Germain au Théâtre d'Aujourd'hui, Montréal, June 2003

Year: 2003
Title: *Le Capitaine Horribifabulo*
Author: Simon Boudrault and Geneviève Simard
Adaptation: *Romeo and Juliet*
Production: Théâtre des Ventrebleus, La Maison Théâtre, February 2003
Notes: Children's literature

Year: 2004
Title: *L'ultime séduction ou L'Alcibiade de William Shakespeare*
Author: Marie La Palme Reyes
Adaptation: Shakespeare as subject, *Coriolanus*
Publication: Online manuscript (August 2004 version) http://marieetgonzalo.files.wordpress.com/2004/07/shakespeare.pdf. Rpt. in *Sept d'un coup (Sept pièces de théâtre réunies en un volume)*. Beaconsfield, QC: Éditions Micro-Éduc, 2006

Year: 2004
Title: *Hamlet-le-Malécite*
Author: Yves Sioui Durand and Jean-Frédéric Messier
Adaptation: *Hamlet*

Publication: Unpublished manuscript (9 September 2004)
Production: Ondinnok, American Can, 1–19 June 2004
Translation: *The Maleceet Hamlet*. Trans. Henry Gauthier. *A Certain William*. Ed. Leanore Lieblein. Toronto: Playwrights Canada P, 2009. 209–61

Year: 2006
Title: *Les mots fantômes*
Author: Michel Nadeau
Adaptation: *Hamlet*
Publication: Unpublished manuscript
Production: Production Théâtre Niveau Parking at Théâtre Périscope, 21 February–18 March 2006

Year: 2007
Title: *Burger Love*
Author: Larry Tremblay
Adaptation: *Romeo and Juliet*, *A Midsummer Night's Dream*
Production: As *Guitare Tatou*, École supérieure de theatre, Université du Québec à Montréal, December 2003. As *Burger Love*, 2007
Notes: First written as *Guitare Tatou* (2003). Very similar to *Roller* (2000)
Translation: *Burger Love*. Trans. Keith Turnbull. *A Certain William*. Ed. Leanore Lieblein. Toronto: Playwrights Canada P, 2009. 263–331

Year: 2007
Title: *Elsemeur*
Author: Katy Veilleux
Adaptation: *Hamlet*
Production: Théâtre Antigun at Salle Fred-Barry du Théâtre Denise-Pelletier, 30 January–17 February 2007

Year: 2011
Title: *Teaching Hamlet*
Author: Keir Cutler
Adaptation: Shakespeare as subject
Production: Montréal Fringe Festival, 2011
Notes: Parody of academia, "authorship question"

Notes

Introduction

1 Although it is not always standard practice in English, I am deliberately choosing to retain French accents on the words "Québec" and "Québécois" in order to highlight the cultural specificity of Québec. Leanore Lieblein, Ric Knowles, Daniel Fischlin, and Robert Schwartzwald all adopt the same practice.

2 "No free Québec without women's liberation! No free women without Québec's liberation!"

All translations in this book are my own, unless otherwise noted (such as when a published translation exists, as is the case for *Hamlet, prince du Québec* and *Les Reines*). I have chosen to translate as literally as possible (even idioms for which I also provide an English equivalent) in order to highlight the differences between the word choice of Québécois adapters and the Shakespearean source text.

3 "To be or not to be free!"

4 "Born for a little roll of bread." "Proceed to action." "A... free... Qué... bec."

5 *Defence and Illustration of the French Language.*

6 "Bill 101." Crafted by Dr Camille Laurin, the minister of cultural development, and passed by the first PQ government in 1977, the Charter of the French Language's purpose is "to make of French the language of Government and the Law, as well as the normal and everyday language of work, instruction, communication, commerce and business." Despite the controversy Bill 101 has often raised in the anglophone media, its preamble states that "the National Assembly intends to pursue this objective in a spirit of fairness and open-mindedness, respectful of the institutions of the English-speaking community of Québec, and respectful of the ethnic

minorities, whose valuable contribution to the development of Québec it readily acknowledges," and it guarantees many rights for Québec's anglophone minority and aboriginal peoples. The Charter also defines fundamental language rights, and it enlarged the mandate of the Office de la langue française (OLF), created in 1961 by Jean Lesage's Liberal government. Often mischaracterized in anglophone media as "the language police," the OLF's role is to define policy on terminology and francization, monitor and report on Québec's linguistic situation, assist civil agencies and businesses, and ensure that French is the normal and everyday language. Since 1977, many of the Charter's articles have been weakened or repealed. The full text of the Charter is available, in French and in English, on the Government of Québec's website.

7 *Life and Death of the Limping King*.

Chapter 1. Postcolonial Shakespeares

1 English Canada's Anglophilia, which distinguishes Canada culturally from the United States, manifests itself not only in notions of "the classics" and "refinement" but also in popular culture. Colonial longing for the mother country must provide at least a partial explanation why 775,000 viewers tune in nightly to CBC Television to watch *Coronation Street*, England's longest running soap opera set in a working-class suburb of Manchester. Ratings data reveal 1 in 5 Canadians watch the show (not counting online viewers). While geographically far removed, an exceptionally large proportion of Canadians find a cultural affinity with the characters of this fictional neighbourhood. The show has aired in Canada for forty years, making it Canada's longest running soap opera. See "Corrie Crazy: Canada Loves Coronation Street," hosted by Debbie Travis, which aired on CBC Television on 9 December 2010, and "Coronation Street at 50" by Andrew Ryan.

2 According to the Government of Québec, "La proportion de personnes de langue maternelle française passe sous la barre de 80% en 2006 (79,6%). Cependant, 81,8% des Québécois déclarent utiliser le français à la maison." [The proportion of persons whose mother tongue is French goes under the 80% mark in 2006 (79.6%). However, 81.8% of Québécois declare that they use French at home] (19). See *Données sociales du Québec: Édition 2009*.

3 The use of "Québécois people" and "Québec nation" is problematic insofar as such terms suggest a homogenous people or a homogenous nation, which was not the case. There have always been anglophones, First Nations, and immigrants living among the francophone majority in

Québec, making Québec a heterogeneous society. As Schwartzwald points out, "Over the past twenty-five years, the presuppositions of social homogeneity of the *peuple québécois* inherent to the anticolonial model have been largely set aside, even if a strong sense still exists that the relations of economic, political, and psychological dependency insisted upon in the discourse of decolonization of the 1960s and 70s retain a fundamental relevance when speaking about Quebec within Canada" ("Rush" 117). The term "peuple québécois" remains, then, an accurate description of the francophone majority and arguably of the inhabitants of different linguistic origins who have also integrated into the Québec nation. Québec was recognized as a nation by the Canadian Parliament on 27 November 2006.

4 "A few half-hectares of snow." *Candide* was written in 1758 and published in 1759 during the Seven Years' War. The context is a conversation in chapter 23 between Candide and Martin who exchange views about France and England. Martin says, "Vous savez que ces deux nations sont en guerre pour quelques arpents de neige vers le Canada, et qu'elles dépensent pour cette belle guerre beaucoup plus que tout Canada ne vaut." [You're aware that these two countries are at war over a few half-hectares of snow in the vicinity of Canada, and that they are spending on this lovely war far more than the whole of Canada is worth] (133). Voltaire made the same claim about New France in similar but slightly different terms in other essays and letters.

5 Michèle Lalonde's essay "La deffence et illustration de la langue quebecquoyse," which I discuss in chapter 4, is a reaction against this colonial attitude vis-à-vis *français de France.*

6 *White Niggers of America,* written while Vallières was in prison in the United States and published in 1968. Vallières compares the Québécois national liberation movement to that of African Americans for civil rights. His Marxist analysis of the Québécois working class, whom he calls a colonized people, calls for armed revolution, which other members of the Front de libération du Québec (FLQ), to which he belonged, undertook in October 1970.

Following the expulsion of *Le Devoir* journalist Guy Lamarche from a press conference held by Maurice Duplessis in 1958, André Laurendeau wrote three articles in which he developed "La théorie du roi nègre" [The Negro-King Theory]. Laurendeau accuses Duplessis of being a negro-king like those in African colonies ruled by Britain who prop up the colonial power and abuse their own citizens: "Les journaux anglophones du Québec se comportent comme les Britanniques au sein d'une colonie d'Afrique. Les Britanniques ont le sens politique, ils détruisent rarement les institutions politiques d'un pays conquis. Ils entourent le roi nègre mais ils lui passent des fantaisies. Ils lui ont permis à l'occasion de couper des têtes: ce sont les moeurs du pays. Une chose ne leur viendrait pas à l'esprit: et c'est de réclamer d'un roi nègre qu'il se conforme aux hauts standards moraux et politiques des Britanniques." [Anglophone newspapers in Québec act like the British within an African colony. The British have good political sense, they rarely destroy the political institutions of a conquered country. They surround the Negro king but they allow him his fantasies. They allowed him to cut off some heads: it is part of the country's customs. One thing does not come to their minds: and it is to demand that the Negro king adopt the high moral and political standards of the British] (Part 1, 4). For more on Laurendeau's comparison of the anglophone newspapers and financial powerhouses with British colonialism, see Claude Bélanger's summary of the situation.

Subsequent analyses of Québec through the lens of colonialism include a special issue of the journal *Parti Pris* called *Portrait du colonisé québécois,* edited by Paul Chamberland (1964), and André d'Allemagne's *Le colonialisme au Québec* (1966).

7 Falardeau's collections of political essays include *La liberté n'est pas une marque de yogourt* (1995), *Les bœufs sont lents, mais la terre est patiente* (1999), and *Rien n'est plus précieux que la liberté et l'indépendance* (2009).

8 Bernard Landry, former leader of the Parti Québécois and premier of Québec, acknowledged his agreement with Falardeau's ideas but not his choice of words: "Je le rencontrais souvent et, chaque fois, je lui disais qu'on pensait à peu près tout le temps la même chose, mais qu'on l'exprimait de façon complètement différente. Cela nous faisait beaucoup rigoler!" [I would meet him often and, each time, I would tell him that we thought pretty much the same thing all the time, but we expressed it in completely different ways. That made us laugh!] Landry also said, "Dans ses écarts, il a sûrement choqué bien des gens, mais il a aussi provoqué des réflexions." [In his bad language, he surely shocked lots of people, but he also provoked thoughts.] See articles by Daphné Cameron and Mathieu Boivin in *La Presse* and *Le Soleil*.

9 "In what way is Québécois literature postcolonial?"

10 See Wes Folkerth's insightful reading of the parallels between *Dry Lips* and *A Midsummer Night's Dream*. Rather than adaptation, it might be more apt, as Folkerth does, to speak of Highway as engaged in an intertextual dialogue with Shakespeare, without trading directly on Shakespeare's cultural authority, since Highway's goal is the recognition of aboriginal cultures in their own right.

11 Daniel David Moses says *Brébeuf's Ghost* could be more accurately described as "inspired by" rather than an "adaptation of" Shakespeare: "I drew the underlining structure of *Brebeuf's Ghost* from the Scottish play. I stole directly from Shakespeare. I usually say it was 'inspired by' because I haven't actually used his language. I think I've gone beyond adaptation." See Melissa McHugh's interview with the author on the *CASP* website.

12 I hesitate, however, to call *Death of a Chief* an adaptation as I define the term in chapter 2. With the exception of a few stage directions and the pronoun shift required by the cross-gender casting, the play does not significantly rewrite Shakespeare's text. The text is Shakespearean; adaptive elements take place only through stage performance.

13 Consult the *CASP* database for further information about these two plays: http://www.canadianshakespeares.ca/Production_Shakespeare/SearchPublicShowPlay.cfm?PlayID=118 and http://www.canadianshakespeares.ca/Production_Shakespeare/SearchPublicShowPlay.cfm?PlayID=115.

14 See Linda Burnett, Peter Dickinson, Ric Knowles ("Othello"), and Ellen McKay for accounts of these adaptations in performance, particularly their treatment of gender and race issues.

15 The text of "The Shakespearean Baseball Game" is available on *CASP*'s site. The black and white video and later colour version are both available on YouTube, as is the video for "Rinse the Blood Off My Toga," whose text has been transcribed as well.

16 *Hamlet on Ice* was written by Grahame Bond, who also co-wrote the rock musical *Boy's Own McBeth* (1979) with Jim Burnett. *The Popular Mechanicals* (1987) by Keith Robinson and Tony Taylor is another farcical Australian adaptation from this period.

17 In addition to the adaptations discussed in this book, a significant number of direct translations of Shakespeare have been produced in Québec.

18 The overwhelming majority of Québécois adaptations take "serious" plays (tragedies, histories, romances) as their starting point and, depending on the adapter, often introduce comical, farcical, or derisive elements into the play. This corpus contains 6 adaptations of *Richard III* (*Vie et mort du Roi Boiteux, Les Reines, Richard moins III, Mon royaume pour un cheval, Dave veut jouer Richard III, Richard III ou la chute du corbeau*), 5 adaptations of *Hamlet* (*Hamlet, prince du Québec, Touchez pas à ma paroisse, Hamlet-le-Malécite, Les mots fantômes, Elsemeur*), 5 adaptations of *Romeo and Juliet* (*À propos de Roméo et Juliette, Roller, La leçon d'Anglaise, Le Capitaine Horribifabulo, Guitare Tatou/Burger Love*), 4 adaptations of *Macbeth* (*Elle, Macbeth de William Shakespeare: Traduit en québécois, Macbean, Le* Making of *de Macbeth*),

2 adaptations of *Othello* (*Sauvée des eaux, Sous l'empire de Iago*), 1 adaptation of *King Lear* (*Lear*), 1 adaptation of *Henry V* (*Henry. Octobre. 1970.*), 1 adaptation of *The Tempest* (*La tempête*), 1 adaptation of *Coriolanus* (*Coriolan*), and 1 adaptation of *Pericles* (*Pericles, Prince of Tyre, by William Shakespeare*). While *The Taming of the Shrew* is considered a comedy, much of the farce relies on misogynist elements not considered comical today; other than Micone's *La mégère de Padova* the only other comedy is Ouellette's *Songe d'une nuit*. Adaptations that take multiple genres as their starting point include *Falstaff*, a combination of the *Henry IV* plays and *Merry Wives of Windsor*, as well as the *38* event, which covers all of Shakespeare's plays. Biographical adaptations about Shakespeare that do not fit into one of his genres include *Shakespeare: un monde qu'on peut apprendre par cœur, William S*, the three *Teaching Shakespeare* plays, *L'aventure de Shakespeare au pays des rêves, L'ultime séduction ou L'Alcibiade de William Shakespeare*, and *Teaching Hamlet*. The preponderance of "serious" plays can arguably be attributed to the adapters' espousal of nationalism; more than comedy, "serious" plays convey legitimacy for such an important topic as the fate of an entire nation. In contrast, many of Shakespeare's comedies interrogate the roles of men and women in society, comedy being an apt genre through which to challenge gender norms before safely marrying off everyone through comic closure. The relative dearth of comedies in this corpus corresponds to greater attention to nation than to gender.

19 In *The Dream of Nation*, Susan Mann Trofimenkoff also makes the analogy between the Conquest and rape: "And yet it was conquest. And conquest is like rape" (31). In concluding her book with the 1980 referendum, she extends the gendering of English Canada and Québec through the metaphor of divorce often applied to sovereignty: "Certainly the reaction of English Canada before the referendum was that of a spurned male: if a frivolous Quebec voted for separation, there would be no question of some new arrangement. For many federalists, indeed, separation was unthinkable precisely because, without quite realizing it, they compared Quebec to a woman. Neither she, nor, by analogy, *la belle province*, had the right to independence. A separate Quebec, they feared, would deny its cultural mission in North America just as certain women were denying their prescribed role in the family to transmit values and refine behaviour. A separate Quebec would abandon French-speaking minorities in other parts of Canada, as horrendous a dereliction of duty as that of a mother abandoning her children. In the eyes of most of English Canada, Quebec had been behaving improperly since the 1960s, flirting with a long discarded French lover from across the sea, flaunting new found economic

and administrative skills, and constantly wheedling more out of the federal government. The cracking of Confederation in the 1960s and 1970s was the cracking of the nineteenth century notion of separate spheres that had placed sexes and peoples, provinces and countries into mutually exclusive but supposedly complementary entities" (330).

20 "We got fucked."

21 *Joual* is Québécois working-class slang. The term *joual* is believed to come from the pronunciation of the word *cheval* [horse] in this dialect. While the term has been mistakenly attributed to the journalist André Laurendeau, its usage dates back much earlier, to at least the 1930s. Although previously stigmatized because it was spoken by the working class, *joual* began to be valorized after the Quiet Revolution, most notably by Michel Tremblay's play *Les Belles-Sœurs* (1968), the first play to be written in *joual*, as well as in popular music, such as Robert Charlebois's songs, and even by some nationalists who saw it as a pride-worthy part of Québec's cultural heritage. In fact, some words considered *joual*, such as *moé* [*moi*; me] and *toé* [*toi*; you], are actually the pronunciations used by royalty prior to the French Revolution. Since Québec was cut off geographically from the rest of France, the *Ancien Régime* pronunciation remained in use in Québec despite evolving into its current form in France.

22 "Faith will be the cement of the nation."

23 "To clear the land."

24 "To be French Canadian meant first to be loyal to the faith of one's ancestors, to keep the family and parish frameworks intact, to stay rooted in the ancestral land, to resist industrialization." See Balthazar's *Bilan du nationalisme au Québec* for a more comprehensive explanation of "la survivance" and a succinct history of nationalist discourses from the founding of New France to the 1980s.

25 *Né pour un petit pain* translates literally as "born for a little roll" of bread as opposed to a loaf. The implication was that French Canadians should be content with what they had already and not strive for more. *La revanche des berceaux* translates literally as "the revenge of the cradles," but the word "revenge" is too strong for the phrase's connotation. The Catholic Church encouraged women to have as many children as possible in order to ensure the survival of the French Canadian nation. A family of twenty children, not counting a few stillborns or early deaths, was common. For an analysis of ultramontane nationalism, see Denis Monière's *Le Développement des idéologies au Québec des origines à nos jours*, especially chapters 4 and 5.

26 "The sky is blue; hell is red."

27 "It's Time for Things to Change." "Masters in Our Own Homes."
28 "Long live free Québec!"
29 For further details, see the Québec government's website commemorating the 50th anniversary of the Quiet Revolution: http://www.revolutiontranquille.gouv.qc.ca.
30 "A childhood of Québec society (until 1837), an adolescence that would correspond to the Quiet Revolution (after a long interruption, a sort of Sleeping Beauty represented by survivalism) and the hope of adulthood with the transition from nation to country."
31 There were, however, exceptions at some levels. In some towns, widows and single, adult women gained the right to vote in municipal elections in 1888 if they were land-owners, and this right was extended to renters in 1892. This right was extended to women separated from their husbands in Montréal in 1908 and to married land-owners in 1931. In school elections, women land-owners had the right to vote until 1899.
32 Abortion became a woman's legal, free choice throughout Canada in 1988 when the Supreme Court, in *R. v. Morgentaler*, struck down Section 251 of the Criminal Code. The Supreme Court ruled that the criminalization of abortion violated Section 7 of the Charter of Rights and Freedoms, which states that "Everyone has the right to life, liberty, and the security of the person and the right not to be deprived thereof except in accordance with the principles of fundamental justice."
33 "A pro-feminist and pro-gay aura."
34 "No free Québec without the freedom of women! No free women without the freedom of Québec!" Various permutations of this slogan exist. It appears in the above form in an FLF document on abortion access dated April 1971 (O'Leary and Toupin 97). In a press release dated 8 May 1970, it appears as "Pas de Québec libre sans femmes libérées" [No free Québec without free women] (71), while a letter dated 4 December 1970 from the FLF to the Women's Liberation Movement in New York ends with "Vive le Québec libre! Vive la lutte de libération des femmes!" [Long live free Québec! Long live the struggle for women's freedom!] (80). The *Manifeste des femmes québécoises*, written by an anonymous "group of women from Montréal," employs the first version of the slogan cited above on the book's back cover. O'Leary and Toupin are careful, however, to disassociate the FLF from the writers of this manifesto, which has erroneously been attributed to the FLF, claiming that "le Manifeste fut écrit par deux femmes de l'extrême gauche d'alors qui, bien que proches de quelques femmes du groupe, n'ont jamais mis les pieds au FLF." [The Manifesto was written by two extreme-left women of the time who, although close to some members of the group, never set foot in the FLF] (53).

35 "A few anglophone students from McGill, enthusiasts of *Women's Lib* and converted to the legitimacy of the struggle for the social and national liberation of Québec."

36 "These radical nationalists were demanding no less than the toppling of patriarchy and Anglo-American imperialism."

37 "Québec being a colonized country, the Québécois woman is thus doubly exploited."

38 "She has lived here for a year and a half and has never been able to communicate directly with us because she still doesn't speak French. She thus in no way can speak in our name nor in that of any Québécois woman."

39 The title is a pun on "la mère patrie," meaning "the mother country," and "amère," meaning "bitter."

40 "Possible to carve out a space as a feminist and to link national emancipation and sexual emancipation"; "significant that, to illustrate the foreignness of the Canadian Alliance in relation to 'Québécois values,' Gilles Duceppe, the leader of the Bloc Québécois, essentially made reference to women's right to abortion and the defence of the rights of gays and lesbians."

The Canadian Alliance was a conservative party that existed from 2000 to 2003. It was first led by Stockwell Day and then Stephen Harper and garnered support primarily from voters in western Canada since it was the successor to the Reform Party of Canada, which was led by Preston Manning from 1987 to 2000. When the Reform Party transformed into the Canadian Reform Conservative Alliance in 2000, it briefly went by the name Canadian Conservative Reform Alliance, which, with the addition of Party, resulted in the humorous acronym CCRAP (pronounced "see-crap" or simply "crap") that many opponents found to be an apt description of the party's policies. The CCRAP nickname stuck with the party until the Alliance merged with the Progressive Conservatives in 2003 to become the Conservative Party of Canada.

Further highlighting CCRAP's cultural estrangement from Québec, the press conference announcing the party's launch took place in front of a large banner with the slogan "Think Big," a phrase that later became the title of Preston Manning's 2003 memoir. Ostensibly, nobody in the CCRAP was aware (or cared?) that "Think Big" was already the slogan of Bob "Elvis" Gratton, a fictional character popularized in the films of Pierre Falardeau. In *Elvis Gratton II: Miracle à Memphis* – the widely popular and highly anticipated cinematic return of the "dead" character that was released on Canada Day in 1999, just one year before the CCRAP's creation – Gratton, who is always portrayed as a clumsy, ignorant redneck worthy of ridicule, frequently utters the "Think Big" slogan in English, often followed by the abbreviated Québécois curse "'sti!" In Québec, "Think Big" invariably evokes Falardeau's scathing critique of American consumerist culture and anti-intellectualism.

41 "The promise of emancipation, which allows them to link the national cause to a series of social causes and to infuse national discourse with the hope of singing tomorrows"; "it also served as a brake on the expression of social diversity."

42 "First, a willingness for complete de-traditionalization of Québec society (since this work was already largely undertaken during the Quiet Revolution). [...] Second, common work building the national welfare state as a stipulation of social solidarity and as a condition of the possibility of the civic nation for nationalists, while for feminists the welfare state permits the politicization of certain injustices that previously were considered private and a political monitoring of sexed social relationships. Third, a convergence in the politicization of identity, even if the two social movements privilege different forms of identitary affiliation."

43 For associations between nationalism and "tribalism," "xenophobia," and "essentialism," see Stephen May's *Language and Minority Rights* (9, 20–3), Michel Seymour's "Québec and Canada at the Crossroads" (2), and Seymour, Couture, and Neilson's "Questioning the Ethnic/Civic Dichotomy" (29n36).

44 Any French speaker living outside Québec knows well that access to government services is rarely what proponents of official bilingualism claim it to be. Official bilingualism applies only to interactions with the federal government but does not provide services to French speakers outside Québec at the provincial level, such as education and healthcare, unless there is a sufficiently large community to warrant French services. The five-year legal battle that francophones in Ontario fought to keep the Montfort hospital open in Ottawa testifies to the difficulties faced by francophones outside Québec. See "Victoire pour l'hôpital Montfort" on Radio-Canada.ca for a recap of the legal saga that lasted from 24 February 1997 to 1 February 2002.

45 In 1996, 52.3 per cent of inhabitants of Montréal had French as a mother tongue, which fell to only 48.8 per cent in 2006. During the same decade, the percentage of "allophones" rose from 26.7 per cent to 31.7 per cent, outnumbering even English speakers whose numbers fell from 18.0 per cent to 16.8 per cent. In the rest of Québec excluding Montréal, the percentage of francophones fell from 93.0 per cent to 92.3 per cent. For Québec overall, the percentage of francophones fell from 80.9 per cent to 79.0 per cent between 1996 and 2006. The discrepancy between the

percentage of people whose mother tongue is French in Montréal where the majority of immigrants settle and the percentage in the rest of Québec testifies to the effect immigration has on the overall decline of French, despite *Loi 101* which obliges immigrant children to attend school in French if they do not have at least one parent who attended school in English. The steady decline of French in Montréal would presumably be even more accelerated than it is now had such protectionist language laws not been put in place by the PQ. See the Government of Québec's *Rapport sur l'évolution de la situation linguistique au Québec*.

46 See "Argumentaire pour la souveraineté" (2008), p 4, on the *Parti Québécois* website.

47 See Monière et al. "Indépendance et croissance économique" for statistics from the World Bank's 1996 report comparing Slovakia to the Czech Republic. Denis Monière, Guy Bouthillier, and Pierre De Bellefeuille demonstrate that, despite the 1991–3 recession, from 1991 to 1996 Slovakia fared better economically than the Czech Republic, and likewise Slovenia and Croatia, newly independent from Yugoslavia, fared better economically than the already independent control group countries of Romania, Bulgaria, and Hungary.

48 Statistics for all thirty-five member countries, as well as the European Union, are available online at http://www.oecd-ilibrary.org.

49 "Il faut reconnaître que l'économie du Québec a connu au cours des derniers mois des progrès spectaculaires. Ils le sont d'autant plus que le Québec a dû, comme bien d'autres, affronter les difficultés économiques qui ont suivi le 11 septembre 2001. On se rappelle que nous avions alors devancé en novembre la présentation du budget 2002–2003 de manière à soutenir la confiance des ménages, notamment, par une accélération des investissements publics. [...] En 2002, la croissance a atteint 3,8% au Québec, dépassant même celle du Canada et celle des États-Unis. Toujours en 2002, Mme la Présidente, le Québec a créé 118 000 emplois sur la moyenne des 12 mois, ce qui veut dire que, de septembre 2001 à décembre 2002, c'est même 170 000 emplois qui ont été créés. Il s'agit de la plus forte création d'emplois enregistrée au Québec depuis 1973." [It must be recognized that Québec's economy has made spectacular progress over the last few months. This progress is even greater given that, like many others, Québec has had to confront the economic difficulties that followed 11 September 2001. Remember that at that time we had advanced to November the presentation of the 2002–2003 budget in order to support the confidence of households, notably by the acceleration of public investments. [...] In 2002, growth reached 3.8% in Québec, exceeding that of Canada and of

the United States. Also in 2002, Mrs. President, Québec created 118,000 jobs on the average of 12 months, which means that from September 2001 to December 2002 it was actually 170,000 jobs that were created. This constitutes the strongest job creation recorded in Québec since 1973.] See the official *Journal des débats de l'Assemblée nationale – 36e législature, 2e session – 11 mars 2003* for Marois's full 2003–2004 budget speech.

50 "Party of ideas."

51 Parizeau's famous phrase has been cited variously as "le vote ethnique" and "les votes ethniques," and the use of a singular or plural article changes the meaning from "an organized vote mandated by specific leaders of ethnic groups directing followers to vote in block" to "individual votes by people of other ethnic origins." In fact, as archival video footage makes clear, Parizeau said "des votes ethniques," which has essentially the latter meaning. The confusion probably arose because the former meaning more accurately reflects the tactics ethnic leaders used to convince members of their communities to vote No.

In *Le Référendum volé*, Robin Philpot describes the hypocritical, ethnically inflected discourse with which the Greek, Italian, and Jewish leaders all pressured their communities to vote No: "Les dirigeants de ces trois communautés, qui ont établi leur coalition dès l'été 1995, ont notamment tenu une conférence de presse le mardi 24 octobre pour inciter les Grecs, les Italiens et les Juifs du Québec à voter NON. Lors de la conférence de presse, Me Athanasios Hadjis, vice-président du Congrès hellénique du Québec, Me Tony Manglaviti, du Congrès national italo-canadien pour la région du Québec, et Me Reisa Teitelbaum, présidente de la section québécoise du Congrès juif canadien, ont vanté le fait que leurs communautés réunissaient quelques 400 000 personnes, soit 6% de la population québécoise, et que celles-ci voteraient à 90% pour le NON. Mais, dans le même souffle et avec un raisonnement qui défie la logique, ils ont mis les dirigeants souverainistes en garde de ne pas faire de distinction entre le vote des minorités et le vote de l'ensemble de la population québécoise. C'est l'histoire du beurre et de l'argent du beurre: d'un côté, on joue la carte ethnique sans broncher pour faire le plein des votes pour le NON, et de l'autre, on crie au racisme à l'idée qu'un souverainiste puisse oser décrire ce qui s'est passé." [The leaders of these three communities, who established their coalition as early as summer 1995, notably held a press conference on Tuesday, 24 October to incite the Greeks, the Italians and the Jews of Québec to vote NO. During the press conference, Maître Athanasios Hadjis, vice-president of the Québec Hellenic Congress, Maître Tony Manglaviti, of the Italian-Canadian Congress for the region of Québec, and Maître Reisa Teitelbaum, president of the Québec section of the Canadian Jewish Congress, bragged about the fact that their communities encompassed about 400,000 people, which is 6% of the Québec population, and that these people would vote at a rate of 90% for the NO. But, in the same breath and with a reason that defies logic, they warned the sovereignist leaders not to make a distinction between the vote of minorities and the vote of the whole Québec population. It is a case of having one's cake and eating it too: on one side, they play the ethnic card without a murmur to fill up on NO votes, and on the other, they cry racism at the idea that a sovereignist could dare describe what has happened] (65).

In his 1997 book *Pour un Québec souverain*, Parizeau implies that his use of the word "nous" on referendum night was about language, not race: "Je demeure convaincu que le seul critère important quant à l'orientation de vote sur la souveraineté, c'est la langue. Ce n'est ni la race ni la couleur; c'est la langue. Je connais beaucoup de souverainistes d'origine haïtienne alors que je n'en connais aucun chez les Jamaïcains…" [I remain convinced that the only important criterion in terms of the orientation of the vote on sovereignty is language. It is neither race nor colour; it is language. I know many sovereignists of Haitian origin while I know none that are Jamaican…] (41). Both, of course, are black, but Haitians speak French while Jamaicans speak English. In his 2009 book *La souveraineté du Québec: Hier, aujourd'hui et demain*, Parizeau reaffirms his openness to immigrants from all origins who want to live in French in Québec while simultaneously denouncing the poisonous discourse of the Greek, Italian, and Jewish Congresses: "J'ai toujours pensé que c'est sur les francophones qu'il faut s'appuyer pour réaliser l'indépendance du Québec et je continue de le croire. Je n'entends pas par francophone le Canadien français de souche, mais tous ceux qui vivent en français, quelle que soit leur origine. Cela ne veut pas dire que les autres Québécois sont des adversaires, mais que la campagne menée pendant des années contre la souveraineté du Québec, appuyée notamment par des Congrès juif, grec et italien, introduisait dans le débat politique une dimension ethnique qui a empoisonné l'atmosphère." [I have always thought that we must count on francophones to achieve Québec's independence and I continue to believe that. I do not mean by francophone the dyed in the wool French Canadian, but all those who live in French, whatever their origin. That does not mean that other Québécois are adversaries, but that the campaign led for years against Québec sovereignty, supported notably by the Jewish, Greek, and Italian Congresses, introduced into the political debate an ethnic dimension that poisoned the atmosphere] (56–7).

Backing up the factual aspect of Parizeau's statement, in *Sortie de secours* Jean-François Lisée describes how the federal government accelerated processing requests for Canadian citizenship leading up to the referendum, knowing that new immigrants would vote overwhelmingly for the No side. In the month prior to the 20 October 1995 deadline for voters to add their names to the voting registry, 11,500 people were naturalized in Québec, a rate of about 580 people for each of the 20 working days. This represents an increase of 250 per cent compared to the month prior, 300 per cent compared to the same month a year earlier, and 440 per cent compared to October 1993. Based on the average rate of naturalization between 1988 and 1998, Lisée calculates that 42,375 immigrants obtained the right to vote prematurely. Based on a participation rate of 84 per cent for new immigrants during the referendum, with 86 per cent of those having arrived for less than ten years voting No, he calculates the No side obtained 30,617 votes it would not have had if the Canadian federal government had not accelerated the naturalization process and given citizenship to these immigrants prematurely.

While the "vote ethniques" part of Parizeau's statement has garnered a lot of attention, much less has been paid to the "argent" part. Philpot interviews Pierre-F. Côté, QC, chief electoral officer of Québec, whom he qualifies as "un juriste prudent et respecté dont la neutralité est légendaire" [a prudent and respected jurist whose neutrality is legendary] (64). Côté deplores the federal government's intrusion into the No campaign, which under Québec law should only have received funding from within Québec: "Les 4,8 M$ versés par Patrimoine Canada, on a fait des enquêtes là-dessus. On n'a jamais été capable de savoir où est allé l'argent. Il y avait un bureau à Montréal quelque part. Ils n'ont jamais voulu répondre à nos questions. On est à peu près certain que les 4,8 M$ ont servi à l'organisation de la marche pour l'unité, le *love-in*." [The $4.8 million paid by Heritage Canada, we investigated that. We were never able to know where the money went. There was an office in Montréal somewhere. They would never answer our questions. We're almost certain that the $4.8 million was used for the organization of the unity march, the "love-in"] (60–1). In addition to the $4.8 million provided illegally by Heritage Canada through the cover-operation Option Canada, Côté calculated another $11.8 million in illegal spending, including donations from private businesses, such as Power Corporation run by the Desmarais family, for a total of over $15 million in illegal spending by the No campaign: "Mon calcul que c'est 11,8 M$, plus les 4,8 M$, plus de 15 M$ avant le référendum. Ce qui est surprenant, c'est que ça ne soulève pas le dégoût!" [My calculation is it is $11.8 million, plus the $4.8 million, more than $15 million before the referendum. What is surprising is that it does not make people sick!] (63). Because of the flat-out refusal of those who violated the law to answer questions and because thirty boxes of documents were reportedly shredded soon after the referendum by Power Corporation (59), the Directeur général des élections du Québec (DGE) was never able to prosecute those responsible for the illegal spending. For further information on this illegal spending, see Normand Lester and Robin Philpot's subsequent investigation *Les secrets d'Option Canada*.

Chapter 2. A Theory of Shakespearean Adaptation

1 Jean Marsden comes close to this conception of "appropriation" when she cites the *OED* definition "to take to one's self" and extrapolates the idea of "making this [desired] object one's own"; however, she ultimately associates the term with its negative connotations of "theft," "possession," "usurpation," and "seizure" (1), failing to conceive the term beyond its traditional usage.

2 Although Part 1 of Julie Sanders's *Adaptation and Appropriation* is subtitled "Defining Terms," her two chapters on "Adaptation" and "Appropriation" tend primarily to describe a host of examples without arriving at a clear definition of these key terms or a justification for her designation of some examples as one or the other. She eventually claims that adaptation is a "transpositional practice, casting a specific genre into another generic mode" (18), may involve "offering commentary on sourcetext" (18), and "can also constitute a simpler attempt to make texts 'relevant' or easily comprehensible to new audiences and readerships via the processes of proximation and updating" (19). Appropriation, she suggests, "frequently affects a more decisive journey away from the informing source into a wholly new cultural product and domain" and "the appropriated text or texts are not always as clearly signalled or acknowledged as in the adaptive process" (26). She offers two subcategories of appropriation – "embedded texts" and "sustained appropriations" – but there is little justification for these subcategories or definition of what they actually are beyond the examples she provides. In casting such a broad definition and trying to categorize such a broad range of examples across media and genres, Sanders's definitions do not actually define the terms.

3 "Transtextual relationships," "intertextuality," "*citation*," "*plagiarism*," "*allusion*"; "paratextuality," "and many other types of accessory signals [...] that provide the text with a (variable) setting and sometimes

commentary"; "*metatextuality*," "the *critical* relationship"; "*architextuality*," "the generic perception [...] guides and determines to a large degree the 'expectation horizon' of the reader, and thus the reception of the work"; "*hypertextuality*." "Relationship uniting a B text ([...] *hypertext*) to an anterior A text ([...] *hypotext*) to which it grafts itself in a manner that isn't commentary."

Translations of Genette are my own in consultation with Channa Newman and Claude Doubinsky's English edition.

4 "It may be of another order, such that B doesn't speak of A at all, but could not however exist as is without A, from which it results through an operation that I will qualify, provisionally, as *transformation*, and which it consequently evokes more or less perceptibly, without necessarily referring to it or citing it. The *Aeneid* and *Ulysses* are undoubtedly, to varying degrees and certainly on different grounds, two hypertexts (among others) of the same hypotext: the *Odyssey*, of course."

5 In *Cybertext: Perspectives on Ergodic Literature*, Espen Aarseth argues that cybertexts, such as hypertext fiction, computer games, and MUDs, are different from "nonergodic literature, where the effort to traverse the text is trivial, with no extranoematic responsibilities placed on the reader except (for example) eye movement and the periodic or arbitrary turning of pages" (1–2). In ergodic literature, such as video games, readers are "constantly reminded of inaccessible strategies and paths not taken, voices not heard" (3), unlike nonergodic literature, such as plays and novels, which is fundamentally linear and does not involve the participation of the reader in determining the outcome of the story. Aarseth warns that theories of literature "have a powerful ability to co-opt new fields and fill theoretical vacuums," which he describes as "a process of colonization" (19). Rather than colonizing video games by recuperating them into the same category of adaptation as plays and novels, as Hutcheon does, recognizing the differences inherent to the medium would pay respect to the processes by which their authors/coders/designers created them.

6 For translation theory in postcolonial contexts such as Québec and how translation differs substantially from adaptation, see Edwin Gentzler, Joseph Graham (ed.), Carol Maier, Rainer Schulte and John Biguenet (eds.), Sherry Simon, and Maria Tymoczko.

7 Lukas Erne argues in *Shakespeare as Literary Dramatist* not only that Shakespeare intended the full versions of his plays to be read as literary texts but also that he, or at least the Lord Chamberlain's Men, had a hand in their publication.

8 For these reasons, although Kidnie discusses Robert Lepage's one-man production of *Elseneur* (1995) as if it were an adaptation (89–102) in

which Lepage performs not Hamlet the character but *Hamlet* the work (99), I exclude it from this book because it is not a textual adaptation of Shakespeare but an innovative stage production. With the exception of the title, the script remains entirely Shakespearean, a standard French translation with cuts and rearrangements, to which Lepage makes no textual additions of his own – startling "not [for] its radicalism, but its utter familiarity" (95). The innovative nature of the play lies in its production on stage since technology allows Lepage to play multiple characters.

Kidnie describes some minor differences between Shakespeare's *Hamlet* and the script of *Elsinore* as played in English in London: "Hamlet's first encounter with Rosencrantz and Guildenstern (2.2.243–378), for example, happened before Polonius showed his love letter to the King and Queen (2.2.86–159), rather than his 'mad' scene with Polonius (2.2.171–211); Ophelia's narrative of Hamlet's visit to her closet was set in counterpoint to Hamlet's 'nunnery' speeches (2.1, 3.1); Gertrude's monologue describing the death of Ophelia (4.7.166–83) was interspersed with snatches of the maid's songs (4.5); and Hamlet's accounts of the pirate attack and his recomposition of the commission to England were conflated (4.6, 5.2)" (183n98). While such rearrangements of scenes do influence the audience's interpretation of the character, they are not as radical as Charles Marowitz's rearrangements and reattribution of lines in his *Measure for Measure* so as to constitute an adaptation. Many other stage productions rearrange the order of scenes, often to facilitate audience comprehension or scene and costume changes for actors, without garnering the label "adaptation."

I also exclude *Romeo & Juliette* (1989), codirected by Robert Lepage and Gordon McCall in Saskatchewan, because the play remains a production and partial translation rather than an adaptation. Although the production was innovative and even controversial in its representation of language politics because Romeo and the Montagues spoke English while Juliette and the Capulets spoke French, the French portion of the play is a direct translation of Shakespeare by Jean Marc Dalpé and the English portion of the script literally consists of photocopied inserts from the Signet edition pasted between the French passages. This bilingual production remains a production of Shakespeare's text, and to deem either of these Lepage productions an adaptation would bring us back to the problem of considering all stage productions that do the least bit of new stage business as adaptations, thereby reducing the term's useful application.

9 Since it is a cinematic rather than a textual adaptation of Shakespeare, I exclude Forcier's Québécois adaptation from this book, but I analyse it in an essay entitled "*Othello* in Québec: Adapting Race and Gender in

André Forcier's *Une histoire inventée,"* forthcoming in *Shakespeare on Screen: Othello.*

10 Likewise, Sanders's "aim is to open out and widen the range of terms and their applications, rather than fixing or ossifying specific concepts of adaptation and appropriation" (13), yet it is difficult to glean a clear definition of the two key terms of her book.

11 In *The Schreiber Theory: A Radical Rewrite of American Film History,* David Kipen uses the Yiddish word for "writer" in order to argue, contrary to auteur theory, that screenwriters have more influence on a film than the director.

Chapter 3. The Quiet Revolution

All quotations in this chapter are taken from the 1968 edition of the play.

1 *Passer à l'action,* meaning literally "to move to action," could be translated as "to take action," but it is a notably Québécois expression that loses in translation its underlying emotional force and its double insistence on action with the verb "passer," "to move," which indicates a forward progress absent from the English expression "to take."

2 In "Entre deux joints" (1973), co-written with RIN leader Pierre Bourgault, Robert Charlebois sings, "Ta sœur est aux États, ton frère est au Mexique/Y font d'l'argent là-bas pendant qu'tu chômes icitte/T'es né pour un petit pain, c'est ce que ton père t'a dit/Chez les Américains, c'pas ça qu't'aurais appris." [Your sister's in the States, your brother's in Mexico/They make money there while you're unemployed here/You were born for a little roll [of bread, as opposed to a loaf], that's what your father said/With the Americans that's not what you'd have learned.] The rejection of the *né pour un petit pain* attitude thus embodies the generational divide between Quiet Revolution youth and their parents, who grew up accepting that they should settle for less, as well as the new generation's growing internationalism.

3 *Étapisme,* meaning "by stages," was adopted by members of the PQ at their Congress, the highest deciding body within the party, held 15–17 November 1974 (Graham Fraser 392). There is a well-known anecdote about how Jacques Parizeau, who disagreed with the idea but rallied to Lévesque's idea, "s'est trompé de micro"; that is, he "mistook" the Against microphone for the For microphone in order to show his disapproval and momentarily raise the tension in the room. *Étapisme* – to achieve independence through a referendum rather than an *élection référendaire,*

that is, through the outcome of a general election – was proposed to René Lévesque by Claude Morin who was later revealed to be a spy working for the Royal Canadian Mounted Police. For Morin's role as a *taupe* [mole], see Normand Lester's *Enquêtes sur les services secrets.*

4 According to Agriculture and Agri-Food Canada, in 2010 Québec exported $221,797,246 in maple sugar and maple syrup products. The next largest exporting province is New Brunswick at $7,645,221, followed by Ontario at $441,308. Québec is the world's largest producer of maple products and represents 95.89 per cent of the $231,298,213 total Canadian exports.

5 "Hamlet is Québec with all its hesitations, with its thirst for freedom, corseted by one hundred years of inaction."

6 "Gravediggers." "A grave [that] can very well be that of Hamlet."

7 "The mire of compromises, of slavery." "The chains that hypocritically [they them]selves forged."

8 "And there are some who say that the revenge of the cradles is over… why don't you try the pill?" "With the salary I make, I don't have the means to buy candies. And plus my wife wouldn't want to… because of the priest."

9 "Have you forgotten who I am? I guided your first steps." "And you blurred my vision."

10 "You guided my steps wisely when my legs were too frail to carry me. Today, still, I listen to you and obey you."

11 "Residences across the country, all more sumptuous one after the other."

12 "Frailty, thy name is priest/dress."

13 In the French version of the text, the compound names are joined by a hyphen and Québec has an accent (Hamlet-Québec). In the English version, the names are joined by a slash and Quebec has no accent (Hamlet/Quebec). I reproduce the character names as they appear in order to distinguish between characters in each version of the text.

14 "Five years ago, day for day, the first separatist bomb exploded in a mailbox. That same day in 1959 Congo rebelled to accede to its indepen…"

15 "Peace-keeping role."

16 "White nigger of America," the title of a book written by FLQ member Pierre Vallières while in prison in New York in 1966–7 and published in 1968. See chapter 1.

17 "I've no education and plus I don't speak English."

18 For francophone content rules and a chronology of changes to Canadian broadcasting rules, see the CRTC website.

19 The Patriots' Rebellion of 1837–8 was principally a demand for responsible government, including the adoption of the 92 Resolutions. Although

sometimes believed to be a war between francophones and anglophones, many anglophones in Lower Canada rebelled against the British Empire alongside the francophones, as they also did in Upper Canada. Gilles Laporte, a history professor at Cégep du Vieux Montréal, lists on his website a total of 42,867 people who participated in the rebellions in Lower Canada.

20 "The tithe was raised and all that money goes to other regions, the same ones that helped the new king get on the throne."

21 "As long as I'm eating scraps, I prefer to eat them at my own table and not someone else's."

22 "Party in favour of independence."

23 "Me, with a guy like that, I'm in. […] If we had held our own back then [at the time of the Patriots of '37]… we wouldn't be there now. I'm sure that we could have."

24 "A burning wound in my side." "Armed aid to firm up our authority in this country."

25 "It only takes a spark to make the powder explode."

26 "It is necessary for your son to submit totally." "Put on iron gloves." "'As of today, the only tolerated language will be that used in the court. Any offender will be severely punished.'"

27 Gurik's portrayal of English Canada's rule of Québec with an iron fist also describes the "Plan B" hard-line tactics employed by the federal government after the close results of the 1995 referendum: punish Québec severely (Bill C-20 also known as the "Clarity Law," fiscal inequality, funds funnelled to federalist organizations in order to challenge Bill 101, funds intended for propaganda as revealed by the sponsorship scandal, etc.) until it accepts its "proper" place within a dialectic of dominance and submission. For an account of these tactics, see Normand Lester's *Le livre noir du Canada anglais*.

28 "One has to face reality… what was is no more."

29 "Quell (or suppress [of a rebellion or terrorists]) them, both him and the people."

30 "Patience often makes causes triumph, even the weakest ones."

31 "[Would] choke him at the foot of the altar so that his death would serve as an example to the other hotheads of the country."

32 "I loved you, now I know that, but the sparkle of honours, the misfortunes that fell upon me, the treacherous tongue of the person largely responsible for our tragedy obscured my reason…"

33 Laurendeau, a Québécois nationalist, noted in the report (which recommended an increase in bilingualism in federal institutions) that the source

of tension between anglophones and francophones in Canada resided in the particular status of Québec. In 1971, Trudeau rejected the recommendations of the commission and instituted instead a policy of multiculturalism, which many consider a strategy to drown out the notion of "two founding nations" in a sea of multiple ethnic identities. See this book's conclusion for a discussion of Canadian multiculturalism versus Québécois interculturalism.

34 Hamlet/Quebec greets the B & B Commission in French. The stage directions indicate he "(stops as if he had just remembered. Looks at the audience)" (20). Rosencrantz/B corrects him, "My honoured lord… (casting an anxious glance at the audience)," and then Hamlet/Quebec "([…] starts the reply anew)" in British English, saying "Good lads, how do ye both?" (21).

35 In her review of the 1968 London performance, Helen Wallace writes: "You don't have to understand French, or even be particularly sympathetic to the French cause to enjoy *Hamlet*. Far from being a propagandist piece of French subtlety fired through with separatist sentiment, it offers, instead a good insight into French-Canadian needs. And it is doubtful anything has been lost in the English translation by Marc Gélinas, since the play adheres so closely to the original Shakespearean text" (142). As Stevenson points out (79), the critic protests too much and seems concerned with calming the audience's fears that they will be exposed to "separatist" discourses that would ruin their enjoyment of the play. The play is ripe with "separatist sentiment," and Gélinas's English translation of Gurik does not adhere closely to the Shakespearean source text. Wallace appears to be reassuring potential playgoers that "it's okay" not to know French or to care about Québec politics at all; they can still "enjoy" the play without having to engage with its underlying nationalist discourses.

36 "Notes that those people are lucky to be bilingual because they can profit from the advantages of both cultures, then he gives a short self-criticism about his own inability to learn French."

37 Gélinas's characterization of the King/The English's duplicity is insightful for 1968. In the aftermath of the 1995 referendum's "love-in," which was quickly followed by the federal government's adoption of the hard-line "Plan B," it takes on added poignancy.

38 "I don't see the light much."

39 "Forced to chain his tongue."

40 "These days, Horatio, the man who wants to survive doesn't lay down his weapons; he fights. But I'm really misplaced to dictate your behaviour."

41 "What to do? Why do it?"

42 "Tramples this land where he is a stranger."

43 As an embodiment of the nation itself, Hamlet-Québec is thus a rape victim too. This victimization explains why the play effeminizes Laertes/Trudeau as a "fédéraste" since Hamlet-Québec's symbolic penetration must be transferred back onto the servant of Le Roi-L'anglophonie.
44 "Awakening." "On one's knees." Both *à genoux* and *prise de conscience* are politically inflected expressions that indicate one's servitude and rejection of servitude respectively, the emotion of which is lost in translation.
45 "Comes to confirm all of his presumptions, all [he felt] without daring to confess it [to himself] openly." "All this anguish, this feeling of oppression, of slavery, of abasement."
46 "I don't put much worth on my life." "Profiteer who could let [him] believe that he understands [him] and loves [him]."
47 "'Those who say tomorrow never think…' that it will not come."
48 "Corset of immobility to numb in him the feeling of vengeance and freedom." "Still tomorrow."
49 "The hope of some future."
50 "Fight!" "Projects born with the most energy and boldness."
51 "If you lie down in the grave, that won't help your sons."
52 "Many men." "A skull… a leader…"
53 "I'm dying… who will come guide us towards the light, for it is not enough to kill the snake but it is also necessary to kill its nest so that on this land can grow freely what must bloom. Will you feel strong enough to do it, courageous enough to want it? It's so much easier to rot in habit. Eat… sleep… die… and never dream… never laugh. Who… who… will get us out of the mire of compromises, of slavery, who will break the chains that hypocritically we ourselves forged. It is necessary that my death serve for others. It is necessary that lives… a… free… Qué… bec."
54 According to Stevenson, in both editions of the French text Hamlet-Québec seems to address Horatio-Lévesque only (72n4). However, in the 1977 Leméac re-edition (as opposed to the 1968 Éditions de l'homme text), Gurik asserts that Hamlet-Québec dies onstage in the arms of both Horatio-Lévesque and L'Officier du Rhin-Bourgault. Their dual support of Hamlet-Québec is significant because it points to how the nation's future depends on Lévesque and Bourgault's mutual collaboration. Indeed, just months after the play they would have to work together when members of Bourgault's RIN merged with Lévesque's MSA to form the PQ. In fact, the PQ's long-standing internal disputes, according to some analysts, originate from tensions between its more radical left-wing members issued from the RIN and its more moderate members coming from Lévesque's centre-left position.

Chapter 4. Tyrants and Usurpers

1 This is, of course, a reductive reading of Shakespeare's text; however, most adaptations take cursory readings of the source text as their starting point. Garneau zeros in on the tyrants and usurpers common to both plays and then tradapts his texts around these elements.

2 As evident in the manifesto's title, Lalonde's adoption of an exaggerated sixteenth-century orthography that both imitates and mocks du Bellay's results in most words being misspelled in contemporary French. Since these words are purposely misspelled to create temporal distance, I have chosen not to mark them with "[*sic*]."

3 "The Defense and Illustration of the Québécois Language." "The Defense and Illustration of the French Language."

4 "Difficulty to express oneself in the language of-one's-mother." "Mother tongue humiliates them personally so strongly."

5 "Alienation." "Insult [her] family and by admiring too much Good Language finish by disrespecting the good people who speak [it]…"

6 "Under the influence of anxiety the behaviour of the ostrich."

7 "Refusing to admit the presence of a Conqueror & foreign Occupier, who dispossesses them a little more each day of the richness of their language and their culture." "Aggressor to cut down."

8 "Occupy their hole." "At the bottom of their own humiliation."

9 "Pride to speak Québécois." "Less and less colonized." "Anyway, the enemy is France!"

10 "Vulgar Québécois." "Reunited under a bold sceptre capable of leading them very, very far."

11 "Surrounded on all sides by powerful foreigners, sometimes English, sometimes American, even, recently, Italian, who […] subject them to their laws, privileges, and rights acquired [from living] on this territory for a more or less long time."

12 "This excellent psychological disposition is truly and surely recognized by any disposition of our laws or proclamation of Independence very real and clear, heard by the United Nations."

13 "The nation that wants to speak does not even manage today to conjugate its strengths in the first person indicative."

14 Garneau's three tradaptations present remarkable differences in terms of the degree of adaptation. *Macbeth*, the first text that was actually published (although not the first he translated), is the most radical both in terms of the language, which constitutes a semantic system in its own right, and the discursive differences produced by this new vocabulary. In contrast,

Coriolan rarely diverges from the Shakespearean source text, and the language contains no *joual* to distinguish it from international French. *La tempête* lies in the middle. The spelling and syntax is mostly regularized, but the text contains distinctly Québécois terms, such as Caliban's insult to Stéphano as "ce niasieux" (5.1.125), and the nationalism is apparent. I limit this discussion to *Macbeth* and *La tempête* since they adapt the Shakespearean source text more significantly than *Coriolan*. The distinction between *Coriolan* and the other two tradaptations holds true in terms of both nation and gender. *Coriolan* does not alter the representation of Shakespeare's women characters, Volumnia, Virgilia, and Valeria, or the masculinity performed by Caius Martius and Tullus Aufidius.

15 Garneau's *Macbeth* has received a great deal of scholarly attention, but this criticism is entirely performance-oriented. See Andrès and Lefèbvre, Hodgdon, Lieblein ("Cette," "Re-making"), and Salter ("Between," "Borderlines"). While these scholars discuss briefly the text's exceptional language, their discussions focus on the play in performance rather than the text itself. Hodgdon and Salter focus on Robert Lepage's 1993 staging with little interest in Garneau's text which is "difficult to understand" for actors and audiences ("Borderlines" 72).

16 "Our home." "Country."

17 See Brisset, chapter 3, esp. pp. 207–22, for a comprehensive discussion of the two passages that Garneau omits.

18 *"I'm skipping from line 38 to line 47 because it's confused and confusing."*

Since Garneau's texts do not provide line numbers, but they do follow Shakespeare's act and scene divisions, references to quotations from Garneau's two tradaptations indicate act, scene, and page numbers.

19 "It would be a blessing and a heavenly justice if our country were liberated from the cursed hand that oppresses it."

As this first citation of a complete sentence of dialogue makes clear, Garneau's phonetic transcription of an eighteenth-century dialect results in most words being misspelled in contemporary French. Since these words are purposely misspelled for phonetic effect, I have chosen not to mark them with "[*sic*]."

20 Following H.L. Rogers in *"Double Profit" in Macbeth* (1964), Muir suggests transposing the lines as follows (xxxiv n.2):

> LORD:That, by the help of these (with Him above/To ratify the work), we may again/Give to our tables meat, sleep to our nights,/Free from our feasts and banquets bloody knives,/Do faithful homage, and receive free honours,/All which we pine for now. (32–7)
>
> LENNOX: Sent he to Macduff? (39)

LORD: He did: and with an absolute 'Sir, not I,'/The cloudy messenger turns me his back,/And hums, as who should say, 'You'll rue the time/That clogs me with this answer.' (40–3)/And this report/Hath so exasperate the King, that he/Prepares for some attempt of war. (37–9)

LENNOX: And that well might/Advise him to a caution, t'hold what distance/His wisdom can provide. (43–5)

21 *"I am not translating from lines 139 to 161* (Oxford University Press edition) *because it's the scene with the doctor in which they talk about the gift of healing of the king of England, a filler scene as we say in film, that has nothing to do with the dramatic action and doesn't even sound very Shakespearean."*

The line numbers of Garneau's Oxford edition correspond to the Oxford edition I use here.

22 "Together, we'll make it!/Our cause cannot be any more just! Victory is waiting for us/At the end of the road."

23 "Our poor country almost has trouble recognizing itself./Our mother country, we can almost no longer call it mother, have to/More closely say grave, mass ditch. It's only naive people/Who know nothing about anything who have the heart to smile in our home./[...]/The only ecstasy that is allowed to reign/Is to have all the pain of the world."

24 Although Brisset notes the deletion of the proper names of Birnam wood and Dunsinan hill (205), she overlooks the discrepancy in the translation of the direction in which the forest moves. While she claims that the play is localized in Québec by the omission of these proper names (205), and she also claims in relation to another passage that the action is associated with the battle of the Plains of Abraham (206), she does not connect the two claims or associate either one with the anomalous translation of the forest's movement, which she does not discuss.

25 All citations from Shakespeare's *Macbeth* refer to the 1998 Oxford edition. Citations from *The Tempest* are taken from the Arden 3rd series edition.

26 "Macbeth won't be beaten until the forest goes down the hill."

27 "You'll tell every soldier to rip off a bush, a shrub,/Or else a little tree to hide himself with, like that they won't have/Any idea of the number we are and besides it's an error that will allow us/To surprise them."

28 Garneau is said to have based his approximation of an eighteenth-century dialect on the language spoken in the mid-1970s in rural Gaspé. Although this dialect was still spoken then with a heavily inflected accent, it is archaic compared to Québécois spoken in the urban centres. A parallel can be drawn between Acadian French spoken in southwest Nova Scotia, which is a mix of sixteenth-century French, Micmac, and English.

Despite being spoken today, this Acadian dialect is archaic compared to standard French because it remains much the same as French spoken in Rabelais's time due to the region's geographic isolation, which prevented the language from developing as it did in France or Québec. The same can be said for some elements of Québécois *joual*, such as words similar to *moi* and *roi* whose pronunciation today as *moé* and *roé* corresponds to how the words were pronounced in France when settlers first immigrated to New France.

29 *Pure laine* is generally translated in English as "dyed in the wool." The term refers to Québécois who are born and raised in Québec, speak with a Québécois accent, and show no traces of any particular immigrant origin.

30 "We'd be better to scram out of here; even more so/That we don't know exactly what to cry about." "I'm like numb in front of this sadness, the pain is coming over me slowly."

31 "Liver of blasphemer."

32 "The source, the river of our blood,/The true resource of our lives, it's all drying up."

33 "Our father the king has suffered murder."

34 "Our father who art in heaven..."

35 " I would like to know if the priests have/Put you to sleep enough that you're going to continue to pray/For the soul of this worthy man."

36 In 1755, in what is known as Le Grand Dérangement, the Acadians were deported from the Maritime provinces of Nova Scotia, New Brunswick, and Prince Edward Island, ostensibly for refusing to swear allegiance to the British but also as part of the larger military campaign against New France during the Seven Years War and as a means to seize the fertile land on which they lived. Scattered to different regions, often separated from family members, Acadians ended up in France, the Thirteen Colonies, and eventually Louisiana where *Cadiens* became Cajuns. Some Acadians resettled in Québec, particularly in the Montérégie, Lanaudière, Centre-du-Québec, Chaudière-Appalaches, and Bas-Saint-Laurent areas.

37 " Betrayed." "Vile betrayal." "Pretty army of hypocrites and traitors." "Bunch of two-sided faces."

38 "Largely crushed by our miseries." "Our story/history breaks my heart."

39 "You lie like a lawyer."

40 "Dirty trick," from "salope" meaning "slut."

41 "And my own brother let himself be tempted/by the devil and my trust in him/met a great lie/and he became master/not only of my revenues/ but also of my power itself/from the habit of lying/he ended up believing his falsehoods/to see them as legitimate." In contrast, Shakespeare's Prospero says, "I thus neglecting worldly ends/[...]/in my false brother/

Awaked an evil nature, and my trust,/Like a good parent, did beget of him/A falsehood in its contrary as great/As my trust was, which had indeed no limit,/A confidence sans bound. He being thus lorded,/Not only with what my revenue yielded/But what my power might else exact, like one/Who, having into truth by telling of it,/Made such a sinner of his memory/To credit his lie, he did believe/He was indeed the duke, out o'th' substitution/And executing th'outward face of royalty/With all prerogative" (1.2.89–105).

42 "From the very heart of the battle/Where the flags of foreigners insult/Our beautiful sky." In contrast, Shakespeare's Ross says, "From Fife, great King,/Where the Norweyan banners flout the sky,/And fan our people cold" (1.2.49–51).

43 The *scandale des commandites*, or sponsorship scandal, revealed in 2004 and subsequently investigated by the Gomery Commission, could be characterized as a "flag war" since federal funding was funnelled inappropriately in order to try to buy a sense of belonging to Canada among Québécois at a cost of $332 million between 1996 and 2004. See "Commandites: La facteur atteint 332 millions" on Radio-Canada.ca.

44 "You can run away, you little failed lords, go/Be gluttonous with the English." In contrast, Shakespeare's Macbeth says, "Then fly, false Thanes,/And mingle with the English epicures" (5.3.7–8).

45 "A woman like they don't make 'em anymore like/A fully encouraging companion."

46 Recent scholarship in French now translates "gender" as "genre" (an improvement on "sociosexuation"), but this practice has only begun in the last decade or so. The word "genre" (which also means "type," as in a literary genre, and is Québécois slang for "sort of") does not always signify "gender" for a general public today and was not used in this sense in 1978 when Garneau published *Macbeth*.

47 "I want nothing more to do with my beautiful, soft sex/gender, I want nothing more to do with/My beautiful, tender sex/gender."

48 In an essay entitled "'Get a Look at Your Wife's Beautiful Cones': Lady Macbeth's Stone Butch Blues and Rural Second-Wave Feminism in *Scotland, PA*," forthcoming in *Shakespeare on Screen: Macbeth*, I demonstrate how Lady Macbeth may be read through the lens of Leslie Feinberg's canonical novel of transgenderism *Stone Butch Blues*. Lady Macbeth's transgenderism transcends her performance of gender to encompass her sexuality as well. Not only does she wish to *be* the opposite sex, but her body's physiological responses to sexually charged experiences suggest that her sexual identity is akin to that of a stone butch, that is, a masculine lesbian who protects herself emotionally by refusing to receive sexual

pleasure. In constructing her character, Shakespeare paints an accurate portrait of a woman whose gender trouble causes significant psychological distress as she is pulled between an essential identity and the social constraints of heteronormativity that deny her the ability to embody that identity.

49 Literally, "to get dressed like many people," but, metaphorically, "to get dressed appropriately as befits people of good standing."

50 "Are you in the process of letting yourself be completely invaded by madness?"

51 "Be all ears."

52 "Night of the long knives." During federal-provincial negotiations about a new Canadian constitution, a common front was formed by the provincial premiers, including Québec's René Lévesque, to reject Pierre Trudeau's proposal. During the night of 4–5 November 1981, after Lévesque retired to his hotel in Hull on the other side of the Outaouais river from Ottawa, the English Canadian premiers broke their agreement with Lévesque, stabbing him in the back, and agreed to Trudeau's proposal for a new Canadian constitution, which was repatriated the next year, but which Québec has not yet signed.

Chapter 5. The First Referendum

1 I have excluded *Falstaff* (1990) from this study of Jean-Pierre Ronfard's Shakespearean adaptations because the text does not contain enough original content to make it relevant here as an adaptation. *Falstaff* abridges and combines the plots of Shakespeare's *1–2 Henry IV* and *The Merry Wives of Windsor* in an almost literal translation. The play contains only one original speech, Falstaff's closing monologue on *la joie de vivre*. In this sense, *Falstaff* is also carnivalesque, but it does not deal with issues of nation and gender.

2 While Ronfard's works, especially *Roi Boiteux*, have garnered much critical attention to date including a special issue of *L'Annuaire théâtral* (2004) and two issues of *Jeu* (1983, 2004), almost all critics have focused on his plays in production to the exclusion of the text, despite both plays having been published. See, for instance, Louise Bouchard, Chassay, Féral, Lapointe, Lavoie and Lefebvre, Le Blanc, and Vigeant. In *Sociocritique de la traduction*, Brisset briefly discusses *Lear* in the context of translation, which she does not distinguish adequately from adaptation, and she too primarily addresses elements of the stage production or plot issues. In "Shakespeare à l'Arsenal," Lafon reads *Roi Boiteux* mainly through its basic plot structure,

from a psychoanalytic – hence arguably anti-feminist – perspective, claiming that *Roi Boiteux* "sert à dénoncer l'impasse du pouvoir des femmes" [serves to denounce the impasse of women's power] (94). This chapter contests Lafon's claim and seeks to fill the void of close textual readings of Ronfard's adaptations and their Shakespearean sources.

3 Carnival has been interpreted by some scholars as a subversion of social order; others see carnival as a safety valve for the release of social tension which is sanctioned by the dominant social order because it re-emerges strengthened and solidified. Among Shakespearean critics, Michael Bristol claims carnival "in no way excludes the possibility of coherent social protest" (*Carnival* 25), while Stephen Greenblatt sees carnival as "a release of pent-up frustrations, a safety valve that would enable the participants to return with renewed obedience" (66). Early modern historian Natalie Zemon Davis suggests carnival can "act both to reinforce order and to suggest alternatives to the existing order" (123). The debate about whether carnival is subversive or a safety valve is thus far-ranging and has not been resolved among critics. Apart from this debate, Québécois critic André Belleau describes Québécois literature, particularly the novel, as strongly influenced by Rabelais and highly carnivalesque, citing the works of Marie-Claire Blais, Roch Carrier, Jacques Godbout, and Jacques Ferron among other examples (54–5). For further work on carnival in North American francophone literatures, see Bourque and Brown.

4 "A bloody and grotesque epic in six plays and an epilogue."

5 See Le Blanc (131–2) for a list of plot parallels, some of which I reproduce here in the list of characters, but some of which oversimplify the two plays and overlook other important similarities.

6 "Our country is sick, profoundly sick."

7 "In this beautiful language that we have left, sign and symbol of our ancestral power."

8 "Culture [...] ties us to the breath and the blood of ancestors like the many-coloured hospital tubes maintain the existence of the dying man who is mummified in his bandages."

9 "I know about the weight (responsibility) of power. Very happy to be rid of it."

10 "It has to change! [...] Excited, crazy women, breasts to the wind, are filling the skulls of their fellow creatures and are starting to bust our ears with their demagogic slogans: 'the old power is dead!', 'long live the right of peoples to order everything!', 'day is breaking...the colour of the sky is changing...welcome the birth of a new order!'. And it's I, (*moans from Violette in her bed.*) well I and my sister, it's we that they expect to bring

about this new order. Imbeciles! Order is order. It doesn't have to be new or old. Order has no colour."

11 *"Bucket of shit." "He starts throwing balls of shit everywhere, particularly on the throne, on the cage of the Shakespeare-Technicians and on the ceiling."* Stage directions are italicized in the texts and appear as such hereafter.

12 "Unnatural time." "Long live bastardry / that knocks down laws / that dirties churches / and dethrones kings."

13 "Power to bastards."

14 The association between carnival and Québec's (neo)colonial status occurs in other nationalist works, the most notable example being Pierre Falardeau's film *Le temps des bouffons* (1993) about the annual Beaver Club supper at the Queen Elizabeth Hotel in Montréal. Falardeau invokes carnival when he implicitly compares Québec and Ghana, but he mocks the notion of carnival since it is temporary and has no lasting political effect: "On est au Ghana en 1957, avant l'indépendance. [...] Chaque année, les membres de la secte [des Haoukas] se réunissent pour fêter. [...] En 1957, le Ghana, c'est une colonie britannique... quelques rois nègres pour faire semblant, mais les vrais maîtres sont anglais. [...] La religion des Haoukas reproduit le système colonial en plus petit, mais à l'envers. Les colonisés se déguisent en colonisateurs, les exploités jouent le rôle des exploiteurs, les esclaves deviennent les maîtres. Une fois par année, les pauvres mangent du chien. Une fois par année, les fous sont maîtres. Le reste du temps, les maîtres sont fous." [We are in Ghana in 1957, before independence. [...] Each year, the members of the [Haoukas] sect gather to celebrate. [...] In 1957, Ghana is a British colony... a few nigger kings to pretend, but the real masters are English. [...] The Haoukas religion reproduces the colonial system smaller but backwards. The colonized disguise themselves as colonizers, the exploited play the role of exploiters, the slaves become masters. Once a year, the poor eat dog. Once a year, the fools are masters. The rest of the time, the masters are crazy] (73). See "*Le Temps des bouffons*, Prise 2" in *La liberté n'est pas une marque de yogourt* for the complete text of the film's voice-over commentary (73–6).

15 "I'm fucked to the bone. [...] Violette, in mocking disregard, has had added to the royal coat of arms, against a heraldic red background, a green-blazoned penis that she claims to have stolen from me for forever. It's hard."

16 In addition to its most well-known usage in *King Lear*, this sense of "nothing" signifying "lack" and hence "vagina" also appears at the end of *Measure for Measure* when the Duke rhetorically asks Mariana, "Why, you are nothing then: neither maid, widow, nor wife?" and Lucio confirms the pun on "nothing" with his witty interjection, "My lord, she may be a

punk, for many of them are neither maid, widow, nor wife" (5.1.177–80). An early modern woman whose sexuality is not properly controlled and sanctioned within the heteronormative economy of marriage is nothing, that is, a prostitute, an empty hole or used-up vagina, or damaged goods whose economic value is nothing.

17 "(*All at once, she takes on an inebriated voice, a guardsman's attitude, and a shithead's look. She adjusts her imaginary balls.*) [...] We told each other: '[...] we've got 'em in our pants, don't we? Of course we've got 'em. Two beautiful big ones like grandfather.'"

18 "Zir" is a gender-neutral pronoun popularly employed by queer and transgendered persons to replace the gendered pronouns "his" and "her." The respectful pronoun to use for transgendered people, people who pass, and drag kings and drag queens is the pronoun of their adopted gender. In keeping with this practice, the correct address for Corneille should be "he" while passing as a man to the king. Gender-neutral pronouns avoid the need for multiple pronouns for the same character, but their relative unfamiliarity with readers (which is indeed part of the point) creates another type of confusion. The following chart provides an example of gender-neutral pronouns and the gendered pronouns to which they correspond:

Subject	Object	Poss. Adj.	Poss. Pro.	Refl.
zie	zim	zir	zirs	zimself
he	him	his	his	himself
she	her	her	hers	herself
they	them	their	theirs	themselves

No consensus has been reached in popular queer culture as to the definitive usage of gender-neutral pronouns and several variations exist. See Williams for a comprehensive overview of the debate, various pronoun sets, and their etymological origins.

19 "They were ripping off their clothes that were burning their skin. Naked, they jumped in place like crippled grasshoppers. They huddled together in the middle of our guys who were laughing at their good luck. 'Hey! I'm the king!' You yelled. 'The flower's mine!' You dropped your pants and the whole army saw it. The whole army saw you in all your force. The women went by you one after the other. Spread eagle by four soldiers who took turns holding them down. You were tireless. You laughed with pleasure. You screamed with rage and fury. And it went on. And it went on. You mounted the last one yawning wide enough to dislocate your jaw.

And you crashed on the ground, instantly fast asleep. I covered you over with my coat. When you woke up, in the early morning of victory, the girl under you was dead.

(*During the whole story, Corneille and the king touch, rub, and excite each other. Corneille straddles the king and wears him out. They end up exhausted on the ground.*)"

20 I develop more fully the theoretical cross-over between Bhabha's idea of colonial mimicry and current approaches to gender imitation that do not adequately distinguish between cross-dressing, drag, and passing in an essay entitled "Cross-Dressing, Drag, and Passing: Slippages in Shakespearean Comedy."

21 "An empty shell, a name with no guarantor."

Citations from *Vie et mort du Roi Boiteux* are referenced by play, scene, and page number.

22 The schoolbook text cited by Lise Payette, who sparked the scandal by calling Claude Ryan's wife an Yvette, is as follows: "Guy pratique les sports, la natation, le tennis, la boxe, le plongeon. Son ambition est de devenir champion et de remporter beaucoup de trophées. Yvette, sa petite soeur, est joyeuse et gentille. Elle trouve toujours le moyen de faire plaisir à ses parents. Hier, à l'heure du repas, elle a tranché le pain, versé l'eau sur le thé dans la théière, elle a apporté le sucrier, le beurrier, le pot de lait. Elle a aussi aidé à servir le poulet rôti. Après le déjeuner, c'est avec plaisir qu'elle a essuyé la vaisselle et balayé le tapis. Yvette est une petite fille obligeante." [Guy plays sports, swimming, tennis, boxing, and diving. His ambition is to become a champion and win lots of trophies. Yvette, his little sister, is joyful and nice. She always finds a way to please her parents. Yesterday, at dinnertime, she sliced the bread, poured water on the tea in the teapot, she set the sugar dish, the butter dish, and the milk. She also helped to serve the roast chicken. After dinner, it's with pleasure that she dried the dishes and swept the rug. Yvette is an obedient little girl] (qtd. in Graham Fraser 247–8).

23 "The absence, in Ronfard's work, of homosexuality, very present in contemporary Québécois literature."

24 In "En contrepoint" [In counterpoint] (1990), Ronfard writes: "Du coup, marchant dans les rues, j'ai commencé à m'interroger: est-ce que l'homosexualité au théâtre, dans la pratique du théâtre est intéressante? À quels niveaux? Est-ce que moi, ça m'intéresse?/Commençons par moi. Peut-être parce que je suis hétérosexuel, donc enfoncé sur ce plan dans ce qu'on appelle la norme, l'homosexualité m'intéresse, privément, au même titre que la cuisine végétarienne, le zen, le vélocipédisme et l'idéologie des non-fumeurs, c'est-à-dire assez peu. [...] Je refuse le slogan fasciste et

bondieusard qui affirme que la vie privée est politique. J'avoue d'ailleurs sur ce point une naïveté totale, probablement par manque d'imagination. [...] Bref, je ne sais jamais qu'un tel est homosexuel, juif ou philatéliste." [At once, walking down the street, I started to ask myself: is homosexuality in the theatre, in the practice of theatre, interesting? On what levels? Does it interest me?/Let's start with me. Maybe because I'm heterosexual, and thus stuck in what we call the norm in this regard, homosexuality interests me, privately, as much as vegetarian cooking, Zen, bicycling, and the ideology of non-smokers, which is to say very little. [...] I refuse the fascist and fundamentalist slogan that the personal is political. In fact, I confess total naivety on this point, probably from a lack of imagination. [...] Briefly put, I never know if so and so is a homosexual, a Jew, or a stamp collector] (123).

While such statements by playwrights may be insightful into their personal views, they should not limit how critics interpret their texts. Ronfard's *Roi Boiteux* clearly does valorize homosexuality through the relationships of Sandy, Nelson, and Freddy and of Catherine and Claire. Although they are not reflected in the text, Ronfard's personal views do point, however, to a broader social disregard or disdain for queers, which, if not homophobic, is at least heterosexist.

25 *"All at once, Catherine gets up and acts with extraordinary brio the role of a photographer's model. She strikes every possible pose, from the magnanimous lady contemplating the universe to the second-rate whore. She and Claire do a dazzling number. They enjoy themselves, laugh, run, spin around, press their bodies against each other. Claire truly makes love to her camera. While heaving moans of cats in heat, they end up rolling around the ground. Claire, genitals against genitals, with Catherine's legs wrapped together around her back, takes one last headshot of Catherine in ecstasy. Enter Richard Premier who sees the scene. [...] Catherine heaves out an immense orgasmic moan."*

26 "Everywhere Eros triumphs, sex, ass."

27 Or not. Albany may either "restore Edgar and Kent to their titles and power as nobles so that they can *sustain* order in the realm" or he may be "inviting them to govern jointly with him" (Foakes, ed. 5.3.319n), an offer which is further complicated by the change between the Quarto and the Folio of the final speech prefix from Albany to Edgar.

28 *"Everyone is thus dead except Laurette. She arrives wearing a large, white shirt, barefoot, hair loose; she no longer has on her fool's make-up. She goes through the centre of the mass grave and finds her way to the throne at the end of the red carpet. She climbs up, settles herself on it, and in a beautiful, quiet gesture, she pulls out her tongue and holds it between her thumb and index finger. She freezes."*

29 "Go on a tour of Africa when it's here where things are happening."

30 "The whole stage clutched to the top of a column."
31 "Coup de théâtre: *one of the Shakespeares, groaning, gets up, pulls out the sword that was penetrating him, drags himself, dying, towards the lighting booth and in a last burst of life turns off the lights while saying*: Fuck!"
Calvaire translates literally as the martyrdom on the road to the cross. Québécois curses generally derive from religious terms in contrast to anglophone curses which are mostly rooted in sexual imagery.
32 "*A typically British umbrella.*" "*Jump into, with eloquence and historical attention* [...] *the long narration of Clarence's dream (authentically excerpted from the great William's* RICHARD III*).*"
33 *Pipi de chat* translates literally as "cat pee," but the phrase can also be an idiom in French with multiple meanings. The phrase is primarily used to compare two things, and it designates something ridiculous or unimpressive similar to the English expression "that's peanuts." It could also refer to a light watering or sprinkling of liquid. Finally, it could mean something stinky or vile.
34 "*The king contemplates a ball of shit that he holds in his hand in a posture that invokes Michelangelo, Rodin, the traditional Hamlet.*"
35 "On their path, they meet the two Shakespeares having come out of their booth out of curiosity. Two worlds confront each other. Silence. Immobility. Question: What are we all doing here? Everyone is engulfed in this theatrical emptiness full of metaphysical angst."

Chapter 6. The Second Referendum

1 "You are feminists." "You are women; you are going to become engineers. You're all just a bunch of feminists; I hate feminists." Cited by Martine Valo in *Le Monde*.
2 "The Killer Was Not a Young Man." "Was as old as all the sexist and misogynist proverbs, as old as all the church fathers who doubted that women had souls. He was the age of all the legislators who forbid university, the right to vote, access to the public sphere to women [...] as old as Man and his contempt for women." "Were young, as young as the gains of feminism [...] as young as life begun again with hope by each generation of women."
3 For an in-depth perspective of Québécois reactions to the Massacre both immediately after the event and more recently, see *Polytechnique, 6 décembre* (ed. Louise Malette and Marie Chalouh) and *Retour sur un attentat antiféministe* (ed. Mélissa Blais et al.), published to commemorate the 1st and 20th anniversaries, respectively. Denis Villeneuve's 2009 film *Polytechnique* dramatizes the events with attention to historical detail, including the after-effects on the survivors.

4 "The softness of Venus's lips... The breathe of Adonis..." "You love that I love you." "Too coward for such a vertiginous dive."

5 "The only being that [he has] loved."

6 While not a full-length play, one of the *38* monologues, *Le Beau Jardin Secret de Jean-Stéphane* by Stéphane Laporte, based upon *The Winter's Tale* (in volume *U*), features a queer narrator, but he is self-loathing and presents a negative image of queerness, far less liberated than Lemieux's out and proud Mercutio.

More positively, Nathalie Claude's burlesque sketch *La leçon d'Anglaise* celebrates lesbianism. However, this short sketch, based on a 14-page unpublished manuscript, was only performed once before a predominantly queer audience within the context of a larger lesbian cabaret show called *Le Boudoir*, which was organized annually by Miriam Ginestier. The sketch is predicated upon an English lesson taught in an all-girls school by "La Professeure d'Anglais, Miss Clitorissa Wet" who, along with the school's director, Mme Baise d'Enfer [Mrs Hell-Fuck], directs the students in an in-class performance of a scene from *Romeo and Juliet*. Thanks to Miss Clit's guidance, the students learn all about "la langue anglaise et les baisers français" [the English tongue and French kisses] (14).

7 Marco Micone's *La mégère de Padova* (1995) could arguably be included here as a play about women, but, as explained in chapter 2, this play barely qualifies as an adaptation. It was first performed as *La mégère apprivoisée* as if it were a straight translation of Shakespeare's *The Taming of the Shrew*. Only *after* Katherine gives her famous last speech, essentially the same as in Shakespeare, does the play diverge from its source text and introduce the possibility that she might not be as tamed as she appears on the surface. Katherine is not resolutely defiant though, and there is nothing particularly feminist about her.

8 Paula de Vasconcelos describes the work of her Pigeons International theatre company as "feminine" in an interview with Denis Salter (76–7).

9 "I am the ghost of Ophelia and I demand peace for her soul."

10 The English translation of *The Queens* by Linda Gaboriau is a literal translation that does not adapt the original text in content or meaning. Unlike the English version of *Hamlet, prince du Québec*, which does change significantly in the English text, it is not an adaptation of an adaptation; therefore, I discuss only the original French text. All English translations of this play are Linda Gaboriau's rather than my own.

11 Saint Sebastian has come to be popularly referred to as the "gay saint." He was a Christian martyr who infiltrated the Roman military (a decidedly homoerotic space) in order to comfort persecuted Christians held prisoner. He was discovered, shot with arrows as punishment, survived,

and returned to confront the Roman Emperor Diocletian, for which he was beaten to death. A cult of Saint Sebastian emerged in the nineteenth century, possibly in reaction to the homoerotic depictions of him in Renaissance art in which he is pierced with phallic arrows and wears an expression of both pleasure and pain. Oscar Wilde adopted the pseudonym "Sebastian Melmoth" upon his release from prison. When the AIDS crisis emerged, Sebastian took on new meaning as a gay icon since he is also a saint with the power to ward off the plague. Sebastian in Shakespeare's *Twelfth Night* also exhibits homoerotic desire.

12 "My country is not a country, it's winter." "Happy about a spring [that does something]."

13 "Woodvilles, [she] first amongst them/Are in the process of inheriting./The treasure of England."

14 "George was a sphere of love/But I reigned in his heart/Ah it must have been painful/To give way to his queen!"

15 "Gasps and groans/Sounds strung together/Words that cannot be found/In any lexicon."

16 "Before time immemorial/You understood that we had been there first/And the world arrived afterwards/You were only our mother/But born after us – ."

17 "Who could better illustrate/The peace in our household?/Yet only months later/This peace had lasted too long."

18 "I have heard tell as well/Of a daughter among these brothers./[...]/It takes you hours/To explain that that girlchild/Was never born."

19 "For lack of giving birth/To a sister for your sons/A daughter who might have been able/To mourn her mother."

20 "To conjure her birth/I promised her everything she could desire/Provided that she arrive inside me/To no avail/She was not inside me."

21 "She is to language/What zero is to numbers." "As sure as you exist/As sure as you stand before my eyes/She is nothing./Nothing. *Rien*."

22 "Your purity is soon to die/Drowned in a cask/This house is no more than a funnel/Where everything mingles and flows/Into the rotten mouth of death." According to Holinshed, George, Duke of Clarence, died from drowning in a butt of malmsey wine (see Oxford edition 1.4n).

23 Antonine Maillet might, at first, appear somewhat out of place in the category of Québécois authors. In "Nation and/as Adaptation," Daniel Fischlin situates *William S* in an "Acadian cultural context" because of Maillet's famous origins in Acadie ("Nation" 333). Yet, this claim overlooks the fact that the play was written and first performed in Montréal,

and, in fact, the play is not nearly as "Acadian" as her other plays since it is written in so-called standard French rather than the Acadian language employed in many of her other texts, such as her novel *Pélagie-la-Charette*. In addition, despite her ethnic origins, Maillet is not only a descendent of deported Acadians but an example of the necessity for most Acadians and French Canadian artists to "immigrate" to Québec. Québec remains the only francophone region of Canada to receive adequate funding for literature and the arts, in large part because it has the demographic base to be self-sustaining and has thus developed many funding agencies in parallel to the "Canadian" organisms which are supposed to promote bilingualism and multiculturalism but which inevitably fall far short of the demand necessary to sustain and promote French culture outside of Québec. It is precisely because of this cultural and economic reality that I have included Maillet's work among "Québécois" adaptations. She represents an important part of the Québécois population: French Canadian immigrants from other provinces. (The music industry best illustrates this cultural and economic reality; we need only think of Edith Butler from Acadie, Zachary Richard from Louisiana, and Wilfred Le Bouthillier, the winner of *Star Académie*, also from Acadie.) Finally, the argument that Québec is the only francophone region of Canada with adequate cultural and economic resources for francophones outside of Québec to follow a career in the arts also extends to academia. Notably, Maillet completed her doctoral dissertation on *Rabelais et les traditions populaires en Acadie* at Université Laval in Québec City in 1970 and was a professor at the Université de Montréal in 1975–6.

24 "See how everything drives me mad!"

25 Here and throughout this discussion "god" is deliberately lower case in a performative gesture of secularization and resistance to christonormativity.

26 "Created, out of nothing, to distract [him]self."

27 "I wanted, like so many others, to have the last word in my dialogue with [... Time]."

28 "Shylock: We demand the author./Fool: The author cannot be found./ Hamlet: The creator cannot be found. God cannot be found!/Falstaff: God is dead and buried."

29 "Nobody made me, except my father and my mother. As for everyone else... authors, creators, God... pointless. Let's talk about serious things."

30 "Conceived a shrew, and put on earth tamed. [...] I am my own opposite. A walking paradox."

31 "We are all his slaves."

32 "For four centuries, my girl, since the beginning of the world, we women have found ourselves in a position of weakness. And what has been done with us?"
33 "We have been loved." "Oh! Oh!! Listen to the gentle pigeon coo. Loved, she says, loved in chains, loved slaves, courtesans, progeny-making machines, male progeny to inherit their goods and titles, and a few females to continue the line. And you call that love, Juliet?"
34 "I was the only one of the two of us who possessed the head, the soul, the heart of a king… but in a woman's body. Why?"
35 "But me in all that, me, your creature, sharpened by ambition, tempted by power, that you endowed with a soul of steel and then to come close it up in an envelope of conventions and laws for men's use, what have you done to me, the woman? You made me precisely that, woman, with all that this condition carries with it of misery and limitations. The woman who won't carry a sword, nor order her man, nor transgress the laws of her sex/gender."
36 "That the male king return to women the usurped power."
37 "When he realized that he created a woman so strong, so free, so independent, the man in him shook for his supremacy. I risked knocking over the order of things. So to cement me in his misogynist view of the world, he folded me in four and broke my backbone. Then he put in my mouth, in me who was gifted with such a splendid frankness, the most boring, insipid, and moralizing speech in world literature."
38 "Not a very good example of his so-called genius. If he had done with me like with you, Falstaff, Hamlet, or Lear, if he had given the Shrew free scope and had let her live to the end of her character, do you think that she would have let herself be tamed, domesticated, reduced to a doormat by her man?"
39 "To the Jew at least he gave the chance to defend himself. Not to the Shrew." "With me, he revealed himself to be a paltry excuse for an author. For by taming the Shrew, he spoiled his play."
40 "Why, yes, brave Jew! You've just spoken the most beautiful speech of my whole work. In the mouth of no other did I place more sublime words. To you I confided the eloquent plea in the defence of a whole people, and you're complaining about me?"
41 "I engendered no Juliet. An angel, two demons, but no Juliet."
42 "The Shrew, sire, the Merry Wife, the Thunder…"
43 "Woman who knows and spreads news." "Gossip." "Indiscrete gossiping." "Piece of gossip." "Slander."
44 "Theatre of resistance because it's an attempt at cultural decolonization." "Ceremonies to heal from violence and escape the abyss of suicide."

These statements appear in Ondinnok's program notes distributed at the performance of *Hamlet-le-Malécite* in Montréal in 2004. The production program has been posted online by *CASP*.

45 "The drama *Sakipitcikan* is that of a love story, that of Shakspeare's Romeo and Juliet of course, but especially that of this love story that we have all wished for ourselves and which, here, is told against a backdrop of chaos, of broken promises, of familial and collective heartbreak that underlies the loss of roots. This work is produced by people for whom this story runs in their veins."

46 Sioui Durand's film *Mesnak* (2012), a cinematic adaptation of *Hamlet-le-Malécite*, also takes place in the fictional village of Kinogamish. The film was shot in 2010 on the Innu reserve of Maliotenam near Sept-Îles in Québec's Côte-Nord region.

47 According to statistics by the Government of Canada, the overall rate of suicide is three times higher among aboriginals than other Canadians, and five to eight times higher among aboriginal youth. See Florence Meney's dossier on Radio-Canada.ca.

48 "Among Native peoples, an internal racism towards Malécites, an unknown nation originally from the St John River valley in New Brunswick."

49 "Nothing but a Malécite." "Too white to play an Indian."

50 "Projects of homosexuality." "Guys in tights."

51 "You could maybe start with *Les Belles-Sœurs* in Attikamek; it's about the only language into which it hasn't been translated."

52 Attikamek is a variant of Cree which is part of the Algonquian language family. Dave's answering machine message begins with the words "Kwé kwé!" (4). At the end of his toast to Gertrude at their wedding reception, Claudius speaks a few "[p]hrases convenues en Attikamek" [conventional phrases] (13). In addition, the play has three "entracte" scene changes during which medieval rats recite excerpts from *Hamlet* in Attikamek (8, 37, 60).

53 "I never knew who my father was. And I don't want to know; he can't do anything for me. When I want to know who I am, I open my wallet... *Laertes gets out his wallet.* ...and inside there's a card that the government of Canada gave me, with my picture on it, which says that I belong to the First Nations, which confers on me the same status as telephone poles and national parks."

54 "I don't pay any taxes and I'm really happy."

55 Accepted in principle in October 2001 and formally signed on 7 February 2002, the *Paix des braves* [Peace of the Braves], an agreement between the Québec government and several Cree nations (deemed "historic" by its initiators but controversial by others), provided $4.5 billion over fifty years

and guaranteed technical jobs in exchange for Hydro-Québec's right to develop new hydroelectric barrages in northern Québec, that is, to make money from water. See Radio-Canada.ca for a full dossier, including original news clips, on the *Paix des braves* agreement.

56 "It's true that Indians today, we've understood: when the settlers arrived, we told them that we couldn't sell our territory, so they took it for free. We got fucked over with the land, but now just watch us get one over with the water. We're slow, but we understand."

57 "Dave wants to act *Hamlet* and for him it's a question of life and death. He fights while situating us in front of his turmoil; it's his way of resisting the collapse of a fake world and that's why he wants to do theatre."

58 The event took place over the course of five nights during which, each night, seven or eight monologues were performed. Each of the thirty-eight authors was under the age of thirty-eight years, and the Shakespearean play which they were assigned to adapt was determined by a random draw from a hat of one of the titles of his thirty-eight plays. They were completely free to do as they pleased in writing their ten-minute monologue and directing an actor of their choice. For a complete list of the playwrights and the titles of their monologues, see the appendix.

59 Literally, "Richard III, poor cabbage," but idiomatically "Richard III, poor, little one."

60 Monologues that engage in authorial navel-gazing or in a metatheatrical reflection on the nature of the performance itself rather than adapting the content of Shakespeare's play include *Titus Andronicus* by François Boulay, *Taxi Actor* by Michel Monty, *Les aut' mots* by Claude Champagne, *Souvenirs d'une auteure malade* by Hélène Boissinot, *Comment vous plairait-il?* by Pascal Brullemans, and *Le beau jardin secret de Jean-Stéphane* by Stéphane Laporte.

61 See Lieblein's "Dave veut jouer *Richard III*" for an account of this play in performance.

62 Support for sovereignty was 40.44 per cent in the 1980 referendum. It rose to as high as 72 per cent following the failure of the Meech Lake Accord. When the 1995 referendum was called, it was at approximately 40 per cent and rose to 49.42 per cent by the end of the campaign. It dipped to 35 per cent in 2002, but surpassed the 50 per cent mark again in 2005 on the ten-year anniversary of the referendum. At any given time, results can range from 35 per cent to 50 per cent depending on which company is doing the polling (whether funded by federalist or by sovereignist interests) and the methodology used (number of people polled, region, language, etc.). See the 2005 report in *Le Devoir* by Gilles Gagné, a sociology professor at Université Laval.

63 As in the case of the tyrants and usurpers found in Garneau's tradaptations, I am not reducing *Henry V* to an unproblematic pro-Henry, pro-English nationalism reading of Shakespeare. As Oxford editor Gary Taylor points out, critics of the play "almost all divide into two camps: partisans of Henry and partisans of pacificism," with the former group interpreting the play as "a blunt straightforward Englishman's paean to English glory" while the latter group "believe Shakespeare (Subtle rather than Blunt, and never straightforward) himself intensely disliked Henry, and tried hard to communicate this moral distaste to the more discerning members of the audience" (1). Likewise, in "Rabbits, Ducks, and *Henry V*," Norman Rabkin shows how some critics of the play may "see an exemplary Christian monarch" while others may "see 'the perfect Machiavellian prince'" (294). Rabkin argues that "the play could scarcely have been anything but a rabbit-duck" optical illusion in which both readings co-exist simultaneously, the memory of one interpretation lingering in the back of one's mind even while one is confronted with the other (280). Indeed, Laurence Olivier's 1944 and Kenneth Branagh's 1989 cinematic productions give viewers two very different representations of Henry and of the war. In arguing that *Henry. Octobre. 1970.* works against "traditional readings of Shakespeare's text as a supposedly rousing elegy to English imperialism," I emphasize "traditional" and "supposedly" since adaptations often take cursory readings as their starting point and then problematize them. *Henry. Octobre. 1970.* is clearly writing back to a pro-English reading of Shakespeare in order to valorize the French.

64 Although I speak here of a Québec with a unified dream of independence, this is clearly not the current socio political reality, nor has it ever been so historically. *Henry. Octobre. 1970.*, however, operates within a Canadian federalist versus Québec sovereignist binary, and this discussion therefore reflects that point of view. For example, the play's positioning of René Lévesque as indirect leader of the FLQ in his role as leader of the French army obviously derives not from historical fact but rather from the process of mapping the October Crisis onto the pre-existing structure of Shakespeare's play. In addition, the English versus French cleavage not only reflects Shakespeare's text but is also one of the ways the adaptation recreates the popular discourse of 1970 in which political positions were much more strongly divided along linguistic lines than is now the case.

65 All quotations from *Henry. Octobre. 1970.* are documented in the body of this essay. The references are to the page numbers of the director's unpublished manuscript and are followed, where applicable, by references to the corresponding passages of Shakespeare's *Henry V*, Arden 3rd series, ed.

T.W. Craik. Thanks to Madd Harold for generously providing a copy of his manuscript.

66 "Speak white/it is so beautiful to hear you/speak of Paradise Lost/ or of the gracious, anonymous profile that shakes in the sonnets of Shakespeare." Lalonde's poem, first read at the *Nuit de la poésie* rather than published, was initially distributed as a *poème d'affiche,* the spirit of which remains today in its distribution on sovereignist websites. References are to the line numbers of the poem.

67 "In the soft language of Shakespeare/with Longfellow's accent/speak a pure and atrociously white French/like in Vietnam and the Congo."

68 Marco Micone claims that giving voice to immigrants was the underlying motivation for his adaptation *La mégère de Padova* (1995): "En tant qu'immigrant, j'ai voulu insister sur l'héterogenéité de cette culture." [As an immigrant, I wanted to insist on the heterogeneity of this culture] (qtd. in Lieblein, "Re-making" 187). Set in Padua, as is *The Taming of the Shrew,* the play mentions Galileo and is clearly Italian but does not diverge significantly from Shakespeare.

69 "We will speak our demise with your words/so that you will not die." "We are one hundred peoples come from afar/to tell you that you are not alone."

70 "Tell the life story of a people of janitors."

71 "But when you really *parlez blanc*/when you *en viens au faits*/to speak of *la vie gracieuse*/and speak of quality of life/and of the Great Society/a little louder then *parlez blanc*/raise your foreman's voices/we're a bit hard of hearing/we live too close to the machines/and only hear our puffing over the tools."

72 This is the condition required to proclaim the War Measures Act legitimately.

73 "Language of curses/[...] not very clean/proper."

74 "Press release./To Robert Bourassa./We have Pierre Laporte./Go fuck yourself with an old groundhog./Piss off./We don't like you./You smell like shit./Horseshit./In a cave./Of an old groundhog?/[...]/Thanks so much, Little Fatty, Little Tall, and Little Young'un/And Pierre Laporte./ Front de Libération du Québec./We will triumph! We will triumph!"

75 "Press release. Robert,/It's us./Guess who?/Can't?/Come on, try?/ Scared?/Wimp?/Fuck off, filth./We will triumph! We will triumph!"

76 "Fag." "Cocksucker." "Does nothing but suck the Boss's dick."

77 See Richard Burt's "New Shakesqueer Cinema" for a discussion of homoeroticism in Kenneth Branagh's cinematic production of *Henry V*.

78 Performed 21–31 August 2002, the play was staged a mere week before the Québec Superior Court released its decision on the constitutionality of

gay marriage on 6 September 2002 in which it struck down the opposite-sex restriction on marriage as an unconstitutional violation of s.15 of the Charter. The general social climate in Québec at the time was favourable of this decision and of queer rights in general, often more so than in English Canada, according to informal opinion polls conducted by newspapers and television news programs.

79 "We got fucked."

80 In addition to the significance of the act of rape itself, it is also pertinent to question why the rapist is Minister Alberta instead of the man who uttered the threats, Henry/Trudeau. The answer, of course, is that the limits of poetic license are quickly reached should one attempt to portray the country's most revered prime minister as a rapist. The outpouring of emotion that marked Trudeau's funeral in 2000, less than two years before the play, clearly placed a social injunction on tarnishing his image so soon after his death. Nonetheless, the rape of Katherine by an English Canadian politician, whether from Alberta or from Ottawa, makes a similar point equating the intrusion of English Canadian politicians in Québécois politics with rape.

Conclusion

1 The combined total exceeds 100 per cent since two plays, *Vie et mort du Roi Boiteux* and *Les Reines*, have been counted in both categories because of the presence of strong women characters even though the nationalist aspects of each play are stronger than the feminist aspects.

2 The following plays deal extensively with the national question: *Hamlet, prince du Québec*; *Lear*; *Macbeth de William Shakespeare: Traduit en québécois*; *Vie et mort du Roi Boiteux*; *La tempête*; *Coriolan*; *Les Reines*; *Henry. Octobre. 1970.*; *Sous l'empire de Iago*; and *Hamlet-le-Malécite*. The first six of these ten plays appear prior to the Montréal Massacre on 6 December 1989. The following plays deal extensively with gender and sexuality: *Vie et mort du Roi Boiteux*; *À propos de Roméo et Juliette*; *Les Reines*; *William S*; *La mégère de Padova*; *Le* Making of *de Macbeth*; *Sauvée des eaux: Texte dramatique sur Ophélie*; and *La leçon d'Anglaise*. The first two of these eight plays appear prior to the Montréal Massacre. As argued in chapter 6, only *William S* is resolutely feminist, while *À propos de Roméo et Juliette* is queer, as is *La leçon d'Anglaise* which was a short sketch within the lesbian cabaret show *Le Boudoir*. The twenty-one other plays listed in the appendix deal with neither nation nor gender. Several have limited Shakespearean content or limited literary appeal as either adaptations or works in their own right.

3 See the *Canadian Adaptations of Shakespeare Project* Online Anthology (ed. Fischlin) for commentary on, and the full text of, many of these plays.
4 "The long walk towards [the achievement of] the country."
5 Anglophone adaptations of Shakespeare in Québec are rare on the whole. The only two authors who have produced adaptations of Shakespeare in Québec each hold a PhD in literature, and the adaptations are not concerned with Québec society or marked in any way as distinctly Québécois. Rather, these adaptations mock academia and scholars similar to the authors themselves. Terrance Ryan Hughes, originally from Vancouver, published 100 copies of *Macbean (or Happiness is a Wet Haggis)* through a small press in Outremont, Montréal, in 1986, having completed a PhD in French literature at McGill in 1980 on Gabrielle Roy and Margaret Laurence. Keir Cutler, from Montréal, wrote *Teaching Shakespeare* parts 1, 2, and 3 in 1999, 2001, and 2006 respectively, followed by *Teaching* Hamlet in 2011. He completed a PhD in theatre at Wayne State University in Detroit, Michigan, but his plays are about bad teaching and about the so-called authorship question, which has been largely dismissed as unscientific by the community of Shakespeare scholars.
6 According to Parizeau's detractors. See the note on "l'argent puis des votes ethniques" in chapter 1. Parizeau claims that "nous" includes anyone who speaks French and shares Québec's common civic values, regardless of birthplace or ethnic origin.
7 For example, on the cultural front, the most popular male artist at the 2004 Gala de l'ADISQ was Rwandan-born Corneille who is well known for his song about immigration, "Parce qu'on vient de loin" [Because we come from afar]. On the political front, the Bloc Québécois's election in January 2006 of four MPs from cultural communities (of fifty-one elected) testifies to a concerted effort of the sovereignist movement to build bridges with voters "from-elsewhere."
8 On an anecdotal side note, and to acknowledge fully the inscription in this book of the binary of English Canada and Québec as two founding nations, I could not help but be struck by the irony that I completed this chapter on what I used to call, when I lived in English Canada, Victoria Day, but which has been officially decreed by the Québec government "La journée nationale des Patriotes" in recognition and celebration of the rebels who took up arms against the rule of Queen Victoria. I don't think, therefore, that an analysis of Canadian and Québécois adaptations within this binary is entirely unjustified today, 175 years after the Patriots' Rebellion of 1837–8.
9 Joanne Tompkins proposes one solution to the problem of "multiculturalism" – a conceptual shift to "polynationalism." Tompkins's neologism

"polynationalism" would "highlight the intersection of the competing forces of nationality, nationalism, ethnicity, identity and subjectivity more accurately addressing the interdependent relationship of theories such as post-colonialism and feminism with multiculturalism. This would also rectify the frequent placement of multiculturalism in isolation or in opposition to a mainstream national paradigm. Poly-nationalism would not pretend to unite disparate groups that have hitherto resisted nationalist stereotypes; instead it would reconsider relationships in contested space" (131n7). In the context of Canada and Québec, polynationalism would require a return by English Canada to the concept of "two founding nations."

10 In Québec the dominance of the English-French divide can be seen in the word used for immigrants from neither of these linguistic traditions. One is either a *francophone*, an *anglophone*, or an *allophone*. *Allophone* literally means "other speaker" and is the category into which all immigrants fall. Hyphenated identifications, such as Irish-American or Asian-Canadian, are not used in Québec.

11 For a comprehensive study of the differences between Canadian multiculturalism, Québécois interculturalism, and French republicanism, see Guillaume Rousseau's *La nation à l'épreuve de l'immigration*. The graphic illustration of the values of these three ideologies is particularly helpful (118).

12 "Policy Statement on Immigration and Integration." "A society in which French is the common language of public life; a democratic society where the participation and the contribution of everyone are expected and encouraged; a pluralist society open to multiple contributions within the limits imposed by the respect of fundamental democratic values and the necessity of intercommunitary exchange."

13 For further scholarship on Québécois interculturalism in contrast to Canadian multiculturalism, see Alain-G. Gagnon's "Plaidoyer pour l'interculturalisme" and Gagnon and Iacovino's "Interculturalism: Expanding the Boundaries of Citizenship."

14 Mario Dumont, leader of the Action démocratique du Québec (ADQ) party, brought the debate to the media forefront by citing a number of examples in a press conference in November 2006: the CLSC in the Parc-Extension area of Montréal denying men access to prenatal classes with their partners so as not to offend Muslim, Hindu, or Sikh women; the Montréal police suggesting women officers call a male colleague so as not to offend Hassidic Jews; the ruling allowing a young boy to wear a kirpan to school. See *Le Devoir*, "Sortie de Dumont."

15 CBC News provides a timeline for the court case at the provincial and federal level and the various judgments and appeals: http://www.cbc.ca/

news/background/kirpan/. Lysiane Gagnon, a columnist for the Toronto-based *Globe and Mail*, explains why Québécois are opposed to the kirpan ruling, citing the reasonable limits Québécois see between security and religious freedom and their hard-won separation of church and state following the Quiet Revolution: http://www.vigile.net/The-kirpan-decision-isn-t-welcome. On 9 February 2011, Québec legislators unanimously voted to ban kirpans within the National Assembly in a PQ-led motion supported by the ruling Liberals and the ADQ and Québec solidaire opposition parties. PQ MNA Louise Beaudoin stated, "Si le multiculturalisme est une valeur canadienne, ce n'est pas une valeur québécoise" [If multiculturalism is a Canadian value, it's not a Québécois value], and she pointed out that German Prime Minister Angela Merkel and British Prime Minister David Cameron had also concluded that multiculturalism was a failure. See Robert Dutrisac's article in *Le Devoir*.

16 In March 2006, in response to a request from the Hassidic Jewish community, the YMCA on the corner of Avenue du Parc and Rue St-Viateur in Montréal replaced its normal windows with frosted glass windows, paid for by the Hassidic community. This was one of the more hotly contested incidents in the reasonable accommodations public debate since the patrons of the YMCA did not request the change and the Hassidic values preventing boys from looking at women were an affront to Québécois values of gender equality. In response to the uproar, the YMCA removed the frosted glass windows in March 2007 but installed blinds as a compromise. See Alexandre Shield's recap in *Le Devoir*.

17 This reasonable accommodation issue arose due to the prohibition against Hassidic Jewish men being alone with a member of the opposite sex in a space with the door closed, which thus made it impossible to take driving tests alone in a car with a woman. The story broke in February 2007, at which time the Charest Liberal government stated that the equality of the sexes must never be questioned. However, the question reared its head again in October 2009 when it was revealed that in January of that year the Commission des droits de la personne had judged it reasonable for the SAAQ to consent to allow people to take driving tests with an examiner of a particular sex for religious reasons. The Liberal government changed its position, agreeing with the commission's findings that the equality of the sexes was not being oppressed by freedom of religion. See Tommy Chouinard's reports in *La Presse*.

18 In January 2007, the municipal council of Hérouxville adopted these "normes de vie" designed to inform immigrants to the town of 1300 inhabitants (which had only one immigrant family at the time) that it was unacceptable to cover one's face in public except on Halloween, to practice

female genital mutilation, or to burn women alive. It also specified that violence against children was prohibited, people dance, drink alcohol, eat non-Kosher meat, and celebrate Christmas, students do not bring anything resembling a weapon to school, schools do not have prayer spaces, and people of the opposite sex study together, work side by side, and swim and exercise together. See the now revised "Normes de vie" on the Municipality of Hérouxville website. In May 2011, André Drouin revealed that he wrote the document so that journalists would jump upon the story and it would have maximum media impact. He stated, "Je riais aux larmes en écrivant ça" [I laughed until I cried while writing that] because the exaggerated ban on practices that have never existed in the small town was absurd. See Laura-Julie Perrault's report in *La Presse*.

19 History professor Jacques Rouillard explains the symbolism of Duplessis's gesture in an article in *Le Devoir*. Daniel Baril, a member of the Mouvement laïque québécois, in an another *Devoir* article explains the contradictions in politicians' choice to keep the crucifix in the National Assembly under the principle of "laïcité ouverte," a term derived from the Bouchard-Taylor report but which Baril posits is impossible to apply to a legal text since it requires making judgments on a case-by-case basis rather than according to legal statutes applicable to everyone.

20 In Ontario, faith-based tribunals had been allowed to settle family law matters since 1991 on the voluntary basis of the participants, most of whom were Catholic or Jewish. A public debate ensued following the release of Attorney General Marion Boyd's report on the Arbitration Act on 20 December 2004 after the Islamic Institute of Civil Justice requested earlier in the year to set up its own Sharia-based arbitration panels under the Arbitration Act. Women's groups, legal groups, and the Muslim Canadian Congress opposed this proposal on the basis that Sharia law does not view women as equal to men and therefore is incompatible with the Canadian Charter of Rights and Freedoms. Ontario Liberal Premier Dalton McGuinty stated on 12 September 2005, "There will be no Shariah law in Ontario. There will be no religious arbitration in Ontario. There will be one law for all Ontarians." See the story by CTV.ca News Staff.

21 On the thirtieth anniversary of the Charter of Rights and Freedoms, Roy Romanow, one of the architects of the Charter and the former NDP premier of Saskatchewan, said, "A new generation of 'Charter kids' and 'Charter judges' is advancing individual rights and diluting the 'communitarian impulses' of Canadians." He added, "When I teach today, I notice that these Charter kids think more individually. They have less of a historical connection to the notion of communitarian impulses. It's almost like a different country now." The consequence of this shift towards

more individualistic thinking is that it may lead to the Americanization of Canada: "Canadians see medicare as a social good. Americans see it as a commodity. That's the sharp, sharp contrast between our societies." The Charter is thus not without its critics, even among its founders. See Haroon Siddiqui for further comments by Romanow.

22 "The percentage of women's plays created on institutional stages is clearly inferior to the percentage of plays written by men. [...] Texts by women dramaturges that dare tackle the still serious problems of the feminine condition or that dramatize the experiences of lesbians or even those of women from cultural communities remain statistically insignificant today in Québec."

23 "If certain feminists intervened in English (Ann-Marie MacDonald) it's that it was entirely natural for them due to language and the cultural reference to be able to integrate Shakespeare in their body of references, whereas in Québec it would have been necessary rather to think of Racine or Molière, neither one nor the other lending himself however like Shakespeare to lesbian or gay slippages of meaning." "No, it never crossed my mind to go through the work of Shakespeare to elaborate my analysis of patriarchy or to elaborate another worldview." Personal communication with the author, 3–4 September 2011.

24 Thanks to Claude Villeneuve, president of the Comité national des jeunes du Parti Québécois in 2005–6, for this insight.

25 "Québécois theatre only exists for the past five years." "French-language theatre in Québec was Canadian theatre first."

26 "Everywhere in the new Québécois theatre, cultural affirmation goes along with affirmation of a national identity."

27 "A society negotiating its change-over in the era of pluralism with the means – that is, the interpretive tools – of a society that preserves a homogeneous image of itself."

28 "They insist on the non-evolving and even regressive character of feminist iconology in terms that go from 'women are always repeating the same thing' to 'sooner or later it will be necessary to move on to another stage.'"

29 Beauchemin argues that the report is a "whitewash": "It essentially tries to show the crisis (over accommodating minorities) was the work of the media, and that, in fact, there is no real problem. This would be the first time in history that a commission of inquiry ends up concluding there's nothing for it to inquire into." See Jeff Heinrich's story in *The Gazette*.

30 Beauchemin's criticisms of Taylor also apply to Gérard Bouchard's views, which Beauchemin sees as dismissive of the francophone majority's right to collective self-affirmation. In an article entitled "Au sujet de l'interculturalisme – Accueillir sans renoncer à soi-même," Beauchemin

characterizes the final report as a slap on the wrist to ordinary Québécois by liberal academics: "pour l'essentiel, le rapport rappelle à l'ordre la majorité franco-québécoise. [...] Ne participe-t-il pas de cet éthos dans lequel l'ouverture à l'autre invite à mettre en veilleuse toute volonté d'affirmation collective?" [Essentially, the report reprimands the franco-Québécois majority. [...] Doesn't it participate in this ethos in which openness to the other invites one to put to sleep any desire for collective affirmation?] He goes on to argue that the francophone majority need not deny its own identity in order to welcome immigrants; rather, a common culture is essential to integration: "Est-il possible, dans ce contexte de célébration emphatique de la diversité, de proposer un modèle d'intégration dans lequel persisterait la conviction que les sociétés forment des mondes de culture, d'histoire et de valeurs singulières? Bouchard associe négativement ce modèle à celui de 'l'assimilation/exclusion'. L'amalgame de ces deux notions est en lui-même significatif. Il implique en effet que d'inviter l'autre à nous rejoindre dans un monde commun et partagé en acceptant de s'y fondre, c'est l'exclure. Mais de quoi au juste? N'est-ce pas au contraire l'inclure dans une proposition de monde commun, d'une communauté de sens?" [Is it possible, in this context of emphatic celebration of diversity, to propose a model of integration in which would persist the conviction that societies form worlds of culture, history, and singular values? Bouchard negatively associates this model with that of 'assimilation/exclusion'. The amalgamation of these two notions is in itself significant. It implies in effect that to invite the other to join us in a common and shared world by accepting to melt into it is to exclude him/her. But from what exactly? Isn't it, on the contrary, to include him/her in a proposal of a common world, a community of meaning?]

31 Sharon O'Dair discusses redistribution, recognition, and Nancy Fraser's work in "Seeing Red, Seeing the Rift in the Left," the conclusion to *Class, Critics, and Shakespeare: Bottom Lines on the Culture Wars* (115–25, esp. 118).

32 In response to the claim that nationalism is less relevant in an age of globalization, Jacques Parizeau argues in his most recent book that globalization makes sovereignty more urgent than ever before: "Je pense qu'au contraire, la mondialisation rend plus nécessaire que jamais le rôle traditionnel de l'État-nation. Face aux menaces, aux abus, aux dérives que, au-delà d'indiscutables avantages, la mondialisation entraîne, le citoyen ne dispose vraiment que d'un seul protecteur: l'État." [I think that on the contrary globalization makes the traditional role of the nation-state more necessary than ever. Against the threats, abuses, drifts that, beyond the indisputable advantages, globalization entails, the citizen really only has a single protector: the state] (67).

33 "Québec feminists, confronted with their double, triple, or quadruple marginalization on the basis of gender, national identity, class, or sexual orientation, are far from having resolved the enigma of the construction of a political strategy adapted to the fragmentation of the identity of the postmodern political subject. But at least they learned that it is pointless to want to simplify the equation from whatever angle one approaches it. If the tensions that are promised to accompany the holding of a third referendum on Québec sovereignty are to be feared, it is less because nationalism covers feminism in its shadow than because feminists, monopolized by countless sectoral causes, are abandoning the central political scene, allowing once again male citizens to decide alone the gender of the nation, without female citizens."

34 See "La présence féminine" on the Québec National Assembly's website for the most recent statistics.

35 The list of ministers appointed on 19 September 2012 can be found on the Radio-Canada.ca website. Cabinet shuffles took place subsequently on 18 October 2012 and 4 December 2012 when Véronique Hivon temporarily left and rejoined the cabinet for health reasons.

36 "She doesn't pass in the public eye."

37 On the latent sexism associated with Marois's image as a "snob" who was "loin des problèmes des gens" [far from people's problems], see Michèle Ouimet's and Tommy Chouinard's articles in the 8 November 2008 edition of *La Presse* which respond to the leak of an internal PQ document about her image the day before in a story by Denis Lessard. Marois acknowledged the latent sexism in politics: "Il y a un regard différent qu'on porte sur les femmes (...). Que ce soit dans le ton de voix qu'on a, dans l'habillement qu'on a. On pardonne plus facilement à un gars d'avoir l'air fatigué. Si c'est une femme, on se demande: est-elle capable de faire la job?" [There's a different look that people take towards women (...). Whether it's in the tone of voice we have, in the clothes we wear. People excuse more easily a man for looking tired. If it's a woman, people ask: is she capable of doing the job?]

Criticism of Marois's personal wealth is particularly ironic in light of her performance as one of Québec's most responsible and efficient ministers of finance in 2002–3 when she steered Québec successfully through the economic aftermath of the 11 September attacks in New York and boosted Québec's economy by 3.8 per cent. See her speech about Québec's economic performance during this period in the note in chapter 1.

38 *La dame de béton* sounds similar to a nickname given to another Québécois politician, Jean Charest, who has often been called "l'homme téflon" [Teflon man] because none of his government's many scandals ever stuck to him.

Works Cited

Aarseth, Espen. *Cybertext: Perspectives on Ergodic Literature*. Baltimore: Johns Hopkins UP, 1997.

Adorno, Theodor, and Max Horkheimer. "The Culture Industry: Enlightenment as Mass Deception." *Dialectic of Enlightenment*. 1944. New York: Verso, 1997. 120–67.

Anderson, Benedict. *Imagined Communities: Reflections on the Origin and Spread of Nationalism*. London: Verso, 1983.

Andrès, Bernard, and Paul Lefèbvre. "Macbeth: Théâtre de la Manufacture." *Jeu* 11 (1979): 80–8.

Ashcroft, Bill, Gareth Griffiths, and Helen Tiffin. *Key Concepts in Post-Colonial Studies*. London: Routledge, 1998.

Assemblée Nationale du Québec. "La présence féminine." Québec. http://www.assnat.qc.ca/fr/patrimoine/femmes1.html.

Atwood, Margaret. "Gertrude Talks Back." *Good Bones*. Toronto: Coach House P, 1992.

Bakhtin, Mikhail. *Rabelais and His World*. 1968. Trans. Hélène Iswolsky. Bloomington: Indiana UP, 1984.

Balthazar, Louis. *Bilan du nationalisme au Québec*. Montréal: Éditions de l'Hexagone, 1986.

Bannerji, Himani. *The Dark Side of the Nation: Essays on Nationalism, Multiculturalism and Gender*. Toronto: Canadian Scholars P, 2000.

Baril, Daniel. "Quand la 'laïcité ouverte' conduit à Duplessis." *Le Devoir*. Montréal. 28 May 2008. http://www.ledevoir.com/societe/ethique-et-religion/191606/quand-la-laicite-ouverte-conduit-a-duplessis.

Barker, Francis. "Nationalism, Nomadism, and Belonging in Europe: *Coriolanus*." *Shakespeare and National Culture*. Ed. John J. Joughin. Manchester: Manchester UP, 1997. 233–65.

Barthes, Roland. "The Death of the Author." 1968. Trans. Stephen Heath. *The Norton Anthology of Theory and Criticism*. Ed. Vincent B. Leitch. New York: W.W. Norton & Company, 2010. 1322–6.

Beauchemin, Jacques. "Au sujet de l'interculturalisme – Accueillir sans renoncer à soi-même." *Le Devoir*. Montréal. 22 January 2010. http://www.ledevoir.com/societe/actualites-en-societe/281502/au-sujet-de-l-interculturalisme-accueillir-sans-renoncer-a-soi-meme.

Bélair, Michel. *Le nouveau théâtre québécois*. Montréal: Leméac, 1973.

Bélanger, Claude. "The Negro-King Theory." 1999. 2006. http://faculty.marianopolis.edu/c.belanger/quebechistory/events/nking.htm.

– "Pierre Elliott Trudeau's Televised Statement on the War Measures Act: October 16, 1970." http://faculty.marianopolis.edu/c.belanger/quebechistory/docs/october/trudeau.htm.

– "Trudeau's 'Just watch me' Interview: Impromptu Interview of Pierre Elliott Trudeau with Tim Ralfe of the CBC and Peter Reilly of CJON-TV on October 13, 1970." http://faculty.marianopolis.edu/c.belanger/quebechistory/docs/october/watchme.htm.

–, trans. "Letter of Pierre Laporte to Robert Bourassa." http://faculty.marianopolis.edu/c.belanger/quebechistory/docs/october/laporte1.htm.

Belleau, André. "Carnavalisation et roman québécois: Mise au point sur l'usage d'un concept de Bakhtine." *Études françaises* 19.3 (1984): 51–64.

Bhabha, Homi. *The Location of Culture*. London: Routledge, 1994.

Bienvenue, Yvan, et al. *38: A. E. I. O. U.* 5 vols. Montréal: Dramaturges Éditeurs, 1996.

Blais, Mélissa, et al., eds. *Retour sur un attentat antiféministe: École Polytechnique de Montréal, 6 décembre 1989*. Montréal. Éditions du remue-ménage. 2010.

Boivin, Mathieu. "Pierre Falardeau: hommages souveranistes… et fédéralistes." *Le Soleil*. Québec. 28 September 2009. http://moncinema.cyberpresse.ca/nouvelles-et-critiques/nouvelles/nouvelle-cinema/9553-pierre-falardeau-hommages-souverainistes-et-federalistes.html.

Boose, Lynda E. "Scolding Brides and Bridling Scolds: Taming the Women's Unruly Member." *Shakespeare Quarterly* 42.2 (1991): 179–213.

Bouchard, Gérard, and Charles Taylor. "Fonder l'avenir: Le temps de la conciliation: Rapport." Commission de consultation sur les pratiques d'accommodement reliées aux différences culturelles. Gouvernement du Québec: Québec, 2008.

Bouchard, Louise. "Lear." *Cahiers de théâtre Jeu* 5 (spring 1977): 107–10.

Bouchard, Reynald. *Touchez pas à ma paroisse*. ms. 1994.

Bourque, Denis, and Anne Brown, eds. *Les littératures d'expression française d'Amérique du Nord et le carnavalesque*. Moncton: Éditions d'Acadie; Chaire d'études acadiennes, 1998.

Brault, Michel, dir. *Les Ordres*. 1974. DVD. 2007.
Brisset, Annie. *Sociocritique de la traduction: Théâtre et altérité au Québec (1968–1988)*. Longueuil: Éditions du Préambule, 1990.
Bristol, Michael. *Big-time Shakespeare*. London: Routledge, 1996.
– *Carnival and Theatre: Plebeian Culture and the Structure of Authority in Renaissance England*. London: Methuen, 1986.
Brossard, Nicole. "Le tueur n'était pas un jeune homme." *La Presse*. Montréal. 21 December 1989. Rpt. *Polytechnique, 6 décembre*. Ed. Louise Malette and Marie Chalouh. Montréal: Éditions du remue-ménage, 1990. 29–30.
– Personal communication with the author. 3–4 September 2011.
Brydon, Diana. "Afterword: Relocating Shakespeare, Redefining Canada." *Shakespeare in Canada*. Ed. Brydon and Makaryk. 395–409.
Brydon, Diana, and Irena R. Makaryk, eds. *Shakespeare in Canada: A World Elsewhere?* Toronto: U of Toronto P, 2002.
Buffery, Helena. *Shakespeare in Catalan: Translating Imperialism*. Cardiff: U of Wales P, 2007.
Bullough, Geoffrey, ed. *Narrative and Dramatic Sources of Shakespeare*. 8 vols. London: Routledge, 1957–75.
Burnett, Linda. "'Redescribing a World': Towards a Theory of Shakespearean Adaptation in Canada." *Canadian Theatre Review* 111 (summer 2002): 5–9.
Burt, Richard. "New Shakesqueer Cinema." *Shakespeare, the Movie: Popularizing the Plays on Film, TV, and Video*. Ed. Richard Burt and Lynda E. Boose. London: Routledge, 1997. Rpt. in "The Love That Dare Not Speak Shakespeare's Name: New Shakesqueer Cinema." *Unspeakable ShaXXXspeares: Queer Theory and American Kiddie Culture*. New York: St Martin's, 1998. 29–75.
Butler, Judith. *Bodies That Matter: On the Discursive Limits of "Sex."* London: Routledge, 1993.
– *Gender Trouble: Feminism and Subversion of Identity*. 1990. London: Routledge, 1999.
Cameron, Daphné. "La mort de Pierre Falardeau suscite des témoignages émus." *La Presse*. Montréal. 28 September 2009. http://moncinema.cyberpresse.ca/nouvelles-et-critiques/nouvelles/nouvelle-cinema/9548-la-mort-de-pierre-falardeau-suscite-des-temoignages-emus.html.
CBC Digital Archives. "Meech Lake: A Vote of Protest." Last updated 30 January 2012. http://www.cbc.ca/archives/categories/politics/the-constitution/constitutional-discord-meech-lake/a-vote-of-protest.html.
CBC News Online. "Timeline: The Quebec Kirpan Case." 2 March 2006. http://www.cbc.ca/news/background/kirpan/.
Centre des auteurs dramatiques. http://cead.qc.ca.
Césaire, Aimé. *Une tempête*. Paris: Seuil, 1969.

Chamberland, Paul, ed. *Portrait du colonisé québécois*. Special issue of *Parti Pris* 1.9–10–11 (summer 1964): 1–174.

Chanady, Amaryll. "Rereading Québécois Literature in a Postcolonial Context." *Québec Studies* 35 (spring/summer 2003): 31–44.

Chassay, Jean-François. "La passion, comme un désert." Vie et mort du Roi Boiteux *de Jean-Pierre Ronfard*. Special issue of *Cahiers de théâtre Jeu* 27.2 (1983): 94–9.

Chaurette, Normand. *Les Reines*. Montréal: Leméac, 1991.

– *The Queens*. Trans. Linda Gaboriau. Toronto: Coach House P, 1992.

Chouinard, Tommy. "Accommodement à la SAAQ: La question soulève un tollé." *La Presse*. Montréal. 2 February 2007. Rpt. *Vigile.net*. http://www.vigile.net/Accommodement-a-la-SAAQ-la.

– "Accommodements raisonnables à la SAAQ: L'opposition proteste." *La Presse*. Montréal. 7 October 2009. http://www.lapresse.ca/actualites/quebec-canada/politique-quebecoise/200910/07/01-909243-accomodements-raisonnables-a-la-saaq-lopposition-proteste.php.

– "Marois victime d'un sexisme latent?" *La Presse*. Montréal. 8 November 2008. http://www.lapresse.ca/actualites/elections-provinciales/200811/07/01-37540-marois-victime-dun-sexisme-latent-.php.

Clark, Sandra, ed. *Shakespeare Made Fit: Restoration Adaptations of Shakespeare*. London: Everyman, 1997.

Clarke, Margaret [Helen M. Buss]. *Gertrude and Ophelia*. *Theatrum* 33 (April/May 1993): S1–S15.

Claude, Nathalie. *La leçon d'Anglaise*. ms. 2002.

Cloutier, Fabien. *L'aventure de Shakespeare au pays des rêves*. ms. 2000.

Cohn, Ruby. *Modern Shakespeare Offshoots*. Princeton: Princeton UP, 1976.

Collectif Clio [Micheline Dumont et al.]. *L'Histoire des femmes au Québec depuis quatre siècles*. Montréal: Quinze, 1982.

Crawford, Robert. "The Bard: Ossian, Burns, and the Shaping of Shakespeare." *Shakespeare and Scotland*. Ed. Willy Maley and Andrew Murphy. Manchester: Manchester UP, 2004. 124–40.

CTV.ca News Staff. "McGuinty Rules Out Use of Sharia Law in Ontario." *CTV News*. 12 September 2005. http://www.ctv.ca/CTVNews/TopStories/20050912/mcguinty_shariah_050911/.

Cutler, Keir. *Teaching Shakespeare; Teaching Detroit (Teaching Shakespeare 2); Teaching* As You Like It *(Teaching Shakespeare 3)*. ms. 1999, 2001, 2006.

– *Teaching Hamlet*. ms. 2011.

d'Allemagne, André. *Le colonialisme au Québec*. Montréal: Éditions RB, 1966. Rpt. Montréal, Lux, 2009.

Dalpé, Jean Marc, Robert Lepage, and Gordon McCall. *Romeo & Juliette*. ms. 1989.

Davis, Natalie Zemon. *Society and Culture in Early Modern France: Eight Essays.* Stanford: Stanford UP, 1975.

de Sève, Micheline. "Féminisme et nationalisme au Québec, une alliance inattendue." *International Journal of Canadian Studies/Revue Internationale d'Études Canadiennes* 17 (1998): 157–75.

Desmet, Christy. "Introduction." *Shakespeare and Appropriation*. Ed. Christy Desmet and Robert Sawyer. London: Routledge, 1999. 1–12.

Desroches, Vincent. "Présentation: En quoi la littérature québécoise est-elle postcoloniale?" *Québec Studies* 35 (spring/summer 2003): 3–12.

Dickinson, Peter. "Duets, Duologues, and Black Diasporic Theatre: Djanet Sears, William Shakespeare, and Others." *Modern Drama* 45.2 (summer 2002): 188–208.

Drouin, Jennifer. "Cross-Dressing, Drag, and Passing: Slippages in Shakespearean Comedy." *Shakespeare Re-Dressed: Cross-Gender Casting in Contemporary Performance*. Ed. James C. Bulman. Madison, NJ: Fairleigh Dickinson UP, 2008. 23–56.

– "Daughters of the Carnivalized Nation in Jean-Pierre Ronfard's Shakespearean Adaptations *Lear* and *Vie et mort du Roi Boiteux*." *Theatre Research in Canada/Recherches Théâtrales au Canada* 27.1 (spring 2006): 10–39.

– "'Get a Look at Your Wife's Beautiful Cones': Lady Macbeth's Stone Butch Blues and Rural Second-Wave Feminism in *Scotland, PA*." *Shakespeare on Screen: Macbeth*. Ed. Sarah Hatchuel, Nathalie Vienne-Guerrin, and Victoria Bladen. Rouen: Publications des universités de Rouen et du Havre, forthcoming.

– "*Hamlet-le-Malécite* (2004)." *Canadian Adaptations of Shakespeare Project*. Ed. Daniel Fischlin. 2005. http://www.canadianshakespeares.ca/a_sioui.cfm.

– "*Macbeth* (1978)." *Canadian Adaptations of Shakespeare Project*. Ed. Daniel Fischlin. 2007. http://www.canadianshakespeares.ca/a_garneau.cfm.

– "Nationalizing Shakespeare in Québec: Theorizing Post-/Neo-/Colonial Adaptation." *Borrowers and Lenders: The Journal of Shakespeare and Appropriation* 3.1 (fall/winter 2007): 23 pp. http://www.borrowers.uga.edu/781655/display. Rpt. "Nationalizing the Bard: Québécois Adaptations of Shakespeare since the Quiet Revolution." *Native Shakespeares: Indigenous Appropriations on a Global Stage*. Ed. Craig Dionne and Parmita Kapadia. Aldershot: Ashgate, 2008. 105–22.

– "*Othello* in Québec: Adapting Race and Gender in André Forcier's *Une histoire inventée*." *Shakespeare on Screen: Othello*. Ed. Sarah Hatchuel and Nathalie Vienne-Guerrin. Rouen: Publications des universités de Rouen et du Havre, forthcoming.

du Bellay, Joachim. *La deffence et illustration de la langue françoyse*. 1549. Ed. Jean-Charles Monferran. Geneva: Droz, 2001.

Dubois, René-Daniel. *Pericles, Prince of Tyre, by William Shakespeare.* ms. 1986.
Dumont, Fernand. *Genèse de la société québécoise.* Montréal: Boréal, 1993.
Durham, John George Lambton, Earl of. *Lord Durham's Report: An Abridgement of* Report on the Affairs of British North America. 1839. Ed. G.M. Craig. Montréal & Kingston: McGill-Queen's UP, 2007.
Dutrisac, Robert. "L'assemblée nationale appuie l'interdiction du port du kirpan." *Le Devoir*. Montréal. 10 February 2011. http://www.ledevoir.com/politique/quebec/316476/l-assemblee-nationale-appuie-l-interdiction-du-port-du-kirpan.
Egervari, Tibor. *Le Marchand de Venise de Shakespeare à Auschwitz.* ms. 1998.
Erne, Lukas. *Shakespeare as Literary Dramatist.* Cambridge: Cambridge UP, 2003.
Falardeau, Pierre. *Les bœufs sont lents, mais la terre est patiente.* Montréal: VLB Éditeur, 1999.
– *La liberté n'est pas une marque de yogourt.* Montréal: Stanké, 1995.
– *Octobre.* Montréal: Stanké, 1994.
– *Rien n'est plus précieux que la liberté et l'indépendance.* Montréal: VLB Éditeur, 2009.
–, dir. *Elvis Gratton II: Miracle à Memphis.* DVD. 1999.
–, dir. *Le temps des bouffons.* 1985. Video. 1993.
–, dir. *Octobre.* DVD. 1994.
Feinberg, Leslie. *Stone Butch Blues.* Ithaca: Firebrand Books, 1993.
Féral, Josette. "L'œuvre ouverte." Vie et mort du Roi Boiteux *de Jean-Pierre Ronfard.* Special issue of *Cahiers de théâtre Jeu* 27.2 (1983): 67–84.
Findley, Timothy. *Elizabeth Rex.* Winnipeg: Blizzard, 2000.
Fischlin, Daniel. "Nation and/as Adaptation: Shakespeare, Canada, and Authenticity." *Shakespeare in Canada.* Ed. Brydon and Makaryk. 313–38.
–, ed. *Canadian Adaptations of Shakespeare Project (CASP).* http://www.canadianshakespeares.ca.
Fischlin, Daniel, and Mark Fortier. "General Introduction." *Adaptations of Shakespeare: A Critical Anthology of Plays from the Seventeenth Century to the Present.* Ed. Daniel Fischlin and Mark Fortier. London: Routledge, 2000.
Fletcher, John. *The Woman's Prize; or the Tamer Tamed.* c.1611. *Adaptations of Shakespeare.* Ed. Fischlin and Fortier. 23–65.
Fleury, Lük. *Richard moins III.* ms. 1998.
Folkerth, Wes. "Goodfellows: Hockey, Shakespeare and Indigenous Spirits in Tomson Highway's *Dry Lips Oughta Move to Kapuskasing.*" *Canadian Shakespeare.* Ed. Susan Knutson. Toronto: Playwrights Canada P, 2010. 199–205.
Forcier, André, dir. *Une histoire inventée.* 1990. DVD. 2012.

Forcier, André, and Jacques Marcotte. *Une histoire inventée*. Montréal: Du Roseau, 1990.

Forsyth, Louise. "*La nef des sorcières* (1976): L'écriture d'un théâtre expérimental au féminin." *L'Annuaire théâtrale* 46 (autumn 2009): 33–56.

Fortier, Mark. "Undead and Unsafe: Adapting Shakespeare (in Canada)." *Shakespeare in Canada*. Ed. Brydon and Makaryk. 339–52.

– "Wild Adaptation." *Borrowers and Lenders: The Journal of Shakespeare and Appropriation* 3.1. (fall/winter 2007): 8 pp. http://www.borrowers.uga.edu/781535/display.

Foucault, Michel. "What Is an Author?" 1969. *The Foucault Reader*. Ed. Paul Rabinow. New York: Pantheon Books, 1984. 101–20.

Fournier, Louis. *FLQ: Histoire d'un mouvement clandestin*. Outremont: Lanctôt, 1998.

Fraser, Graham. *Le Parti Québécois*. Trans. Dominique Clift. Montréal: Libre Expression, 1984.

Fraser, Nancy. *Justice Interruptus: Critical Reflections on the Postsocialist Condition*. London: Routledge, 1997.

– *Scales of Justice: Reimagining Political Space in a Globalizing World*. New York: Columbia UP, 2009.

Fraser, Nancy, and Axel Honneth. *Redistribution or Recognition? A Political-Philosophical Exchange*. Trans. Joel Golb, James Ingram, and Christiane Wilke. London: Verso, 2003.

Gagné, Gilles. "Dix ans après le référendum de 1995 – Un appui ferme à la souveraineté." *Le Devoir*. Montréal. 20 October 2005. http://www.ledevoir.com/non-classe/92982/dix-ans-apres-le-referendum-de-1995-un-appui-ferme-a-la-souverainete.

Gagnon, Alain-G. "Plaidoyer pour l'interculturalisme." *Possibles* 24.4 (autumn 2000): 11–25.

Gagnon, Alain-G., and Raffaele Iacovino. "Interculturalism: Expanding the Boundaries of Citizenship." *Democracy, Nationalism and Multiculturalism*. Ed. Ramón Máiz and Ferran Requejo. London: Frank Cass, 2005. 25–42.

Gagnon, Lysiane. "The Kirpan Decision Isn't Welcome in Quebec." *The Globe and Mail*. Toronto. 13 March 2006. Rpt. *Vigile.net*. http://www.vigile.net/The-kirpan-decision-isn-t-welcome.

Garneau, Michel. *Coriolan*. Montréal: VLB Éditeur, 1989.

– *Macbeth de William Shakespeare: Traduit en québécois*. Montréal: VLB Éditeur, 1978.

– *Shakespeare: un monde qu'on peut apprendre par cœur*. ms. 1991.

– *La tempête*. Montréal: VLB Éditeur, 1989.

Genette, Gérard. *Palimpsestes: La littérature au second degré*. Paris: Éditions du Seuil, 1982.

– *Palimpsests: Literature in the Second Degree*. Trans. Channa Newman and Claude Doubinsky. Lincoln: U of Nebraska P, 1997.

Gentzler, Edwin. *Contemporary Translation Theories*. London: Routledge, 1993.

Germain, Jean-Claude. *Rodéo et Juliette*. ms. 1970.

Girard, Jacques, and Reynald Robinson. *Roméo et Julien*. Québec: Éditions du Théâtre de la Bordée, 1982.

Golder, John, and Richard Madelaine. "'To dote thus on such luggage': Appropriating Shakespeare in Australia." *O Brave New World: Two Centuries of Shakespeare on the Australian Stage*. Ed. John Golder and Richard Madelaine. Sydney: Currency P, 2001. 1–16.

Gouvernement du Québec. *Au Québec pour bâtir ensemble: Énoncé de politique en matière d'immigration et d'intégration*. Québec: Ministère des Communautés culturelles et de l'Immigration du Québec, Direction des communications, 1990. http://www.micc.gouv.qc.ca/publications/fr/ministere/Enonce-politique-immigration-integration-Quebec1991.pdf.

– *Charte de la langue française*. Québec: Office québécoise de la langue française, Éditeur officiel du Québec, à jour au 1 mai 2013. http://www2.publicationsduquebec.gouv.qc.ca/dynamicSearch/telecharge.php?type=2&file=/C_11/C11.html.

– *Charter of the French Language*. Québec: Office québécoise de la langue française, Éditeur officiel du Québec, Updated to 1 May 2013. http://www2.publicationsduquebec.gouv.qc.ca/dynamicSearch/telecharge.php?type=2&file=/C_11/C11_A.html.

– *Données sociales du Québec: Édition 2009*. Québec: Institut de la statistique du Québec, 2009. http://www.stat.gouv.qc.ca/publications/conditions/pdf2009/donnees_sociales09.pdf.

– *Rapport sur l'évolution de la situation linguistique au Québec: Faits saillants du suivi démolinguistique Septembre 2011*. Québec: Office québécois de la langue française. 9 September 2011. http://www.oqlf.gouv.qc.ca/etudes2011/20110909_faits_saillants.pdf.

Government of Canada. "Canadian Maple Syrup." Ottawa: Agriculture and Agri-Food Canada. http://www.ats.agr.gc.ca/pro/4689-eng.pdf.

– "CRTC Origins: History and Chronology." Ottawa: Canadian Radio-television and Telecommunications Commission. http://www.crtc.gc.ca/eng/backgrnd/brochures/b19903.htm.

– "French-language Music and Canadian Content on Radio." Ottawa: Canadian Radio-television and Telecommunications Commission. http://www.crtc.gc.ca/eng/cancon/r_french.htm.

Grady, Hugh, and Terence Hawkes, eds. *Presentist Shakespeares*. London: Routledge, 2007.

Graham, Joseph F., ed. *Difference in Translation*. Ithaca & London: Cornell UP, 1985.

Graves, Warren. *Chief Shaking Spear Rides Again or The Taming of the Sioux*. Toronto: Playwrights Co-Op, 1975.

Greenblatt, Stephen. *Learning to Curse: Essays in Early Modern Culture*. London: Routledge, 1990.

Gurik, Robert. *Hamlet, prince du Québec*. Montréal: Éditions de l'homme, 1968.

– *Hamlet, prince du Québec*. Montréal: Leméac, 1977.

– *Hamlet, Prince of Quebec*. Trans. Marc F. Gélinas. Toronto: Playwrights Guild of Canada, 1968.

Harold, Madd, and Anthony Kokx. *Henry. Octobre. 1970*. ms. 2002.

Hawkes, Terence. *Shakespeare in the Present*. London: Routledge, 2002.

Heinrich, Jeff. "Dissident Decries 'Whitewash.'" *The Gazette*. Montréal. 17 May 2008. http://www2.canada.com/components/print.aspx?id=d86da0a9-822d-454e-be4e-a87cdee372f9.

Highway, Tomson. *Dry Lips Oughta Move to Kapuskasing*. Calgary: Fifth House, 1989.

Hobsbawm, E.J. [Eric J.]. *Nations and Nationalism since 1780: Programme, Myth, Reality*. Cambridge: Cambridge UP, 1990.

Hodgdon, Barbara. "Macbeth at the Turn of the Millenium." *Shakespearean Illuminations: Essays in Honor of Marvin Rosenberg*. Ed. Jay L. Halio and Hugh Richmond. Newark: U of Delaware P, 1998. 147–63.

Hughes, Terrance Ryan. *Macbean*. Outremont, QC: Ormond House, 1986.

Hutcheon, Linda. *A Theory of Adaptation*. London: Routledge, 2006.

Jameson, Fredric. "Third World Literature in the Era of Multinational Capitalism." *Social Text* 15 (fall 1986): 65–88.

Jubinville, Yves. "Inventaire après liquidation: Étude de la réception des *Fées ont soif* de Denise Boucher (1978)." *L'Annuaire théâtrale* 46 (autumn 2009): 57–80.

Kidnie, Margaret Jane. *Shakespeare and the Problem of Adaptation*. London: Routledge, 2009.

Kiernander, Adrian. "John Bell and a Post-colonial Australian Shakespeare, 1963–2000." *O Brave New World: Two Centuries of Shakespeare on the Australian Stage*. Ed. John Golder and Richard Madelaine. Sydney: Currency P, 2001. 236–55.

Kipen, David. *The Schreiber Theory: A Radical Rewrite of American Film History*. Brooklyn, NY: Melville House Books, 2006.

Knowles, Ric. "*Othello* in Three Times." *Shakespeare in Canada*. Ed. Brydon and Makaryk. 371–95.

– *Shakespeare and Canada: Essays on Production, Translation, and Adaptation*. Brussels: Peter Lang, 2004.

–, ed. *The Shakespeare's Mine: Adapting Shakespeare in Anglophone Canada.* Toronto: Playwrights Canada P, 2009.

Lafon, Dominique. "Shakespeare à l'Arsenal ou Comment une filiale rompt avec la société mère." *L'Annuaire théâtrale* 24 (1998): 85–99.

Lalonde, Michèle. "La deffence et illustration de la langue quebecquoyse." 1973. *Défense et illustration de la langue québécoise suive de prose et poèmes.* Paris: Change/L'Hexagone/ Laffont, 1980. 9–34.

– "Speak White." 1970. *Défense et illustration de la langue québécoise suive de prose et poèmes.* Paris: Change/L'Hexagone/ Laffont, 1980. 37–40.

Lamoureux, Diane. *L'amère patrie: Féminisme et nationalisme dans le Québec contemporain.* Montréal: Éditions du remue-ménage, 2001.

– "Nationalisme et féminisme: Impasse et coïncidences." *Possibles* 8.1 (1983): 43–59.

Lanier, Douglas. *Shakespeare and Modern Popular Culture.* Oxford: Oxford UP, 2002.

Lapointe, Gilles. "Le 'Roi boiteux': Un théâtre 'look.'" Vie et mort du Roi Boiteux *de Jean-Pierre Ronfard.* Special issue of *Cahiers de théâtre Jeu* 27.2 (1983): 85–93.

– "*Vie et mort du Roi Boiteux* de Jean-Ronfard." *Canadian Drama* 9.2 (1983): 220–5.

Laporte, Gilles. *Les Patriotes de 1837 @ 1838: Les Rébellions du Bas-Canada.* http://cgi2.cvm.qc.ca/glaporte/index.shtml.

Laurendeau, André. "La théorie du roi nègre." *Le Devoir.* Montréal. 4 July 1958. 4. Rpt. http://faculty.marianopolis.edu/c.belanger/quebechistory/docs/AndreLaurendeau-Theorieduroinegre.html.

– "La théorie du roi nègre – II." *Le Devoir.* Montréal. 23 October 1958. 4.

– "La théorie du roi nègre – III." *Le Devoir.* Montréal. 18 November 1958. 4. Rpt. http://faculty.marianopolis.edu/c.belanger/quebechistory/docs/AndreLaurendeau-latheorieduroinegreIII.html.

Lavoie, Pierre, ed. Vie et mort du Roi Boiteux *de Jean-Pierre Ronfard.* Special issue of *Cahiers de théâtre Jeu* 27.2 (1983): 62–138.

Lavoie, Pierre, and Paul Lefebvre. "Les entrailles du 'Roi boiteux.'" Vie et mort du Roi Boiteux *de Jean-Pierre Ronfard.* Special issue of *Cahiers de théâtre Jeu* 27.2 (1983): 113–32.

Le Blanc, Alonzo. "Ronfard: Dérive organisée et conflit des cultures." *Études Littéraires* 18.3 (winter 1985): 123–41.

Lefebvre, Paul. "Chronologie et crédits." Vie et mort du Roi Boiteux *de Jean-Pierre Ronfard.* Special issue of *Cahiers de théâtre Jeu* 27.2 (1983): 133–8.

Legault, François. "Finances d'un Québec souverain." *Publications du Parti québécois.* May 2005. 49 pp. http://pq.org. Rpt. http://pq-labelle.ca/images/PDF/finance_quebec.pdf.

Lemieux, Pierre-Yves. *À propos de Roméo et Juliette.* ms. 1989.
Lepage, Robert. *Elseneur.* Montréal. ms. 1996.
Lépine, Marc. "Lettre de Marc Lépine." *La Presse.* Montréal. 24 November 1990. Rpt. http://www.philo5.com/Textes-references/LepineMarc_TexteIntegralDeSaLettre_891206.htm.
Lessard, Denis. "Marois: Entre snobisme et persévérance." *La Presse.* Montréal. 7 November 2008. http://www.lapresse.ca/actualites/elections-provinciales/200811/06/01-37094-marois-entre-snobisme-et-perseverance.php.
Lester, Normand. *Enquêtes sur les services secrets.* Montréal: Éditions de l'homme, 1998.
– *Le livre noir du Canada anglais.* Montréal: Éditions des Intouchables, 2001.
Lester, Normand, and Robin Philpot. *Les secrets d'Option Canada.* Montréal: Éditions des Intouchables, 2006.
Lévesque, Solange. "Théâtre – L'imaginaire comme territoire." *Le Devoir.* Montréal. 29 May 2004. http://www.ledevoir.com/culture/theatre/55640/theatre-l-imaginaire-comme-territoire.
Lieblein, Leanore. "Cette Belle Langue: The 'Tradaptation' of Shakespeare in Quebec." *Shakespeare and the Language of Translation.* Ed. A.J. Hoenselaars. London: Arden, 2004. 255–69.
– "Dave veut jouer *Richard III*: Interrogating the Shakespearean Body in Québec." *Canadian Theatre Review* 111 (2002): 15–21.
– "The Ghost of Ophelia and the Presence of Absence." Seminar paper on "Shakespeare Spin-offs," Shakespeare Association of America Conference, Washington, DC, April 2009.
– "'Le Re-making' of le Grand Will: Shakespeare in Francophone Quebec." *Shakespeare in Canada.* Ed. Brydon and Makaryk. 174–91.
– "Shakespeare and the Quebec Nation." *The Elizabethan Theatre XV.* Ed. C.E. McGee and A.L. Magnussan. Toronto: P.D. Meany, 2002. 261–77.
–, ed. *A Certain William: Adapting Shakespeare in Francophone Canada.* Toronto: Playwrights Canada P, 2009.
Lisée, Jean-François. *Sortie de secours.* Montréal: Boréal, 2000.
Lorde, Audre. "The Master's Tools Will Never Dismantle the Master's House." *Sister Outsider: Essays and Speeches.* Trumansburg, NY: Crossing P, 2004. 110–13.
MacDonald, Ann-Marie. *Goodnight Desdemona (Good Morning Juliet).* Toronto: Coach House P, 1990.
Maier, Carol. "Toward a Theoretical Practice for Cross-Cultural Translation." *Between Languages and Cultures: Translation and Cross-Cultural Texts.* Ed. Anuradha Dingwaney and Carol Maier. Pittsburgh: U of Pittsburgh P, 1995.

Mailhot, Laurent. "Sur le *Chemin du roy* avec *Hamlet, prince du Québec.*" *Théâtre québécois II: Nouveaux auteurs, autres spectacles*. Ed. Jean-Cléo Godin and Laurent Mailhot. Montréal: Hurtubise HMH, 1980. 57–75.

Maillet, Antonine. *William S.* Montréal: Leméac, 1991.

Malette, Louise, and Marie Chalouh, eds. *Polytechnique, 6 décembre*. Montréal: Éditions du remue-ménage, 1990.

Mansour, Kadar. *Sous l'empire de Iago*. ms. 2002.

Marois, Pauline. "Discours sur le budget 2003–2004." *Journal des débats de l'Assemblée nationale – 36e législature, 2e session – 11 mars 2003*. http://www.assnat.qc.ca/fr/deputes/marois-pauline-79/interventions.html.

Marowitz, Charles. *Measure for Measure*. 1975. *Adaptations of Shakespeare*. Ed. Fischlin and Fortier. 188–207.

Marsden, Jean, ed. *The Appropriation of Shakespeare: Post-Renaissance Reconstructions of the Works and the Myth*. New York: Harvester Wheatsheaf, 1991.

Martin, Alexis. *Dave veut jouer Richard III*. ms. 2001.

May, Stephen. *Language and Minority Rights: Ethnicity, Nationalism, and the Politics of Language*. Harlow, UK: Pearson, 2001.

McClure. J. Derrick, "Scots for Shakespeare." *Shakespeare and the Language of Translation*. Ed. Ton Hoenselaars. London: Arden Shakespeare, 2004. 217–39.

McHugh, Melissa. "The Influence of Shakespeare on Aboriginal Theatre: An Interview with Daniel David Moses on *Brébeuf's Ghost*." *Canadian Adaptations of Shakespeare Project*. Ed. Daniel Fischlin. nd. http://www.canadianshakespeares.ca/i_ddmoses.cfm.

McKay, Ellen. "The Spectre of Straight Shakespeare." *Canadian Theatre Review* 111 (summer 2002): 10–14.

Mealing, S.R., ed. *The Jesuit Relations and Allied Documents: A Selection*. Ottawa: Carleton, Library Series, 1990.

Meney, Florence. "Les Autochtones du Québec: Ce mal qui ronge les jeunes autochtones du Québec." Radio-Canada. http://www.radio-canada.ca/nouvelles/dossiers/autochtones/mal.html.

Mercier, Serge. *Elle*. Ottawa: Leméac, 1974.

Messier, Jean-Frédéric, and Paula de Vasconcelos. *Le* Making of *de Macbeth*. ms. 1996.

Micone, Marco. *La mégère de Padova*. ms. 1995.

– "Speak What." *Jeu: Revue de Théâtre* 50 (1989): 83–5.

Monière, Denis. *Le Développement des idéologies au Québec des origines à nos jours*. Montréal: Québec/Amérique, 1977.

– *Pour comprendre le nationalisme au Québec et ailleurs*. Montréal: Presses de l'Université de Montréal, 2001.

Monière, Denis, et al. "Indépendance et croissance économique ne sont pas aussi incompatibles qu'on le laisse croire: Les scénarios catastrophistes prennent l'eau." *Le Devoir*. Montréal. 4 July 1998. A9.

Moses, Daniel David. *Brébeuf's Ghost: A Tale of Horror in Three Acts*. Toronto: Exile, 2000.

Moss, Laura, ed. *Is Canada Postcolonial? Unsettling Canadian Literature*. Waterloo: Wilfred Laurier UP, 2003.

Municipalité de Hérouxville. "Normes de vie." http://municipalite.herouxville.qc.ca/normes.pdf.

Nadeau, Michel. *Les mots fantômes*. ms. 2006.

Naipaul, V.S. *The Mimic Men*. Harmondsworth: Penguin, 1969.

Ngũgĩ wa Thiong'o. *A Grain of Wheat*. London: Heinemann, 1967.

– *Moving the Centre: The Struggle for Cultural Freedoms*. London: James Currey, 1993.

Nielsen, Kai. "Un nationalisme culturel, ni ethnique ni civique." *Le pays de tous les Québécois: Diversité culturelle et souveraineté*. Ed. Michel Sarra-Bournet. Montréal: VLB Éditeur, 1998.143–59.

Nkunzimana, Obed. "Le débat postcolonial et le Québec." *Québec Studies* 35 (spring/summer 2003): 63–87.

Nolan, Yvette, and Philip Adams. *Shakedown Shakespeare*. Toronto: Playwrights Union of Canada, 1997.

Nolan, Yvette, and Kennedy Cathy MacKinnon. *The Death of a Chief*. 2005. *The Shakespeare's Mine*. Ed. Knowles. 379–427.

Novy, Marianne, ed. "Introduction." *Transforming Shakespeare: Contemporary Women's Re-Visions in Literature and Performance*. New York: St Martin's P, 1999. 1–12.

Nussbaum, Martha. "Human Functioning and Social Justice: In Defense of Aristotelian Essentialism." *Political Theory* 20.2 (May 1992): 202–46.

O'Dair, Sharon. *Class, Critics, and Shakespeare: Bottom Lines on the Culture Wars*. Ann Arbor: U of Michigan P, 2000.

O'Leary, Véronique, and Louise Toupin, eds. *Québécoises deboutte! Une anthologie des textes du Front de libération des femmes (1969–1971) et du Centre des femmes (1972–1975)*. Vol. 1. Montréal: Les Éditions du remue-ménage, 1982.

Ondinnok. "Ondinnok présente hamlet LE MALÉCITE." *Canadian Adaptations of Shakespeare Project*. Ed. Daniel Fischlin. http://www.canadianshakespeares.ca/spotlight/pdf/ondinnokprogram.pdf .

– "Réalisations: Sakipitcikan." *Ondinnok*. http://www.ondinnok.org/fr/index.php?m=notre-theatre&mm=realisations#7.

Organisation for Economic Co-operation and Development. www.oecd.org.

Ouellette, Michel. *Songe d'une nuit*. ms. 1995.

Ouimet, Michèle. "Pauline la victime." *La Presse*. Montréal. 8 November 2008. http://www.lapresse.ca/debats/chroniques/michele-ouimet/200811/08/01-37557-pauline-la-victime.php.

Parizeau, Jacques. *Pour un Québec souverain*. Montréal: VLB Éditeur, 1997.

– *La souveraineté du Québec: Hier, aujourd'hui et demain*. Montréal: Les éditions Michel Brûlé, 2009.

Parti Québécois. "Argumentaire pour la souveraineté." *Parti Québécois*. 2008. https://d.pq.org/sites/default/files/ArgumentairePourLaSouverainete2008.pdf.

Paster, Gail Kern. *The Body Embarrassed: Drama and the Disciplines of Shame in Early Modern England*. Ithaca: Cornell UP, 1993.

Perrault, Laura-Julie. "Hérouxville: un coup monté?" *La Presse*. Montréal. 26 May 2011. http://www.lapresse.ca/actualites/quebec-canada/national/201105/25/01-4402851-herouxville-un-coup-monte.php.

Philpot, Robin. *Le Référendum volé*. Montréal: Éditions des Intouchables, 2005.

Plato. *The Symposium*. Trans. Christopher Gill. London: Penguin, 1999.

Rabkin, Norman. "Rabbits, Ducks, and *Henry V*." *Shakespeare Quarterly* 28.3 (summer 1977): 279–96.

Radio-Canada.ca. "Candidatures féminines: La CAQ se classe 3e avec 24% de femmes." *Radio-Canada Information*. 7 August 2012. http://www.radio-canada.ca/sujet/elections-quebec-2012/2012/08/07/031-candidatures-femmes-caq-troisieme-rang.shtml.

– "Commandites: La facteur atteint 332 millions." *Radio-Canada Information*. 25 May 2005. http://www.radio-canada.ca/nouvelles/special/nouvelles/commandites/200505/24/005-juricomptables-gomery2.shtml.

– "Paix des braves: Les Cris achetés?" *Archives de Radio-Canada*. 19 January 2002. http://archives.radio-canada.ca/politique/droits_libertes/dossiers/1119-6120/.

– "Pauline Marois présente ses ministres." *Radio-Canada Information*. 19 September 2012. http://www.radio-canada.ca/nouvelles/Politique/2012/09/19/001-parti-quebecois-pauline-marois-annonce-conseil-ministres.shtml.

– "Victoire pour l'hôpital Montfort." *Archives de Radio-Canada*. 1 February 2002. http://archives.radio-canada.ca/politique/langue_culture/clips/12750/.

Reyes, Marie La Palme. *L'ultime séduction ou L'Alcibiade de William Shakespeare*. ms. 2004. http://marieetgonzalo.files.wordpress.com/2004/07/shakespeare.pdf. Rpt. *Sept d'un coup (Sept pièces de théâtre réunies en un volume)*. Beaconsfield, QC: Éditions Micro-Éduc, 2006.

Ronfard, Jean-Pierre. "En contrepoint." *Cahiers de théâtre Jeu* 54 (1990): 123–5.

– *Falstaff*. ms. 1990.

– *Lear*. *TRAC* (1977).
– *Vie et mort du Roi Boiteux*. 2 vols. Montréal: Leméac, 1981.
Rouillard, Jacques. "Le crucifix de l'Assemblée nationale." *Le Devoir*. Montréal. 27 January 2007. http://www.ledevoir.com/non-classe/128878/le-crucifix-de-l-assemblee-nationale.
Rousseau, Guillaume. *La nation à l'épreuve de l'immigration*. Québec: Éditions du Québécois, 2006.
Ryan, Andrew. "Coronation Street at 50: 86 Weddings, 37 Births, 118 Deaths and 775,000 Canadian Fans." *The Globe and Mail*. Toronto. 7 December 2010. http://www.theglobeandmail.com/news/arts/television/coronation-street-at-50-86-weddings-37-births-118-deaths-and-775000-canadian-fans/article1826993/.
Salter, Denis. "Acting Shakespeare in Postcolonial Space." *Shakespeare, Theory and Performance*. Ed. James C. Bulman. London: Routledge, 1996. 113–31.
– "Between Wor(l)ds: Lepage's Shakespeare Cycle." *Theater* 24.3 (1993): 61–70.
– "Blood ... Sex ... Death ... Birth: Paula de Vasconcelos's *Le Making of de Macbeth*: An Interview." *Australasian Drama Studies* 29 (October 1996): 67–83.
– "Borderlines: An Interview with Robert Lepage and Le Théâtre Repère." *Theater* 24.3 (1993): 71–9.
Sanders, Julie. *Adaptation and Appropriation*. London: Routledge, 2006.
Sarra-Bournet, Michel, ed. *Le pays de tous les Québécois: Diversité culturelle et souveraineté*. Montréal: VLB, 1998.
Schulte, Rainer, and John Biguenet, eds. *Theories of Translation: An Anthology of Essays from Dryden to Derrida*. Chicago: U of Chicago P, 1992.
Schwartzwald, Robert. "Fear of Federasty: Québec's Inverted Fictions." *Comparative American Identities: Race, Sex and Nationality in the Modern Text*. Ed. Hortense J. Spillers. London: Routledge, 1991. 175–95.
– "Rush to Judgment? Postcolonial Criticism and Quebec." *Québec Studies* 35 (spring/summer 2003): 113–32.
– "'Symbolic' Homosexuality, 'False Feminine,' and the Problematics of Identity in Québec." *Fear of a Queer Planet: Queer Politics and Social Theory*. Ed. Michael Warner. Minneapolis: U of Minnesota P, 1993. 264–99.
Sears, Djanet. *Harlem Duet*. 1996. *Adaptations of Shakespeare*. Ed. Fischlin and Fortier. 285–317.
Seymour, Michel. "Quebec and Canada at the Crossroads: A Nation within a Nation." *Nations and Nationalism* 6.2 (2000): 227–55.
Seymour, Michel, with Jocelyne Couture and Kai Neilsen. "Questioning the Ethnic/Civic Dichotomy." *Rethinking Nationalism*. Ed. Jocelyne Couture, Kai Nielsen, and Michel Seymour. Calgary: U of Calgary P. *Canadian Journal of Philosophy* 22 (supplementary 1996): 1–61.

Shakespeare, William. *Hamlet*. Ed. Harold Jenkins. Arden Ser. 2. London: Thomson Learning, 1982.

– *King Henry V*. Ed. T.W. Craik. Arden Ser. 3. London: Routledge, 1995.

– *King Henry V*. Ed. Gary Taylor. Oxford: Oxford UP, 1982.

– *King Lear*. Ed. R.A. Foakes. Arden Ser. 3. Walton-on-Thames: Thomas Nelson, 1997.

– *King Richard III*. Ed. Antony Hammond. Arden Ser. 2. Walton-on-Thames: Thomas Nelson, 1981.

– *Macbeth*. Ed. Nicholas Brooke. Oxford: Oxford UP, 1990.

– *Macbeth*. Ed. Kenneth Muir. Arden Ser. 2. Walton-on-Thames: Thomas Nelson, 1984.

– *Measure for Measure*. Ed. N.W. Bawcutt. Oxford: Oxford UP, 1991.

– *The Tempest*. Ed. Virginia Mason Vaughan and Alden T. Vaughan. Arden Ser. 3. Walton-on-Thames: Thomas Nelson, 1999.

Sherlow, Lois. "Normand Chaurette's *Les Reines*: Shakespeare and the Modern in the Alchemical Oven." *Shakespeare in Canada*. Ed. Brydon and Makaryk. 353–70.

Shields. Alexandre. "Accommodements raisonables – Des fenêtres claires munies de stores pour le YMCA du Parc." *Le Devoir*. Montréal. 20 March 2007. http://www.ledevoir.com/societe/actualites-en-societe/135813/accommodements-raisonnables-des-fenetres-claires-munies-de-stores-pour-le-ymca-du-parc.

Siddiqui, Haroon. "Siddiqui: Is the Charter Changing Canada for the Worse?" *The Toronto Star*. Toronto. 17 April 2012. http://www.thestar.com/printarticle/1162569.

Simard, Francis. *Pour en finir avec Octobre*. Montréal: Stanké, 1982.

Simon, Sherry. *Gender in Translation*. London: Routledge, 1996.

– "The Language of Cultural Difference: Figures of Alterity in Canadian Translation." *Rethinking Translation: Discourse, Subjectivity, Ideology*. Ed. Lawrence Venuti. London: Routledge, 1992. 159–76.

– "Translating and Interlingual Creation in the Contact Zone: Border Writing in Quebec." *Post-colonial Translation: Theory and Practice*. Ed. Susan Bassnett and Harish Trivedi. London: Routledge, 1999.

Sioui Durand, Yves. *Sakipitcikan*. ms. 1996.

–, dir. *Mesnak*. DVD. 2012.

Sioui Durand, Yves, and Jean-Frédéric Messier. *Hamlet-le-Malécite*. ms. 2004.

Smiley, Jane. *A Thousand Acres*. New York: Ballantine Books, 1991.

"Sortie de Dumont contre les accommodements." *Le Devoir*. Montréal. 17 November 2006. http://www.ledevoir.com/societe/justice/123021/sortie-de-dumont-contre-les-accommodements.

Squires, Nick. "Aussie Larrikins in Serious Trouble." *Telegraph.co.uk*. 3 July 2004. http://www.telegraph.co.uk/news/worldnews/australiaandthepacific/australia/1466099/Aussie-larrikins-in-serious-trouble.html.

Stevenson, Melanie. "À qui appartient Shakespeare? Les tiraillements au sujet du *Hamlet, prince du Québec* de Robert Gurik." *L'Annuaire théâtrale* 24 (1998): 69–84.

Tate, Nahum. *The History of King Lear*. 1681. *Adaptations of Shakespeare*. Ed. Fischlin and Fortier. 66–96.

Taylor, Charles. "The Politics of Recognition." *Multiculturalism: Examining the Politics of Recognition*. Ed. Amy Gutmann. Princeton: Princeton UP, 1994. 25–73.

Thomas, Nancy. *Richard III ou la chute du corbeau*. ms. 2002.

Thompson, Daphné. *Sauvée des eaux: Texte dramatique sur Ophélie*. ms. 2000.

Tompkins, Joanne. "Inter-referentiality: Interrogating Multicultural Drama in Australia." *Our Australian Theatre in the 1990s*. Ed. Veronica Kelly. Amsterdam: Rodopi, 1998. 117–31.

Travis, Debbie. "Corrie Crazy: Canada Loves Coronation Street." CBC Television. 9 December 2010. http://www.cbc.ca/player/Shows/ID/1691175212/.

Tremblay, Larry. *Roller. Théâtre à lire et à jouer* 4. Manage, Belgium: Éditions Lansman, 2000.

Tremblay, Michel. *Les Belles-Sœurs*. 1968. Montréal: Lémeac, 1972.

Trivedi, Poonam. "Introduction." *India's Shakespeare: Translation, Interpretation, and Performance*. Ed. Poonam Trivedi and Dennis Bartholomeusz. Newark: U of Delaware P, 2005. 13–41.

– "'It is the bloody business which informs thus...': Local Politics and Performative Praxis, *Macbeth* in India." *World-wide Shakespeares: Local appropriations in film and performance*. Ed. Sonia Massai. London: Routledge, 2005. 47–54.

Trofimenkoff, Susan Mann. *The Dream of Nation: A Social and Intellectual History of Québec*. Toronto: Gage, 1983.

Tymoczko, Maria. "Post-colonial Writing and Literary Translation." *Post-colonial Translation: Theory and Practice*. Ed. Susan Bassnett and Harish Trivedi. London: Routledge, 1999.

Un groupe de femmes de Montréal. *Manifeste des femmes québécoises*. Montréal: L'Étincelle, 1971.

Vallières, Pierre. *Nègres blancs d'Amérique*. 1968. Montréal: Parti pris, 1969.

Valo, Martine. "Antiféminism: le massacre qui a traumatisé le Québec." Paris. 11 December 2009. http://www.lemonde.fr/ameriques/article/2009/12/11/

antifeminisme-le-massacre-qui-a-traumatise-le-quebec_1279096_3222.html. Rpt. http://www.lapresrupture.qc.ca/ArchivesLettresOuvertes.html.

Vigeant, Louise. "Aventure du côté du carnaval: *Vie et mort du Roi Boiteux.*" *Theatre Research International* 17.3 (fall 1992): 203–16.

– "(Im)Pure Theatre." *Canadian Theatre Review* 50 (spring 1987): 14–19.

Vigeant, Louise, and Lorraine Camerlain. "Les voyages d'ici à la pourtant en ce même lieu." Vie et mort du Roi Boiteux *de Jean-Pierre Ronfard*. Special issue of *Cahiers de théâtre Jeu* 27.2 (1983): 100–12.

Villeneuve, Denis, dir. *Polytechnique*. DVD. 2009.

Vogel, Paula. *Desdemona: A Play about a Handkerchief*. 1977. *Adaptations of Shakespeare*. Ed. Fischlin and Fortier. 233–54.

Voltaire. *Candide, ou, L'Optimisme, traduit de l'Allemand de Mr. Le Docteur Ralph*. 1759. Paris: Hachette Livre, 1991.

Wallace, Helen. "French-Canadian Political Satire Resounding Success for LLT." 1968. Rpt. in Gurik, *Hamlet, prince du Québec*. Ottawa: Leméac, 1977. 141–3.

Warrington, Lisa. "Comedy and Irreverence: Rewriting Shakespeare in Aotearoa/New Zealand." *Shakespeare's Legacy: The Appropriation of the Plays in Post-Colonial Drama*. Ed. Norbert Schaffeld. Trier: Wissenschaftlicher Verlag Trier, 2005. 125–40.

Wayne, Johnny, and Frank Shuster. "Rinse the Blood Off My Toga." 1955. http://www.informalmusic.com/latinsoc/rinse.html. http://www.youtube.com/watch?v=rR_5h8CzRcI .

– "The Shakespearean Baseball Game: A Comedy of Errors, Hits, and Runs." 1958. 1971. http://www.canadianshakespeares.ca/anthology/baseball.pdf. http://www.youtube.com/watch?v=Uzl6LEfouEE. http://www.youtube.com/watch?v=mhQ9aeCE8Oo .

Whelehan, Imelda. "Adaptations: The Contemporary Dilemmas." *Adaptations: From Text to Screen*. Ed. Deborah Cartmell and Imelda Whelehan. London: Routledge, 1999. 3–19.

Williams, John. "Gender-Neutral Pronoun FAQ." http://www. aetherlumina.com/gnp/.

Wolf, Susan. "Comment." *Multiculturalism: Examining the Politics of Recognition*. Ed. Amy Gutmann. Princeton: Princeton UP, 1994.

Women's Theatre Group, and Elaine Feinstein. *Lear's Daughters*. 1987. *Adaptations of Shakespeare*. Ed. Fischlin and Fortier. 215–32.

Index